New Case Law Referencer on DISHONOUR *of* CHEQUES

New Case Law Referencer on DISHONOUR *of* CHEQUES

Second Edition

Hari Dev Kohli
M.A., B.T., B.L. (Gold Medalist), M.L. (Gold Medalist), Ph.D.

Author of
Supreme Court on Hindu Law
Case Law Ready Referencer on Law of Limitation
New Case Law Referencer on Arbitration and Conciliation Act
Hinduism and Divorce
Law and Illegitimate Child

Universal
Law Publishing Co. Pvt. Ltd.
NEW DELHI - INDIA

First Edition : 2007
Second Edition : 2010

ISBN : 978-81-7534-955-1

Published by
UNIVERSAL LAW PUBLISHING CO. PVT. LTD.
C-FF-1A, Dilkhush Industrial Estate,
(Near Azadpur Metro Station) G.T. Karnal Road,
Delhi-110 033
Tel : 011-27438103, 27215334, 42381334
Fax : 011-27458529
E-mail *(For sales inquiries)* : sales@unilawbooks.com
E-mail *(For editorial inquiries)* : edit@unilawbooks.com
Website : www.unilawbooks.com

Recommended citation: *New Case Law Referencer on Dishonour of Cheques*, Hari Dev Kohli, 2nd Edn. (New Delhi: Universal Law Publishing Co. Pvt. Ltd., 2010)

Computer Typeset **at Aesthetic &** *Printed* at Taj Press, New Delhi.

PREFACE TO THE SECOND EDITION

Law relating to "Dishonour of Cheque" has close proximity or near blended relationship with the commercial activity which has attained significant role in global perspective and in this distinctive relationship, role of cheque can be called "*sine qua non*" of commercial transactions based on the concept of "repose and trust and dishonour of cheque is the breach of trust over which the commercial world raised the superstructure of domestic and international trade. Thus new provisions were added to the Negotiable Instruments Act to give it biting teeth. It is common knowledge that when new provisions are added with the motive of suppressing mischief, they also usher in new problems which are bound to be subjected to Judicial Scrutiny and thereby judicial interpretation becomes more important and judge made law becomes significant. Since law is dynamic so is the judicial interpretation, thus multitude of judicial decisions has come over the years since its first edition which was published in 2007.

So it became incumbent to add those judicial decisions to bring the book up-to date because the sick case law enhances the practical utility of the book, especially for professionals and the corporate Sector. It is hoped that his edition will be useful for the Bench and the Bar and will serve as beacon light.

July 2010 **HARI DEV KOHLI**

INTRODUCTION

Old order changeth, yielding place to new. Temples of Babylon used as banks were the most powerful Greek banking institutions. But with the end of the civilization of antiquity, disappearance of relics of ancient time was a natural consequence. The seeds of modern banking system were sown by the innovative goldsmiths which ultimately blossomed into a fruit bearing plant and the concept of Banking saw the light of the day in 1694 in England with limited activities which with Peel's Act of 1844 had its activities enlarged and growth of Deposit Bank and cheque currency ushered in and it became ever expanding so much so that the activities of the banks became multifarious resulting in the creation of a nerve center of commercial hospitable hub.

Ancient India was never lagging behind. It was never a stranger to the conception of banking as the verses from the works of Manu, Gautma, Brihaspati, Baudhayana and Kautilya reveal the rules which governed the policy of loan and rates of interest. Gradually and gradually the banking system in some concrete shape started laying its foundation stone and the Indian banker earned a very high and respectable esteem when the common precept prevailed, "No Salvation except through the preceptor, no credit except through the banker".

But after the fatal combinations of Banking with commercial enterprise which led to reckless speculation and forgetfulness of the norm of safety of the money as of top priority, many changes from time to time were brought to give stability to the banking institution and the classical "Lex Mercatoria" after Lord Mansfield's ruling appeared in the shape of Bill of Exchange largely based on the customs and usages prevalent at the time followed by the Merchants and Negotiable Instruments Act, in India, though, drafted in 1866, came into existence in 1881 which recognized usages and certain customs prevailing among the Indian merchants. This Act has been amended several times but still it is not that comprehensive as it should be.

However, an amendment of far reaching consequence was brought by Banking, Public Financial Institutions and Negotiable Instruments Laws (Amendment) Act, 1988 (66 of 1988) by which section 80 and section 117 were amended to the extent of rate of interest and new Chapter XVII was added containing section 138 to section 142. This new Chapter was added specifically to enhance the acceptability of cheques in settlement of liabilities by making the drawer liable for penalties in case of bouncing of cheques due to insufficiency of funds in the accounts or for that reason that it exceeds the arrangements made by the drawer. In fact this Chapter would indicate that it is primarily to provide an additional criminal remedy over and above the civil remedies available to the payee or the holder in due course of the cheque with adequate safeguards to prevent harassment of honest drawers based on the principle of "Condonation" and "*locus poenitentia*" embodied in clause (c) of proviso to section 138 of the Act.

But the evil practice of issuing cheques without there being adequate amount in the accounts became so rampant and galloping that the amendments of 1988 could not obstruct the gushing flow of bouncing of cheques. Sections 138 to 142 in Chapter XVII have been found deficient in dealing with dishonour of cheques. Not only that the punishment provided in the Act has proved to be inadequate and also the procedure prescribed for the Courts to deal with such matters has been found to be cumbersome. The courts are unable to dispose of such cases expeditiously in a time bound manner in view of the procedure obtained in the Act which led to the magnitude of back-log of such cases rising menacingly. Keeping in view the large number of complaints under the said Act pending in various courts, a Working Group was constituted to review section 138 of the Negotiable Instruments Act, 1881 and make recommendations as to what changes were needed to effectively achieve the purpose of that section.

The Report of the Working Group making certain recommendations, consideration of the representations of various institutions and organizations, consultation with the Reserve Bank of India and other legal experts resulted in the introduction of a Bill, namely, the Negotiable Instruments (Amendment) Bill, 2001 in the Lok Sabha on 24th July, 2001. The Bill was referred to Standing Committee of Finance which made certain recommendations in its report submitted to Lok Sabha in November, 2001.

As a result of this cumulative considerations the Negotiable Instruments (Amendment and Miscellaneous Provisions) Act, 2002 (55 of 2002) was enacted further to amend the Negotiable Instruments Act, 1881, the Banker's Books Evidence Act, 1891 and the Information Technology Act, 2000 and came into force with effect from 6-2-2003.

With the present structure of the Negotiable Instruments Act, 1881, the required legal push has been given and the preservation of its sanctity of the cheque rests on the will and wisdom of the society so that the instrumentality to dislodge the good faith disappears once for all in view of the wide avenues opened for restoration of faith by the introduction of section 147 in the Act. Firmness of the Judiciary will be an added impetus to keep the faith reposed in the issue of cheques unshaken.

CONTENTS

CHAPTER II

PRESUMPTION OF LAW – BUT REBUTTABLE

CHAPTER III

MENS REA - NOT A DEFENCE

CHAPTER IV

OFFENCE COMMITTED BY COMPANIES AND LIABILITY OF DIRECTORS

CHAPTER V

COMPETENCY OF COURT – ITS POWERS AND COGNIZANCE OF OFFENCES

CHAPTER VI
DISHONOUR OF CHEQUE – SUMMARY TRIAL IF REQUIRED

CHAPTER IX

BANK'S CHEQUE RETURNING MEMO – MANDATORY PRESUMPTION OF DISHONOUR OF CHEQUE BUT REBUTTABLE

CHAPTER X

DISHONOUR OF CHEQUE – A COMPOUNDABLE OFFENCE

CHAPTER XI
DISHONOUR OF CHEQUE AND OTHER ASPECTS

DRAFTING OF NOTICE AND COMPLAINT

TABLE OF CASES

A

B

D

E

F

G

H

K

L

M

N

O

P

Q

R

S

T

U

V

CHAPTER I

DISHONOUR OF CHEQUE – A CRIMINAL LIABILITY

Section 138. Dishonour of cheque for insufficiency, etc., of funds in the accounts.—Where any cheque drawn by a person on an account maintained by him with a banker for payment of any amount of money to another person from out of that account for the discharge, in whole or in part, of any debt or other liability, is returned by the bank unpaid, either because of the amount of money standing to the credit of that account is insufficient to honour the cheque or that it exceeds the amount arranged to be paid from that account by an agreement made with that bank, such person shall be deemed to have committed an offence and shall, without prejudice to any other provision of this Act, be punished with imprisonment for [a term which may be extended to two years], or with fine which may extend to twice the amount of the cheque, or with both:

Provided that nothing contained in this section shall apply unless—

(a) the cheque has been presented to the bank within a period of six months from the date on which it is drawn or within the period of its validity, whichever is earlier;

(b) the payee or the holder in due course of the cheque, as the case may be, makes a demand for the payment of the said amount of money by giving a notice in writing, to the drawer of the cheque, [within thirty days] of the receipt of information by him from the bank regarding the return of the cheque as unpaid; and

(c) the drawer of such cheque fails to make the payment of the said amount of money to the payee or as the case may be, to the holder in due course of the cheque within fifteen days of the receipt of the said notice.

Explanation.—For the purposes of this section, "debt or other liability" means a legally enforceable debt or other liability.

INTRODUCTION

Section 138 has many ingredients. These ingredients must be satisfied in order to fasten the liability on the drawer of the cheque when it is dishonoured and then the payee has to observe the further requirements in order to launch prosecution against the drawer of the cheque. Thus, each ingredient is to be discussed in the light of statutory and judicial perspectives.

I. CHEQUE

Cheque has been defined under section 6 of the Negotiable Instruments Act, 1881 which stipulates:—

'A "cheque" is a bill of exchange drawn an a specified banker and not expressed to be payable otherwise than on demand and it includes the electronic image of a truncated cheque in the electronic form.

Explanation I.—For the purpose of this section, the expressions—

(a) "A cheque in the electronic form" means a cheque which contains the exact mirror image of a paper cheque, and is generated, written and signed in a secure system ensuring the minimum safety standards with the use of digital signature (with or without biometrics signature) and asymmetric crypto system;

(b) "a truncated cheque" means a cheque which is truncated during the course of a clearing cycle, either by the clearing house or by the bank whether paying or receiving payment, immediately on generation of an electronic image for transmission, substituting the further physical movement of the cheque in writing.

Explanation II.—For the purpose of this section, the expression "clearing house" means the clearing house managed by the Reserve Bank of India or a clearing house recognised as such by the Reserve Bank of India.'

BILL OF EXCHANGE

In the definition of cheque an expression "Bill of Exchange" is used which needs illustration. This expression is defined under section 5 of the Act which says:—

'**5. "Bill of exchange".**—A "bill of exchange" is an instrument in writing containing an unconditional order, signed by the maker, directing a certain person to pay a certain sum of money only to, or to the order of, a certain person or to the bearer of the instrument.

A promise or order to pay is not "conditional", within the meaning of this section and section 4, by reason of the time for payment of the amount or any instalment thereof being expressed to be on the lapse of a certain period after the occurrence of a specified event which, according to the ordinary expectation of mankind, is certain to happen, although the time of its happening may be uncertain.

The sum payable may be "certain", within the meaning of this section and section 4, although it includes future interest or is payable at an indicated rate of exchange, or is according to the course of exchange, and although the instrument provides that, on default of payment of an instalment, the balance unpaid shall become due.

The person to whom it is clear that the direction is given or that payment is to be made may be a "certain person", within the meaning of this section and section 4, although he is mis-named or designated by description only.'

Section 138 only speaks of cheque. Though section 13 of the Negotiable Instruments Act also speaks about "Negotiable Instrument" which means a promissory note, bill of exchange or cheque payable either to order or to bearer. Thus, if all these provisions are read together, section 138 only deals with cheque and not other negotiable instruments. However, keeping the definition of cheque in view as given under section 6 of the Act, still there is a need to go through the judicial pronouncements as discharge of debt or other liability can be by other instruments and that whether those instruments come within the purview of section 138 of the Act and the following case laws illustrate this point very vividly.

CHEQUE AND ITS DIFFERENT ASPECTS

POST-DATED CHEQUE

***Ashok Kumar Rajesh Kumar* v. *Manmohan Singh,* (1997) 1 Bank LJ 12: (1997) 1 BC 570: 1997 Cr LJ 3273 (P&H)**

Cases referred:

(1994) 1 Rec Cri R 150 (SC) (followed); (1994) 3 Rec Cri R 366 (AP); (1994) 1 Rec Cri R 220 (P&H); 1993 Cr LJ 744 (P&H); 1991 Cr LJ 3253; (1991) 1 All Cri LR 965 (P&H) (distinguished).

Facts of the case.—In this case many issues were raised and one of the issues was that, "the cheque in question was a post-dated one." The contention was that since the cheque was post-dated, if at all, is only a bill of exchange and had not become a cheque and thus does not attract section 138 of the Act and that it is only a civil liability and relied upon 1993 Cr LJ 744 (P&H) where it was *held* that if a cheque issued by the accused to clear an outstanding liability is dishonoured by the Bank, it is only a breach of promise and a civil liability. The High Court relied on (1994) 1 Rec Cri R 150 (SC) wherein the Supreme Court said that, "the post-dated cheque is not payable till the date which is shown on the face of the said document. It will become cheque only on the date shown on it and prior to that it remains a bill of exchange under section 5 of the Act. As a bill of exchange post-dated cheque remains negotiable but it will not become a "cheque" till the date when it becomes "payable on demand." Hence, *held* that there are no grounds to quash the proceedings.

***Peacock Industries (P.) Ltd.* v. *State of Rajasthan,* 2002 Cr LJ NOC 156 (Raj): (2001) 2 Raj Cri C 958: (2002) 1 Raj LR 701**

In this case it was *held* that post-dated cheque shall be deemed to have been drawn on date it bears as per Supreme Court's decision cited 1993 Cri LR (SC) 739.

***Ashok Yeshwant Badeve* v. *Surendra Madhavrao Nighojakar*, (2001) 3 SCC 726: AIR 2001 SC 1315: (2001) 105 Comp Cas 167: 2001 Cr LJ 1674 (SC)**

Cases referred:

(1993) 4 SCC 424: 1993 SCC (Cri) 1243; AIR 1967 SC 1118: (1967) 1 SCR 190: 36 Comp Cas 866; *Brian* v. *Dwyer*, (1979) 53 Australian Law Journal Reports 123; *Aylmer N. Keys* v. *Royal Bank of Canada*, 1947 SCR 377 (Supreme Court of Canada); *Pollock* v. *Bank of New Zealand*, (1902) 20 New Zealand Law Reports 174; *Royal Bank of Scotland* v. *Tottenham*, (1894) 71 LT 168: (1894) 2 QB 715; *Palmer* Ex Parte *Richdale (in re:)*, (1882) 19 Ch D 409; *Gatty* v. *Fry*, (1877) 2 Ex D 265; *Ball* v. *O. Sullivan*, (1871) LR 6 QB 209; *Hinchcliffe* v. *Ballart Banking Company*, (1870) 1 VR (1) 229; *Enamel* v. *Robarts*, (1868) 9 B&S 121.

Held: After referring to various foreign decisions and also Supreme Court's earlier decision cited (1993) 4 SCC 424: 1993 SCC (Cri) 1243, that a post-dated cheque is not payable till the date which is shown thereon arrives and will become a cheque on the said date and prior to that date the same remains "Bill of Exchange".

WHETHER INTEREST WARRANT IS A CHEQUE

***Ashok Chaturvedi* v. *Dr. Nirmala Jayawant Patil*, (2003) 2 Bank CLR 746: (2003) 2 Crimes 398: 2003 Cr LJ 3824 (Bom)**

Cases referred:

AIR 2000 SC 145: (2000) 1 SCC 1: 2000 Cr LJ 373: (2000) 1 KLT 141; 2000 AIHC 1649; (1999) 5 SCC 693: 1999 SCC (Cri) 1034: (1999) 78 Comp Cas 573: 1999 Cr LJ 3498 (SC); 1997 All MR 413; AIR 1984 SC 1824: (1984) 4 SCC 352: 1984 SCC (Cri) 620; AIR 1971 SC 447: (1970) 3 SCC 491: 1971 Cr LJ 418.

Facts of the case.—Besides, various issues, one of the issue was that the "Interest Warrant" is not a cheque as contemplated by section 138 of the said Act. The High Court negatived this contention along with other contentions raised by the petitioner stating that the interest warrant is a bill of exchange and as such definition of cheque as given in section 6 of the Act is also a bill of exchange. Thus, dishonour of interest warrant is also covered by section 138 of the Act.

***Vinod Baid* v. *S.G.K. Oriental Degree College*, (2003) 1 Bank C 459: (2003) 2 Civ LJ 589: 2003 Cr LJ 810 (AP)**

Facts of the case.—The issue before the Court was that the document issued is not a cheque and it is only a Demand Warrant. It is also contended that "Cheque" is defined under section 6 of the Negotiable Instruments Act and Demand Warrant does not come within the said definition. The court referred to sections 5 and 6 of the Act and also referred the book *Introduction to Negotiable Instruments* by James McLoughlin (1975 Edn., page 130) and the book *Negotiable Instruments Act* by Bhashyam and Adiga (16th Edn., page 117) and *held* that when there is no mention in the document that it is payable on demand, the said document does not fall within the definition of cheque. So when the said document is not a cheque then it is not covered by section 138 of the Act. *Held* that "Demand Warrant" is not a cheque and hence section 138 does not apply.

PAY ORDER AND CHEQUE

***Punjab and Sind Bank* v. *Vinkar Sahakari Bank Ltd.*, (2001) 7 SCC 721: 2001 SCC (Cri) 1395: AIR 2001 SC 3641: (2001) 3 KLT 533: 2002 Cr LJ 93 (SC)**

Cases referred:

AIR 1962 Ker 210: (1962) 82 Comp Cas 1122; AIR 1956 Cal 615; AIR 1948 Bom 1: 49 Bom LR 309; AIR 1930 Pat 239: 9 Pat 717; *Capital and Counties Bank* v. *Gorden*, 1903 AC 240: 8 Comp Cas 221.

Facts of the case.—The issue raised was as to whether Pay Order is a cheque within the meaning of section 138 of the Act and the contention was that "Pay Order" is only a draft issued by the Bank and it may at best be a promisory note but not a cheque. The court referred to the definition of "Bill of Exchange" as contained in section 5 of the Act and then referred to section 85A of the Act which deals with drafts drawn by one bank upon another branch of the same bank for a sum of money payable to order on demand purports to be endorsed by or on behalf of the payee, the bank is discharged by payment in due course. It is evident that the section renders such draft a Negotiable Instrument. Then referred to section 131A which makes all the provisions of crossing of cheques applicable to drafts also and then section 17 of the Act was referred. *Held,* that Pay Order is a cheque and is within the purview of sections 138 of the Act.

AMOUNT OF CHEQUE MORE THAN THE LIABILITY

***P.V. Kochayippa* v. *P.N. Suprasidan, Rajni Dhawan,* (2002) 3 Rec Cri R 352: 2002 Cr LJ 4803 (Ker)**

Cases referred:

AIR 2001 SC 3871; 2001 Cr LJ 1674: AIR 2001 SC 1315: (2001) 3 SCC 720: (2001) 105 Comp Cas 167; (1994) 1 Crimes 379.

Facts of the case.—It is a case where the liability was of Rs. 80,000 but the cheque issued was for Rs. 1,00,000 and dishonoured. Since there is difference of Rs. 20,000 in the cheque and liability it is not within the purview of section 138 of the Act. *Held,* that it is immaterial whether the amount of the cheque is more or less than the liability. Only thing is that the whole amount of the cheque is necessary to discharge the debt or legal liability and in this case the explanation for Rs. 20,000 is given as being the interest agreed to be paid. Thus the accused cannot get an acquittal. The case was remanded back to pass sentence after hearing the accused.

REVALIDATION OF CHEQUE

***Veera Exports* v. *T. Kalavathy,* (2002) 1 SCC 97: 2002 SCC (Cri) 85: AIR 2002 SC 38: 2002 Cr LJ 203 (SC)**

Case referred:

(2001) 1 Mad LW (Cri) 322 (Reversed).

Facts of the case.—It is a case where section 87 of the Act was discussed which deals with the material alterations in the cheque. It is *held* that invalid cheque can be revalidated voluntarily by altering the date so that to give fresh life to cheques for another 6 months.

CHEQUE NOT ISSUED VOLUNTARILY

***Taher N. Khamhati* v. *Vinayak Enterprises, Secundrabad,* (1996) 86 Com Cas 471: 1995 Cr LJ 560 (AP)**

Facts of the case.—It is a case where the loan was advanced and a cheque was taken from the debtor with a view to make use of it, as a threat for realisation of amount. *Held,* that the cheque is not issued voluntarily and hence the accused are acquitted and the decision was upheld by the High Court.

Note.—*This decision appears to militate against section 139 of the said Act.*

***Anant Ram* v. *Ram Krishan,* 2010 (1) Crimes 424 (HP)**

Cases referred:

ICDS Ltd. v. *Beena Shabeer,* (2002) 6 SCC 426; *Kumar Exports* v. *Sharma Carpets,* (2009) 2 SCC 513; *Rajendran* v. *Jose,* 2002 Cr LJ 3911; *Hari Kishan and State of Haryana* v. *Sukhbir Singh,* AIR 1988 SC 2127; *Suganthi Suresh Kumar* v. *Jagdeeshan,* (2002) 2 SCC 420; *Anil Kumar Neotia* v. *Union of India,* AIR 1988 SC 1353.

In this case the court held that where forcible execution of cheque could not be probabilised and statutory presumption has not been rebutted, accused cannot escape conviction.

NON-ISSUE OF CHEQUE

***R. Asokiyaraj* v. *G. Murli Krishna,* 2003 Cr LJ NOC 38 (Mad)**

Facts of the case.—It is a case where the accused denied the issuance of cheque in favour of the complainant. He filed an application for sending the cheque to an expert for examination. He filed the application on the day he was examined under section 313, the Cr. P.C. The application was rejected on the ground of delay. *Held,* Not Proper.

Note.—Refer 1997 Cr LJ 479 (Ker); 1994 Cr LJ NOC 262 (Overruled); (1993) 2 Ker LT (SN) 29 (followed).

II. DEBT OR OTHER LIABILITY

This ingredient is found in section 138 of the Act but this expression has been particularly specified under *Explanation* to section 138 of the Act which says:—

'For the purpose of this section, "Debt or other liability" means a legally enforceable debt or other liability. So for the purpose of "debt or other liability" the expression is cabined and confined within the cage of *Explanation* and has to be interpreted in the same sense. So, for, the purpose of interpretation we have to seek shelter under the judicial pronouncements.'

CHEQUE AND TIME-BARRED PROMISSORY NOTE

***S. Krishnamurthy* v. *A.R. Rajan,* (1996) 87 Comp Cas 212: 1996 Cr LJ 3552 (Mad)**

Facts of the case.—In this case three issues were raised:—

(i) Complaint not filed by the Payee or the Holder in due course.

(ii) The cheque was not signed by the accused.

(iii) Cheque was issued against time-barred promissory note.

The High Court negatived all the issues. Adverting to the 3rd issue, it was said that besides the concurrent finding of the courts below, the perusal of the record would as well make clear that in respect of the alleged two time-barred pronotes, the accused has paid interest on various dates and thereby the two disputed pronotes have not become time-barred, and hence the cheques were issued in discharge of the legally enforceable debts. The revision was dismissed.

***Kiran Finance Co., Hoshiarpur* v. *Sukhdev Krishan*, 2006 Cr LJ 766 (P&H)**

Limitation – Material showing that cheque was issued by respondent when debt liability had become time barred. Section 19 of the Limitation Act cannot be invoked.

CHEQUE *VERSUS* NO DEBT OR OTHER LIABILITY LEGALLY ENFORCEABLE

***Uplanche Mallikarjun* v. *Rat Kanti Vimla*, (1997) 4 Crimes 139: (1997) 2 APLJ 389: 1997 Cr LJ 4237 (AP)**

Case referred:

1996 Cr LJ 636 (followed).

Facts of the case.—In this case the cheque was issued by "Kanyaka Parmeshwari Charitable Marriage Trust" which was dishonoured with an endorsement, "Insufficient funds". The case of the accused was that there is no averment in the complaint that the cheque was issued in discharge of debt or other liability and that if the cheque is given as a gift or in charity, it does not amount to an offence under section 138 of the Act. *Held,* that the complaint is not maintainable.

***A. Bhoosan Rao* v. *Purshotamdas Pantani*, (1998) 2 CCC 655: 1998 Cr LJ 906 (AP)**

Facts of the case.—It was a case wherein the complainant could not discharge the initial proof of debt or liability so much so that he had not produced the cheque which is alleged to have been issued. Even his statement before the Court was highly contradictory. The lower court acquitted the accused. The complainant filed criminal appeal. The High Court *held* that the order of acquittal is proper as the complainant could not prove that he had sufficient capacity and that the accused has drawn such amount. *Held,* the criminal appeal is not maintainable.

***K.N. Sudagopan* v. *T.C. Govindarajan*, (1998) 1 BC 557: 1998 Cr LJ 143 (Mad)**

Cases referred:

(1997) 1 Crimes 4 (SC); 1992 Supp (1) SCC 335: 1992 SCC (Cri) 426: AIR 1992 SC 604: 1992 Cr LJ 527 (SC); *Amar Chand Agarwalla* v. *Shanti Bose*, AIR 1973 SC 799 (1973) 4 SCC 10: 1973 Cr LJ 577: 1973 SCC (Cri) 651.

Facts of the case.—In this case the issues raised were that:

(i) There was no enforceable debt.

(ii) No notice of demand was made.

(iii) There is inconsistency in endorsement by bankers.

But the accused raised these pleas after a lapse of three years when the trial had almost reached at the final stage. The High Court did not enter into the enquiry of the issues raised but only one issue was considered as to whether the petitioner was entitled to the reliefs prayed for. The High Court referred to the above cited cases and *held* that the allegations in the complaint are not absurd but *prima facie* show that they constitute an offence. *Held,* that the petitions be dismissed.

***Narinder Anand* v. *Maruti Udyog Limited,* (1998) 1 CCC 535: (1998) 37 Bank LJ 270: 1998 Cr LJ 759 (Del)**

Cases referred:

(1996) 3 Crimes 85 (SC); AIR 1992 SC 2206: (1992) 1 SCC 217: (1992) 1 KLT 1: (1992) 2 Punj LR 35; (1979) 44 STC 239 (Mad); (1975) 36 STC 582.

Facts of the case.—In this case the complainant filed statement of account not disclosing any other amount due except for alleged Sales Tax liability. The accused had submitted 'C' forms prior to passing order summoning accused. The original cheques and cheque returning memos were returned to the accused. The contention of the accused was that the cheques were returned after adjustment of accounts. It was only a Sales Tax liability which has been wiped out after submission of 'C' forms. Moreover, the assessment has still not been done. *Held,* that there is no cause to proceed against the petitioners under section 138 of the Act as there was no amount due or debit outstanding or the liability for which the cheques were dishonoured.

***Adithya Alkalads Ltd.* v. *NCC Finance Ltd.,* (2000) 2 Andh WR 29: (2001) 1 BC 539: (2001) 3 Civ LJ 260: (2000) 4 Crimes 186: 2001 Cr LJ 1585 (AP)**

Facts of the case.— The accused issued a cheque to be deposited as security against the bill discounting amount. Later on, this cheque was made use of by putting the date as 18-2-1997. Subsequently, an hire purchase agreement came into force by which the accused issued 36 cheques. If there is any default in the payment of instalments the complainant is at liberty to use any cheque out of the 36 cheques but not by putting a date 18-2-1997 on a cheque which was not issued against any debt or other liability but only by way of a security. The conviction and sentence was set aside.

***Genious Financial Services Ltd.* v. *Sarthi Studios Private Ltd.,* (2001) 1 Crimes 584: (2000) 2 Andh LJ (Cri) AP 400: 2001 Cr LJ 293 (AP)**

Facts of the case.—In this case there was absence of express averment in the complaint about existence of legally enforceable liability whereas the plea was that in course of business the accused had availed intercorporate deposit facility and that amount was due and owed by the accused and the cheque was issued for settlement of that amount. *Held,* that requirements of section 138 are complied with and hence the complaint cannot be quashed.

***Essar Projects Ltd.* v. *WPIL Ltd.,* (2002) 2 CHN 345: 2002 CWN 921: 2002 Cr LJ 4637 (Cal)**

Facts of the case.—The issue raised in this case was that the cheque was not issued against discharge of liability. The cheques are given towards advance payments to the complainant. So the same does not fall under section 138 of the Negotiable Instruments Act. It was *held* that whether the cheques were issued towards discharge of liability or not is to be decided in the trial after recording evidence. Proceedings initiated against the accused cannot be quashed in exercise of inherent powers. It appears that the High Court relied on section 139 of the said Act.

***Gopi S/o Vasudevan* v. *Sudershan, S/o Chakarpani*, (2002) 3 BC 426: (2002) 4 Crimes 32: (2002) 2 KLT 606: 2002 Cr LJ 4194 (Ker)**

Cases referred:

(1999) 3 Ker LT 849; 1995 Cr LJ 560; (1993) 2 Ker LT 326; (1992) 2 Ker LT 40.

Facts of the case.—It is a case wherein during the trial the accused contended that the cheque was given by him to the complainant but it was devoid of consideration. The case was that Sivadasan Chandran took a loan from the complainant and when demanded the accused intervened and gave his own cheque. It was agreed by the complainant that if the amount is paid by Shivdasan Chandran by 31-3-1972, no action will be taken on the said cheque. The amount was not paid and as such the cheque was presented and dishonoured. The issue involved was whether the cheque covers the third party's liability and falls under section 138 of the Act. The court *held* that the cheque issued for discharge of another man's liability also comes within the scope of section 138 of the Negotiable Instruments Act. The court relied on (1993) 2 Ker LT 326 wherein it is said that if the intention of Parliament had been otherwise, the words "of any debt or other liability", appearing in section 138 of the Act would have been further qualified by the words, "of the drawer". The order of the lower Court was upheld.

Note.—*Another person's debt or liability falls within the scope of section 138 of the Negotiable Instruments Act.*

***A.V. Murthy* v. *B.S. Nagabasavanna*, (2002) 2 SCC 642: AIR 2002 SC 985: 2002 Cr LJ 1749 (SC)**

Facts of the case.—The contention of the respondent seems to be that the loan was taken four years back prior to the issue of cheque, the debt or liability for which the cheque was drawn by him had ceased to be legally enforceable and, therefore, no complaint should have been filed by him. The Supreme Court referred to section 118 and section 139 of the said Act and section 25(3) of the Indian Contract Act, 1872 and further relying upon the balance sheet as on 31-3-1997 showing the amount borrowed by the respondents which means acknowledgement of debt. At this stage it is premature to agitate these contentions. The case is remanded back to the trial court to proceed with the complaint according to law.

Note.—*Plea of debt or other liability, legally enforceable or not is a matter of evidence during trial.*

***V. Sreelatha alias Raja* v. *Makanchand Bothra*, (2002) 2 SCC 263: (2002) 2 Crimes 19: (2002) 1 Mad W 271: 2003 Cr LJ 1938 (Mad)**

Cases referred:

Pankajbhai Nagjibhai Patel v. *State of Gujarat*, AIR 2001 SC 567: (2001) 2 SCC 595: 2001 SCC (Cri) 369: (2001) 1 KLT 517; (2001) 3 Crimes 218 (SC); (1999) 1 Crimes 70 (Mad); AIR 1999 SC 3762: (1999) 7 SCC 510: 1999 SCC (Cri) 1284; AIR 1988 SC 2127: (1988) 4 SCC 551: 1988 SCC (Cri) 984; AIR 1977 SC 1177: (1977) 3 SCC 25: (1977) 3 SCR 513: 1977 Cr LJ 964; (1975) 2 SCC 406: 1976 Cr LJ 1721: AIR 1976 SC 2205; AIR 1973 SC 786.

Facts of the case.—In this case various issues were raised but one of the issue was pertaining to "debt or other liability". According to the complainant the accused received a loan of Rs. Five lakh and when demanded, the accused issued two post-dated cheques and the same were returned dishonoured as "Not arranged". The accused executed a promissory note also to this effect. The contention of the accused was that the loan had already been discharged. The High Court *held* that where such defence is taken it is for the accused to adduce oral and documentary evidence to establish that the entire amount has been paid back but in this case no steps were taken to prove the same by the accused. In view of sections 118 and 139 of the Act and the decision of the Supreme Court cited 2001 (3) Crimes 218 (SC), it has to be *held* that the cheques have been issued in discharge of the liability and then the same had been dishonoured. The criminal appeal by the appellant/ accused is dismissed.

***Pawan Enterprises* v. *Satish H. Varma*, (2003) 3 BC 198: (2003) 3 Rec Cri R 350: 2003 Cr LJ 2146 (Bom)**

Cases referred:

2001 Cr LJ 972 (Distinguished); 2001 Cr LJ 4745 (Distinguished).

Facts of the case.—In this case the accused purchased T.V. for Rs. 22,760. Paid cash of Rs. 5000 at the time of purchase and a cheque for balance amount of Rs. 17,745 dated 8-1-1998. This said cheque was dishonoured on presentation. In between, the accused paid instalments in cash amounting to Rs. 6,965 which did not figure in the notice issued by the complainant. The High Court *held* that the cheque was issued on 4-4-1996. The cheque was dated 8-1-1998. Had the accused paid all the instalments the complainant would have not filed this complaint. Thus, the cheque issued was not in discharge of liability but towards security. The Revision filed by the complainant was dismissed.

Note.—*Liability and Security are two distinct entities.*

***Geeta Srivastava* v. *Bhanu Sharma*, (2003) 2 Civ LJ 587: (2002) 101 DLT 321: (2003) 66 DRJ 108: 2003 Cr LJ 801 (Del)**

Facts of the case.—The petitioner is a government teacher. She is not engaged in the business of her husband. The loan was taken by her husband by way of cheque and it was her husband who is the drawer of the cheque which was dishonoured. Merely because the petitioner accompanied her husband when he took the loan as the complainant happened to be her friend, would in no way saddle the petitioner with the liability of the offence under section 138 of the Act. The High Court further said that if the concept propounded by the learned counsel "company" means "Association of individuals", is accepted then every member of the family of a person who is engaged in a particular business can be roped in being, "Association of individuals".

***H. Rajgopala* v. *D.C. Mehta*, (2003) 3 BC 329: (2003) 3 Crimes 131: 2003 Cr LJ NOC 140 (AP)**

Facts of the case.—It is a case of dishonour of cheque for Rs. 5,16,700 but there are no commas immediately after '5' and '16'. There appears a stroke "/" between "516" and "700". Writing of "516" is entirely different from writing of "700". The contention of the respondent was that he issued the cheque only for Rs. 516 without filling up other particulars which looks plausible. Moreover, it was proved by evidence that the cheque was issued in discharge of legally enforceable debt as stated by complainant. The cheque appears to be doubtful. *Held,* complaint is not maintainable.

***Nutech Organic Chemicals Ltd.* v. *G.M.R. Technologies and Industries Ltd.*, 2003 Cr LJ 1462: (2003) 1 Andh WR 688: (2003) 3 Civ LJ 39 (AP)**

Cases referred:

(2002) 1 SCC 234: (2002) 108 Comp Cas 48: 2002 Cr LJ 266 (SC); (1999) 1 SCC 113; (1999) 2 Andh LD 669; 1997 Cr LJ 1942 (AP); (1995) 1 Andh LT 468.

Facts of the case.—There is a clear averment in the complaint that the cheques in question were issued for the discharge of an existing liability. But the contention of the accused is that the cheques have been issued in lieu of the earlier cheques. *Held,* that it is a matter to be decided as to whether the cheques were given towards security or in lieu of understanding reached, after taking evidence. At this stage there are absolute no grounds to quash the proceedings.

***Bangaru Packaging Company* v. *Marwel Organics*, (2003) 1 Andh WR 673: (2003) 3 BC 352: 2003 Cr LJ 2498 (AP)**

Case referred:

2000 Cr LJ 2386.

Facts of the case.—In this case two contentions were raised:

(1) There is no averment in the complaint that the cheques are issued towards discharge of liability.

(2) That the liability is not legally enforceable in view of section 69(2) of the Partnership Act, 1930.

The High Court *held* that both the contentions are disputed one and can be decided after taking evidence. There are no grounds to quash the proceedings.

***C. Antony* v. *K.G. Raghvan Nair*, (2003) 1 SCC 1: AIR 2003 SC 182: 2003 Cr LJ 411 (SC)**

Cases referred:

Dharamdeo Singh v. *State of Bihar*, AIR 1976 SC 832: (1976) 1 SCC 610: 1976 Cr LJ 638; AIR 1974 SC 286: (1974) 3 SCC 762.

Facts of the case.—The trial court acquitted the accused. The High Court converted acquittal into conviction. The reasoning of the trial court was:—

(1) The cheque was misused by the complainant.

(2) The ink of the signature and other particulars filled is different.

(3) The witness is not examined before whom the cheque was issued.

(4) Advancement of money was not proved.

The High Court convicted the accused on different grounds which is reappraisal of the evidence. The Supreme Court *held* that the trial Court has given cogent reasons for not accepting the evidence led on behalf of the complainant and could not establish his case. The Supreme Court allowed the appeal and upheld the judgment of the trial Court.

Note.—*If there is denial, then the liability has to be established by the complainant.*

***Devamma* v. *A.R. Raghu*, (2004) 3 BC 167: (2004) 121 Comp Cas 322: (2004) 2 Kant LJ 244: 2004 Cr LJ 1357 (Karn)**

Facts of the case.—The contention of the accused was that the cheque was issued for securing peaceful possession only and not for discharge of any liability. It is contended that whole amount has been paid as can be seen from the sale-deed whereas the complainant stressed that there is a legal liability towards which the cheque is issued. It is *held* that the case falls under section 138 read with sections 118 and 139 of the Negotiable Instruments Act and the complaint cannot be quashed as the contentions can be thrashed out at the full dressed trial.

***Thekkan and Company* v. *M. Anitha*, (2004) 1 BC 435: (2004) 1 Ker LJ 188: (2003) 3 KLT 870: 2004 Cr LJ 58 (Ker)**

Case referred:

(2002) 3 Ker LT 852: 2002 (2) Ker LJ 711.

Facts of the case.—In this case accused has borrowed Rs. 1,25,000 from the complainant and agreed to repay the same in 10 monthly instalments. To discharge the said liability the accused issued 11 cheques. Ten cheques were of Rs. 12,500 each and one cheque was for the entire amount of Rs. 1,25,000. The condition was that if the entire amount was not paid before the agreed date, the 11th cheque of Rs. 1,25,000 shall be presented. The accused paid only Rs. 37,500. Balance amount remained unpaid even after the expiry of 15 days from date of receipt of demand notice. It was *held* that the cheque in issue is issued for the discharge of a legally enforceable liability and it was presented in pursuant to the understanding between the parties. The lower court took the view that the 11th cheque was by way of security. However, the High Court *held* that ingredients of section 138 are satisfied. The accused is at liberty to adduce evidence to rebut the presumption under section 139 of the Act. Resultantly, the appeal of the complainant was allowed and the impugned order was set aside. The respondent was found guilty, convicted and sentenced to pay a sum of Rs. 87,500 and an imprisonment till the rising of the Court.

***Abdul Raheem* v. *U.P.K. Mohammad Haneefa*, (2004) 4 Rec Cri R 17: (2004) 3 All Cri R 714: 2004 Cr LJ 2812 (Mad)**

Facts of the case.—The allegation is that the cheque was issued by accused to complainant in discharge of hand loan of Rs. 60,000 borrowed by the accused from the complainant. Plea of the complainant of hand loan looked improbable due to strained relations between the parties and pendency of litigation between the parties. The plea of the accused was that complainant along with some other persons had snatched away a series of cheques from him. *Facts of the complaint in terms of evidence did not prove the liability* and the accused was acquitted and the High Court did not interfere in the matter as the appeal had no merit and was bound to fall.

***Kurapati Nageshwara Gupta* v. *Madam Shekhar*, (2004) 4 BC 518: (2004) 4 IC 333: (2004) 2 Rec Cri R 218: 2004 Cr LJ 1856 (AP)**

Cases referred:

(2002) 2 Andh LT (Cri) 353; AIR 1996 SC 2239.

Facts of the case.—In this case there were two allegations:

(1) That the cheque was issued towards return of advance by K.K. Raja Mallshwar Rao on failure of registering a sale-deed for the purchase of 325 sq. yds. of land. Thus, the cheque was issued towards discharge of liability which was dishonoured.

(2) That A1 acted on behalf of A2 to A4 and thus they were vicariously liable.

But the complainant could not prove the allegation against A2 to A4 as the accused failed to adduce evidence to bring the case within the scope of section 141 of the Act. Hence, the petitioners/accused A2 to A4 are *held* not liable as they are in no way concerned with the liability.

***Lalan Parshad* v. *State of Jharkhand*, (2004) 2 BLJR 1556: (2004) 3 East Cri C 192: 2004 AIR Jhar CR 2417: 2004 Cr LJ 3622 (Jhar)**

Cases referred:

(2001) 2 East Cri C 353 (Pat) (Followed); 2000 Cr LJ 1988; 1999 Cur Cri R 424.

Facts of the case.—In this case a dispute arose between the Directors of the Company. Property of one of the Directors was with the Bank as Collateral Security. He died. A meeting of Arbitrators was held in which it was awarded that the collateral security be released from the Bank and handed over to the deceased's legal heirs and till then a cheque for Rs. 55 lakh be issued as security for the release of Title Deeds. When he failed to get the documents released by 10-8-2002, the complainant presented the cheque which was dishonoured due to "Payment Stopped". It was represented as advised by the accused, it was again dishonoured with the remarks, "Payment Stopped". The issue was that when the cheque was issued, there was no existing liability. Further, it was found that some manipulations were made in page 6 of the complaint and thus the complainant committed forgery alongwith Advocate. Moreover it was a case of civil nature, being breach of terms of agreement. Hence, the order taking cognizance was quashed.

***Sri Murugan Financiers* v. *P.V. Perumal*, 2005 Cr LJ 269 (Mad)**

Held, that legally enforceable liability was not proved. Cheque issued as guarantee.

***Jagdish Rao Agarwal* v. *State of Andhra Pradesh*, 2005 Cr LJ 314 (AP)**

It is to be proved by the accused that cheque is not issued towards discharge of liability.

***V. Munikrishaniaha* v. *C. Janki Ram Naidu*, 2005 Cr LJ 1093 (AP)**

Drawer of cheque is to prove that there is no liability. Cheque was not issued towards liability. Rebuttal of presumption under section 139.

***Jagmohan* v. *State of Uttar Pradesh*, 2005 Cr LJ 1361 (All)**

Non-existence of liability is to be proved by the accused.

***Sufala Finance (P) Ltd.* v. *B. Narsimha Reddy*, 2005 Cr LJ 1291 (AP)**

Complainant could not establish liability. Matter remanded giving additional opportunity to prove liability.

***M.S. Raghunathan* v. *Rajesh Shah & Co.*, 2005 Cr LJ 2077 (Guj)**

The drawer could not prove that there is no liability.

***Goa Handicrafts, Rural and Small Scale Industries Development Corporation* v. *Samudra Ropes (P) Ltd.*, 2005 Cr LJ 4072 (Bom)**

Accused rebutted the presumption. Cheque given by way of security. Sections 118/139, the Negotiable Instruments Act.

***J. Daniel* v. *State of Kerala*, 2005 Cr LJ 4095 (Ker)**

Cheque issued for compounding an offence which is not compoundable. Dishonour will not constitute offence as being no liability.

***Asoo Haji* v. *K.I. Abdul Latif*, 2005 Cr LJ 640 (Ker)**

Blank cheque issued. Amount filled after finding the balance in the account outstanding. Liability established.

***General Auto Sales* v. *Vijya Laxmi D*, 2005 Cr LJ 1454 (Ker)**

Blank cheque given: Amount filled after seeing the account in the ledger. No rebuttal. Liability established.

SECTION 138

***R. Priyadharshini (A-2)* v. *LIC Housing Finance Ltd.*, 2006 (1) JCC (NI) 12 (Mad)**

Cases referred:

1998 (3) Crimes 543; I (2005) BC 273; 1992 (1) KLT 1; I (2005) BC 315 (MP); CDJ 2004 AP HC 173; (2001) Cr LJ 3120 (Mad); (1997) BC 480; (1994) 1 Mad LW (Ori) 337; 1995 (1) Crimes 226 (Bom); 2002 Cr LJ 2760 (Del); 2001 Comp Cas 794; (2002) 108 Comp Cas 503 (Ker).

It is case of *No Liability*. Husband and wife are joint account holder. Accused No. 1 drew cheque to discharge his liability. Cheque being dishonoured, complaint was filed against husband and wife. Accused No. 2 (wife) filed petition to quash the summoning order. The petition is allowed and summoning order is quashed.

***J. Daniel* v. *State of Kerala*, 2006 (1) JCC (NI) 48 (Ker)**

It is a case of *No Liability*. In this case cheque was issued out of an agreement compounding the offence punishable under section 376 of the IPC which is not compoundable and is hit by section 23 of the Contract Act. The cheque in question was issued for a consideration which is unlawful. It is not a claim arising out of an enforceable debt or other liability. Hence, it will not come under section 138 of the Negotiable Instruments Act.

***Jyanti Bhai Vijya Bhai Kataria* v. *Kamlakar*, 2006 (2) JCC (NI) 174 (MP)**

Case referred:

State of Punjab v. *Kasturi Lal*, AIR 2004 SC 4087.

It is a case under section 138 read with Section 9 of the Negotiable Instruments Act. *Held*, that the cheque was presented by the complainant. The cheque is "Payable to self". It is premature to hold whether the accused is guilty or not. No ground is made for quashment of proceeding pending before CJM under section 138 against the petitioner/accused.

***K.A. Prakash Rao* v. *W. Indra Devi*, 2006 (3) JCC (NI) 281 (AP)**

Cases referred:

(2001) 8 SCC 458; (2001) 6 SCC 16; (2003) 3 SCC 232.

It is a case of *No Liability*. The plea of the complainant is that the cheque was issued towards settlement of his account as he retired from the partnership. The accused's plea is that the complainant has not yet retired from the partnership. PW-1 admits that he has not informed the Registrar of firms about his retirement. Since he failed to prove his retirement, the conclusion is that there is no existing liability.

***Virender Singh* v. *Laxminarayan*, 2007 (1) JCC (NI) 6 (Del)**

Cases referred:

2006 (1) LRC 408 (Ker); (1986) 2 SCC 378; AIR 1968 SC 534; (1974) 2 SCC 533; (1998) 3 SCC 471.

If a cheque is issued in respect of debt or liability which is not legally enforceable then section 138 would not apply. According to doctrine of *"pari delicto"* the court will refuse to enforce an illegal agreement at the instance of a person who himself is a party to an illegality or fraud.

***Bishan Dayal* v. *Dinesh Kumar Singal*, *2007* (2) JCC (NI) 150 Del**

Cases referred:

(2001) 10 SCC 218; (2004) 13 SCC 366; (2002) 1 SCC 234.

Held, that whether a legally enforceable debt exists in favour of the complainant or not should not be pre-judged by the court. It is open to be considered in the trial. The disputed questions do not qualify as ground calling for interference under section 482 of the Cr. P.C.

Also refer

M/s. Pine Product Industries v. *M/s. R.P. Gupta & Sons*, 2007 (1) JCC (NI) 28 (Del); *M/s. Collage Culture* v. *Apparal Expart Promotion Council*, 2007 (4) JCC (NI) 388; *Shyam Gopal Gupta* v. *Sanjeev Bhargava*, 2007 (4) JCC (NI) 405 (Del).

***P. Suresh Kumar* v. *R. Shankar*, *2007* (1) JCC (NI) 106 (SC)**

Cases referred:

(2001) 2 SCC 595; (1999) 7 SCC 510; (2002) 6 SCC 462; (2002) 6 SCC 663; (2006) 3 SCC 178.

It appears from a plain reading of the complaint-petition that the respondent had admitted his liability to the extent of Rs. 7 lakh. Respondent had to issue the cheque under some threat or coercion in the Police Station could not be accepted.

Appeal is dismissed.

Note.—*The Apex Court directed that having regard to the relevant facts of the case, as envisaged under section 357 of the Cr. P.C., must be considered by the courts.*

***Vijya Ganesh Gandholekar* v. *Indranil Jairaj Damale*, 2008 Cr LJ 657 (Bom)**

Cases referred:

AIR 2006 Bom 1096; AIR 2002 SC 38; (1999) 1 Bank Cas 519.

In this case the plea was taken that it was a time-barred debt. Drawer has revalidated the cheque from time to time. It could be said that on each occasion there was a fresh promise as envisaged by section 25 of the Contract Act. It is an acknowledgement within meaning of section 18 of the Limitation Act if revalidation was made within period of limitation. Proceedings for dishonour of cheque were initiated within three years from last date of revalidation.

Debt was not time-barred debt.

***Natesha Securities* v. *Vinayak Waman Mokashi,* 2008 Cr LJ 1115 (Bom)**

Cases referred:

(2000) 3 All ER 182; (1995) 3 All ER 918; AIR 1988 SC 2267; 1915 AC 705.

The fact that the demand draft was dream in favour of the applicant-firm and that it was credited in the account of the applicant lead me to hold that the applicant/accused was a debtor and the complainant was a creditor. The cheque of Rs. 1,00,000 was given by the accused to the complainant discharge of his legal liability. Thus none of the contentions raised by Mr. Gupta can be accepted. *The complainant has proved beyond doubt his legally enforceable liability as revealed by the evidence. The revision is, therefore, without merit.*

***M/s. Surana Securities Ltd.* v. *G. Kamlakar,* 2008 Cr LJ 1221**

Cases referred:

AIR 2002 SC 182; AIR 1998 SC 596; AIR 1984 SC 5; AIR 1960 Mad 240; AIR 1956 Nag 8; AIR 1938 Mad 723; (1913) 14 Cr LJ 529; (1908) 7 Cr LJ 499 (Mad).

Two issues were raised in the complaint and answered by the court.

(i) Complaint if made in the name of incorporeal person like company it is necessary that a natural person represents such juristic person.

(ii) In a letter addressed by the accused to the complainant it was categorically stated that he had verified the account statement and stated that it is true and correct. The accused pleaded in the letter that the complainant should bear with him for the delay. *Now it is not open to the accused to plead that there was no legally enforceable debt.*

***A.R.M. Nizmathuallah* v. *Vaduganathan,* 2008 Cr LJ 880 (Mad)**

It is a case of debt duly acknowledged in terms of section 25(3) *Illustration (e)* of the Contract Act. So the cheque issued becomes a promise made in writing to pay furnishing fresh cause of action. So proceedings cannot be quashed. Moreover, it is a triable issue which can be decided under section 482 Cr. P.C. The court relied on 2005 STPL (DC) 82 (Ker).

***K.S. Bakshi* v. *State,* 2008 (3) JCC (NI) 267 (Del)**

Cases referred:

AIR 2006 SC 3366; AIR 2002 SC 3014; (1967) 1 AC 361; (1987) QB 527; AIR 1966 SC 193; AIR 1981 SC 1271.

In this case the ambit and scope of "other liability" was discussed.

The word "other liability" means "debt". Under the doctrine of "*ejusdem generis*" there must not be a distinct genus. It takes its meaning from the other expression used. When words pertaining to a class, category, or genus are followed by general words, in such a case the general words take their meaning from the preceding particular words.

***Sudhir Kumar Bhalla* v. *Jagdish Chand,* 2008 (2) JCC (NI) 241 SC**

In this case the trial Court dismissed the complaint but the High Court convicted the accused. High Court did not give cogent, satisfactory and convincing reasons for disbelieving and discarding the pre-charge evidence of the appellant, corroborated by the evidence of the expert opinion in regard to interpolation and fabrication of the cheque. Appellant cannot be convicted. Hence, the judgment and order of the High Court is set aside.

***Titanor Components Ltd.* v. *Techno Engineers,* 2009 (3) Crimes 133 (Bom)**

It is an appeal against acquittal. The facts are that the complainant supplied the plant to the accused but finally the buyer did not place order for the purchase of machinery. The court accepted the plea that so long as the order is not placed the machinery shall belong to the complainant and not to the proposed buyer. *Held,* that the Magistrate cannot be faulted with. There is no liability on the part of the proposed buyer (accused). There is no ground to interfere with acquittal.

***Bansal Paper Mart* v. *State,* 2009 (2) JCC (NI) 82 (Del)**

In *lieu* of cheque the payment was made by two pay orders. Thus there was no liability at the time of filing the complaint. The liability *qua* the cheque stood liquidated.

***M/s. Vijya Polymers Pvt. Ltd.* v. *M/s. Vinnay Agarwal,* 2009 (2) JCC (NI) 144 Del**

In terms of Section 18 of the Limitation Act, the debt was time-barred. Hence, it is not legally recoverable and was not legally recoverable at the time of issue of the cheque.

Refer. *Smt. Ashwini Satish Bhat* v. *Sri Jeevan Divakar Lalienkar,* 2000 (5) Bom CR 9.

***P. Venugopal* v. *Madan P. Sarathi,* 2009 (1) JCC (NI) 27 (SC)**

Case referred:

Krishna Janardhan Bhat v. *Dattatraya G. Hegde,* 2008 (4) SCC 54.

It is held that all the courts below have arrived at a concurrent finding that the complainant has been able to prove his case of grant of a loan. The burden of proof got shifted to the accused and the burden of proof does not extend to the extent that the cheque was issued for the discharge of any debt or liability which is required to be proved by the complainant. It is essentially a question of fact.

***M/s. Kumar Exports* v. *M/s. Sharma Carpets,* 2009 (1) JCC (NI) 34 (SC)**

In this case the word "Presumption" was explained as" taking as true without examination or proof". But it is rebuttable. The evidence of the Sales Tax Department showed that there was no transaction of woollen carpets. Thus, the plea of the accused had given blank cheques as advance payment is probable. There was no existing liability.

***Smt. Nanda w/o Dharmnandanwar* v. *Nand Kishore S/o Talakram*, 2010 (1) Crimes 708 (Bom)**

Cases referred

Krishna Janardhan Bhatt v. *Dattatraya G. Hedge*, AIR 2008 SC 1325; *Kusum Ingots & Alloys Ltd.* v. *Pennar Peterson Securities Ltd.*, (2002) 2 SCC 745.

It is held that only legally enforceable debt or liability can be enforced in the proceedings under section 138 of the said Act, because the *Explanation* to the Penal provision is abundantly clear that the dishonoured cheque must have been received by the complainant against a legally enforceable debt or liability. A money lender cannot enforce a loan transaction lawfully without production of valid money lending licence operative at the time of transaction of loan to be recovered.

***S.K. Sales* v. *Jay Ambe Industries*, 2010 (1) Crimes 177 (Bom)**

In this case judgment of acquittal in passed. Principal amount was paid by the accused. Statement of account showed balance amount on account of commission. How such commissions is payable is not shown. The Trial Court took the view that cheque was given in security of the loan amount and entire amount has been paid. The court held that where two views one possible the view taken by Trial Court would not be liable to interference is appeal.

III. DISHONOUR OF CHEQUE

This topic is covered under sections 91 and 92 of the Negotiable Instruments Act. Section 91 deals with "Dishonour by non-acceptance" and section 92 deals with "Dishonour by non-payment". Section 138 is to be read in conjunction with section 92. Section 92 reads as follows:—

> "A promissory note, bill of exchange or cheque is said to be dishonoured by non-payment, when the maker of the note, accepter of the Bill or drawee of the cheque default in payment upon being duly required to pay the same".

Section 64 of the said Act says:—

> "It embodies the principles that promissory note, bills of exchange and cheques must be presented for payment to the maker, acceptor or drawee thereof by the holder or any body authorised by him."

It is to be supplemented with section 31 of the Act which says that a general liability is on the Banks (Drawee of cheques) that all cheques be paid normally, provided there is sufficient money in the account of the drawer and his signatures not differ. The Drawee Bank has no right to refuse payment of the cheque on unfair excuses particularly when there is restraint order of any court.

(*Refer* AIR 1988 Cal 265).

But section 31 is to be read further to know that the cheque can be dishonoured only when there is insufficiency of funds, otherwise the cheque is not dishonoured but it is called, "Return of cheque". The banks have a cheque returning memo which contains various reasons for "return of cheque" but there is only one reason of dishonour of cheque which is "insufficiency of funds".

Section 138 has stated two reasons for dishonour of cheque, *i.e.*,

(1) insufficiency of funds.

(2) exceeds arrangement.

However, judicial pronouncements have added more reasons for dishonour of cheque which come within the scope of section 138 of the Act. Now we shall look to all those reasons for dishonour of cheque falling within the ambit of section 138 of the Act as judicial pronouncements are binding in nature.

IV. REASONS FOR DISHONOUR

INSUFFICIENCY OF FUNDS/REFER TO DRAWER

The term "refer to drawer" is widely used by the Banks to cover various grounds of return of cheque including the ground of dishonour of cheque being short of funds. M.S. Parthasarthy in his book *Cheques in Law and Practice* (3rd Edition) has said that the term "refer to the drawer" is not a damaging expression but when the cheque is returned it generally means return due to shortage of balance in the Bank in the account of the Drawer.

In *V.S. Krishnan* v. *V. Narayanan,* 1990 LW (Cri) 66, this expression "Refer to Drawer" was specifically dealt with and while comparing it with section 138 giving reasons for dishonour, the court *held* that the expression "Refer to Drawer" be not used generally or carelessly but the specific expression be used to avoid confusion. It was by way of a judicial advice. However, the term, "Refer to Drawer" is commonly considered as alternative to "Insufficiency of Funds.".

***A.C. Raj, Inchivila, Thottathu Veedu, Parasala* v. *M. Rajani, Ezha Kudi-vila Veedu,* (1997) 1 CCC 170: (1997) 1 Ker LJ 168: (1997) 2 BC 59: (1997) 1 Ker LT 302: 1997 Cr LJ 1939 (Ker)**

Case referred:

(1996) 2 Ker LT 886 (relied on).

Facts of the case.—There were two issues involved:—

(1) Cheque returned with endorsement, "Refer to Drawer". It could mean any reason including "insufficiency of funds". It is for the complainant to prove that the said endorsement means that there was "insufficiency of funds." No evidence is adduced in this regard. Hence; not proved.

(2) Notice given by the complainant does not make mention of the amount of cheque but a different amount including interest thereon without specifying rate of interest and amount of interest claimed. The notice is defective in terms of section 138(a). The court relied on 1996 (2) Ker LT 886. This decision was rendered by the Calcutta High Court. It is a case of no evidence and hence the petition fails on merits.

***Ram Nath* v. *Jagdish Parshad Garg,* 1999 Cr LJ 2136 (Raj)**

Case referred:

(1998) 3 SCC 249: (1998) 1 KLT 582: 1998 Cr LJ 1397: AIR 1998 SC 1057.

Facts of the case.—In this case the cheque was dishonoured for "insufficiency of funds". The complainant produced sufficient evidence to prove the culpability of the accused. The lower court sentenced him to three months simple imprisonment with fine of Rs. one lakh and in default to further undergo simple imprisonment for another ten days. The matter went in appeal before Additional Sessions Judge. There was no arguments on the case but made two submissions:—

(1) That the accused had already undergone three months simple imprisonment

(2) That he is not in a position to pay the fine of Rs. one lakh as directed by the trial Court.

The appellate Court did not interfere. The matter went to the Higher Court. It also did not interfere but *held* that there is no alternative provided in the provision and as such the complainant has to file a civil suit to recover this amount and the suit if filed within 4 months, the same should be decided within 4 months. The petition was found infructuous and hence dismissed.

***M. Subramanyam* v. *P. Rathina Kumar*, 1995 Cr LJ 3098 (Mad)**

Case referred: 1990 Mad LW (Cri) 67 (relied on).

Facts of the case.—In this case two issues were raised:

(1) That the allegations in the complaint are so vague that cognizance could not have been taken by the trial Magistrate.

(2) That the endorsement by the Banker, "refer to drawer" cannot be *held* to be either due to insufficiency of funds in the accounts to honour the cheque or because the amount shown in the cheque exceeds the arrangement.

The High Court negatived both the contentions and said that 'in Banking parlance the reason "Refer to Drawer", when cheques are returned unpaid is used generally for returning the cheques for want of funds or because of garnishee order. This, again, is a matter of evidence. The bank would be able to justify before the court the reasons for which the cheques were returned. If in banking parlance, "Refer to Drawer", is used for the purpose of insufficiency of funds, the ingredients of the section would be attracted.'

***Voltas Ltd.* v. *Hiralal Agarwalla*, (1991) 71 Comp Cas 273: 1991 Cr LJ 609 (Cal)**

Cases referred:

(1983) 3 SCC 25: 1983 SCC (Cri) 553: 1983 Cr LJ 159 (SC); 1983 Cr LJ 172 (SC) (relied on); 1982 Lah IC 1777 (Cal); 1979 Cr LJ 86 (Cal); 1978 Lah IC 898; 1918 AC 777.

Facts of the case.—In this case two issues were raised:

(1) That the accused at the top of the hierarchy of officers of the company and not responsible for day-to-day business of the company is not to be *held* liable.

(2) That the cheque returned with remarks, "Refer to Drawer", means cheque returned not for want of funds.

The High Court negatived both the pleas raised by the petitioner presently. Reverting to the terminology, "Refer to the Drawer," the High Court *held* that it is pre-mature to hold that the accused persons have not committed the offence and that can be brought out only in the regular trial of the case as, "Refer to Drawer" is subjected to various interpretations. The petition fails.

***Syed Rasool and Sons* v. *Aildas & Company*, (1993) 78 Comp Cas 738: 1992 Cr LJ 4048 (AP)**

Cases referred:

(1992) 1 An WR 372 (overruled); (1992) 1 An WR 502 (affirmed); (1992) 1 Crimes 23 (Ker); (1991) 1 KLT 595; (1991) 1 Crimes 226 (Karn); (1991) 71 Comp Cas 273 (Cal); (1991) 71 Comp Cas 536 (Mad); (1990) 2 Bank CLR 416 (P&H); *State of Bihar* v. *Deokaran Nenshi*, AIR 1973 SC 908: (1972) 2 SCC 890: 1973 SCC (Cri) 114: 1973 Cr LJ 347; AIR 1960 SC 866: (1960) 3 SCR 388: 1960 Cr LJ 1239; *London Joint Stock Bank Ltd.* v. *Macmillan*, 1918 AC 777.

Facts of the case.—The issue involved is that whether, "Refer to Drawer", means cheque returned unpaid for want of funds or otherwise. In this case various citations were referred. The High Court *held* that there can be various reasons for dishonour of cheque but the words, "Refer to Drawer", in their ordinary meaning amounted to a statement by the Bank, "we are not paying, go back to the drawer and ask him "why" or else "go back to the drawer and ask him to pay". *We are of the firm view that, "Refer to Drawer", necessarily means, as per banking parlance, that the cheque has been returned for want of funds in the account of the drawer of the cheque.*

***K.P. Sahadevan* v. *T.K. Sreedharn*, 1996 Cr LJ 1223 (Ker)**

Cases referred:

1994 MLJ (Cri) 91 (followed); (1993) 2 Ker LJ 704; (1992) 1 Ker LT 812.

Facts of the case.—In this case two issues were raised:—

(1) Whether the Judicial Magistrate First Class can impose fine more than Rs. 5,000 in view of *non-obstante* clause in section 142. (*Held* in the affirmative).

(2) "Refer to Drawer" and Burden of Proof.

The High Court *held* as follows:—

That when the cheque was returned with endorsement, "Refer to Drawer", the burden of proof is on the complainant to show that the cheque was returned either for insufficiency of funds or the amount exceeds the amount arranged to be paid. In this case the Bank Manager is not called as a witness. The High Court remanded back the case to the Trial Court to decide afresh in the light of such evidence and the earlier evidence available on record. The Manager may be examined along with documents connected with the return of cheques.

***Lilly Hire Purchase (P) Ltd.* v. *Darshan Lal*, (1997) 2 Bank LJ 258: (1997) 89 Comp Cas 663: 1997 Cr LJ 4603 (P&H)**

Cases referred:

1996 Cr LJ 3316 (P&H); (1994) 2 Rec CR 82 (P&H); (1994) 2 Rec CR 135 (P&H); (1977) 4 SCC 551: 1978 Cr LJ 165: AIR 1978 SC 47 (followed); AIR 1968 SC 733 (1968) 2 SCR 685: 1968 Cr LJ 876 (followed).

Facts of the case.—The cheque was dishonoured on two grounds: (1) Refer to Drawer, (2) Signatures do not tally. The trial Magistrate came to the conclusion that the case has been made out and passed summoning order. The Sessions Judge reversed the order of the Trial Magistrate. The High Court *held* that "Refer to Drawer" means, "Insufficiency of Funds", "signatures do not tally" is a fact which can be decided in the trial on the basis of evidence adduced.

***Francis Savio* v. *State Bank of Kerala*, 1998 Cr LJ 4735 (Ker)**

Cases referred:

(1998) 3 SCC 249: (1998) 92 Comp Cas 88: (1988) 1 KLT 582: 1998 Cr LJ 1397 (SC); 1996 Cr LJ 1692 (SC); 1994 Cr LJ 674 (Ker) (overruled by Supreme Court).

Facts of the case.—There were three issues in this case

(1) Ingredients of section 138 are not specifically averred in the complaint.

(2) Refer to Drawer.

(3) Section 357, the Cr. P.C.

The High Court *held* as follows:—

(1) That the words used "stop payment" for dishonouring of cheque is already overruled by the Supreme Court. It falls under the ambit of section 138, the Negotiable Instruments Act.

(2) In view of the statement of the Bank Manager that there was insufficiency of funds it is sufficient to construe that 'Refer to drawer' means for want for sufficient funds.

(3) The Magistrate is vested with power to award compensation under section 357, the Cr. P.C.

***Pradip Tibrewal* v. *State of Gujarat*, (1998) 3 CCC 190: (1998) 3 Rec Cri R 53: 1998 Cr LJ 559 (Guj).**

Facts of the case.—In this case three issues arose:—

(1) Refer to Drawer.

(2) Cause of action. (The complaint is pre-mature.)

(3) Whether criminal proceeding can be initiated in view of civil suit.

All the issues are negatived. On the point of dishonour of cheque, the court has *held* that the endorsement on the cheque while returning, "Insufficient funds" and asking the complainant to refer to the drawer. Thus, reading the two endorsements it is clear that "Refer to Drawer" means "Insufficiency of Funds" for dishonouring the cheque. The petition is dismissed with a direction to the trial court to dispose of the case expeditiously.

Note.—*"Refer to Drawer" generally means, "Insufficiency of Funds," but it needs to be proved by the complainant. This ground "Refer to Drawer" does not fall within the cover of "Presumption" that it is due to "Insufficiency of Funds" that the cheque is dishonoured.*

ACCOUNT CLOSED

***S. Prassana* v. *R. Vijayalakshmi*, (1992) 2 CCR 1325: 1992 Cr LJ 1233 (Mad)**

Case referred:

(1991) 1 Crimes 226 (followed).

Facts of the case.—It is a case where the cheque was dishonoured on the ground of "Account closed". The court followed 1991 (1) Crimes 226 (Karn) where it is *held* that ground of dishonour of cheque "Account Closed" does not fall within the cover of section 138 of the Negotiable Instruments Act which speaks:—

(1) Insufficiency of funds.

(2) Exceeds arrangements.

Thus, the petition was dismissed that such ground "Account closed" is not covered by section 138 of the Act.

***Shavindera Sansguiri* v. *Adineo*, 1996 Cr LJ 1816 (Bom)**

Cases referred:

(1994) 1 Crimes 379 (Ker) (dissented from); 1993 Cr LJ 680 (Bom).

Facts of the case.—In this case the cheque issued was post-dated. Account was closed after issue of cheque. Thus, the cheque was dishonoured on the ground, "Account closed". The court *held* that ground for dishonour of cheque is not material. If a debtor, with ulterior motive issues a cheque and then closes the account to avoid discharge of debt, he is doing so on his own risk. The court *held* that such practice is not only violating the Banking Regulation Act but also falls within the ambit of section 138 of the Act. In short, the view of the court is that the paramount requirement of the section is the acceptability of the cheque and its dishonouring is against the object of the provision.

***J. Krishnan Nair* v. *P. Jaseentha*, (1998) 3 CCC 206: (1998) 4 Rec Cri R 154: 1998 Cr LJ 3913 (Ker)**

Cases referred:

(1994) 1 KLT 111 (dissented); (1993) 2 KLT 141.

Facts of the case.—It is a case where a post-dated cheque is issued.

Before the cheque reached the bank, the account was closed. The court took the view that closure of account amounts to "Insufficiency of Funds" and such case falls within the ambit of section 138 of the Act.

***NEPC Micon Ltd.* v. *Magma Leasing Ltd.*, (1999) 4 SCC 253: 1999 SCC (Cri) 524: AIR 1999 SC 1952: 1999 Cr LJ 2883 (SC)**

Cases referred:

AIR 1988 SC 1057; AIR 1966 SC 2339; 1996 Cr LJ 1816 (Bom); (1995) 4 Crimes 379 (AP); 1995 Cr LJ 1882 (Mad); 1994 Cr LJ 2874 (Guj); (1994) 1 Crimes 379 (Ker); 1993 Cr LJ 680 (Bom); 1992 Cr LJ 1233 (Mad); (1991) 1 Crimes 226; AIR 1988 SC 79: (1987) 4 SCC 203: (1987) 2 LLN 911; AIR 1975 SC 1871: (1975) 4 SCC 745: 1975 Tax LR 1935: (1976) 1 SCR 38; 1974 Cr LJ 472; AIR 1965 SC 871: (1965) 1 SCR 7; *Seaford Court Estate Ltd.* v. *Asher*, (1949) 2 KB 481: (1949) 2 All ER 155 (CA); *Heydan's* case, 76 ER 637.

Facts of the case.—It is a case of dishonour of cheque on the ground of "Account closed". *Held*, that it is an offence by drawer of cheques envisaged in section 138. The discussion centered around interpretation of Statutes, Penal Statutes and Legislative intention. The Supreme Court said that even though section 138 is a penal statute, it is the duty of the court to interpret it consistent with the legislative intent and purpose so as to suppress the mischief and advance the remedy. Section 138 of the Act has created a contractual breach as an offence and the Legislative purpose is to promote efficacy of Banking and of ensuring that in commercial or contractual transaction cheques are not dishonoured and credibility in transacting business is maintained. *Held*, that "Account Closed" amounts to "Insufficiency of Funds".

Note.—*This ground "Account closed", for dishonour of cheque be read in section 138 as being introduced judicially.*

***G. Venkataramanaiah* v. *Sillakallu Venkteshwarlu*, 1999 Cr LJ 1219 (AP)**

Cases referred:

(1992) 3 Crimes 306 (Bom) (dissented from); (1991) 1 Crimes 226 (Karn) (dissented from).

Facts of the case.—The cheque was dishonoured on the ground that the account is closed. The court *held* that a dishonest person after issuing a cheque or even before issuing a cheque (as in this case) can any time at his own will close the account and in such situation section 138 shall in effect become inoperative. This has not been the intention of the Parliament. *Held,* that the offence under section 138 is committed even if the cheque is returned on the ground of closure of account.

***Rajender Basantrao Khade* v. *Laxmikant Shantilal Choudhari*, 2000 Cr LJ 1195 (Bom)**

Cases referred:

(1999) 4 SCC 253: (1999) 96 Comp Cas 822: 1999 SCC (Cri) 524: 1999 Cr LJ 2883 (SC) (followed); 1996 Cr LJ 1816; 1992 Mah LJ 302; 1991 Cr LJ 1603 (Ori).

Facts of the case.—It is a case under section 138, the Negotiable Instruments Act read with section 420, the I.P.C. The cheque in question was dishonoured as the account is closed. The main argument was that "closure of account" is the ground which is not covered by section 138 of the Act. The High Court referred to (1999) 4 SCC 253: (1999) 96 Comp Cas 822: 1999 SCC (Cri) 524: 1999 Cr LJ 2883 (SC) wherein the Supreme Court has observed that section 138, the Negotiable Instruments Act has to be interpreted taking into consideration the legislative intent and purpose. When a cheque is returned unpaid with an endorsement "Account closed", it amounts to returning the cheque because of insufficiency of funds. The order of the Sessions Judge is set aside and the matter is remanded back to the trial court to proceed further according to law on other points raised therein.

***Thirumala Agencies* v. *Samala Mareppa and Sons*, (2001) 2 BC 105: (2001) 3 CCC 423: (2001) 3 Crimes 400: 2001 Cr LJ 2692 (Karn)**

Facts of the case.—In this case three issues were raised:—

(1) That refusal to accept notice amounts to service according to law.

(2) Cheque dishonoured with an endorsement "Account closed".

(3) Cause-of-action arises only after the expiry of 15 days provided in the notice.

These points raised by the petitioner are negatived. The High Court *held* that the fact of service of notice is a matter of fact which need not be considered as being finding of fact. Regarding dishonour of cheque on the ground "Account closed", it is *held* that if the cheque came to the presented and it was returned with an endorsement "Account closed", it amounts to dishonesty and it comes within the definition of section 138, the Negotiable Instruments Act. Regarding "Cause-of-action" the court referred to and relied on 1995 Cr LJ 1904 (Karn) wherein it was said that cause-of-action arises only after the expiry of 15 days.

***Hashmikant M. Seth* v. *State of Gujarat*, (2004) 3 Crimes 233: (2004) 2 Guj LJ 783: 2004 Cr LJ 3628 (Guj)**

Cases referred:

AIR 2003 SC 2035: (2003) 3 SCC 232: 2003 Cr LJ 1723: (2003) 114 Comp Cas 644; 2003 Cr LJ 3292; 1999 Cr LJ 2883; (1992) 2 Crimes 171 (AP); 1998 Cr LJ 1680 (Karn); 1996 Cr LJ 1816 (Bom); (1994) 21 Cr LJ 546: 1995 (1) Guj LH 458; 1993 Cr LJ 680 (Bom); 1991 Cr LJ 1347 (SC).

Facts of the case.—In this case the cheque was issued after "Closure of Account". The High Court, referred to various case laws and *held* that the offence in terms of section 138 stands committed even if cheque is issued after closure of account as the amount standing to the credit of that account would be "Nil". So it cannot be said that the cheque issued after the closure of account is not covered by section 138 of the Act and further *held* that *Urban Co-operative Credit Society, Borsad* v. *State of Gujarat*, 2003 Cr LJ 3292, decided by single Judge of this court is *per incuriam.* It has no binding force.

***P.N. Salim* v. *P.J. Thomas*, (2005) 1 BC 41: (2004) 4 ICC 618: (2004) 3 Ker 384: (2004) 1 KLT 816: 2004 Cr LJ 3096 (Ker)**

Cases referred:

2004 Cr LJ 414 (Ker); (2003) 3 SCC 232: (2003) 114 Comp Cas 644: 2003 Cr LJ 1723 (SC) (Relied on); (2002) 3 Ker LT 852; (2000) 2 Ker LJ 679; (1999) 4 SCC 253: 1999 SCC (Cri) 524: (1999) 96 Comp Cas 822: AIR 1999 SC 1952 (relied on); 1996 Cr LJ 1816 (Bom) (relied on); (1993) 2 Ker LJ 96.

Facts of the case.—It is an appeal against the order of acquittal and the quantum of punishment awarded. The High Court *held* that the accused failed to discharge the burden and to rebut the presumption under section 138, the Negotiable Instruments Act, and hence the impugned judgment of acquittal is set aside and recommended to take a lenient view on the point of sentence as imposition of substantive punishment has no penological object to be achieved in a case like the one.

***Jaspal Singh Bedi* v. *State of Punjab*, 2005 Cr LJ 1061 (P&H)**

Cheque issued from closed account. No explanation by the accused. High Court held acquittal is not proper.

***Vijya Kumar Gupta* v. *R.S. Traders*, 2005 Cr LJ 3860 (J&K)**

Account closed before cheque reached Bank. Amounts to Insufficiency of Funds.

Note.—*It is felt that if a cheque is post-dated and the account is closed due to some circumstances and the party (Payee) is informed well in advance prior to the date of presentation of the cheque and a willingness is shown to replace the cheque already issued, from the account now maintained by the drawer and still the cheque is presented, this situation may not be covered by section 138 of the Act. In such cases the drawer of the cheque must comply with Proviso (c) to section 138 of the Act as non-compliance with Proviso (c) of section 138 gives rise to cause-of-action and not mere dishonouring of cheque.*

PAYMENT STOPPED

***Thomas Varghese* v. *P. Jerome,* (1992) 2 Crimes 919: (1992) 2 CCR 2191: 1992 Cr LJ 3080 (Ker)**

Cases referred:

(1991) 1 Ker LT 269; ILR 1990 Karn 3881; (1990) 2 BC 305; AIR 1981 SC 1922: (1981) 4 SCC 173: (1981) 131 ITR 597.

Facts of the case.—Cheque issued by the drawer was dishonoured with the endorsement "Payment stopped by drawer." *Held,* that if the cheque is dishonoured with such endorsement and the complaint is specific that there was no funds in the account and that the drawer stopped the payment with ulterior motive and mischievously and maliciously, the proceedings initiated under section 138 of the Act cannot be quashed.

***Bhageerthi* v. *Veena,* (1992) 3 Crimes 663: 1992 Cr LJ 3946 (Ker)**

Facts of the case.—In this case the cheque was dishonoured with the remarks, "Payment stopped by the Drawer", but there is no averment in the complaint that the cheque was dishonoured for want of adequate money. *Held,* section 138 of the Act is not attracted.

***Safiq Ahmed* v. *Ahsan Halim,* 1993 Cr LJ 3823 (Sikkim)**

Cases referred:

(1992) 2 BC 35 (P&H) (Followed); (1990) (2) BC 305 (P&H) (Followed).

Facts of the case.—Cheque was dishonoured with the remarks, "Payment stopped by the drawer". But there is no averment in the complaint about "insufficiency of funds". Thus, there is no allegation in the complaint which could make it a *prima facie* case under section 138 of the Act. The complaint and the proceedings initiated thereto are quashed. The complainant is at liberty to resort to another proceedings before the competent authority in connection with other offences.

***Rama Gupta* v. *Bakeman's Home Products Ltd.,* (1994) 79 Comp Cas 473: 1993 Cr LJ 744 (P&H)**

Cases referred:

(1991) 2 RCR 535 (distinguished); (1990) 2 RCR 335 (followed); (1987) 2 RCR 263 (relied on); (1984) 2 CLR 496 (distinguished).

Facts of the case.—The cheque was dishonoured with the remarks, "Payment Stopped by the Drawer." There is sufficiency of funds to honour the cheque. There is also no allegation of cheating in the complaint. *Held,* that continuance of proceedings amounts to abuse of the process of court. The impugned complaint, summoning order and further proceedings were quashed.

***S. Ashok* v. *Vasudevan Moosad,* (1995) 82 Comp Cas 665: 1993 Cr LJ 2486 (Ker)**

Cases referred:

(1993) 1 Ker LT 13; AIR 1992 SC 604: 1992 Supp (1) SCC 335: 1992 Cr LJ 527; AIR 1992 SC 1379: (1992) 3 SCC 317: 1992 Cr LJ 1956: 1992 SCC (Cri) 636; 1992 Cr LJ 3946 (Ker); (1991) 1 Ker LT 269; AIR 1977 SC 1754: (1977) 1 SCC 505: 1977 SCC (Cri) 132; AIR 1976 SC 1947: (1976) 3 SCC 736: 1976 Cr LJ 1533.

Facts of the case.—Cheque returned with endorsement, "Stop Payment". There is no specific allegation in the complaint that the cheque was bounced for want of sufficient funds and as such the offence under section 138 is not made out and the complaint can be quashed under section 482, Cr.P.C.

***Dr. P.K. Mohammad Rasheed* v. *State of Kerala,* (1994) 1 APLJ 73: (1993) 2 KLT 1027: 1994 Cr LJ 674 (Ker)**

Cases referred:

1993 Cr LJ 2486 (relied on); (1993) 1 Ker LT 13; (1993) 2 Ker LT 237; 1992 Supp (1) SCC 335: 1992 Cr LJ 527: AIR 1992 SC 604 (followed); (1992) 3 SCC 317: 1992 Cr LJ 1956: 1992 SCC (Cri) 636: AIR 1992 SC 1379 (followed); 1992 Cr LJ 3080 (distinguished); 1992 Cr LJ 3946 (relied on); AIR 1975 AP 158; AIR 1967 Ker 97; AIR 1951 SC 115: 1951 SCR 145: 30 Pat 329; *Queen* v. *Commissioner for Special Purposes of Income-tax,* (1888) 21 QBD 313.

Facts of the case.—Bank returned the cheque with endorsement, "Payment Stopped". The complaint was filed without alleging cause of dishonour of cheque. *Held* that all dishonour of cheques are not made punishable under section 138 of the Negotiable Instruments Act. Only the dishonour of cheque on account of circumstances mentioned in section 138 of the Act is made punishable and this ingredient of section 138 must be pleaded, *i.e.,* "Insufficiency of Funds" or "Exceeds Arrangement". In the absence of such pleading the complaint is not maintainable.

***Sri Bhaskar Fertilizers* v. *Dinkal Agro Chemicals (P) Ltd., Hyderabad,* 1996 Cr LJ 1103 (AP)**

Cases referred:

(1995) 1 ALD 393 (explained and distinguished); (1994) 3 Crimes 579 (Bom); 1994 Cr LJ 674 (Ker) (explained and distinguished); (1994) 2 Andh LT (Cri) 326 (Ker); (1994) 79 Comp Cas 335 (P&H) (dissented from); (1994) (3) Crimes 308 (Raj); 1993 Cr LJ 2486 (Ker); (1993) 76 Comp Cas 241 (P&H) (dissented from); 1993 Cr LJ 3823 (Sikkim) (explained and distinguished); 1992 Cr LJ 4048; (1992) 1 Andh WR 372 (followed); 1992 Cr LJ 3080 Ker (followed).

Facts of the case.—In this case there are two aspects:—

(i) Cheque was dishonoured with an endorsement on the cheque, "Stop Payment by the Drawer".

(ii) There was categorical allegation that the cheque was issued towards the discharge of a liability and it was dishonoured on the ground that there were no funds in the account of the Drawer.

The High Court referred to various case laws and *held* that even in the absence of any allegation to the effect that the cheque had been returned unpaid for want of funds, the court should take cognizance of the offence. Also the complaint cannot be thrown out at the threshold without trial and the enquiry has to go on to find out whether, irrespective of the expression used in the banking parlance, the cheque was returned for want of funds. The High Court observed that the Drawer might play mischief and ask the banker to stop payment finding no funds in his account to evade punishment and the section 138 of the Act. Moreover, in this case a very heavy stress is laid on the "Dishonour of Cheque".

***S.K. Jain* v. *Narinder Singh*, 1996 Cr LJ 1834 (P&H)**

Cases referred:

1994 Cr LJ 674 (Ker); 1993 ISJ (Banking) 511 (P&H); 1993 ISJ (Banking) 126 (Ker) (relied on); 1992 ISJ (Banking) 5177 (Ker) (relied on); (1992) 1 KLT 812; 1992 Cr LJ 3946 (Ker); 1992 ISJ (Banking) 7334 (P&H).

Facts of the case.—This petition is filed under section 482, the Cr. P.C. for quashing the complaint and the summoning order. The cheque was dishonoured with endorsement "Payment Stopped" but the allegation in the complaint was that the petitioner (accused) with *mala fide* intention issued the cheque to cheat the respondent (complainant) and he had no funds in the bank and as such intentionally got the payment of the cheque stopped. The High Court *held* that countermanding of a cheque by "stop memo" hardly affects the rights of the respondent to initiate the proceedings under the Act. If the circumstances contemplated in section 138 are made out, the court has to examine whether the cheque was returned for want of sufficient funds or not and the same can be decided after taking the evidence. The petition is dismissed.

***Electronics Trade and Technology Development Corporation Ltd.,* v. *Indian Technologists and Engineering (Electronics) (P.) Ltd.,* (1996) 2 SCC 739: 1996 SCC (Cri) 454: 1996 Cr LJ 1692 (SC)**

Facts of the case.—The cheque is returned with the endorsement "Instructions for non-payment". The Supreme Court went more forward in asserting that "stop payment" virtually means "insufficiency of funds". Even if it is so, the payment can be made within 15 days of the receipt of notice issued by the payee or holder in due course. Even then non-payment amounts to dishonest intention which is inferable. Hence, section 138 is attracted.

***Anil Kumar Parolia* v. *Md. Shafique Khan,* (1997) 2 CCC 20: (1997) 2 BC 669: 1997 Cr LJ 717 (Cal)**

Cases referred:

(1996) 3 SCC 87; (1995) 1 Cal HN 370.

Facts of the case.—Cheque was dishonoured for, "Payment stopped". There is allegation of negligence on the part of the payee causing loss to the drawer of the cheque. Civil suit is pending in the court for damages. The High Court *held* that the matter cannot be disposed of within limited purview of section 138. Criminal

Proceedings are liable to be stayed till disposal of the civil suit under compelling circumstances.

***S.V. Rajendera Singh* v. *Lahari Recording Co. Pvt. Ltd.*, 1998 Cr LJ 1680 (Kant)**

Cases referred:

(1996) 2 SCC 739: 1996 SCC (Cri) 454: 1996 Cr LJ 1692 (SC); 1995 Cr LJ 1384 (FB) (Ker); 1994 Cr LJ 3515 (Ker); ILR 1994 Ker 2689; 1992 Cr LJ 3779 (relied on); 1992 Cr LJ 4048 (AP); (1991) 4 SCC 139; AIR 1973 SC 908: (1972) 2 SCC 890: 1973 SCC (Cri) 114: 1973 Cr LJ 347.

Facts of the case.—Many issues are raised but here we are concerned with the dishonour of cheque on the ground, "Stop Payment". The High Court referred to the decision of the Supreme Court cited as 1996 Cr LJ 1692 SC wherein it is said that there are not only two grounds but other endorsements of the bank dishonouring of the cheque would also be available to petitioner (drawee) to proceed against the drawer of the cheque where dishonest intention can be presumed.

***Mahindra A. Dadia* v. *State of Maharashtra*, (1998) 4 All Mah LR 115: 1998 Cr LJ 4361 (Bom)**

Cases referred:

1998 AIR SCW 842; 1997 AIR SCW 4084; (1996) 2 SCC 739: AIR 1996 SC 2339: 1996 SCC (Cri) 454; 1996 Cr LJ 1692 (SC); (1995) 1 Crimes 226 (relied on); AIR 1992 SC 2206: (1992) 1 SCC 217: (1992) 1 KLT 1.

Facts of the case.—The cheque was dishonoured with the endorsement, "Stop Payment". The drawer also sent a prior notice that the cheque may not be presented as the same is given by way of security. Also the issue of *mens rea* was also raised. The High Court relying on the *ratio decidendi* of the various Supreme Court decisions *held* that if the cheque is dishonoured for any reason, dishonest intention is inferable and section 138 is attracted. *Mens rea* is ruled out under section 140 of the Act.

***Sangeeta Pande* v. *State of Uttar Pradesh*, 1998 All LJ 422: 1998 Cr LJ 1978 (All)**

Case referred:

AIR 1996 SC 2339: (1996) 2 SCC 739: 1996 SCC (Cri) 454.

Facts of the case.—Cheque was dishonoured with endorsement (Stop Payment). It is alleged that the accused specifically told the payee that the cheque was issued for satisfying him for time being. The High Court referred to the Supreme Court decision 1996 Cr LJ 1692 (SC) that once the cheque is issued, it is presented and dishonoured, and any instruction given thereafter the issue of cheque will not be of any help to the drawer of the cheque. It amounts to dishonour of cheque within the meaning of section 138 of the Act.

***Modi Cements Ltd.* v. *Kuchil Kumar Nandi*, (1998) 3 SCC 249: AIR 1998 SC 1057: (1998) 92 Comp Cas 88: (1998) 1 KLT 582: 1998 Cr LJ 1397 (SC)**

Cases referred:

1997 Cr LJ 805 (reversed); 1996 AIR SCW 840 (overruled); 1996 SCC (Cri) 1340: (1996) 6 SCC 369 (overruled).

Facts of the case.—It is a case where the cheque was dishonoured on the ground of "Stop Payment". The Supreme Court in this case propounded that:—

(i) Once a cheque is dishonoured, the presumption under section 139 follows.

(ii) Presumption under section 139 is rebuttable.

(iii) Sections 138 to 142 promote the efficacy of Banking operations and to ensure credibility in transacting business through cheques.

(iv) Any instructions issued to the bank to dishonour the cheque after it is issued, does not fit in with the object and purpose for which the provisions are brought in.

***K.I. George* v. *Muhammed Master*, 1999 Cr LJ 3121 (Ker)**

Cases referred:

(1998) 3 SCC 249: (1998) 1 KLT 582: AIR 1998 SC 1057: 1998 Cr LJ 1397 (SC); (1993) 2 KLT 1027.

Facts of the case.—The cheque was dishonoured for reason that payment of cheque was stopped by drawer. No averment was made in the complaint that cheque was dishonoured for insufficiency of funds. The High Court in the light of the decision of the Supreme Court in (1998) 3 SCC 249: (1998) 1 KLT 582: AIR 1998 SC 1057: 1998 Cr LJ 1397 (SC) *held* that mere stoppage of payment by the drawer will not preclude an action under section 138 of the Negotiable Instruments Act. The acquittal of the accused is converted into conviction and imposed a simple imprisonment for three months.

***Indra Baxi* v. *Sunita Goel*, 2001 Cr LJ NOC 13 (MP)**

Facts of the case.—Cheque was dishonoured on basis of directions of "Stop Payment". Plea of absence of liability was taken as accounts stood settled between the parties subsequent to the issue of cheque. Though no material or documents were produced but the plea of settlement is not disputed. The issue is whether liability is subsisting or stands discharged and this can be established in the trial court and not in a proceeding under section 482, the Cr. P.C. Matter remitted to the Trial Court.

***Urban Co-operative Credit Society* v. *State of Gujarat*, (2003) 2 Guj LH 629: (2003) 3 Guj LR 2207: 2003 Cr LJ 3292 (Guj)**

Cases referred:

2002 Cr LJ 3935 (SC); (2002) 7 SCC 655: 2003 SCC (Cri) 151; (2002) 7 SCC 150: 2002 SCC (Cri) 1626; 2001 Cr LJ 3582 (Karn); AIR 2001 SC 2651: (2001) 6 SCC 30: 2001 SCC (Cri) 974; (2001) 7 SCC 541; (2001) 10 SCC 218; 2000 Cr LJ 1988; (2000) 3 Guj LH 468 (relied on); (1999) 4 SCC 253: 1999 SCC (Cri) 524: 1999 Cr LJ 2883: AIR 1999 SC 1952 (relied on); (1999) 2 Crimes 171 (dissented from); 1996 Cr LJ 1816 (Bom) (dissented from); (1993) 4 SCC 424: 1993 SCC (Cri) 1243; (1992) 1 SCC 217: (1992) 1 KLT 1: AIR 1992 SC 2206: 1992 Cr LJ 3779 (followed); AIR 1983 SC 67.

Facts of the case.—In this case post-dated cheque was issued by the company. Before the issuance of the cheque the company was closed and all its amount was transferred to another institution. Thus, the account of the company was closed. The cheque when presented was dishonoured. Person signing the cheque has no account on that day with the Bank. The High Court *held* that when the account was not in existence on the date of issue of cheque then in that case it would not amount to an offence under section 138 since the initial requirement of section 138 is not said to have been satisfied. Thus, the petition stands dismissed. The High Court relied on 1999 Cr LJ 2883 (SC).

***Goa Plast (P) Ltd.* v. *Chico Ursula D'Souza,* AIR 2004 SC 408: (2004) 1 Bank LLR 733: (2004) 1 BC 246: 2004 Cr LJ 664 (SC)**

Cases referred:

AIR 2003 SC 1723: (2003) 3 SCC 232: 2003 Cr LJ 1723; AIR 2001 SC 1315: (2001) 3 SCC 726: 2001 Cr LJ 1674; AIR 2001 SC 3897: (2001) 6 SCC 16: 2001 SCC (Cri) 960; AIR 2001 SC 2895: (2001) 8 SCC 458: 2002 SCC (Cri) 14; AIR 2002 SC 182: (2002) 1 SCC 234: 2002 SCC (Cri) 121: 2002 Cr LJ 266; AIR 1998 SC 1057: (1998) 3 SCC 249: 1998 Cr LJ 1397; AIR 1996 SC 2339: (1996) 2 SCC 739: 1996 SCC (Cri) 454; AIR 1977 SC 666.

Facts of the case.—It is a case of dishonour of cheque on the ground of "Stop Payment". The Supreme Court observed as follows:—

(1) In the first place there must be funds in the account for honouring the cheque.

(2) That there is no subsisting debt or other liability. Mere denial will not do. Section 139 must be rebutted.

The Supreme Court found that both the courts below failed to appreciate that there was subsisting liability. There were no sufficient funds needed for the honour of the cheque. Hence, *held* that the decision of the lower court is legally perverse and dismissed the petition.

***Gorantala Venkateshwara Rao* v. *KollaVeera Raghava Rao,* 2006 Cr LJ 1 (AP)**

Legally enforceable Debt – Mere loss of demand promissory note on its non-production by itself would not be sufficient to conclude that there was no legally enforceable debt.

***Om Parkash Tiwari* v. *State,* 2009 (2) JCC (NI) 137 (Del)**

It is a case of dishonour of post-dated chaque by "Stop Payment" by the petitioner. Issue raised that the payment has been made has to be raised as a defence in the trial. It is not a case to quash the proceedings.

See also: AIR 2009 (NOC) 136 MP.

OTHER CONSIDERATIONS

***S. Prithviraj Kukkillaya* v. *Mathew Koshy,* (1991) 71 Comp Cas 131: 1991 Cr LJ 1771 (Ker)**

Cases referred:

1990 Mad LJ (Cri) 178 (relied on); (1989) 2 Ker LT 740 (approved).

Facts of the case.—It is a case where the cheque was issued prior to the commencement of the Act but failure to pay the amount of the dishonoured cheque on demand was subsequent to the commencement of Act. In this case Article 20(1) of the Constitution of India was discussed and found that it is not applicable in view of proviso to section 138 (b) and (c) and section 142 of the Act. *Held,* that the complaint is maintainable.

***Babulal Nainmal Jain* v. *Khimji Ratanshi Dedhis,* (2001) 105 Comp Cas 849: 1998 Cr LJ 4750 (Bom)**

Facts of the case.—In this case the cheque was returned unpaid due to structural defects and the drawer of the cheque refused to replace the cheque. The remarks of the Bank while returning the cheque was, "Refer to Drawer". The cheque in question was returned not due to insufficiency of funds but due to structural defects in the cheque. Structural defect means any defect in its form, want of signature, date has not been properly written a figure of the amount has been over written or erasure of the drawer's name, etc. *Held,* that such dishonouring does not fall within the scope of section 138 of the Act.

MATERIAL ALTERATION

***Kunjamma Cheriyan* v. *Solomon,* 2005 Cr LJ 1588 (Ker)**

Material alterations amount in words subsequently inserted. Accused acquitted.

***Ram Chandran* v. *K. Dineshan,* 2005 Cr LJ 1237 (Ker)**

Material Alterations. Cheque is for Rs. 25,000, is added to make it 1,25,000 ordered acquittal; 1998 Cr LJ 3228; AIR 1977 SC 366: (1976) 4 SCC 572: 1977 Cr LJ 225; (1989) 2 Ker LT 932 (followed).

Note.—*Section 138 if to be invoked, requires satisfaction of the following ingredients:—*

(1) *Issue of cheque by a drawer.*

(2) *On an account maintained by the person with the bank.*

(3) *To discharge the debt or other liability.*

(4) *In part or full.*

(5) *The said cheque is dishonoured on the ground of insufficiency of funds or exceeds arrangement.*

(6) *These two grounds are judicially supplement with other grounds such as Refer to Drawer, Account closed, Payment stopped.*

(7) *These judicially introduced grounds are normally considered as insufficiency of funds.*

(8) *But these grounds are rebuttable. If rebutted then section 138 of the Act shall not be attracted.*

(9) *In fact, dishonour of cheque accompanied with dishonest intention is the basis of section 138.*

PROVISO (a) TO SECTION 138

INTRODUCTION

Proviso (a) to section 138 is to be read with other provisions of the Act given below:—

Section 64.—Promissory notes, bills of exchange and cheques must be presented for payment to the marker, acceptor or drawee thereof respectively, by or on behalf of the holder as hereinafter provided. In default of such presentation the other parties thereto are not liable thereon to such holder...........

Section 68.—A promissory note, bill of exchange or cheque made, drawn or accepted payable at a specified place and not elsewhere must, in order to charge any party thereto, be presented for payment at that place.

Section 72.—Subject to the provisions of section 84 a cheque must, in order to charge the drawer, be presented at the Bank upon which it is drawn before the relation between the drawer and his banker has been altered to the prejudice of the drawer.

Section 84(2).—In determining what is a reasonable time, regard shall be had to the nature of the instrument, the usage of trade and of bankers and the facts of the particular case.

Section 118(b).—That every negotiable instrument bearing a date was made or drawn on such date.

Section 138, Proviso (a).—The cheque has been presented to the bank within a period of six months from the date on which it is drawn or within the period of its validity whichever is earlier.

Now these provisions present that the cheque: (1) must be presented, (2) on the bank on which it is drawn, (3) be presented on the particular place mentioned in the cheque, and (4) must be presented within six months from the date of the cheque or its validity whichever is earlier. It is said that provisions of the Penal laws must be construed strictly and nothing is to be added from our own side to the prejudice of the accused. Thus, proviso (a) to section 138 is to be read now in the light of Judicial pronouncements as to its real interpretation.

CASE-LAW

***Manoj K. Seth* v. *R.J. Fernandez*, (1992) 73 Comp Cas 441: 1991 Cr LJ 3253 (Ker)**

Cases referred:

1991 Cr LJ 1771; 1990 TLNJ (Cri) 121 (dissented from); (1989) 2 Ker LT 740; AIR 1967 SC 118.

Facts of the case.—It is a case of post-dated cheque bearing date 6-3-1990 but was drawn on 1-3-1986. The cheque was presented only on 2-8-1990 and was dishonoured. Looking to the date of cheque, *i.e.*, 6-3-1990, it was presented within six months. The High Court *held* that it is the date on the cheque and not the date on which it is drawn and issued that matters under section 138, proviso (a). The High Court dissented from 1990 TLNJ (Cr) 121. The appeal is dismissed.

***Richard Samson Sherrat* v. *State of Andhra Pradesh*, (1993) 78 Comp Cas 28: 1992 Cr LJ 2566 (AP)**

Cases referred:

(1992) 1 Crimes 23 (dissented from); (1991) 2 ALT 10; (1991) 1 KLJ 335 (followed); AIR 1975 SC 1039: (1975) 4 SCC 22: (1975) 3 SCR 743.

Facts of the case.—In this case the issue was as to whether there can be repeated presentation of cheque and if so whether there will be a new cause-of-action on new presentation.

In *Kumaresan* v. *Ameerappa*, (1992) 1 Crimes 23, it was held that the payee cannot have a second cause-of-action on the same cheque when once he had failed to institute a complaint on the strength of the first cause-of-action.

But Kerala High Court in *Mahadevan Sunil Kumar* v. *Bhadran*, (1991) 1 KLJ 335, took the stand that there can be no second cause-of-action on the same cheque if the payee has fulfilled all other conditions.

Thus, the High Court in this case *held* that for presentation of cheque the number of times is not restricted and that every subsequent presentation and dishonour gives rise to fresh cause-of-action for filing a complaint.

***Syed Rasool & Sons* v. *Aildas and Company*, (1993) 78 Comp Cas 738: 1992 Cr LJ 4048 (AP)**

Cases referred:

(1992) 1 An WR 502 (affirmed); (1992) 1 Crimes 23 (Ker); (1991) 1 KLJ 335; (1991) 1 KLT 595; (1991) 1 Crimes 226 (Kant); (1991) 71 Comp Cas 273 (Cal); (1991) 71 Comp Cas 536 (Mad); (1990) 2 Bank CLR 416 (P&H); AIR 1973 SC 908: (1972) 2 SCC 890: 1973 Cr LJ 347; AIR 1960 SC 866: (1960) 3 SCR 388: 1960 Cr LJ 1239; *London Joint Stock Bank Ltd.* v. *Macmillan*, 1918 AC 777.

Facts of the case.—In this case two issues were raised:—

(1) Refer to drawer.

(2) Repeated presentation of cheque.

Regarding repeated presentation of the cheque the High Court *held* that during the validity period the cheque can be presented any number of times but the action by filing a complaint under section 138 read with section 142 can be taken only once and affirmed (1992) 1 An WR 502.

***Madan Mohan* v. *K.M. Menon*, (1994) 79 Comp Cas 710: 1993 Cr LJ 2654 (Del)**

Cases referred:

1992 Cr LJ 2566 (AP) (relied on); (1992) 2 CCR 2129 (Ker) (relied on).

Facts of the case.—The High Court *held* that clause (a) of the proviso to section 138 does not lay down as to "how many or number of times" a cheque can be presented to the Bank. It only talks about the presentation of cheque within a period of six months. Relying on the decisions cited above it, it is *held* that it is not desirable to read any such restriction as to number of times and the complaint can be filed after issue of notice and non-payment of amount within 15 days of the receipt of notice.

***Javid Ahmed* v. *Syed Azamthulla Hussaini*, 1993 Cr LJ 2359 (AP)**

Cases referred:

1992 Cri MP No. 8855 of 1991, D/21-1-1992 (P&H) (relied on); 1991 Cr LJ 3253 (Ker) (dissented from); 1990 Cri MC No. 1714 of 1990, D/14-6-1990 (Mad) (relied on).

Facts of the case.—The issue in this case is that the post-dated cheque was drawn and the date on the cheque was beyond a period of six months and delivered to payee. It was *held* that such a cheque falls out of the purview of clause (a) of the proviso to section 138 and prosecution under section 138 in respect of cheques presented beyond six months of delivery thereof is liable to be quashed. In this case the cheques were issued on 23-6-1990, bearing a date on the cheques as 15-12-1991, 18-12-1991, 19-12-1991 and 23-12-1991. The cheques were presented on 18-1-1992.

Note.—*In this case the period of six months was considered from the date the cheques are drawn and not from the date that is written on the cheque.*

***Company of Management for Baranagar Jute Factory* v. *Atis Dispankar Chowdhari*, 1993 Cr LJ 2165 (Cal)**

Cases referred:

1992 C Cri LR 14 (Cal) (followed); (1992) 1 Crimes 23 (Ker) (dissented from); (1992) 2 Cal HN 434; (1992) 1 Cal HN 299; 1991 Cr LJ 1771; 1991 C Cri LR 311 (Cal); (1990) 1 Cal HN 222; 1990 C Cri LR 145 (Cal); (1989) 2 Ker LT 740; AIR 1984 SC 1824: (1984) 4 SCC 352: 1984 SCC (Cri) 620; 1960 Cr LJ 902: AIR 1960 (Cal) 444; (1955) 59 Cal WN 481; AIR 1932 Cal 768.

Facts of the case.—It is a case of dishonour of cheque which was repeatedly presented and dishonoured. It is *held* that in case of dishonour of cheque a second presentation of returned cheque to the bank for payment before serving notice under section 138(b) is not barred.

***Dynamatic Forgings India Ltd.* v. *Nagarjuna Investment Trusts Ltd.*, (1994) 79 Comp Cas 583: 1993 Cr LJ 1206 (AP)**

Cases referred:

1992 ISJ (Bom) 111; (1992) 1 Anm 372; 1992 Cr LJ 739 (P&H); 1992 Cr LJ 2566 (AP); 1991 Cr LJ 609 (Cal); 1991 Cr LJ 2594 (P&H); (1990) 2 Mad WN (Cri) 47; (1990) 1 Mad WN (Cri) 76.

Facts of the case.—It is a case of presentation of cheque for the second time. The High Court *held* that the presentation of the cheque for the second time within the stipulated period of six months is not unwarranted, and it cannot he said that the second presentation in this case is an excuse to save the limitation.

***Satishkumar* v. *Krishnagopal*, 1994 Cr LJ 887 (Bom)**

Cases referred:

1993 Cr LJ 680 (Bom); 1992 Cr LJ 2566 (AP) (relied on); (1992) 1 Crimes 23 (Ker) (dissented); (1992) 73 Comp Cas 590 (Cal) (relied on); (1991) 1 KLT 335.

Facts of the case.—*Held* that clause (a) of proviso to section 138 does not enjoin that a cheque should be presented to the bank for payment only once. There is no restriction on number of times it may be presented. A cheque can be presented twice or more times within the period of six months or the period of its validity and then on such dishonour of cheque a fresh right accrues in favour of the complainant every time and he can enforce that right by initiating proceedings under section 138 of the Act.

***Mallapa Sangappa Desai* v. *Laxmanappa Basappa Whoti*, 1995 Cr LJ 715 (Karn)**

Cases referred:

1994 Cr LJ 887 (Bom); 1993 Cr LJ 680 (Bom); 1993 Cr LJ 2165 (Cal); 1993 Cr LJ 2566 (AP); 1991 Mad LW (Cri) 481.

Facts of the case.—In this case the issue was that notice was not issued to the drawer within 15 days from the date the cheque was returned first. But it was issued within 15 days after the last return of the cheque. *Held,* the case falls under section 138 of the Act.

***S.K.D. Laxmanan Fireworks Industries* v. *K.V. Sivarama Krishnan*, (1995) 84 Comp Cas 447: 1995 Cr LJ 1384 (Ker) (FB)**

Cases referred:

(1991) 1 Ker LT 839 and 1993 Cr LJ 3515 Ker (overruled); (1994) 79 Comp Cas 125 (Ker) (dissented from); (1994) 2 Ker LT 997 (dissented from); 1992 Cr LJ 4048 (AP) (followed); 1993 Cr LJ 680 (Bom) (followed); 1991 Cr LJ 609 (Cal) (followed); (1991) 1 Ker LT 651 (followed); (1994) 2 KLT (SN) 22 Case No. 29 (followed); (1994) 1 Ker LT (SN) 25, Case No. 23 (followed).

Facts of the case.—After discussing various case laws the High Court *held* that there is nothing in the provisions in Chapter XVII of the Act which will preclude the creation of successive causes of action on the basis of one and the same cheque and that the complaint will be maintainable in spite of the fact that he has not filed any complaint in time on the basis of one or more cause of actions accrued to him earlier, but only one prosecution and conviction or acquittal is possible in view of section 300 of the Cr. P.C.

***G. Ekantappa* v. *State of Karnataka*, (1997) Kar 1014: (1997) 2 Kant LJ 63: 1997 Cr LJ 1274 (Karn)**

Cases referred:

(1995) Cr Rev Petn. No. 14 of 1995, D/3-4-1995 (Karn); *D. Puttaswami* v. *N. Ramakrishna*; 1994 Cr LJ 31515 (Ker); 1992 Cr LJ 4048 (AP); 1992 Cr LJ 2566 (AP); (1991) 2 SCC 141: 1991 SCC (Cri) 315: (1991) 1 LLN 970; AIR 1984 SC 1688: (1984) 4 SCC 222: 1984 Lab IC 1578.

Facts of the case.—In this case there was dishonour of cheque twice and the demand notice was also issued twice. It was *held* that the complaint made on a second dishonour is maintainable provided clauses (b) and (c) of the proviso to section 138 and section 142 is complied with.

Note.—*The complaint can be filed even on the second dishonour of cheque irrespective of the fact that all the essentials are complied with even on the dishonour of cheque for the first time.*

***S.V. Rajendra Singh* v. *Lahari Recording Co. Pvt. Ltd.*, 1998 Cr LJ 1680 (Karn)**

Cases referred:

AIR 1996 SC 2339: (1996) 2 SCC 739; Cri R.P. No. 146/95, D/3-4-1995 (Karn) (*held per-incuriam*); 1995 Cr LJ 1384 (FB) (Ker); ILR 1994 Ker 2698; 1994 Cr LJ 3515 (Ker); AIR 1992 SC 2206: (1992) 1 SCC 217: 1992 SCC (Cri) 88: (1992) 1 KLT 1 (relied on); 1992 Cr LJ 4048 (AP); (1991) 4 SCC 139; AIR 1973 SC 908: (1972) 2 SCC 890: 1973 Cr LJ 347: 1973 SCC (Cri) 114.

Facts of the case.—One of the issues involved was as to how many times the cheque can be presented and with what consequences. It was *held* that the complainant can file a complaint for the offence under section 138 read with section 142 of the Act after the dishonouring of the cheque for the first time or he may choose to present the cheque at the request of the drawer within the said period of 6 months from the date of the cheque any number of times but the action to be taken by him by filing the complaint only once.

***Rama Bangia* v. *Pushpa Builders Ltd.*, (1998) 3 Chand Cri C 89: 1998 Cr LJ 4385 (Del)**

Cases referred:

1995 Cr LJ 1384 FB (Ker); (1994) 56 DLT 66; 1993 Cr LJ 265 (Del); (1992) 1 Crimes 23 (Ker); (1988) 4 AD (Del) 197.

Facts of the case.—Held, that so long as a cheque remains unpaid, the payee or holder in due course will certainly be entitled to present the cheque again, of course within a period of six months from the date on which it was drawn or within the period of its validity, whichever is earlier and if the cheque is again dishonoured no express provision in Chapter XVII of the Act expressly preclude the payee or holder in due course from issuing a notice of demand under clause (b) of proviso to section 138 of the Act and in case of default in making payment as demanded, from filing a complaint on the basis of fresh course of action which accrues to him thereby for a second or third time as the case may be.

***Premlata Chadda* v. *Surendra Kumar Soni*, (1998) 4 Civ LJ 104: (1998) 2 MPLJ 54: 1998 Cr LJ 3657 (MP)**

Cases referred:

1997 Cr LJ 1274 (Karn); 1997 Cr LJ 1545 (Raj); 1995 Cr LJ 1384 (Ker) (FB); 1994 Cr LJ 3515 (Ker); (1992) 1 Crimes 23 (Ker).

Facts of the case.—A cheque can be presented for payment any number of times until it has become stale. There is no provision precluding the payee from doing so. Even if he does not take steps to file complaint for the first time he can do so subsequently as a second innings after complying with the procedural requirements within the stipulated time. Successive cause-of-action can arise on repeated presentation and dishonour of cheque. It cannot be said that more than one cause-of-action on the same cheque is not contemplated. Such a construction would neither suppress the mischief nor advance the remedy. That would be against the plain meaning of the statutory provision.

***Sadanandan Bhadran* v. *Madhavan Sunil Kumar*, (1998) 6 SCC 514: 1998 SCC (Cri) 1471: AIR 1998 SC 3043: 1998 Cr LJ 4066 (SC)**

Cases referred:

1995 Cr LJ 1384 (Ker) (FB); (1991) 1 Ker LT 893.

Law propounded by the Supreme Court:

(1) That on each presentation of cheque and its dishonour a fresh right – and not cause-of-action – accrues in favour of the payee.

(2) He may, therefore, without taking pre-emptory action in exercise of his right under clause (b) of proviso to section 138, go on presenting the cheque so as to enable him to exercise such right at any point of time during the validity of the cheque.

(3) But, once he gives a notice under clause (b) of proviso to section 138, he forfeits such right, for, in case of failure of the drawer to pay the money within the stipulated time he would be liable for the offence and the cause-of-action for filing the complaint will arise.

(4) The period of one month for filing the complaint with be reckoned from the day immediately following the day on which the period of fifteen days from the date of receipt of the notice by the drawer expires.

***K.V. Muhammed Kunhi* v. *P. Janardhan*, (1998) 3 CCC 501: (1998) 2 KLT 207: 1998 Cr LJ 4330 (Ker)**

Cases referred:

(1994) 2 Ker LT (SN) 4; 1991 Cr LJ 3253 (Ker); AIR 1970 AP 234 (followed); AIR 1967 SC 1118: (1967) 1 SCR 190: 36 Comp Cas 866; ILR (1962) 1 All 761; AIR 1951 Cal 316 (followed); ILR (1906) 29 Mad 75.

Facts of the case.—In this case the issue of "six months" as stipulated in clause (a) of proviso to section 138 and its calculation was discussed. The High Court referred to section 3(35) and section 9 of the General Clauses Act, 1897 (10 of 1897) and *held* as follows:—

(1) That the date of limitation will commence only from the date found in the cheque.

(2) Period of "six months" prescribed for in clause (a) of proviso to section 138 means British Calendar month as used in section 3(35) of the General Clauses Act, 1897.

(3) Date of cheque cannot be excluded in calculating the period of six months.

***A.B.K. Publications Ltd.* v. *Tamil Nadu Newsprint and Papers Ltd., Madras*, (1999) 3 Crimes 97: 1999 Bank J 918: 1999 Cr LJ 2741 (Mad)**

Case referred:

(1997) 3 Crimes 433.

Facts of the case.—The issue involved was whether the word "Bank" used denotes "Drawer's Bank" or "Payee's Bank". The High Court *held* that the word "Bank" as contained in proviso (a) to section 138 would clearly show that the presentation of the cheque would be made in the bank which could entertain the same. The banks, which could entertain the cheque, are either the drawer's bank or the payee's bank. While the payee presents the cheque in the payee's bank in order to forward it to the drawer's bank, virtually, the payee's bank acts as an agent of the drawer's bank on whose behalf the amount is being disbursed by the Payee's bank. Therefore, the reading of proviso (a) to section 138 of the Act would clearly show that the cheque can be presented either in payee's bank or in the drawer's bank and the date of presentation in the respective bank will be reckoned for calculating the period of six months from the date on which it is drawn.

***Nagdev Sons* v. *State of Uttar Pradesh,* 1998 All LJ 2510: (2001) 107 Comp Cas 226: (1999) 2 BC 409: 1999 Cr LJ 518 (All)**

Cases referred:

1996 AAC (Cri) 22 (overruled); 1995 All Cri C 239 (approved); (1994) 1 Crimes 845 (P&H); (1992) 1 Crimes 23 (Ker).

Facts of the case.—It is a case of successive presentation of cheque. It is *held* that the presentation (successive) of cheque is permissible and the period of limitation would start running from the date of last presentation and dishonouring of the cheque.

***Kesavan Thankappan* v. *State of Kerala,* (1998) 1 Bank CLR 404: 1999 Bank J 482: (1998) 93 Comp Cas 574: 1999 Cr LJ 714 (Ker)**

Facts of the case.—The cheque was issued on 15-7-1989 and it was presented by the appellant for encashment on 26-12-1989. As per the Treasury Code, Vol. I, Rule 245(b), a cheque shall remain current only for three months from the date of issue. *Held,* that a cheque which is issued with the reduced validity period has to be presented for encashment within the expiry of that period so as to attract the provisions of section 138 of the Negotiable Instruments Act. [*See* proviso (a) to section 138 of the Negotiable Instruments Act.]

***Arunbhai Nilkanthrai Nanavati* v. *Jayaben Prabhudas,* (2000) 100 Comp Cas 828: (1999) 2 Guj LH 168: (2000) 1 Bank CLR 73: (2000) Bank J 376: 2000 Cr LJ 1152 (Guj)**

Cases referred:

1999 Cr LJ 2883; (1998) Cri Revn Application No. 452 of 1997, D/21-1-1998 (Guj); 1998 Cr LJ 4758 (Mad); (1998) 92 Comp Cas 398 (P&H); (1995) 1 Cur Cri R 363 (Karn) (distinguished); 1992 Cr LJ 4048 (AP) (distinguished).

Facts of the case.—In this case the discussion was on the word used "presentation" in proviso (a) to section 138 and *held* that "presentation" means, presentation of the cheque in the drawer's bank in terms of section 138 read with section 72 of the Act. The presentation to the collecting bank is of no value. The word "presentation" will serve no purpose if the cheque is presented at any other bank or branch as it amounts in "entrustment" or "tender" and not "presentment". So the cheque be presented at the paying bank, *i.e.,* drawer's bank within six months. If it is presented at the drawer's bank after the expiry of six months for whatever reasons, it is time barred and does not fall within the purview of section 138 [proviso (a)].

Note.— *See 1999 Cr LJ 2741 (Mad) where it is held that "Bank" means "Payee's Bank" or "Drawer's Bank".*

***Shri Ishar Alloys Steels Ltd.* v. *Jayaswals Neco Ltd.*, (2001) 3 SCC 609: 2001 SCC (Cri) 582: AIR 2001 SC 1161: 2001 Cr LJ 1250 (SC)**

Cases referred:

(1999) 3 Crimes 252 (Guj): 2000 Cr LJ 1152; 1999 Cr LJ 2741; (1998) 92 Comp Cas 398 (P&H).

Facts of the case.—The issue was, what is meant by "Bank" as mentioned in clause (a) of proviso to section 138 of the Negotiable Instruments Act.

Note.—*"A combined reading of sections 72 and 138 of the Act would leave no doubt in our mind that the law mandates the cheque to be presented at the bank on which it is drawn if the drawer is to be held criminally liable. Such presentation is necessarily to be made within six months at the bank on which the cheque is drawn, whether presented personally or through another bank, namely, the collecting bank of the payee."*

***V. Venkatesa Subbu* v. *Jaya Bhaskaran & Co.*, (2004) 3 Civ LJ 160: (2004) MLJ (Cri) 48: 2004 Cr LJ 855 (Mad)**

Case referred:

1998 Cr LJ 4066 (SC).

Facts of the case.—It is a case where the accused was acquitted by the trial court on two grounds:—(1) The complainant has not produced any record to show that he is the partner of the firm. (2) That the cheque was dishonoured on the reason that the account was closed and thus section 138 is not attracted. The High Court *held* that the grounds for acquitting the accused are not valid but, however, there is another ground on which the acquittal is sustainable.

The facts are that the cheque was presented on 31-3-1994 and the same was dishonoured and returned on 5-4-1994. In respect of the said dishonoured cheque the complainant sent notice on 18-4-1994. The said notice was received by the accused who in terms sent a reply on 30-4-1994. Thereafter the complainant presented the same cheque second time on 31-5-1994 and same was dishonoured for the reason, "Account closed". The complainant sent notice on 23-6-1994 which was replied by the accused on 14-7-1994, which was also received by the complainant. Thereupon, the complaint was filed. The High Court, referring to the decision of the Supreme Court, 1998 Cr LJ 4066 SC, *held* that there cannot be second cause-of-action on 23-6-1994 when the cause-of-action has already arisen on 18-4-1994 when notice was sent on first dishonour of cheque. Hence, the appeal was dismissed and the order of acquitted was upheld.

***K. Annaji Rao* v. *N. Krishna Raju Sekhar*, (2004) 121 CC 831: (2004) 4 Andh LT 491: (2005) 1 Bank LLR 185: 2004 Cr LJ 2911 (AP)**

Cases referred:

1998 Cr LJ 4066 (SC); 1998 AIR SCW 4112; 1998 Cal Cr LR 283 (distinguished); 1997 Cr LJ 4275 (distinguished); (1997) 6 Andh LD 202 (followed).

Facts of the case.—In this case the cheque was presented on 12-10-1995 but no mention was made in the complaint. However, on dishonour, no demand notice was issued. The cheque was presented for the second time on 22-1-1996 and was dishonoured and thereupon issued a demand notice and then for non-payment, the complaint was filed. The trial court acquitted the accused on two grounds:—

(1) There was no proof of service of notice.

(2) The cheque was presented twice but no complaint was filed on the dishonour of the cheque for the first time.

The High Court *held* the second ground unsustainable in view of 1998 Cr LJ 4066 SC but agreed with the trial court for non-maintainability for want of service of notice. The appeal is dismissed.

SECTION 138, PROVISO (A)

***Vijya Chaudhary* v. *Gian Chand Jain*, 2008 (3) JCC (NI) 291 (Del)**

Cases referred:

2008 (2) CCC 099 (Ker); 2008 (1) CCC 442 (Del); 2007 (4) CCC 387 (Kant); 1993 (1) Crimes 51; IR 1998 SC 1057; 1999 Cr LJ 2883; 2007 (2) Crimes 467 (MP); 2002 (1) Crimes 104; II (2007) DLT (Cri) 630; 130 (2006) DLT 534 (SC); (1996) 2 SCC 739; 1993 Ori LJ 680; (2000) 2 SCC 745; 136 (2007) DLT 308.

In this case many issues were involved but one of the issues was the date of presentation of cheque. In the instant case there was sufficient time gap of nearly one year and eight months between the date of alleged issuance of cheque and date of its presentation. In such circumstances section 138 of the Negotiable Instruments Act is not attracted.

***Arti Mittal* v. *State*, 2009 (2) JCC (NI) 96 (Del)**

Case referred:

Shri Ishar Alloy Steels Limited v. *Jayaswals NE Co. Limited*, 2001 (2) JCC (SC) 17: AIR 2001 SC 1161.

The cheque was issued on 1-1-2007. It was presented on 2-7-2007, *i.e.*, beyond the period of 6 months. In that view of the matter the petitioner stands discharged in both complaint cases.

Note.—It is hit by section 138 proviso (a).

***S.L. Construction* v. *Alapati Srinivasa Rao*, AIR 2009 SC 1538**

Cases referred

(2005) 4 SCC 417; (2004) 13 SCC 498; AIR 1998 SC 3043; 1998 Cr LJ 4066.

Section 138, proviso(a) stipulates that what is prohibited is presentation of the cheque within the mentioned period and not the number of times it is presented. It is, therefore, immaterial whether for one reason or the other the complainant had to present the cheque for the third time or not.

***Surendrapal Singh Chawla* v. *State of Gujarat*, 2010 (1) Crimes 397 (Guj)**

Cases referred

Arunabhai Nilkanthraj Nanavati v. *Jayaben Prahladbhai through her power of Attorney*, 1999 (3) Crimes 252; *Shri Ishar Alloy Steels Ltd.* v. *Jayaswals NE Co. Ltd.*, 2001 (1) Crimes 284 (SC); *Krishna Janardhan Bhatt* v. *Dattatraya G. Hegde*, AIR 2008 SC 1325.

In this case the issue was that the cheque was not presented in the branch of the Bank on which it was drawn. It was held that where sufficiency of funds in the account of the drawer is ascertained due to core banking systems or on-line banking system, non-presentation of the cheque on the branch of the cheque on which it was drawn would not mean that cheque was not presented.

Note.—*Dishonour of cheque is by itself not an offence under section 138. To bring the case within the purview of the section certain other requirements have to be fulfilled. The first-part of the requirements is present in the main section itself,* i.e.:

(1) *The cheque has to be towards payment of an amount for the discharge in whole or in part of any debt or any other liability;*

(2) *The cheque is returned by the bank unpaid;*

(3) *The reason for non-payment of the cheque should be insufficiency of funds or amount of cheque exceeding the amount arranged to be paid from the account.*

The second part of the requirements is covered by clauses (a), (b) and (c) of proviso to section 138 to be further read with section 142(b) and the proviso thereto.

Clause (a) of proviso to section 138 is, like other clauses (b) and (c) of proviso are conditions precedent which are mandatory and binding on the payee. Violation of these clauses of proviso deprives the payee of the right to file the complaint and section 142(b) binds him further.

PROVISO (b) TO SECTION 138

INTRODUCTION

Section 92 of the Negotiable Instruments Act speaks of Notice on dishonour by non-payment. A promissory note, bill of exchange or cheque is said to be dishonoured by non-payment when the maker of the note, accepter of the bill or drawee of the cheque makes default in payment upon being duly required to pay the same. According to section 93, when a promissory note, bill of exchange or cheque is dishonoured by non-acceptance or non-payment, the holder thereof, or some party thereto who remains liable thereon, must give notice that the instrument has been so dishonoured to all other parties, whom the holder seeks to make severally liable thereon, and to someone of the several parties whom he seeks to make jointly liable.

Now these provisions have been incorporated in *clause (b) of proviso to section 138* whereby the payee or the holder in due course of the cheque, as the case may be, makes a demand for the payment of the said amount of money by giving notice in writing, to the drawer of the cheque within fifteen days (*now within thirty days*) of the receipt of information by him from the bank regarding the return of the cheque as unpaid.

The object of issuing notice indicating the factum of dishonour of cheque is to give an opportunity to the drawer to make the payment within fifteen days so that the payee need not initiate any criminal action though the cheque is dishonoured. [*See* AIR 2001 SC 518: (2001) 1 SCC 631: 2001 SCC (Cri) 229: 2001 Cr LJ 708 and (1999) 8 SCC 221: 1999 SCC (Cri) 1411: AIR 1999 SC 3607: (1999) 98 Comp Cas 712.]

The provision of section 138, proviso (b) is indispensable and breach of the same would result in the dismissal of the complaint filed by the complainant. [*See* 2001 Cr LJ 211 (Karn) and 2002 Cr LJ 4176 (MP).]

The notice thus to be given is to be looked from two angles, *i.e.*,

(1) Non-issue of Notice/Non-service of Notice,

(2) Issue of Defective Notice,

with the help of judicial pronouncements made in the light of statutory provision.

VALIDITY OF NOTICE

***Sri Satyanarayana Gowda* v. *B. Rangappa*, 1996 Cr LJ 2264 (Karn)**

Cases referred:

AIR 1995 Karn 219; 1992 (Supp) MWN (Cri) 38 (All).

Facts of the case.—It is a case where the advocate sent the notice but it was unsigned. Reliance was placed on AIR 1995 Karn 219. It was *held* that it is to be seen that whether the purpose is achieved, is the only question that arises for consideration. Similar is the object under section 80 of the C.P.C. From the detailed information given in the notice it is abundantly clear that the petitioner had come to know of the purpose for which the notice is given by the advocate. *Hence, the notice given by the advocate without his signature is not invalid in the eye of law.*

***Syed Hamid Bafaky* v. *Moideen*, (1993) 85 Comp Cas 267: 1996 Cr LJ 1013 (Ker)**

Cases referred:

1994 Cr LJ 3439 (Ker) (relied on); 1993 Cr LJ 2196 (Ker).

Facts of the case.—It is a case where the notice was issued but its service was disputed. The trial court presumed that the accused was evading service. *Held,* it is a question of fact to be decided in the trial. The complaint could not be quashed.

***P.A. Verghese* v. *M.A.A. Communications Pvt. Ltd.*, (1997) 2 CCC 711: (1997) Ker 1747: 1997 Cr LJ 4208 (Karn)**

Cases referred:

1996 Cr LJ 2927 (Cal); 1994 Cr LJ 3115 (Karn); 1993 Cal Cri LR 225; AIR 1984 SC 718: (1984) 2 SCC 500: 1984 Cr LJ 647; AIR 1983 SC 67: (1983) 1 SCC 1: 1983 Cr LJ 159.

Facts of the case.—Many issues were raised and one of them pertained to issue of notice. The complainant got issued a legal notice to the accused company. It was served on the company but there was no reply to the said notice, either admitting or denying the liability or specifying the person who was incharge and responsible for the affairs of the company. Hence, the complainant impleaded all the Directors. At this point the summoning order could not be quashed.

***Padmaja Marketing Enterprises* v. *V.S.R. Murthy Proprietor*, (1997) 4 Crimes 106: (1998) 36 Bank LJ 77: 1998 Cr LJ 881 (AP)**

Facts of the case.—That the accused owed an amount of Rs. 44,117 to the complainant as on 31-3-1991. The said amount was legally recoverable. The complainant issued a notice on 30-8-1991 after receipt of information of return of cheque by the bank unpaid. The accused received the notice but chose to remain silent without accepting or denying the version of the complainant. No doubt, the accused, after the issue of cheque, paid Rs. 5,000 and a further sum of Rs. 5,000 after filing the complaint but still Rs. 34,000 was balance payable. *Held,* that the acquittal of the accused was improper and the matter was remanded back for fresh trial.

***Satyavan Chaplot* v. *Rajendra*, (1998) 3 Civ LJ 740: (1998) 2 Raj LW 1139: (1998) 2 WLC 190: 1998 Cr LJ 2309 (Raj)**

Case referred:

1994 Cr LJ 3115 (Karn).

Facts of the case.—It is a case of alleged defective notice. In the notice instead of 15 days 7 days were given to make payment for the dishonoured cheque. It was *held* that there was no mention of period in clause (b) of proviso and the payment could be made any time but before 15 days which was mentioned under clause (c) of proviso. Hence, the purpose of Notice is to give information to the drawer of the bouncing of cheque and demand of payment and thereby the notice given is valid.

***Jose Antony Kokkad* v. *Official Liquidator, High Court of Kerala, Kochi*, (2000) 100 Comp Cas 811: 1998 Cr LJ 4095 (Ker)**

Cases referred:

AIR 1998 Ker 278; (1997) 2 Ker LJ 243; AIR 1966 SC 135: (1965) 3 SCR 665: (1965) 2 Comp LJ 90.

Facts of the case.—The issue involved was that whether section 446 of the Companies Act is applicable in a proceeding initiated under section 138, the Negotiable Instruments Act. *Held,* that the proceedings initiated against the company under section 138 are not in conflict with section 446 of the Companies Act, 1956. Sections 138 to 142 have been brought for inflicting punishment for violation of the Negotiable Instruments Act and not to affect the assets of the company as per section 446 of the Companies Act. The proceedings could not be stayed.

***L. Sonkadhir* v. *P. Thiyagarajan*, 1998 Cr LJ 3903 (Mad)**

Cases referred:

1996 Cr LJ 180 (Mad); (1994) 2 MWN (Cri) 231; 1992 Cr LJ 1233 (Mad).

Facts of the case.—The issue involved is whether deemed receipt can be construed as a receipt as contemplated under section 138 of the Act. A reference was made to clause 27 of the General Clauses Act wherein it is stated that unless a different interpretation appears the service shall be deemed to be effected by properly addressing, prepaying and posting by registered post, a letter containing the document and unless a contrary is proved. *Held* that in view of clause 27 of the General Clauses Act, the deemed receipt is presumed and the fact of actual receipt can be taken up in the trial. The petition stands dismissed.

***Jayachandran* v. *Babu Raj*, (2000) 101 Comp Cas 154: (1998) 3 CCC 455: (1998) 2 KLT 224: 1998 Cr LJ 3671 (Ker)**

Cases referred:

(1997) 2 Ker LT 539; 1994 Cr LJ 3439 (Ker); 1993 Cr LJ 2196 (Ker).

Facts of the case.—In this case, the issue was that when the postman went to the residence of the respondent on five occasions, the respondent was not available. Therefore, the notice was returned unserved. So it was on the respondent to prove this fact by examining the postman. This issue was not raised during the trial and now this issue was raised after a lapse of six years. The appeal against acquittal was dismissed. The appellant would have examined the postman during the trial and now he cannot be allowed to fill the *lacuna* which is totally forbidden in criminal law.

***S.S. Srikumar* v. *M.M. Ibrahim*, (1998) 4 Civ LJ 214: 1998 Cr LJ 2492 (Ker)**

Facts of the case.—It is a case of service of notice wherein the only ground pleaded was that there was no proper service of notice on the basis of which the judgment of the lower court was questioned.

The complainant sent a demand notice on 27-4-1992 for which the reply was sent by the respondent through advocate. The lower court found the service of notice improper and acquitted the accused. The High Court examined the evidence and found that there was proper service of notice and remanded the case to the lower court for fresh trial.

***Ravinder Kumar Mahajan* v. *Sohan Lal*, 1998 Cr LJ 3273 (P&H)**

Cases referred:

(1997) 1 Rec CR 412; 1997 Cr LJ 1939 (distinguished); 1996 ISJ (Banking) 542 (distinguished); 1995 ISJ (Banking) 35 (relied on); (1995) 83 Comp Cas 245 (Mad); (1995) 83 Comp Cas 473 (Mad); 1993 (Supp) Civil CC 106.

Facts of the case.—It is an appeal against the order of the lower court dismissing the complaint on the plea that the demand notice was given demanding the payment in lieu of bounced cheque within 7 days. The High Court *held* that even if the complainant gave a notice demanding payment of the cheque within 7 days, it will not invalidate the notice under section 138(b) of the Act as the respondent accused were entitled to make the payment within 15 days of the receipt of notice. [Refer also 1998 Cr LJ 2309 (Raj) in this regard.]

***G.S. Srikanth* v. *Lakshmi Financiers*, 1999 Bank J 900: (1999) 1 Civ LJ 782: (1999) 98 Comp Cas 321: 1999 Cr LJ 329 (AP)**

Cases referred:

(1997) 2 Andh LT (Cri) 1 (relied on); (1997) 6 Andh LD 202 (distinguished); AIR 1997 SC 1540: (1996) 9 SCC 471; (1996) 1 JT (SC) 669; (1994) 1 Andh LT (Cri) 603 (relied on); 1992 Cr LJ 1233 (Mad) (relied on); 1991 Cr LJ 3010 (All) (distinguished); AIR 1989 SC 630: (1989) 1 SCC 264.

Facts of the case.—In this case section 114 of the Evidence Act and clause 27 of the General Clauses Act, 1897 were discussed. The facts were that the notice was sent but neither the acknowledgement due nor the postal cover were received back. Moreover, the complainant did not file the postal receipt but filed the copy of notice. The High Court *held* that it being a matter of trial, the complaint cannot be quashed. The presumption could be rebutted in the trial.

***Bhanwar Lal* v. *State of Rajasthan*, (1998) 3 Raj LW 1803: (1999) 4 Civ LJ 174: (1999) 1 Crimes 695: 1999 Cr LJ 949 (Raj)**

Cases referred:

(1998) 2 WLC 304 (Raj) (relied on); 1996 Raj Cri C 508 (explained); AIR 1989 SC 630: (1989) 1 SCC 264 (relied on).

Facts of the case.—It is a case where the notice sent by the complainant could not be served on the accused persons. It was returned unserved. Thereafter, the complaint was filed and the Magistrate took cognizance of the case and issued process. The High Court *held* that the complainant had discharged his responsibility which is statutorily imposed on him and the notice has been sent on the correct address known to the complainant. The accused had all the opportunity to raise all his objections during the trial. The appeal was dismissed.

***Y. Srinivasa Reddy* v. *A.V. Arunadevi*, 1999 Bank J 909: (1999) 97 Comp Cas 246: (1999) 3 Crimes 423: 1999 Cr LJ 3644 (AP)**

Case referred:

(1994) 79 Comp Cas 150.

Facts of the case.—The case of the complainant was that the statutory notice was sent through registered post and through certificate of posting. The contention of the accused was that he did not receive the demand notice demanding money. The High Court *held* that it was a matter of fact which could be gone into during trial. The petition was dismissed.

***P.V.R.S. Manikumar* v. *Krishna Reddy*, (1999) 3 Crimes 312: (1999) 4 Rec Cri R 34: (1999) 2 BC 353: 1999 Cr LJ 2010 (Mad)**

Cases referred:

(1998) 1 CTC 229 (Mad); 1997 Cr LJ 1939 (Ker); 1997 Cr LJ 1942 (AP); 1997 Cr LJ 4237 (AP); (1995) 82 Comp Cas 368 (Ker); 1995 Cr LJ 3412 (Cal); (1994) 1 Mad WN (Cri) 114 (Mad); (1994) 3 Crimes 262 (Mad); 1994 Mad LJ (Cri) 360; (1994) 2 Cur Cri R 858 (Mad) (relied on); 1994 AIR SCW 4994; (1991) 2 Mad WN (Cri) 110 (Mad); AIR 1984 SC 110: (1984) 2 SCC 556; AIR 1978 SC 1019: (1978) 2 SCC 165: 1978 SCC (Cri) 168: 1978 Cr LJ 778; *Wright* v. *Bennett*, (1948) 1 All ER 227.

Facts of the case.—Many issues were raised but one of them pertained to notice:

(1) Demand notice in which interest was also added.

(2) Period of 15 days is not mentioned in the notice.

(3) The complaint did not mention the existing liability.

The High Court negatived all the contentions based on fact and on law. The petition is dismissed.

***Baroda Ferro Alloys and Industries Ltd.* v. *Span Overseas Pvt. Ltd.*, (1999) 2 Mah LJ 220: (1999) 4 Rec Cri R 443: (1999) 5 Bom Cr 249: 1999 Cr LJ 1820 (Bom)**

Cases referred:

1998 Cr LJ 4066 (SC); (1992) 75 Comp Cas 372 (Mad) (distinguished); AIR 1954 Nag 38.

Facts of the case.—It was a case of limitation based on notice. The cheque was dishonoured as per bank advice dated 4-8-1993. Notice was sent on 9-8-1993. Complaint was filed on 30-10-1993 and, therefore, the complaint was barred by time. He presented the cheque second time and gave notice on 15-9-1993. So period of one month was calculated from 15-9-1993. On the other hand it was contended the first notice was by Fax informing about dishonour of cheque and about making alternate arrangement, which is not a demand notice. Furthermore, there was M.O.U. by which the accused gave an undertaking that he would pay the amount within 30 days. This M.O.U. gave a fresh cause-of-action and as such the notice given second time is valid and the petition is liable to be rejected. *Held,* that the filing of complaint on the basis of second notice is not barred by limitation.

***D. Ramaswami* v. *P. Mohan Babu*, (1999) 3 Andh LT 664: (2001) 707 Comp Cas 396: 1999 Cr LJ 3929 (AP)**

Cases referred:

(1997) 1 Andh Lt (Cri) 795; 1997 Cr LJ 4275; 1994 Cr LJ 3439 (Ker); 1992 (Supp) Mad WN (Cri) 214; AIR 1989 SC 630: (1989) 1 SCC 264; AIR 1981 MP 76; AIR 1964 AP 314; AIR 1957 (MB) 151.

Facts of the case.—It was a case where the notice was sent to the accused on the correct address but was returned unserved. There was no rebuttal by the accused that he was not in the town and that the postal endorsement is not correct. *Held,* that the notice is deemed to be served.

***Bilakchand Gyanchand Co.* v. *A. Chinnaswami*, (1999) 5 SCC 693: 1999 SCC (Cri) 1034: AIR 1999 SC 2182: 1999 Cr LJ 3498 (SC)**

Facts of the case.—In this case the cheques were issued in favour of the Appellant by and on behalf of Shakti Spinners Ltd. and signed by the Managing Director A. Chinnaswami. The cheques were dishonoured for want of sufficient funds. The notice was sent but was refused by the respondent. This was followed by a complaint under section 138 read with section 142 of the Negotiable Instruments Act. Process was issued by the Trial Magistrate. The High Court found that the notice was not sent to the company and quashed the proceedings. *Held,* that the High Court erred in quashing the proceedings and further *held* that there is no infirmity in sending the notice to the Managing Director of the Company who has signed the cheques. The appeal was allowed and the order of the High Court was set aside.

***Central Bank of India* v. *Saxons Farms*, (1999) 8 SCC 221: AIR 1999 SC 3607: 1999 Cr LJ 4571 (SC)**

Facts of the case.—In this case the validity of notice was questioned. The expression used in the notice was, "kindly arrange to make the payment to avoid the unpleasant action of my client." There was a further expression that the drawee will take action under the provisions of the Indian Penal Code by informing the police. The Supreme Court observed that the High Court ignored the last line of the notice which read: "kindly arrange to make the payment to avoid unpleasant action of my client," but the High Court considered that there was no demand of payment in the notice. The Supreme Court *held* that the notices were valid and proper. The appeals were allowed and the impugned order of the High Court was quashed.

***Suman Sethi* v. *Ajai K. Churiwal*, (2000) 2 SCC 380: 2000 Cr LJ 1391**

Cases referred:

(1999) 8 SCC 221: (1999) 98 Comp Cas 712: AIR 1999 SC 3607: 1999 Cr LJ 4571 (SC); AIR 1963 SC 1116: 1963 Supp (2) SCC 724: (1963) 2 Cr LJ 186; *Dyke* v. *Elliot*, 17 ER 373: 1872 LR 4 AC 184.

Facts of the case.—In this case the payee claimed cheque amount and incidental charges. *Held*, that if the cheque amount and incidental charges are severable, presumption as contemplated in section 139 in favour of holder will arise only in respect of cheque amount. Regarding other amount, *i.e.*, incidental claim, civil suit is necessary. *Held*, that the notice was valid.

***Subrata Kumar Dash* v. *Pradeep Kumar Sen*, 2000 Cr LJ 3614 (Ori)**

Cases referred:

1999 Cr LJ 1822: AIR 1999 SC 1090: (1999) 3 SCC 1: 1999 SCC (Cri) 329; (1994) 1 Cur Cr R 587 (Mad) (followed); AIR 1991 AP 74.

Facts of the case.—The cheque was dishonoured for insufficiency of funds. Notice was sent but returned unserved. Facts and circumstances reveal that the petitioner left the place of his residence in order to avoid receipt of notice. However, this point can be gone into during the trial. The complaint cannot be quashed.

***S.G. Pandalai* v. *Jacob C Alexander*, (2000) 3 Crimes 232: (2000) 2 Ker 650: (2000) 2 KLT 759: 2000 Cr LJ 2155 (Ker)**

Cases referred:

(1999) 3 SCC 614: 1999 SCC (Cri) 455: AIR 1999 SC 1385: 1999 Cr LJ 2092 (SC) (distinguished); (1996) 1 Ker LT 389 (*held per-incuriam*); (1993) 2 Ker LT 265.

Facts of the case.—There were two issues:

(1) Particular form of notice.
(2) Issuance of notice on the instructions of the Power-of-Attorney of the payee given to the advocate.

Held, that no particular form of notice is required. Notice issued calling upon the drawer to pay the cheque amount within 15 days of the receipt of notice is valid and further *held* that the power-of-attorney holder of the payee can give instructions to the advocate and such instruction does not make the notice invalid.

***A. Sathyanarayana* v. *C. Nagaraj*, 2000 Cr LJ 2341 (Karn)**

Cases referred:

1999 Cr LJ 4606 SC; 1998 AIR SCW 4112; (1998) 4 Crimes 120 (Raj); (1997) Cr LJ 4275 (AP); (1997) 2 Bank CLR 73 (AP); (1996) 1 JT (SC) 669; (1995) Cri Rev P No. 327 of 1991, decided on 16-1-95 (Karn).

Facts of the case.—In this case the notice was sent to the drawer on the address given in the Memorandum of Understanding by registered post. The said postal cover returned with postal endorsement as "not-found" on all the seven days on which notice was taken for service. *Held,* that such service could be construed as deemed service. The High Court referred to section 27 of the General Clauses Act, 1897 (10 of 1897) in this regard. The judgment of Appellate Court was set aside and the judgment of the trial court was upheld.

***Uniplas India Ltd.* v. *State,* (2001) 6 SCC 8: 2001 SCC (Cri) 955: AIR 2001 SC 2625: (2001) 106 Comp Cas 669: 2001 Cr LJ 3326 (SC)**

Cases referred:

AIR 1999 SC 1609: (1999) 4 SCC 567: 1999 Cr LJ 2276: (1999) 97 Comp Cas 575; AIR 1998 SC 3043: (1998) 6 SCC 514: (1998) 2 KLT 765.

Facts of the case.—In this case section 138(b) along with sections 433 and 434 of the Companies Act, 1956 was discussed. Section 433(2) contains one of the six clauses for which the company can be wound up by court, *i.e.,* if the company is unable to pay its debts. Section 434 states that the creditor is to make a demand requiring the company to pay the amount due to the creditor. The mode of making such demand is also delineated in the section. Clause (b) of proviso to section 138 of the Negotiable Instruments Act also contemplates the making of a demand of payment of the cheque amount. If any notice is given under section 434 of the Companies Act within 15 days of the information from the bank regarding return of cheque drawn by a company as unpaid, such a notice would as well be good enough under clause (b) of proviso to section 138 of the Negotiable Instruments Act. But in this case notice under section 434 was not given within 15 days of the date of earlier dishonour of the cheque, if so the said dishonour remained without any further escalation and need not snowball into a cause of action. So the cheque represented and notice thereby given as dishonour creates a cause-of-action for launching a complaint.

***VIF Airways Ltd.* v. *Aishu Finance Ltd.,* (2002) 2 BC 274: (2002) 2 Crimes 205: 2002 Cr LJ NOC 385 (AP)**

Facts of the case.—In this case the notice came back unserved with endorsement that party is not available by postal authority. Petitioner deliberately evaded to receive the said notice to escape from payment of liability of dishonoured cheque amount. There was no assertion that the notice was sent on wrong address.

***C.E.I. Consultancy* v. *Modi World Infotech,* (2002) 3 BC 438: 2002 Cr LJ 2731 (AP)**

Cases referred:

(2001) 6 SCC 338: 2001 Cr LJ 2566: 2001 Cr LJ 2566 (SC); (2001) 1 Andh LT (Cri) 175; (1997) 4 SCC 241: 1997 SCC (Cri) 544: (1997) 1 Mah LJ 509: 1997 Cr LJ 1519 (SC); (1995) 5 SCC 751; 1993 Cr LJ 680 (Bom); AIR 1992 SC 1379: (1992) 3 SCC 317: 1992 Cr LJ 1956; AIR 1991 SC 1260: 1992 Supp 1 SCC 222: 1992 SCC (Cri) 192.

Facts of the case.—In this case the High Court *held* that notice of dishonour need not be sent by Registered Post. Notice can be sent also by certificate of posting.

Notice sent by certificate of posting can be presumed to have been received by addressee. In this case notice was sent by Regd. Post AD and under certificate of posting. It is presumed that the letter sent under certificate of posting must have been received by the addressee in terms of section 114 of the Evidence Act, 1872. However, this fact could be gone into during the trial.

***N.E. Verghese* v. *State of Kerala,* (2002) 1 Ker LJ 109: (2002) 1 KLT 488: 2002 Cr LJ 1712 (Ker)**

Facts of the case.—In this case notice of dishonour was sent under Registered Post and under Certificate of Posting on correct address. It was returned with the Postal endorsement "Not Claimed" Notice was *held* to be duly served.

***Arvind Bhat Selarka* v. *Dilip Cogad,* 2003 Cr LJ 3360 (P&H HC)**

Cases referred:

2001 Cr LJ 1674; 2001 Cr LJ 3632 (followed); 1999 Cr LJ 4606 (followed).

Facts of the case.—In this case notice was sent to the accused. Notice was returned with the endorsement "Refused". It amounted to receipt of Notice. The High Court observed that it must be borne in mind that the court should not adopt an interpretation which helps a dishonest evader and clips an honest payee as that would defeat the very legislative measure.

***Vijya Kumar Sethi* v. *Kanwar Bhupinder Singh,* (2003) 2 BC 321: (2003) 3 Rec Cri R 538: 2003 Cr LJ 2124 (HP)**

Cases referred:

(2000) 2 SCC 380: 2000 SCC (Cri) 414: AIR 2000 SC 828: 2000 Cr LJ 1391 (SC); (2000) 1 Cr LJ (HP) 169; (2000) 1 Cr LJ (HP) 304; (2000) 2 Civ Court Cases 457; (1998) 2 Civ Court Cases 219; AIR 1993 SC 1126: 1995 Supp (4) SCC 469: 1994 SCC (Cri) 1762; AIR 1986 SC 1436: (1986) 2 SCC 585: 1986 Cr LJ 1070; AIR 1979 SC 663: (1979) 1 SCC 328: 1971 (MLJ) Cri 456; AIR 1978 SC 1; AIR 1977 SC 1621: (1977) 3 SCC 512; AIR 1975 SC 1960: (1975) 4 SCC 649: 1975 Cr LJ 1732; AIR 1973 SC 799: (1973) 4 SCC 10: 1973 Cr LJ 577; AIR 1973 SC 2145: (1973) 2 SCC 583: 1973 Cr LJ 1404; AIR 1954 SC 726: 1954 Cr LJ 1808.

Facts of the case.—In this case many issues were raised:—

(1) Whether cognizance can be taken in the absence of proof of date of notice by the accused.

(2) Whether cognizance can be taken in spite of the plea that immediately on receipt of notice the amount was sent by two demand drafts by Registered Post A.D.

(3) Non-grant of permission to examine Advocate of the Complainant.

(4) Whether demand of extra amount over and above the cheque amount makes the notice invalid.

(5) Imposition of fine of Rs. 17,200.

(6) Whether compensation to the complainant can be awarded.

The High Court *held* the accused guilty but on the point of fine, the High Court *held* that it is illegal and reduced it to Rs. 5,000 and directed to pay compensation to the complainant a sum of Rs. 10,000 and if not paid, to be realised as permitted under law.

***Kavuri Suwarna Bala Sundaram* v. *Karmati Poorna Chandra Rao,* (2004) 2 CLR 360: (2004) 2 BC 571: (2004) 119 Comp Cas 156: (2004) 3 Rec Cri R 8: 2004 Cr LJ 712 (AP).**

Cases referred:

2001 Cr LJ 4157 (distinguished); AIR 2000 SC 828: (2000) 2 SCC 380: 2000 SCC (Cri) 414; (1997) 1 Andh LT (Cri) 678.

Facts of the case.—It is a case where in the notice correct amount is specified but wrong number of the dishonoured cheque is mentioned. The High Court referred to sections 5, 6 and 138 and *held* that typographical mistake of cheque No: mentioned in the notice cannot be the ground for quashing the proceedings. Hence, the revision was dismissed.

***Rozy Kukreja* v. *Finance Associates,* (2004) 2 JKJ 256: (2004) 4 Rec Cri R 845: 2004 Cr LJ 3700 (J&K)**

Cases referred:

1998 Cr LJ 4066 (SC); 2000 Cr LJ 112 (Pat); 1997 Cr LJ 4275 (AP); (1992) 1 Crimes 60.

Facts of the case.—The cheque was dishonoured. Notice of demand of payment was not served, *i.e.,* it came back unserved. The accused was informed and he assured that the cheque shall be honoured on representation. On representation it got bounced for the reason *"Account closed on Advice"*. Thereupon, the complainant issued notice. The plea of the petitioner was that the complaint was barred by time. The High Court *held* that the first notice was not served. The so-called "notice is served" is deemed to be first notice and the complaint is not barred by time from the date of the second notice as this notice has only given cause-of-action.

***G. Valappan* v. *S. Madhavan Pillai,* 2004 Bank J 202: (2003) 4 Rec Cri R 589: 2004 Cr LJ NOC 230 (Mad)**

Case referred:

1995 Cr LJ 3412 (Cal) (distinguished).

Facts of the case.—There was a variation in the amount of cheque and amount claimed in the notice. Amount spent towards issuing of notice was also claimed in addition to the cheque amount. *Held,* that proceedings cannot be quashed on the ground that there was demand of more amount than the amount mentioned in the cheque.

***Neelesh Kumar @ Neelesh Jain* v. *Janardhana,* 1 (2005) CCR 405 (Karn)**

Cases referred:

AIR 1966 SC 330: (1964) 7 SCR 618: (1965) 1 MLJ (SC) 105; (2000) 3 CCC 82 (Karn); ILR 2000 (Karn) 2726; ILR 2000 (Karn) 1255 (relied on); (1995) 2 Karn LJ 175; 2000 Cr LJ 1005 (AD) (relied on); JT (1996) 1 SC 669 (relied on); ILR 2002 (Karn) 181 (relied on).

Facts of the case.—It is a petition under section 482, the Cr. P.C. for quashing the proceedings. The case of the petitioner is that there is no demand notice served on him. The case of the respondent is that the notice was sent by Registered Post Acknowledgment Due but returned with an endorsement—"No Such Addressee". The demand notice sent under certificate of posting was duly served on the petitioner/accused and he personally approached seeking more time as being in financial difficulties. The issue is whether the said notice was served on the petitioner/accused. The High Court *held* that when there is dispute as to the service of notice, the matter cannot be quashed under section 482, the Cr. P.C. It is a matter to be decided in the trial being a matter of deemed service of notice.

***B. Kiranmaye* v. *Prasoona Traders,* (2005) 1 CCR 349 (AP)**

Cases referred:

(1993) 3 Crimes 175; 1 (2004) CCR 371; IV (2000) CCR 121 (SC); (1997) 2 ALT (Cri) 1 (AP); AIR 1989 SC 630 (relied on); IV (1999) CCR 63 (SC) (relied on).

Facts of the case.—Notice was sent but returned with the remarks "Addressee Not Found". *Held,* that seeking quashing of proceedings for want of due service of notice is but abuse of the process of court. This court cannot take into consideration the plea of defence of the accused under section 482, the Cr. P.C. but will go by allegations in complaint and documents produced by the complainant. Petitioner is at liberty to take all pleas raised in the petition in the trial. Criminal Petition was dismissed.

***V. Raja Kumari* v. *P. Subarama Naidu,* (2004) 8 SCC 774: (2004) 3 KLT 799: 2005 Cr LJ 127 (SC)**

Notice by Post with correct address. Deemed to be served.

***Vuppla Venkata Nageshwar Rao* v. *Tulluri Chit Funds (P) Ltd.,* 2005 Cr LJ 575 (AP)**

Notice contains more amount than the cheque amount which included collection charges. It does not invalidate the Notice.

***Yaswitha Construction (P) Ltd.* v. *C. Subha Reddy,* 2005 Cr LJ 1518 (AP)**

Complaint cannot be quashed under section 482, the Cr. P.C. on the plea of invalid service of notice. It has to be proved in Trial.

***V. Kishore* v. *S. Ajai Kumar,* 2005 Cr LJ 2383 (AP)**

Notice to be given within 30 days. Intimation from Bank is essential than only the period of 30 days will start. It is a case of acquittal.

***Mazaffar Alam Ansari alias M.A. Ansari* v. *State of Jharkhand,* 2005 Cr LJ 1534 (Jharkhand)**

Notice issued much beyond expiry period. Order taking cognizance and issuing of non-bailable warrant of arrest is improper and quashed.

***M. Shamsudheen* v. *V.P. Sunder Rajan,* 2005 Cr LJ 1278 (Ker)**

In the Notice interest and notice charges were also claimed. Notice is valid.

***P.K. Radha Kirshna* v. *Vijyan Nambiar,* 2005 Cr LJ 4184 (Kant)**

Notice sent by U.P.C. Not returned. Deemed to be served. Dismissal of complaint not proper.

SECTION 138, PROVISO(B)

***V. Raja Kumari* v. *P. Subarama Naidu*, AIR 2005 SC 109**

Cases referred:

(2002) 9 SCC 415; 1999 Cr LJ 4571; AIR 1999 SC 3762; 1998 (93) Comp Cas 843 (AP); (1996) 7 SCC 523; AIR 1992 SC 1604; 1994 Cr LJ 3439; AIR 1981 SC 1284.

Held

(i) Notice despatched by the sender by post with correct address on it is deemed to be served on sendee unless he proves that it was not really served.

(ii) Complaint cannot be dismissed at the threshold on the ground that there was no proper service of notice. Question has to be decided during the trial.

***Gyan Chand* v. *State of Rajasthan*, 2006 (3) JCC (NI) 269 (Raj)**

Case referred:

Jose Anthony Kokkad v. *Official Liquidator*, 1998 Cr LJ 4095.

Section 138 of the Negotiable Instruments Act overrides section 446 of the Companies Act and hence the order of the Judicial Magistrate is set aside.

***C.S. Madhusudhan* v. *B Eswaramma*, 2006 (3) JCC (NI) 276 (AP)**

Cases referred:

2006 (2) JCC (NI) 161; 1999 (2) JCC (SC) 552; (2004) 8 SCC 774.

It is a case of non-service of notice. The accused proved that the notice was sent on the wrong address. The court *held* that rule of purposive construction or mischief rule must be applied, *i.e.*, in interpreting the statute court must adopt that construction which suppresses the mischief and advances the remedy. The court can still presume deemed service of notice. Also Refer 2006 (3) JCC (NI) 239 (AP).

***V.K. Jain* v. *Sharad Jagtiani*, 2006 (3) JCC 252 (Del)**

Cases referred:

(1994) 4 SCC 445; 1998 (92) Comp Cas 517; 2002 (2) JCC 1171; 2003 (2) JCC (NI) 132; 1999 (2) JCC (Del) 383.

If notice is served through Registered Post or UPC on the correct address, presumption of service arises. It is a disputed matter which can be seen during the trial only.

***V.K. Gupta* v. *M/s. Dimension & Designers (P) Ltd.*, 2006 (3) JCC (NI) 271 (Del)**

Cases referred:

2001 (6) SCC 8; (1999) 4 SCC 567; (1998) 6 SCC 514; (2005) 12 SCC 502.

Complaint was filed on 22.5.1998

Cheque dishonoured on 4-4-1998

Notice issued on 15-4-1998

The complaint is filed within time. The cheque was presented twice and dishonoured. Notice is given only when the cheque was dishonoured for the second time and thus is within time.

***M/s. Laltech Engineering Projects Pvt. Ltd.* v. *M/s. Gypsum Structural India Pvt. Ltd.*, 2006 (1) JCC (NI) 1 (Del)**

Case referred:

Central Bank of India v. *M/s. Saxons Farms*, 1999 Cr LJ 4571.

It is case where the notice sent is not a demand notice of the amount of the dishonoured cheques but it is a notice regarding the dues payable. The notice is not in time with section 138(b) proviso. However, the cheques were presented for the second time and this time the notices sent were valid and thus the complaint is maintainable. The petition is dismissed.

***D. Vinod Shivappa* v. *Nanda Belliappa*, 2006 (2) JCC (NI) 161 SC**

Cases referred:

(1999) 7 SCC 510; (2001) 6 SCC 463; (2004) 8 SCC 774; (2005) 4 SCC 417; (1998) 6 SCC 514.

It is *held* that the question has to be answered by reference to the facts of the case and no universal application can be laid down that in all cases where notice is not served on account of non-availability of the address, the court must presume service of notice.

***Ashwani Kumar Julka* v. *Lt. Col. Parthojit Chowdhary (retd.)*, 2007 (1) JCC (NI) 32 (Del)**

Cases referred:

1992 (1) Crimes 60; 1993 (3) Recent Criminal Report 542; 2001 DCR 275; 1999 (1) JCC 256; 1999 (7) SCC 510.

Held that 15 days' period is to be calculated from the date when a notice is returned by the sendee as unclaimed. It is clear that as per the endorsement on the envelope, registered envelope was lastly taken by the postman at the residential address of the accused on 29-11-1996 and at his official address on 28-11-1996 and thereafter made the endorsement. The period of 15 days cannot be calculated from 30-11-1996 when envelopes were received back by the respondent/complainant. If the limitation is to be counted from 28-11-1996/29-11-1996 the last date for filing the complaint is 13/14-1-1997. The complaint was filed on 16-1-1997 which is barred by limitation. The provision for condonation of delay was not there then, hence the court is helpless.

***Smt. Krishna Gupta* v. *Sri Sita Ram Singhal*, 2007 (4) JCC (NI) 399**

Held, that it is settled law that procedure is hand made of justice. The hyper-technicalities cannot be allowed to defeat the substantive Justice. There is no particular requirement that a notice must mention the position held by the person in the company. If an individual who signed the cheque is informed about the dishonour of cheque, even if it is not mentioned in the notice that he was secretary of the company. The notice will remain a valid notice.

***Sri Kumar Chakraborty* v. *Data Con Systems Pvt. Ltd.*, 2007 (1) JCC (NI) 41 (Cal)**

Cases referred:

2001 (1) CHN 235; 1999 (2) JCC 552 (SC).

Held: Prescribed period for filing complaint can neither he extended by section 473, the Cr. P.C., nor by section 5 of the Limitation Act Admittedly notice as required was sent within 15 days of the return of the cheque. The notice returned on 23-7-2002 with postal remarks "Not Claimed". Complaint was filed and cognizance was taken on 7-8-2002 by virtue of section 142(b). It is held that actual date of accrual of cause-of-action in such cases has to be analysed in the context of factual details. The High Court directed the trial Court to expedite the trial of the case.

***M/s. J.R.V. Electronics Co Pvt. Ltd.* v. *M/s. M.G. Electronics Ltd.*, 2007 (2) JCC (NI) 123 Del**

Cases referred:

2002 (62) DRJ 378; (1998) 6 SCC 514; AIR 2001 SC 676; 1999 Cr LJ 1820; (2005) 4 SCC 417; 2002 (1) DCR 154 (Del); 2002 (108) Cr LJ 3001.

It is held that legal position regarding a cause-of-action in dishonour of cheque, it is well-settled if dishonour of cheque has once snowballed into a cause-of-action it is not permissible for a payee to create another cause-of-action with the same cheque.

***Charanjeet Verma/Aero Club* v. *State*, 2007 (2) JCC (NI) 132 (Del)**

Cases referred:

2000 Cr LJ 3280; (2003) 10 SCC 521; (2005) 10 SCC 336.

Notices issued but could not be issued on the drawer. Prescribed time frame is not followed. *Held*, summoning orders are rightly not issued.

***C.C. Alavi Hazi* v. *Palapatty Muhammed*, 2007 (2) JCC (NI) 225 (SC)**

Cases referred:

(2006) 6 SCC 456; (1999) 7 SCC 510; AIR 1992 SC 1604; (1996) 7 SCC 523; (2004) 8 SCC 774.

It is held that giving of notice is process of which receipt is the accomplishment. It is for the payee to perform the former process by sending notice to the drawer at correct address and the drawer to comply with clause (e) of proviso to section 138 of the Negotiable Instruments Act. It has to be seen that whether there is non-receipt of notice or deliberately avoided service of notice.

***M/s. Sarav Investment & Financial Consultants Pvt. Ltd.* v. *Lloyds Register of Shipping India Office Staff Provident Fund*, 2007 (4) JCC (NI) 350 (SC)**

Cases referred:

JT 2007 (7) SC 498; (1999) 7 SCC 510; JT 2007 (9) SC 496; (2007) 9 SCALE 371.

In this case service of notice was not sought to be effected under Registered cover with Acknowledgement Due. The agent of the complainant sought to serve the notice through their own employees. Metropolitan Magistrate presumed service of notice which was not accepted by the High Court. Judgment of the High Court is set aside. Appeal is allowed stating that notice is served according to law.

***M/s. Rahul Builders* v. *M/s. Arihant Fertilizers & Chemical*, 2007 (4) JCC (NI) 377 SC**

Cases referred

(2000) 2 SCC 380; (2003) 8 SCC 300.

It is held that an *omnibus* notice without specifying as to what was the amount due under the dishonoured cheque would not subserve the requirement of law. In the instant case no demand was made for payment of the cheque amount. The impugned judgment cannot be faulted. In this case the demand was made for the whole of Rs. 8,72,409 which was due and not Rs. 1,00,000 the amount of the dishonoured cheque.

***Som Nath* v. *State of Punjab*, 2008 (2) JCC (NI) 164 (P&H)**

Cases referred:

1992 (2) Recent Criminal Reports 199 (Mad); 2007 (3) Raj 177 (SC).

In this case section 27 of the General Clauses Act was invoked. Notice sent to the accused but he did not receive and return it as "unclaimed". It is deemed to be constructive service of notice.

***First Learning Quest Private Ltd.* v. *Tera Construction Private Ltd.*, 2008 (3) JCC (NI) 274 (Del)**

Cases referred:

AIR 1997 SC 987; AIR 1988 SC 709; AIR 1977 SC 1754; AIR 2006 SC 2872; 20 (1981) DLT 302; AIR 1961 SC 1494; AIR 2006 SC 2179; AIR 2007 (NOC) 131 (Ker); AIR 2006 (NOC) 1244 (All); I (1996) BC 530; 1993 Comp Cas (Vol 78) 507; 1996 Comp Cas (Vol 86) 205; I (1998) BC 677; 1993 Comp Cas (Vol 83) 172; AIR 2007 (NOC) 1372 (Bom); 2000 Cr LJ 1251; I (1999) BC 506; 2007 (2) JCC (NI) 150; 2004 (1) JCC 420; 134 (2006) DLT 315; AIR 1999 SC 3762; 99 (2000) DLT 244; 2001 Cr LJ 4745 (SC).

In this case various aspects of Notice were discussed:—

(i) Notice sent UPC is deemed to have been served when sent on the last address known.

(ii) Deemed Service of notice requires evidence.

(iii) The burden of proving that there is no debt or liability is on the accused. This duty has to be discharged in the trial.

***Maharaji Educational Trust* v. *Housing & UDC Ltd.*, 2008 (3) JCC (NI) 281**

Cases referred:

2007 (3) AD (Del) 606; 1997 (1) Crimes 55; 1996 SCC (Cri) 454.

It is seen that the notice was served on the correct address but the stamp on the Acknowledgement was put that of "Santosh Rana Medical College" which shows *mala fide* intention of the petitioners by putting a wrong stamp although the notices, were sent on the correct address. Notice is duly served on the petitioners. Petition is dismissed.

***R. Sridhar* v. *T.K. Rajendra Sha,* 2008 (3) JCC (NI) 305 (Mad)**

Case referred:

V. Raja Kumari v. *P. Subharamma Naidu,* 2004 (3) JCC (NI) 226 (SC).

The notice was sent through courier service on the correct address. Returned unserved with the remaks "Refused". It is promised that the notice is deemed to have been served on the accused. Appeal is allowed.

***Satish Grover* v. *State of Uttar Pradesh,* 2008 Cr LJ 3228**

Cases referred:

2007 Cr LJ 3214; 2001 AIR SCW 2307.

In this case demand notice was sent by Registered Post. Along with the complaint copy of notice, and photo copy of Registry was also filed. A plea was taken that the complaint did not disclose date of service of notice. The plea is not tenable. The complaint is not liable to be quashed on that ground.

***Mrs. Fatima Begam* v. *Md. Sajid Alam Chowdhry,* 2008 Cr LJ 1227 (Gau)**

It is held that if adequate averments are made in the complaint to the effect that notice of demand was sent by Registered Post on the correct address of the accused, it is deemed to have been served on the accused in view of section 27 of the General Clauses Act and section 114 of the Evidence Act. Furthermore, it is a triable issue that can be gone in the trial.

Cases referred:

2007 Cr LJ 3214; AIR 2001 SC 676; AIR 1999 SC 1609.

***B.K. Sarkar* v. *State of Gujarat,* 2008 Cr LJ 1230 (Guj)**

It is *held* that provisions of the statute, in particular section 138 of the Negotiable Instruments Act are required to be complied with strictly and any deviation would entail consequences of non-maintainability of the complaint. Delay can be condoned with regard to delay in filing the complaint as provided under section 142(b) proviso. It does not extend to section 138(b).

***Kapil Upadhyay* v. *M/s. Milan Auto,* 2008 Cr LJ 1242 (MP)**

Cases referred:

AIR 1999 SC 1090; AIR 1998 SC 3043.

It is held that cause-of-action is not continuous or recurring. Cheque is dishonoured, notice issued but complaint is not filed within time. The cheque was again presented and dishonoured. Complaint was filed on the basis of second notice. The complaint is not maintainable.

***Dr. Premish Verma* v. *Lokesh Sharma,* 2008 Cr LJ 1246 (Chhat)**

Cases referred:

2006 Cr LJ (NOC) 547; (2006) 9 SCC 340; (2005) 4 SCC 417; AIR 2001 SC 2752; AIR 2001 SC 36; AIR 1999 SC 1090; AIR 1999 SC 1609; AIR 1996 SC 1491; AIR 1972 SC 1293; AIR 1970 SC AP 234; AIR 1967 Bom 138; AIR 1965 Ori 71; AIR 1962 Mys 117; AIR 1953 Nag 81.

In this case the discussion was on the word "of" used in section 138 (proviso) and section 142(b) of the Negotiable Instruments Act. It is held that the word "if" is akin to "from" section 9 of the General Clauses Act and section 12 of the Limitation Act were referred.

***Anil Kumar Goel* v. *Kishan Chand Kaura*, 2008 (1) JCC (NI) 36 SC**

Cases referred:

2004 (7) SCC 338; AIR 1984 SC 87.

The facts of the case are that the cheque was issued on 31-3-1998. It was presented on 11-4-1998. Notice dated 27-4-1998 was duly served on the appellant on 27.4.1998. On the assurance the cheque was again presented and it was dishonoured on 30-9-1998. Notice dated 13-10-1998 was served but no payment was made. The Supreme Court decided as follows:—

(i) Clause (a) of proviso gives the right that the payee can successively present the cheque during its validity.

(ii) But once a notice was issued and received but payment is not made, the cause-of-action arose.

(iii) New Amendment of proviso to Section 142(b) is not retrospective.

Hence, the complaint filed is barred by limitation.

***Subhod S. Salaskar* v. *Jaya Parkash M. Shah*, 2008 (3) JCC (NI) 330 (SC)**

Cases referred:

2007 (4) SCC 70; (2007) 3 SCC 693; 2008 (8) SCALE 54; 2006 (9) SCC 340; (2007) 6 SCC 555; (2007) 9 SCC 650; 2008 AIR SCW 295; (2005) 9 SCC 15; JT 2008 (1) SC 340; 2007 (12) SCALE 364.

The Apex Court explained the following issues:—

(i) Section 142(b) proviso inserted by the Amendment Act, 2002 is a substantive and not a procedural provision.

(ii) It is not a restrospective provision.

(iii) Any complaint filed with delay before this Amendment of 2002 will not have the benefit of the amendment of 2002.

(iv) The Magistrate shall have no jurisdiction to take cognizance unless all the ingredients for taking cognizance are satisfied.

(v) Section 27 of the General Clauses Act will apply if the notice is sent by post within 30 days of the dishonour of cheque.

(vi) As per Order V, Rule 9(5), if the notice does not come back within 30 days, it is presumed to have been served.

(vii) Presumption, under such circumstance can also be presumed under section 114 of the Evidence Act.

***M/s. Indo Automobiles* v. *M/s. Jai Durga Enterprises*, 2008 (3) JCC (NI) 351 (SC)**

Cases referred:

1999 (7) SCC 510; 2004 (8) SCC 774.

(i) Once the notice is sent by Registered Post with acknowledgement due on the correct address, it must be presumed that it has been served.

(ii) On the question of interpretation of the endorsement made on the envelope can be considered in the trial in the background of the facts of the case.

***National Co-operative Bank Ltd.* v. *M.V. Rangachar,* 2009 (3) Crimes 136 (Kar)**

Cases referred:

2002 Cr LJ 4176 (MP); (1999) 4 SCC 567.

It is said that provision of section 138(b) of the Act regarding giving of notice to the accused within the stipulated period is mandatory. Non-compliance whereof would make the complaint liable to be dismissed.

***HDFC Bank Ltd.* v. *Amit Kumar Singh,* 2009 (3) JCC (NI) 185 (Del)**

Cases referred:

AIR 1999 SC 3782; 2007 (6) SCC 555; 1990 Cr LJ 1594; 1990 Cr LJ 2265; 2000 Cr LJ 3998; 2006 (6) SCC 456; 2004 (7) SCC 338; 2008 (16) SCALE 317; 2001 (6) SCC 463; AIR 1966 SC 1313; (1969) 3 SCC 28.

It is *held* that the complainant must satisfy the Magistrate at the stage of pre-summoning about the service of notice on the accused. Anything short of this will not fall within the ambit of "deemed service".

M/s. Boss Gears Ltd.* v. *M/s. Mohta Bright Steels

In this case the accused on receipt of demand notice replied the same along with consolidated draft within 15 days of stipulated period. This consolidated amount included the amount of dishonoured cheque. Thus the liability is discharged within the stipulated period. So there is no cause-of-action to prosecute the petitioners.

***Bashir Ahmed Mir* v. *Abdul Ahmed Ganai,* 2009 Cr LJ (NOC) 815 (J&K)**

It is a case of dishonour of cheque. Demand notice though dispatched but there is nothing on record to suggest that it was sent on correct postal address and served upon the alleged accused. Mandatory requirements are not met with complaint is not maintainable.

The High Court relied on:—

(i) AIR 2007 SC (Supp) 1705.

(ii) AIR 2007 SC (Supp) 1688.

***Shiv Kumar* v. *Natarajan,* 2009 (3) JCC (NI) 175 (SC)**

Cases referred:

2008 (16) SCALE 317; 2001 (6) SCC 588; 1998 Cr LJ 4330; 2008 (1) KLJ 327.

In this case the discussion was on the expression, "within a period of receipt of information." Notice was issued on the 31st day and not within a period of 30 days from the date of receipt of intimation from the Bank. Reference was made to section 9 of the General Clauses Act which is not applicable to section 138(b) proviso.

***M/s. Indo Automobiles* v. *M/s. Jai Durga Enterprises*, AIR 2009 SC 386**

Cases referred:

AIR 2005 SC 109; AIR 1999 SC 3762.

Notice was sent through Registered Post and under certificate of posting on their correct address. It must be presumed that service of notice has become effective. Service of notice cannot found to be not valid merely because there is endorsement by postal peon. Moreso, when the postal peon in not examined quashing of complaint that notice was not served on them is liable to be set aside.

***R.K. Chawala* v. *Goa Antibiotics and Pharmaceuticals Ltd.*, 2010 (1) Crimes 178 (Bom)**

Cases referred:

Prem Chand Vijay Kumar v. *Yashpal Singh*, (2005) 4 SCC 417; *Anil Kumar Goel* v. *Kishan Chand, Kaura*, (2009) 1 SCC (Cri) 209.

In this case the complaint was dismissed on two grounds *i.e.* firstly, the notice was not sent within 15 days of the receipt of information from the bank of dishonour of cheque and secondly, the complainant earlier had made a demand in writing by notice dated 25.11.1998. The appellant raised the issue of amendment of from 15 days to 30 days. It was held that that amendment is w.e.f. 6.2.2003 and it is prospective in nature and not retrospective. Held that dismissal of complaint on first ground cannot be faulted.

Note.—*(1) Issue of Demand Notice for payment of cheque amount is a must.*

(2) It must be served or deemed to be served on the drawer of the cheque.

(3) The notice should not be defective to lose its validity.

(4) Dispute about notice can be agitated in the trial and not under section 482, the Cr. P.C.

(5) Notice once served under clause (b) of proviso to section 138 of the Negotiable Instruments Act is the beginning of cause-of-action culminating after 15 days of its receipt by the drawer of cheque.

(6) It is legally desirable to send the notice both by Registered Post Acknowledgment Due and UPC.

(7) Technicalities of notice will not destroy the Legislative measure.

(8) Clause (b) of proviso to section 138 is indispensable and its breach will result in dismissal of complaint.

(9) Its object is to give chance to honest drawer of cheque to rectify the omission and to protect himself from the rigours of a criminal trial.

PROVISO (c) TO SECTION 138

INTRODUCTION

Proviso (c) to section 138 of the Negotiable Instruments Act says:—

"The drawer of such cheque fails to make payment of the said amount of money to the payee or as the case may be to the holder in due course of the cheque within fifteen days of the receipt of the said notice."

Section 142(b) says, "such complaint is made within one month of the date on which the cause-of-action arises under clause (c) of proviso to section 138."

In proviso (c) to section 138 the expression used is, "Whether Fifteen Days Of The Receipt Of The Said Notice." It has two aspects:

(1) within fifteen days.

(2) of receipt of notice.

The period of fifteen days envisaged in proviso (c) to section 138(c) of the Negotiable Instruments Act, 1881 will begin to run on the day next to the day on which the service of notice has been effected. For instance, notice is received on 1-1-1990. The period of fifteen days for making payment of the dishonoured cheque will start from 2-1-1990 and will expire on 16-1-1990 and cause-of-action for filing the complainant will being from 17-1-1990. [*See* 2000 Cr LJ 3547 (Guj) (FB).]

Pertaining to "receipt of notice", it is not the "giving" of notice which makes the offence but it is the "receipt" of notice by the drawer which gives the cause-of-action to the complainant to file the complaint. Fifteen days are to be counted from the "receipt" of information regarding the return of the cheque as unpaid. For instance the notice is issued on 5-10-1995 but received by the drawer of the cheque on 8-10-1995. The starting point will begin from 9-10-1995. [*See* AIR 2001 SC 676: 2001 (6) Sic 463: (2001) 1 KLT 528 and (2001) 6 SCC 582: 2001 SCC (Cri) 1184: (2001) 106 Comp Cas 730.]

Clause (b) of section 142 carries a restrictive meaning. Only one fact will give rise to the cause-to-action and that is the failure to make payment within 15 days from the date on which notice is received by the drawer of the cheque. Second presentation of cheque and issue of second notice will not revive cause-of-action. [*See* 1995 Cr LJ 1904 (Karn); 2000 Cr LJ 122 (Guj); (1998) 91 Comp Cas 599 (Cal).]

CASE LAW

***Aruna Bai* v. *Surrendra Babu*, 1995 Cr LJ 1904 (Karn)**

Facts of the case.—

Cheque issued on 30-11-1991.

Cheque presented on 11-4-1992.

Intimation of dishonour 11-4-1992 for insufficient funds.

Issue of Notice on 23-4-1992.

Notice received by drawer on 25-4-1992.

Payment to be made by 10-5-1992.

Cause of action starts from 11-5-1992.

The complaint filed on 3-6-1992 (within one month).

The trial Magistrate dismissed the complaint as time barred. It appears that the trial Magistrate considered "receipt of notice" as the cause-of-action. The Revision Petition was allowed as being within time.

***Swaroop Vegetable Products Industries Ltd.* v. *Vindhya Soya Ltd.*, 1996 Cr LJ 1150 (MP)**

Cases referred:

1994 Cr LJ 2874 (Guj); 1993 Cr LJ 670 (Bom); 1992 Cr LJ 4048 (AP); 1992 Cr LJ 3080 (Ker); AIR 1976 SC 1947: (1976) 3 SCC 736: 1976 Cr LJ 1533; AIR 1963 SC 1430: (1963) 2 Cr LJ 397: (1964) 1 SCR 639.

Facts of the case.—

Cheque issued on 14-2-1991.

Cheque returned on 30-3-1991.

The payee issued notice within prescribed period and waited for 15 days for the payment. There was no reply from the drawer of the cheque. The payee filed the complaint on 23-5-1991 within one month from the due date of accrual of cause-of-action.

The learned trial magistrate took cognizance of the complaint which was challenged on two grounds:—

(1) The order does not disclose the date of the cheque and the amount of the cheque.

(2) The order does not disclose the date on which the cause-of-action arose, and hence such a cryptic is liable to be set aside.

The High Court *held* that for determining the question whether any process is to be issued or not, what the Magistrate has to be satisfied is whether there is sufficient ground for proceeding or not, whether there is sufficient ground for conviction. Whether the evidence is adequate for supporting the conviction can be determined only at the trial and not at the stage of enquiry under section 202, the Cr. P.C. *Held*, that the Magistrate has not committed any error in taking cognizance of the case and issuing process. The Revision Petition was dismissed.

***N. Venkata Sivaram Prasad* v. *Rajeshwari Constructions*, 1996 Cr LJ 3409 (AP)**

Cases referred:

(1995) 2 APLJ 488; (1994) 1 Andh LT 510 (explained and distinguished); (1991) 1 Andh LT 22 (explained and distinguished); AIR 1972 SC 2639: (1973) 3 SCC 753: 1973 SCC (Cri) 521.

Facts of the case.—

Cheque issued on 30-4-1991.

Cheque dishonoured on 7-5-1991.

Intimation received on 13-5-1991.

Notice issued on 25-5-1991.

Notice not received as per endorsement 27-5-1991.

Period of 15 days expired on 11-6-1991.

Complaint filed on 3-6-1991.

Cause-of-action arose on 12-6-1991.

Held, that the complaint filed is premature. There was no cause-of-action on 3-6-1991. The learned Magistrate should have either returned the complaint or dismissed the complaint as there was no cause-of-action on 3-6-1991 and the complaint on 3-6-1991 is no complaint in eye of law.

***Ashok Hegde* v. *Jathin V. Attawan,* (1997) 3 Crimes 445: (1997) 3 Kant LJ 208: (1997) 3 Cur Cri R 776: 1997 Cr LJ 3691 (Karn)**

Facts of the case.—

Cheque issued on 31-7-1989.

Cheque returned unpaid on 13-9-1989.

("Payment stopped")

Notice issued on 13-9-1989.

Notice received back on 21-9-1989.

(Addressee refused)

Period of 15 days expired on 5-10-1989.

Complaint filed on 27-9-1989.

The trial Magistrate took cognizance and directed to issue process which was challenged. *Held,* that date of issuance of notice is not to be taken into account. The cause-of-action had not arisen on 27-9-1989 when the complaint was filed. The complainant filed was premature. Hence, the proceedings pending on the file of the Magistrate was quashed. [Refer 1996 Cr LJ 3409 (AP)]

***Lallu Lal Aggarwal* v. *Damodar Gupta,* 1997 Cr LJ 1545 (Raj)**

Cases referred:

1996 Cr LJ 1692 (SC) (relied on); (1996) 6 SCC 369: 1996 SCC (Cri) 1340; (1996) WLC 215 (Raj); (1995) 1 Cur Cri R 521 (P&H) (dissented from); (1992) 3 Crimes 594 (P&H) (dissented from).

Facts of the case.—In this case the cheque was dishonoured but on first dishonour the notice was not delivered. By virtue of this the payee did not lose his right of second or third presentation. The cause-of-action arose on first dishonour of cheque but the payee had to go through clauses (b) and (c) of proviso to section 138 of the Act to have the right to file a complaint. Thus, the cause-of-action arose only on the expiry of 15 days from the receipt of notice. Hence, the petition was dismissed.

***Devender Kumar Rai* v. *Ram Gopal Rai,* 1999 All LJ 376: (1999) 1 Bank CLR 298: (1998) 2 BC 583: 1999 Cr LJ 1349 (All)**

Facts of the case.—Two points were raised in the petition:

(1) The cheque issued is not a payment towards any debt.

(2) The notice was issued to make payment within 30 days but the complaint is filed before the expiry of 30 days.

The cheque was dishonoured when presented on the ground of shortage of funds and other technical grounds. The notice was issued which was refused on 12-3-1996. No payment came up to 30-3-96 and hence the complaint was filed on 30-3-1996. It was found that the payee complied with all the requirements of proviso (a), (b) and (c) of section 138 and section 142(b). Hence, the petition was dismissed.

***Kumari Sunita Charak* v. *Ajay Kumar Sharma*, (2000) 4 Civ LJ 38: 2000 Cr LJ 2572 (J&K)**

Cases referred:

1999 Cr LJ 949 (Raj) (Dissented from)

Facts of the case:

The cheque was dishonoured on 30-6-1998.

Intimation of dishonoured received on 3-7-1998.

Cheque was again presented on 12-8-1998.

Intimation of dishonoured received on 24-8-1998.

Notice was issued on 2-9-1998.

Complaint was filed on 9-9-1998.

The learned Magistrate took cognizance of the case and summoning order was passed against the drawer of the cheque which was challenged. *Held,* that the complaint is pre-mature. Hence; the petition was disallowed.

Amina* v. *Baby*, *1 (2005) CCR 233 (Ker)

Facts of the case.—Two cheques dated 19-8-1996 and 3-1-1997 were presented but were dishonoured. The drawer of the cheque was informed on 25-1-1997. However, the notice was dated 11-2-1997 and posted on 13-2-1997. If the date was to be taken as 25-1-1997, the notice was issued after the expiry of 15 days, but whereas in the complaint the date of intimation was mentioned as 3-2-1997. If the date 3-2-1997 was taken, the notice sent on 13-2-1997 was within time. The court *held* as follows:—(1) He shall undergo imprisonment for a day to be decided by the Magistrate. (2) He shall pay compensation of Rs. 72,000 to be paid to the payee if realised, failing the accused will undergo imprisonment for 3 months.

***Mahesh Mehta HUF* v. *State of Goa*, 2006 Cr LJ 1142 (Bom) (Goa Bench)**

Mere return of cheque dishonoured simpliciter does not become an offence under section 138. Said offence gets completed after notice was served and payment as required by notice was not made.

Displacement of presumption under section 139 lies on the accused.

SECTION 138(E)

***D. Vinod Shivappa* v. *Nanda Belliappa*, AIR 2006 SC 2179**

Cases referred:

(2005) 4 SCC 417; AIR 2005 SC 109; AIR 2001 SC 676; AIR 1999 SC 3762; AIR 1998 SC 3043; 76 ER 637.

Regarding section 138, proviso (c) the Apex Court said that it is well-settled law that in interpreting a statute the court must adopt that construction which suppresses the mischief and advances the remedy. This is a rule laid down in *Heydan's* case (76 ER 637) also known as the rule of purposive construction or mischief rule. Presumption in all cases cannot be drawn where notice is not served on account of non-availability of addressee. No such rule of universal application can be laid down and question depends on facts and circumstances of each case.

***Subhash Chand Barjatya* v. *The State*, 2006 (2) JCC (NI) 212 (Del)**

In this case section 138(c) and sections 91 and 311, the Cr. P.C. were discussed. There were applications under sections 91 and 311, the Cr. P.C. for summoning of cheque returning register and the other was for recalling CW1 for further cross-examination. The applications were rejected. Revision was filed. It was found that CW2 has changed his earlier stand and as such the summoning of document is necessary. When there was cross-examination of CW-1 was done, at that time document CW-2/D2 was not on record. So the recall petition is justified.

***Teja Seeds Corporation, Warrangal* v. *Nandi Seeds Pvt. Ltd., Mahboobnagar*, 2007 (2) JCC (NI) 135 (AP)**

Cases referred:

AIR 2000 SC 828; 2000 (2) ALD (Cri) 855.

Notice was issued on 19.10.2005

Notice received on 24.10.2005

Reply received by the Complainant along with D/D of Rs. 1,00,000 on 12.11.2005

Complaint is filed on 6-12-2005

It is *held* that the payment should have been made 8-11-2005, *i.e.*, within 15 days but made on 12-11-2005, offence is said to have been committed on the expiry of 15 days from the receipt of notice.

***M/s. Tide Water Oil Co. (I) Ltd.* v. *M/s. Greaseoil (I)*, 2007 (1) JCC (NI) 116**

Cases referred:

1998 (6) SCC 514; 2005 (4) SCC 417.

Cheques were issued on 31-8-1999

Cheques present in the Bank on 3-9-1999

Legal Notice issued on 17-9-1999

On 4-9-1999 a letter was received that the cheques be presented on 30-9-1999. The cheques were again presented but returned dishonoured. Two notices were issued on 23-10-1999 and 6-11-1999 but payment was not received. The complaint was filed on 2-12-1999. The whole story indicated that the complainant ignored letter dated 4-9-1999. As being the case the complainant would have filed the complaint on the basis of notice dated 17-9-1999 on 2-11-1999 but was filed on 2-12-1999 which is time-barred.

***Ramesh Chand* v. *Ravinder Singh Chandel*, 2007 Cr LJ 1313 (HP)**

Cases referred:

AIR 2006 SC 2179 (followed); AIR 2005 SC 109 (followed).

Held, that in case the complainant wants the court to presume service of notice upon the respondent, he must lead evidence to show that the endorsement made on the postal envelope is either false or it has been wrongly procured by the accused or there is other sufficient material on record to show that the accused was aware of the issuance of notice and has managed to procure the said endorsement on the postal envelope. The burden of proof is on the complainant.

Note.—*Section 138 comprises of the following essentials to make dishonour of cheque punishable as an offence:*

(1) *The cheque has to be towards payment of an amount of money for the discharge in whole or in part of any debt or other liability.*

(2) *Debt or other liability means a legally enforceable debt or other liability.*

(3) *The cheque is returned by the Bank unpaid.*

(4) *The reason for non-payment of the cheque should be insufficiency of funds or exceeds arrangement.*

(5) *Any other reason such as Refer to drawer, stop payment, Account closed, etc., when amounting to shortage of funds in the account.*

(6) *The cheque is presented within 6 months or within the validity period whichever is earlier from the date on the cheque.*

(7) *The payee or holder in due course issues a notice in writing within 15 days of the intimation of dishonour of cheque from the Bank. (Now read 30 days)*

(8) *The drawer fails to make payment within 15 days of the receipt of Notice.* [See *1995 Cr LJ 1222 Del; AIR 2000 SC 954.]*

(9) *The burden of proof his on the complaint by leading evidence of the receipt of intimation that the cheque is dishonoured,* i.e., *that the demand notice is received where there is doubt regarding receipt of demand notice.*

NO NOTICE/DEFECTIVE NOTICE

***Rajiv Kumar* v. *State of Uttar Pradesh,* (1993) 78 Comp Cas 507: 1991 Cr LJ 3010 (All)**

Facts of the case.—In this case the information about non-payment of cheque was received on 27-2-1990. The notice was sent within the prescribed period. But there was no evidence that the notice is served on the accused. The document produced showed that it was received by one Guddu and not the drawer of the cheque. The said acknowledgement does not show that it was addressed in the name of the accused. In absence of service of notice under section 138(b) of the Negotiable Instruments Act, no prosecution and cognizance of offence was permissible.

***Gopa Devi Ojha* v. *Sujit Paul,* (1995) 2 CHN 37: 1995 Cr LJ 3412 (Cal)**

Cases referred:

(1994) 2 All CR 644; (1993) 1 Cal HN 298 (followed); (1993) 3 Crimes 1064 (SC); AIR 1992 SC 1379: (1992) 3 SCC 317: 1992 Cr LJ 1956; 1990 TLNJ (Cr) 121; 1979 Cr LJ 998.

Facts of the case.—In this case the cheque amount was Rs. 5,79,000 whereas the amount claimed in the notice is Rs. 6,50,000. That was not the cheque amount and as such the notice was vague and insufficient and the said notice could not be sustained in law.

***B. Adhikari* v. *Panraj,* (1996) 86 Comp Cas 431: 1996 Cr LJ 180 (Mad)**

Facts of the case.—The petitioner was found guilty and convicted. He filed a criminal appeal before the Additional Sessions Judge and lost. This was a Revision Petition challenging the impugned order of the A.S.J. on the ground of non-service of notice on the accused. *Held,* that for the mere reasoning of failure in compliance with the in-built mandate in clause (b) of proviso to section 138 of the Act the conviction and sentence was not sustainable.

***Inderjeet Kaur* v. *Gandotra Trading and Leasing Corpn. Jammu,* 1998 Cr LJ 3659 (J&K)**

Cases referred:

(1997) 1 Shimla LJ 336; AIR 1992 SC 604: 1992 Supp (1) SCC 335: 1992 Cr LJ; AIR 1960 SC 866: (1960) 3 SCR 388: 1960 Cr LJ 527 1239.

Facts of the case.—It is not mere the dishonour of cheque but the service of demand notice and non-payment by the drawer of the cheque within 15 days of the receipt of notice, which leads to the filing of the complaint. The High Court *held* that receipt of notice by the accused assumes significance because it is after expiry of 15 days of this date the complaint can be maintained. This aspect is missing both in the complaint as well as in preliminary evidence. Hence, the petition was allowed.

***Tomy Jacob Kattikkaran* v. *Dr. Thomas Manjalay,* (1997) 11 SCC 24: 1997 SCC (Cri) 1184: AIR 1998 SC 366: 1998 Cr LJ 661 (SC)**

Facts of the case.—The respondent issued a cheque for Rs. 3,00,000 being the amount due to the appellant. It was dishonoured on presentation. The appellant then sent a notice to the respondent demanding the amount but it came back unserved with an endorsement that he was absent. Thereafter another similar notice was sent and served upon the respondent but he did not pay when this case was pending, the respondent filed another complaint under sections 380, 465, 467, 468 and 471, the I.P.C. In the first complaint there was conviction and in the second complaint there was discharge of the appellant under section 245(1), the Cr. P.C.

The Supreme Court agreed with the acquittal of the appellant by the Sessions Judge and the High Court as that before filing the complaint no notice was issued within the period prescribed under section 138 of the Act and for the second complaint upheld the decision of the trial Magistrate of discharge as evidence being insufficient. This order of the trial Magistrate was reversed by the High Court.

***Ganesh Dass* v. *Narender Kumar,* (1993) 3 CCC 605: (1999) 1 Raj LW 725: 1999 Cr LJ 3362 (Raj)**

Case referred:

1993 Cr LJ 1751 (Ori).

Facts of the case.—It is a case of dishonour of cheque, but for dishonour of cheque no notice was sent to the drawer of the cheque demanding payment. This notice is mandatory as the object of this provision is to give chance to make payment within 15 days of the receipt of the said notice. Omission to send notice is fatal to the complaint and hence the proceedings were quashed.

***Bipin J. Shah* v. *Niru B. Mehta*, (2001) 2 Mah LJ 632: 2001 Cr LJ 4819 (Bom)**

Facts of the case.—In this case the notice was sent to Ashok Mehta accused No. 1 and not to Bipin Shah accused No. 2. The cheque was signed by Ashok Mehta. The complaint was filed against both. The trial Magistrate considered that notice to one accused is sufficient for cause-of-action against the other accused. *Held,* that cause-of-action against the other accused on the basis of the notice issued to accused No. 1 is erroneous. There is no cause-of-action against accused No. 2 and his application is allowed.

***N.G. Narayanswami* v. *Vijyanand Roadlines Ltd.*, (2001) 4 ICC 517: (2001) 2 BC 323: 2001 Cr LJ 211 (Karn)**

Case referred:

AIR 1991 SC 441: (1991) 1 SCC 113: (1991) 70 Comp Cas 1.

Facts of the case.—The short question was that whether the complaint under section 138, the Negotiable Instruments Act was maintainable in law in the absence of a notice to the drawer of the cheque under proviso (b) to section 138(b) of the Act. Proviso to section 138 stipulates: "Provided that nothing contained in this section shall apply unless—"

There are three clauses (a), (b) and (c). They are mandatory. Clause (b) is the heart of the section. Its breach will result in dismissal of the complaint. Hence, the petitioner succeeded as there was violation of clause (b) of proviso to section 138 of the Act.

***S.V. Murthye* v. *State*, (2002) 3 BC 82: (2002) 3 Crimes 91: 2002 Cr LJ 3219 (Del)**

Cases referred:

1999 Cr LJ 1221 (AP); AIR 1999 SC 1609: (1999) 4 SCC 567: 1999 SCC (Cri) 600: 1999 Cr LJ 2276; (1999) 80 DLT 660; 1998 Cr LJ 4066 (SC); 1998 Cr LJ 3539 (Karn); (1998) 4 AD 197 (Del); (1995) 59 DLT 284.

Facts of the case.—Intimation of dishonour of cheque was received on 29-7-1994 in respect of Ch. No. 09757729 dated 10-3-1994 and for Ch. No. 09757731 dated 15-3-1994 on 20-7-1994 and for Ch. No. 09757732 dated 20-3-1994 on 25-7-1994. The notice was issued on 24-9-1994 which was much beyond 15 days and the plea taken was that the Magistrate had the power to condone the delay under section 473, the Cr. P.C. and the delay was deemed to have been condoned when he issued the summoning order. Thus, the court *held* that there was no provision of condonation of delay under section 138 of the Act and as such neither section 473, the Cr. P.C. nor section 5 of the Limitation Act shall apply. There was no cause-of-action on 24-9-1994 when the notice was issued. The complaint was quashed.

***Pattabirama Reddy* v. *Nageshwar Reddy*, (2002) 3 All Cri R 61: (2001) 2 MLW (Cri) 781: 2002 Cr LJ NOC 185 (Mad)**

Facts of the case.—Failure to issue notice by letter. Demand was made through a telegram. Even no confirmatory letter was sent. *Held,* that telegram could not be accepted as statutory notice. Thus there was non-compliance with statutory provisions.

***Devender Kumar Surana* v. *Lalit Porwal*, (2002) 3 BC 408: 2002 Cr LJ 4176 (MP)**

Cases referred:

(2002) 2 Bank Cas 239 (MP); AIR 1999 SC 1609: (1999) 4 SCC 567: 1999 SCC (Cri) 600: 1999 Cr LJ 2276.

Facts of the case.—The case of the complainant was that petitioner could not send the Notice on the 15th day being public holiday.

Evidence showed that Post Office was functioning on that day for urgent and essential work. *Held,* that notice could have been sent by Fax or Courier or through personal service.

Notice was sent beyond 15 days resulting in dismissal of the complaint.

***Sunrise Oleo Chemicals Ltd.* v. *K.M. Enterprises*, (2003) 3 ALT 106: (2003) 2 Crimes 228: 2003 Cr LJ 3135 (AP)**

Cases referred:

(2002) 1 Andh LT (Cri) 151; 1998 Cr LJ 4066 (SC); (1993) 78 Comp Cas 512 (Mad); (1992) 1 Crimes 1233 (Cal).

Facts of the case.—In this case the cheque was dishonoured and notice was issued which was returned unserved with the endorsement that "No such person was residing in the said address for seven days". After the expiry of 15 days he again presented the cheque to save limitation. The High Court *held* that the complainant either on the premise of deemed notice or on the premise that there has been no service of notice, could have filed the complaint. In the former case it is barred by time and in the latter case there is no cause of action. Hence, the petition was dismissed and the conviction and sentence was set aside.

***Subhash Chander* v. *Pritam Singh Machinewala*, (2003) 3 All Cri R 989: 2003 Cr LJ 2157 (J&K)**

Case referred:

(1999) 9 SCC 192: 1999 SCC (Cri) 1141: AIR 2000 SC 3639.

Facts of the case.—In this case a cheque was dishonoured on 20-5-1997. A notice of demand for payment, in writing, after dishonour of cheque was given on 3-6-1997. It is neither borne out from complaint nor the evidence was adduced as to when the notice was received by the accused. One of the indispensable factor is that the complaint is to be filed within one month after the cause-of-action arises under clause (c) and this cause-of-action arises after 15 days of the receipt of notice issued under clause (b) of proviso to section 138. It is not possible to compute a period of 15 days unless date of receipt of notice is made out for accrual of cause-of-action. Thus, this acquittal appeal was *held* devoid of merit.

***K. Dev Raj* v. T.K. Koya, (2003) 2 Civ LJ 318: 2003 Cr LJ 520 (Mad)**

Case referred:

1990 Mad LJ (Cri) 178.

Facts of the case.—The notice is said to have been sent but there is no whisper about the non-payment of the amount by the accused. So one of the essential ingredient of section 138 is missing. Reliance was placed on 1990 Mad LJ (Cri) 178 and *held* that the complaint is not maintainable.

***Padmini Polymers Ltd.* v. *Unit Trust of India*, (2002) 101 DLT 376: (2002) 65 DRJ 705: 2003 Cr LJ 1053 (Del)**

Case referred:

1998 Cr LJ 4066: AIR 1998 SC 3043: (1998) 6 SCC 514: 1998 SCC (Cri) 1471: (1998) 2 KLT 765.

Facts of the case.—It is a case where the letter was written by the complainant to the accused making him aware of fact of dishonour of cheques but there was no demand to make payment within 15 days. The letter was dated 5-7-2001 which did not speak of payment. The notice sent through the advocate was dated 17-11-2001 which contained all the ingredients of clause (b) of proviso to section 138 of the Act. The cheques were dishonoured and brought to the notice of the accused on 5-7-2001 which was not a notice of demand and demand notice dated 17-11-2001 was time-barred. Hence, the petition had no merit.

***M. Laxmipathi* v. *Employees State Insurance Corporation*, (2003) 1 BC 328: (2002) 5 Kant LJ 451: 2003 Cr LJ 354 (Karn)**

Facts of the case.—In this case the notice was issued to the petitioner-accused on 5-7-1990 and received by him on 10-7-1990. Within 15 days, therefrom, the petitioner should have tendered the amount pursuant to the notice, *i.e.*, by 25-7-1990. Whereas before the expiry of 25-7-1990 the petitioner took a stay order against the recovery of the arrears in respect of which the cheque in question was issued. The stay order granted was till 27-7-1990 and continued until further orders. Thus the payment within 15 days was suspended by a court order and by virtue of this the payee or holder in due course cannot lodge a complaint. Thus, the complaint lodged suffered from cause of action. The order of conviction and sentence was set aside.

***M. Murugan* v. *Queen Jhansi Vetrikodi*, (2004) 3 BC 242: (2004) 2 CTC 530: 2004 Cr LJ 3184 (Mad)**

Cases referred:

2002 Cr LJ 185; (1999) 4 SCC 567: 1999 SCC (Cri) 600: (1999) 97 Comp Cas 575: 1999 Cr LJ 2276 (SC); 1993 Cr LJ 3677 (SC).

Facts of the case.—It is a case where notice was sent by telegram and was not authenticated by a subsequent letter within a period of limitation. The notice was not valid and the Revision was dismissed.

***Om Parkash Kapoor* v. *State of Bihar (now Jharkhand)*, (2004) 2 BLJR 1282: (2004) 4 BC 431: (2004) 3 Cur Cri R 519: 2004 Cr LJ 3229 (Jhar)**

Case referred:

1997 Cr LJ 2122 (Mad).

Facts of the case.—This is a Criminal Revision Petition against the conviction and sentence. The issue involved was that Notice required under section 138 of the Act was not served on the revisionist. The accused issued four post-dated cheques No. 216451 dated 30-7-1989, No. 216452 dated 30-8-1989, No. 216454 dated 30-9-1989 and No. 216455 dated 30-10-1989, all of Rs. 15,000 each. These cheques, when presented, were dishonoured. On assurance, the cheques were represented but again got dishonoured and thereupon a notice was issued but got no reply. Finally, the complaint was filed on 3-11-1989. Further facts were that the first cheque was dishonoured on 14-8-1989. The second cheque was dishonoured on 1-9-1989. The third cheque was dishonoured on 4-10-1989. Regarding first and second cheque the Advocate's notice was sent which came back unserved with the remarks, "*Ranchi Se Bahar Gaye Huhi Hai*". Notice regarding 3rd cheque was sent which returned with the remarks. "Refused". This endorsement was dated 21-10-1989. The complaint was filed on 3-11-89. It was a composite notice for three cheques. As per dates mentioned notice regarding first two cheques was barred by time and for the third cheque the complaint was premature as the accused had time to make payment upto 5-11-1989 whereas the complaint was filed on 3-11-1989 itself. Hence, the complaint was not maintainable. The conviction and sentence passed by the lower court was set aside.

***K.R. Indira* v. *Dr. G. Adinarayana*, (2003) 8 SCC 300: 2003 SCC (Cri) 2002: AIR 2003 SC 4689: (2003) 117 Comp Cas 407: 2004 Cr LJ 5 (SC)**

Cases referred:

(2000) 2 SCC 380: 2000 SCC (Cri) 414: AIR 2000 SC 828: 2002 Cr LJ 1391 (SC); 1999 Cr LJ 4571 (SC).

Facts of the case.—In this case two issues were raised:—

(1) Consolidated demand notice in respect of four dishonoured cheques was sent.

(2) There was no specific demand for payment covered by four dishonoured made in the notice.

The Supreme Court *held* that the consolidated demand notice does not invalidate the notice. Regarding the second issue, the Supreme Court found that the amount claimed was different than that of the amount covered by the four dishonoured cheques and thus there was no demand of the amount covered by the cheques. Hence, the Appeal was dismissed.

***Abdur Rehman M. Mulgand* v. *Mohammad Hashan Mulgand*, 2006 Cr LJ 1159 (Bom) (Goa Bench)**

No specific format of Notice. Requisite condition of valid notice is that it should be in writing and must demand for value of the cheque. Minor discrepancies do not make the notice invalid; 1998 Cr LJ 4750 (Bom) (relied on).

Notes.—

1. *Issue of notice is a condition precedent.*
2. *It must be made within 15 days (now 30 days) of the receipt of information of the dishonour of cheque.*
3. *The payee has to call for the payment for the amount covered by the dishonoured cheque.*

4. *It is desirable not to ask for incidental or other charges, but if required they must be shown separately or may be severable from the cheque amount.*
5. *The notice must be in writing.*
6. *It must be sent on correct address.*
7. *Deemed service is also a notice served on the drawer of the cheque.*
8. *It is desirable to send the notice by Registered Post AD as well as by UPC.*
9. *If the payee enters the second stage of proviso (b) of section 138 of the Act, he has to wait for proviso (c) and should not revert to proviso (a) to create a new cause-of-action.*
10. *Consolidated demand notice for more than one cheque does not invalidate the notice provided the prescribed period of 30 days is not breached.*

CHAPTER II

PRESUMPTION OF LAW – BUT REBUTTABLE

Section 139. Presumption in favour of holder.—It shall be presumed, unless the contrary is proved, that the holder of a cheque received the cheque of the nature referred to in section 138, for the discharge, in whole or in part, of any debt or other liability.

PRESUMPTION

Section 4 of the Evidence Act, 1872 speaks of three classes of presumptions, *viz.*, (1) presumption of law, (2) presumption of fact, and (3) mixed presumptions. A presumption of law is a rule of law that a particular inference shall be drawn by a court from a particular circumstance. The second class of presumption consists of those which are commonly known as presumptions of fact. A presumption of fact is a rule of law that a fact otherwise doubtful may be inferred from a fact which is proved. The term "presumption of fact" is used to designate an inference, affirmative or disaffirmative of the existence of some fact, drawn by a judicial Tribunal by a process of probable reasoning from some matter of fact, either judicially noticed, or admitted, or established by legal evidence to the satisfaction of the Tribunal. "Presumption of mixed law and fact" holds an intermediate place between presumptions of law and presumptions of fact. They consist chiefly of certain inferences which, from their strength, importance, and frequent occurrence, attract, as it were the observation of the law and from being constantly recommended by Judges, become in time as familiar to the courts as presumption of law and occupy nearly as important a place in the administration of justice.

However, section 4 of the Evidence Act, 1872 has used three phrases, *i.e.*, (1) "may presume", (2) "shall presume", and "conclusive proof". The question of presumption has to be kept distinct from question of proof. The presumptions may be rebuttable or irrebuttable. But presumptions arising under section 114 of the Evidence Act are not presumptions of law but of fact. They are rebuttable. (AIR 1921 Nag 39; AIR 1928 All 16; AIR 1952 Assam 97). *Illustration* (c) to section 114 of the Evidence Act, 1872 says, "that a bill of exchange, accepted or endorsed, was accepted or endorsed for good consideration." This presumption, being presumption of fact under section 114 of the Evidence Act, has received the status of a *presumption of law under section 118 of the Negotiable Instruments Act, 1881* and has been made applicable to all Negotiable Instruments (AIR 1935 Mad 769; AIR 1988 Cal 54). The Supreme Court in AIR 1965 SC 920: (1965) 1 SCR

254, has said that the special rules of evidence laid down in section 118 apply only as between parties to the instrument or those claiming under them. In other cases presumption will only be in terms of section 114 of the Evidence Act [*See* also AIR 1961 SC 1316; AIR 1967 Punj 331; AIR 1976 Goa 8; AIR 1959 Raj 1 (FB); (1969) 1 Mys LJ 217; 1978 Ker LT 868; AIR 1982 Ori 264; AIR 1979 Gau 46].

Law of the Negotiable Instruments Act, 1881 has been amended from time to time but the Banking, Public Financial and Negotiable Instruments Laws Amendment Act, 1988 (66 of 1988) and the Negotiable Instruments (Amendment and Miscellaneous Provisions) Act, 2002 (55 of 2002) were brought to enhance the acceptability of cheques in settlement of liabilities by making the drawer liable for penalties in case of bouncing of cheques due to specified grounds and *section 139, has given teeth to section 138 by shifting the burden of proof of liability on the person who issued the cheque.* So section 4 and section 114, *Illustration* (c) of the Evidence Act, 1872 and section 118(a) and section 139 of the Negotiable Instruments Act, 1881 be read conjunctively.

JUDICIAL VIEW

***S. Mohan Singh* v. *Madan Lal,* 1996 Cr LJ 681 (J&K)**

The High Court *held* that section 139 creates a statutory presumption that a cheque, received in the nature referred to under section 138, is always issued in discharge of debt or other liability. Therefore, it is not necessary for a complainant to specifically plead that the cheque which was issued to him and dishonoured by the Bank was in fact issued in the discharge of a debt or a liability. By reading sections 138 and 139 of the Act together, it becomes abundantly clear that it is for the accused to show that the cheque issued by him and dishonoured by the bank was not in the discharge of any debt or liability.

***Goa Plast Pvt. Ltd.* v. *Chico Ursula D'Souza,* 1996 Cr LJ 2344 Bom (Goa Bench)**

Cases referred:

Bratinderanath Banerjee, Director, Standard Chartered Bank v. *Hiten P. Dalal,* (1994) 4 Bom CR 237. (relied on); *Prithvi Raj* v. *Bhupendra,* (1994) 3 Crimes 579; *Alexander* v. *Joseph Chacko,* (1994) 1 Crimes 388; *Adapa Bhogi Raju* v. *S.G. Ramayya,* (1994) 1 Crimes 351; *Ram Krishna Bedu Rane* v. *State of Maharashtra,* AIR 1973 SC 246: 1973 Cr LJ 287: (1973) 1 SCC 366; *V.D. Jhingan* v. *State of Uttar Pradesh,* 1966 Cr LJ 1357; *Dhanvantrai Balwantrai Desai* v. *State of Maharashtra,* AIR 1963 SC 575: 1963 Supp (1) SCR 485: (1964) 2 Cr LJ 437: 65 Bom LR 332; *State of Ajmer (now Rajasthan)* v. *Shivaji Lal,* 1959 Supp (2) SCR 739: 1959 Cr LJ 1127: AIR 1959 SC 847; *State of Madras* v. *Vaidyanath Iyer,* AIR 1958 SC 61: 1958 Cr LJ 232; *Bacha Prasad* v. *Janki Rai,* AIR 1957 Pat 380 (FB); Dr. P.W. Rege *"Law of Negotiable Instruments."* (referred).

The High Court said:—Before invoking presumption under section 139, the Negotiable Instruments Act, it has to be proved by the prosecution that:—

(i) The liability of the nature specified existed.

(ii) It was the liability of the accused.

(iii) The cheque was given towards that liability.

Held: The complainant failed to prove the case to attract the provisions of section 138 of the Act, the question does not arise to rebut the presumption under section 139 of the Act.

***R. Sankaralingam* v. *Union of India*, 1996 Cr LJ 3387: (1996) 86 Comp Cas 709**

Held: The law can impose presumptions when certain basic facts and circumstances exist. Sections 138 and 139 of the Act are based on such presumptions which arise on the existence of certain facts and circumstances and the presumption is to the effect that the holder of the cheque received the cheque of the nature referred to in section 138 of the Act for the discharge, in whole or in part, of any debt or other liability.

***Bhaskaran Chandrasekhran* v. *V. Radakrishnan*, (1998) 3 Civ LJ 889: (1998) 4 Crimes 156: (1998) 2 Ker LJ 86: (1998) 1 Ker LT 881: 1998 Cr LJ 3228 (Ker)**

Cases referred:

Jayanti Lal v. *Zubeda Khanum*, AIR 1986 AP 120; *Loonkaran Sethia* v. *Ivan E. John*, AIR 1977 SC 336: (1977) 1 SCC 379: (1977) 1 SCR 853; *Kirmani* v. *Aga Ali Akbar*, AIR 1928 Mad 919.

Held: When a cheque is issued for valid consideration with no dispute regarding signature, amount and name, it cannot be said that putting a date on the cheque by the payee who is the holder of the cheque in due course would amount to material alteration rendering the instrument void. In this case section 118(a) of the Negotiable Instruments Act, 1881 and section 114 of the Evidence Act, 1872 were discussed.

***Sailesh Kumar Agrawal* v. *State of Uttar Pradesh*, (2000) 2 Bank LLR 519: (2004) 4 Civ LJ 237: (2000) 4 Rec Cri R 432: 2000 Ori LJ 2921 (All)**

Cases referred:

Suman Sethi v. *Ajai Kumar Churiwal*, AIR 2000 SC 828: (2000) 2 SCC 380; *Maruti Udyog Ltd.* v. *Narendra*, (1999) 1 SCC 113; *Sadanandan Bhadran* v. *Madhavan Sunil Kumar*, AIR 1998 SC 3043: (1998) 6 SCC 514: (1998) 2 KLT 765.

Held: Many issues were raised and one of the issues was that the cheque was not for discharge of any debt or liability and further said that when once the cheque is issued, the presumption is in favour of the complainant that the cheque is regarding discharge of the liability and it is for the applicant to prove the contrary. The High Court relied on (1999) 1 SCC 113.

***Suman Sethi* v. *Ajai K. Churiwal*, (2000) 2 SCC 380: 2000 SCC (Cri) 414: AIR 2000 SC 828: 2000 Cr LJ 1391 (SC)**

Cases referred:

Central Bank of India v. *Saxon Farms*, AIR 1999 SC 3607: (1999) 8 SCC 221: (1999) 98 Comp Cas 712; *M. Narayanan Nambiar* v. *State of Kerala*, AIR 1963 SC 1116: 1963 Supp (2) SCR 724: (1963) 2 Cr LJ 186: 1963 Ker LT 1015; *Dyke* v. *Elliot*, 1872 LR 4 AC 184.

Held: In this case the issue agitated was that whether the notice issued under proviso (b) to section 138 of the Act was valid or not. While discussing the issue, section 139 of the Act was also discussed. The Supreme Court *held* that section 139 has to be read with section 138 and reading both the sections together it would appear that presumption would arise only in respect of the "said amount". Impliedly, application of section 139 depends on the full satisfaction of the ingredients of section 138 of the Act.

***Hiten P. Dalal* v. *Bratinderanath Banerjee,* (2001) 6 SCC 16: 2001 SCC (Cri) 960: (2001) 106 Comp Cas 574: 2001 Cr LJ 4647 (SC)**

Cases referred:

AIR 2000 SC 1488: (2000) 6 SCC 427; AIR 1998 SC 831: (1998) 2 SCC 418: 1998 SCC (Cri) 645: (1998) 91 Comp Cas; AIR 1977 SC 666; AIR 1973 SC 246: (1973) 1 SCC 366: 1973 Cr LJ 287; AIR 1968 SC 1292; AIR 1964 SC 575: 1963 Supp (1) SCR 485: (1964) 1 Cr LJ 437; AIR 1966 SC 1742; AIR 1961 SC 1316: (1963) 1 MLJ (SC) 85; AIR 1958 SC 61.

Held: Sections 138 and 139 require that the court "shall presume" the liability of the drawer of the cheques for the amounts for which the cheques are drawn. It is obligatory on the court to raise this presumption in every case where the factual basis for the raising of the presumption had been established. It introduced an exception to the general rule as to the burden of proof in criminal cases and shifts the onus on to the accused. Such a presumption is a presumption of law as distinguished from a presumption of fact which describes provisions by which the court "may presume" a certain state of affair. Presumptions are rules of evidence and do not conflict with the presumption of innocence because by the latter all that is meant is that the prosecution is obliged to prove the case against the accused beyond reasonable doubt. The obligation on the prosecution may be discharged with the help of presumption of law or fact unless the accused adduces the evidence showing the reasonable possibility of the non-existence of the presumed fact.

***V.P. Venkatesulu* v. *K.P. Mani Nayar,* (2001) 104 Comp Cas 348: 2001 Cr LJ 745 (Karn)**

Held: A plain reading of section 139 goes to show that the presumption created by it, is a rebuttable presumption. That presumption may get displaced by the prosecution evidence on record itself, or the accused may choose to lead independent evidence in rebuttal thereof.

If the circumstances of suspect character emerge proved from the prosecution evidence which are found to be badly damaging the credibility of the prosecution case, they are sufficient to displace the presumption available to the complainant under section 139. Once that presumption gets dislodged by such suspicious circumstances borne out by prosecution evidence, then heavy burden lies on the complainant to prove by independent positive evidence the most material fact of existence of debt or other liability against the accused drawer of the cheque in respect of that particular cheque amount. The court *held* that the legal infirmities in the story of the claimant effectively displaces and successfully rebuts the presumption under section 139 of the Act available to the complainant in favour of existence of debt or liability against accused. The revision is dismissed.

***K.N. Beena* v. *Muniyappan*, (2001) 107 Comp Cas 459: (2001) 8 SCC 458: 2002 SCC (Cri) 14: 2001 Cr LJ 4745 (SC)**

Case referred:

2001 AIR SCW 3861.

Held: In this case the Supreme Court took an identical stand as taken in 2001 AIR SCW 3861. *Held,* that the court took an erroneous view that the burden of proof lies on the complainant and that the learned Judge lost sight of sections 118 and 139 of the Act. Under section 139 the court has to presume, unless the contrary was proved, that the holder of the cheque received the cheque for discharge, in whole or in part of a debt or liability. The presumption is rebuttable. However, the burden of proving that a cheque had not been issued for a debt or liability is on the accused. The impugned judgment was set aside and the conviction and sentence as awarded stood.

***Vinod Tanna* v. *Zaheer Siddiqui*, (2002) 1 Crimes 104: 2001 Cr LJ 2297 (Bom)**

Cases referred:

AIR 1998 SC 1057: (1998) 3 SCC 249: 1998 Cr LJ 1397; (1996) 2 SCC 739: 1996 SCC (Cri) 454: AIR 1996 SC 2339; (1996) 6 SCC 369: 1996 SCC (Cri) 1340; 1993 Cr LJ 680 (Bom).

Held: The Supreme Court discussed the scope of sections 118 and 138 of the Act and then by referring to various decisions of the apex Court, it was *held* that whether petitioner had issued blank cheques, whether those were written by the petitioner, or those were written beyond instructions of the respondent, whether amount due is less than the amount endorsed on the cheque, these and such issues are matter of defences and further said.........because once the cheque is issued by the drawer, a presumption under section 139 must follow.

***Joseph Jose* v. *J. Baby Pathuval Puravidan Poothoppu*, (2003) 1 BC 180: (2002) 2 Ker LJ 334: 2002 Cr LJ 4392 (Ker)**

Case referred:

Bhaskaran v. *Balan,* (1999) 3 Ker LT 440.

Held: That there is no burden on complainant to prove before court entire details of transaction resulting in issuing of cheque. There is a presumption that cheque was issued for discharge of debt or other legal liability. Section 118(a) and section 139 are to the effect to be presumed that, in the absence of any contrary evidence, the complainant received the cheque for discharge in whole or in part of a debt or other legal liability. *Held,* that the acquittal of the accused is unjustified and the matter is remitted back to trial court for passing fresh judgment in accordance with law.

***Bharathbai K. Patel* v. *C.L. Verma*, (2002) 3 Guj LR 1713: 2002 Cr LJ 3469 (Guj)**

Cases referred:

2002 Cr LJ 266; 2001 Cr LJ 4745; AIR 1999 Guj 193; 1995 Cr LR (Guj) 223.

Held: It was a case under section 482, the Cr. P.C. The High Court, firstly took a common stand that at the initial stage of proceedings the High Court is not justified in entertaining and accepting the plea that there was no debt or liability. However, the High Court *held* that when the accused had successfully rebutted the presumption at initial stage itself and pointed out basic infirmity as to the maintainability of the proceedings, there was no use asking the accused to face the trial till it was concluded and allowed the petition for quashing of criminal proceedings.

***Shamsul Islam* v. *16th Additional Sessions Judge, Kanpur Nagar*, 2002 All LJ 2268: (2002) 3 All WC 2468: 2002 Cr LJ 4564 (All)**

Held: It was a case under section 482, the Cr. P.C. The criminal proceedings were initially started against two accused but criminal proceedings against one accused was dismissed by the trial court and also by the Revision Court. The petition under section 482, the Cr. P.C. was filed by the other accused for quashing the proceedings. The High Court *held* that subsequently the payment was made in a subsequent transaction cannot be considered in a petition under section 482, the Cr. P.C. as there is presumption that the cheque is issued to discharge the debt or liability and if the debt or liability is already discharged by the accused, it is a matter of evidence which must be adduced by the accused and that proceedings cannot be quashed on this ground.

***Steel Authority of India* v. *B.D. Aggarwal & Sons Ltd.*, 2002 Cr LJ 382 (P&H)**

Cases referred:

2001 AIR SCW 3861; AIR 1999 SC 1952: (1999) 4 SCC 253: (1999) 96 Comp Cas 822; AIR 1998 SC 1057: (1998) 3 SCC 249: 1998 Cr LJ 1397.

Held: This was a petition under section 482, the Cr. P.C. In a case of dishonour of cheque the Trial Court passed the summoning order and the same was set aside and thus this petition was for quashing the order of the Revision Court. The High Court, while referring to the above cited cases decided by the Supreme Court, *held* that the presumption under section 139 of the Act could not be rebutted at the initial stage and that rebuttal could be at the appropriate stage by proving the contrary.

***Raghunathan* v. *Selvaranjan*, 2002 MLJ (Cri) 257: 2002 Cr LJ 3848 (Mad)**

Cases referred:

(2001) 6 SCC 16: 2001 SCC (Cri) 960: (2001) 106 Comp Cas 574: AIR 2001 SC 3897; AIR 2001 SC 2895: (2001) 8 SCC 458: 2002 SCC (Cri) 14; 1998 Cr LJ 4237 (AP).

Held: In this case the trial court convicted the accused and sentenced him to undergo simple imprisonment for 3 months and to pay a fine of Rs. six thousand. On appeal the accused was acquitted. The case came before the High Court and sections 118 and 139 of the Act were vigorously agitated. The High Court relying on the above decisions *held* that the court in complaint under section 138 has to presume, unless the contrary was proved that the holder of the cheque received the cheque for discharge in whole or in part, of a debt or liability and in this case the judge lost sight of section 118 and section 139 of the Act. *Held*, that the acquittal order was wrong and the order of the Trial Court was restored.

***V.A. Sivaraman* v. *Vasu,* (2003) 3 BC 73: (2003) 2 Civ LJ 594: (2003) 2 Rec Cri R 445: 2003 Cr LJ 929 (Ker)**

Held: It was a case where the cheque was issued not in discharge of liability but at the intervention of the police threatening custodial assault and further circumstances revealed that the issuance of cheque is cloudy. The court *held* that it is true that a presumption would arise under section 139 of the Negotiable Instruments Act that the holder of the cheque received it for the discharge in whole or in part of any debt or liability but the evidence that came to light rebutted the presumption and accordingly the appeal against acquittal is dismissed.

***Waterbased Ltd.* v. *K. Ravindera,* (2002) 3 BC 1: (2003) 2 Civ LJ 595: (2003) 115 CC 752: 2003 Cr LJ 967 (AP)**

Cases referred:

AIR 2002 SC 182: (2002) 1 SCC 234: 2002 Cr LJ 266; AIR 2001 SC 3897: (2001) 6 SCC 16: (2001) 106 Comp Cas 574; 2001 Cr LJ 2178 (AP); (2000) 3 Andh WR 117; (1999) 1 SCC 113; 1998 Cr LJ 856; 1998 Cr LJ 419; (1997) 2 Crimes 115; (1992) 3 Crimes 1094.

Held: This case was discussed in the light of section 60 of the Contract Act, 1872 which speaks about "application of payment where debt is to be discharged is not indicated". The presumption under section 139 of the Negotiable Instruments Act arises that drawer issued the cheque against legally enforceable debt or liability. The accused could not prove by documentary evidence that subsequent issuance of cheque resulted in discharge of amount covered by the dishonoured cheque. The lower court found the accused not guilty but the High Court negatived the contentions of the lower court on the basis of which the accused was acquitted and found the accused guilty and looking to the circumstances of the case the accused is sentenced to pay a fine of Rs. 5,000 and in default to undergo simple imprisonment for a period of three months.

***Mandadi Ram Reddy* v. *State of Andhra Pradesh,* 2003 Cr LJ 3647 (AP)**

Cases referred:

AIR 2002 SC 182: (2002) 1 SCC 234: 2002 SCC (Cri) 121: 2002 Cr LJ 266; AIR 2002 SC 985: (2002) 2 SCC 642: (2002) 108 Comp Cas 838: 2002 Cr LJ 1479; AIR 2002 SC 3014: (2002) 6 SCC 426: (2002) 111 Comp Cas 742: (2002) 3 KLT 218; (2001) 1 MPLJ 229.

Held: It is a Criminal Miscellaneous Petition filed under section 258, the Cr. P.C. for stopping further proceedings in the case and to discharge the accused. That petition being dismissed, a revision petition was filed against the order of the learned Judicial Magistrate. The High Court *held* that this case fell under "other liability" and it could be presumed that the cheque was received for discharge of liability. It becomes obligatory on the part of the accused petitioner to prove contrary to rebut the presumption. Plea of non-existence of liability and non-enforceability can be raised at the stage of trial. *Held* that the complaint could not be quashed.

***Abdul Hameed* v. *State of Rajasthan*, (2003) 4 Raj LW 2618: (2002) 2 BC 529: 2003 Cr LJ 1047 (Raj)**

Cases referred:

1997 Cr LJ 4237 (AP); 1996 Cr LJ 636 (AP); 1995 Cr LJ 560 (AP); (1993) 1 WLN 388; AIR 1991 SC 1020: (1991) 1 SCC 412: (1991) 1 MLJ (SC) 46; AIR 1980 Mad 7; AIR 1963 SC 1165: (1964) 1 SCR 316.

Held: It is a revision petition under section 401, the Cr. P.C. It was a case where the partnership was dissolved and the accounts were settled. The accused issued cheque in favour of the complainant after the accounts were settled. The accused was found guilty under section 138 of the Negotiable Instruments Act. In this case section 4 and section 139 of the Negotiable Instruments Act were discussed. The presumption is drawn that the cheque is issued for discharge of debt or liability. The complainant has discharged his initial burden but accused petitioner failed to establish that the cheque was issued not of the nature referred to in section 138 of the Negotiable Instruments Act. The High Court *held* no merit in the case and dismissed the petition.

***Jayam Company, Chennai* v. *Ravichandran*, (2003) 2 BC 584: 2003 Cr LJ 2890 (Mad)**

Cases referred:

AIR 2002 SC 681: (2002) 2 SCC 420: 2002 SCC (Cri) 344: (2002) 1 KLJ 444; AIR 2001 SC 3897: (2001) 6 SCC 16: 2001 SCC (Cri) 960: (2001) 106 Comp Cas 574; AIR 2001 SC 2895: (2001) 8 SCC 458: 2002 SCC (Cri) 14; AIR 1958 SC 61.

Held: In this case the accused was acquitted on two grounds:—

(i) That there was no legally enforceable liability since the cheque was obtained by force with the help of the police.

(ii) That the complaint was barred by limitation.

The High Court negatived both the contentions and *held* that the judgment of the trial court suffers from patent errors of law and perversity in approach and set it aside. The emphasis of the High Court was on presumption under section 139, the Negotiable Instruments Act which the court must draw as it was a presumption of law by which the burden of proof shifted on to the accused and the accused must adduce evidence showing reasonable possibility of the non-existence of the presumed fact.

***U.K. Rajah* v. *Dr. V. Ramanathan*, (2003) 4 All Cri R 439: 2003 Cr LJ 3388 (Mad)**

Cases referred:

AIR 2002 SC 3014: (2002) 6 SCC 426: 2002 SCC (Cri) 1342: (2002) 111 Comp Cas 742; (1982) 2 Mad LW (Cri) 478.

Held: It was a petition to call for the record and to quash the proceedings. The case of the petitioner was that the issuance of cheque is under pressure exerted by the complainant. The High Court *held* that the presumption under section 139 that the drawer has issued the cheque only for the debt or liability incurred by him operates. Consequently the criminal original petition was dismissed as having no merit.

***Goaplast Pvt. Ltd.* v. *Chico Ursula D'Souza,* (2003) 2 SCC 232: 2003 SCC (Cri) 603: 2003 Cr LJ 1723 (SC)**

Cases referred:

AIR 2001 SC 1315: (2001) 3 SCC 726: 2001 Cr LJ 1674; AIR 1999 SC 1952: (1999) 4 SCC 253: 1999 SCC (Cri) 524: (1999) 96 Comp Cas 822; AIR 1998 SC 1056 (followed); AIR 1996 SC 2339: (1996) 2 SCC 739; (1993) 4 SCC 424: 1993 SCC (Cri) 1243 (distinguished).

Held: It is a case of issuance of post-dated cheque and stoppage of its payment before due date of payment. *Held,* that once a cheque is issued by a drawer, a presumption under section 139 which says that "holder of cheque receives it in discharge in whole or in part, of any debt or other liability," must follow and merely because the drawer issued notice to the drawee or to the bank for stoppage of payment before due date of payment, it will not preclude an action under section 138 by the drawee or holder of cheque in due course.

***L. Mohan* v. *Mohan Naidu,* (2004) 4 ICC 631: AIR 2004 Kant 2182: 2004 Cr LJ 3177 (Karn)**

Cases referred:

AIR 2001 SC 1161: (2001) 3 SCC 609: 2001 Cr LJ 1250; AIR 2001 SC 2895: (2001) 8 SCC 458: 2002 SCC (Cri) 14; AIR 2000 Karn 169.

Held: It was a revision petition. Once the party admits regarding the issuance of a cheque and also admits the signature in it, then burden of proof shifts on him. The accused had to prove in the trial, by leading cogent evidence that there was no debt or liability and the revision petitioner has failed to discharge this burden and as such the revision petition is liable to be dismissed.

***M.P. Abdul Nazar* v. *S.V. Dileep Kumar,* (2004) 4 ICC 859: (2004) 2 Ker LJ 406: (2004) 3 Ker LT 264: 2004 Cr LJ 4707 (Ker)**

Case referred:

(2002) 3 Ker LJ 853.

Held: That execution of the cheque having been proved, the presumption under section 139 of the Negotiable Instruments Act comes into play and no worthwhile attempt had been made to rebut that presumption. However, the High Court took a serious note that in spite of the dictum in *Anil Kumar* v. *Shammi,* (2002) 3 Ker LT 853, the courts below had not chosen to invoke the powers under section 357(3), the Cr. P.C. nor has reasons been shown to justify that course. The High Court modified and reduced the sentence imposed and directed to pay a sum of Rs. 27,500 as compensation under section 357(3), the Cr. P.C. and in default to undergo simple imprisonment for a period of 45 days.

***Nagisetty Nagaiah* v. *State of Andhra Pradesh,* 2004 Cr LJ 4107 (AP)**

Cases referred:

AIR 2003 SC 182: (2003) 1 SCC 1; AIR 2001 SC 3897: (2001) 6 SCC 16: (2001) 106 Comp Cas 574; AIR 2001 SC 2895: (2001) 8 SCC 458: 2002 SCC (Cri) 14; 1996 Cr LJ 636 (AP); AIR 1976 SC 832; AIR 1974 SC 286: (1974) 3 SCC 762: 1974 SCC (Cri) 238.

Held: The point in issue was that the lower court committed an error in coming to the conclusion that cheque was not issued for the discharge of legally enforceable debt and since the complainant failed to discharge the initial burden by establishing that the cheque was issued for discharging a legally enforceable debt or liability and as such the presumption under section 139 of the Negotiable Instruments Act cannot be drawn. The High Court *held* that the initial burden does not mean that it is a burden on the part of the complainant to prove that there was a legally enforceable debt or liability by leading evidence. The mere basic facts of the case should inspire the invocation of the legal presumption under section 139 of the Act. The lower court could not be said to have erred in holding that the initial burden was not discharged by the complainant which was absent in this case and as such the criminal appeal failed.

***B.V. Rangam* v. *B. Govinda Reddy,* (2004) 3 BC 485: (2004) 4 ICC 627: 2004 Cr LJ 3170 (AP)**

Cases referred:

(2002) 1 Andh LD (Cri) 817; AIR 2001 SC 3897: (2001) 6 SCC 16: (2001) 106 Comp Cas 574; AIR 2000 SC 145: (2000) 1 SCC 1: 2001 SCC (Cri) 174: 2000 Cr LJ 373; AIR 1977 SC 666: (1975) 4 SCC 761: 1977 Cr LJ 254.

Held: It is an appeal against the order of the lower court acquitting the accused under section 255(1), the Cr. P.C. for the offence under section 138 of the Negotiable Instruments Act, 1881, on the ground that the complainant could not prove that the issuance of the cheque was in discharge, in whole or in part, of the legally enforceable debt or other liability. The High Court *held* that the cheque in possession of the complainant is itself a discharge of initial burden as to legally enforceable debt and the accused has to prove that the said cheque was not issued for the purpose of any legally enforceable debt or liability. There was no rebuttal of the presumption by the accused. The High Court *held* that acquittal was not proper. The respondent was found guilty.

***C. Manohar* v. *B.R. Poornima,* 2004 Cr LJ 4436 (Mad)**

Case referred:

AIR 1998 SC 1057: (1998) 3 SCC 249: 1998 Cr LJ 1397: (1998) 1 KLT 582.

Held: It was an appeal against the order of the trial court acquitting the accused. The complaint was filed by an advocate against his client for issuance of cheque towards his legal fee and expenditure towards stamp duty and the cheque on presentation was dishonoured. It was *held* that the complainant had not discharged the initial burden that the cheque was issued in whole or in part of discharge of debt or liability legally enforceable and by virtue of which the legal presumption under section 139 of the Negotiable Instruments Act could not be drawn. The appeal is bereft of merits and was bound to fail.

***Bharat Sales Corporation, Parsudih, Jamshedpur* v. *State of Jharkhand*, 2004 Cr LJ 4569 (Jhar): AIR 2004 Jhar 2755**

Case referred:

AIR 1988 SC 1998: 1988 Supp SCC 686: 1989 SCC (Cri) 48.

Held: This is the complainant's appeal on special leave granted by this court under the provisions of section 378(4) of the Cr. P.C. against the order of acquittal passed by the lower court. It is a case where the learned Judge did not apply her mind and there is no discussion on sections 138 and 139 of the Negotiable Instruments Act. The High Court particularly referred to the judgment of the Supreme Court in *State of Uttar Pradesh* v. *Anil Singh*, AIR 1988 SC 1998: 1989 SCC (Cri) 48, wherein it was said that, "it is necessary to remember that a judge does not preside over a criminal trial merely to see that no innocent man is punished. A Judge also presides to see that a guilty man does not escape. One is as important as the other. Both are public duties which the Judge has to perform." The High Court remitted back the case to the trial court for reconsideration of all the material and evidence on record as well as the provisions of law and to dispose of the case in accordance with law.

***General Auto Sales* v. *Vijyalaxmi D.*, 2005 Cr LJ 1454 (Ker)**

Cases referred:

(2002) 6 SCC 426: 2002 SCC (Cri) 1342: (2002) 111 Comp Cas 742: (2002) 3 KLT 218: AIR 2002 SC 3014 (followed).

Held: This appeal was against the order of acquittal. The complainant contended that the stand of the accused that a blank cheque was issued by him as a security was no longer available to the accused in view of Supreme Court decision in *ICDS Ltd.* v. *Beena Shabeer*, AIR 2002 SC 3014: (2002) 6 SCC 426: (2002) 111 Comp Cas 742: (2002) 3 KLT 218. The High Court *held* that in this case there was really a presumption available in favour of the complainant in terms of sections 118 and 139 of the Negotiable Instruments Act and against the accused and the accused, who had admitted the signature in the cheque (Exh P-1) and also admitted the business dealings between the complainant and the accused, had not discharged his burden to rebut that presumption and thus the acquittal was set aside.

***Usha Singh* v. *R.V. Shashidharan*, 2006 Cr LJ 904 (Karn)**

Issuance of cheque and acceptance of signature is sufficient to invoke presumption under section 139 but it is rebuttable presumption.

Note.—*(i) Dishonour of cheque is by itself not an offence under section 138. To come within the purview of the section, certain other requirements as stipulated therein are to be complied with by the complainant which amounts to discharge of initial burden which lies on the shoulders of the complainant.*

REFER: (a) *Canbank Financial Services Ltd.* v. *Gitanjali Motors Ltd.*, 1995 Cr LJ 1222 (Del).

(b) *Kusum Ingots & Alloys Ltd.* v. *Pennar Peterson Securities Ltd.*, AIR 2000 SC 954: (2000) 2 SCC 745: 2000 SCC (Cri) 546: 2000 Cr LJ 1464.

(c) *B. Mohan Krishna* v. *Union of India*, 1996 Cr LJ 636 (AP).

(d) *Rajindera Steels Ltd.* v. *Union of India*, 2000 Cr LJ 625 (Del).

(e) *Narinder Kumar* v. *Harnam Singh*, 2000 Cr LJ 257 (HP).

(ii) *Thereupon, the court shall presume that the cheque was issued in discharge of, in whole or in part, of debt or any liability legally enforceable. It is a presumption of law.*

(iii) *This presumption of law is rebuttable by the accused during trial with cogent evidence.*

(iv) *If the complaint is loaded with legal infirmities, it can be thrown out at the initial stage itself.*

SECTION 139

***Goa Handicrafts, Rural & SSIDC Ltd.* v. *Samudra Ropes, (Bom)*, 2006 (2) JCC (NI) 78 (Bom)**

In this case the High Court considered the ratio laid down in *Modi Cements Ltd.* v. *Kuchil Kumar Nandi*, (1998) 3 SCC 249; *Goa Plast (P) Ltd.* v. *Chico Ursula D'Souza*, 2003 (3) JCC (NI) 305 and *M.M.T.C. Ltd.* v. *Medchl Chemicals and Pharma P Ltd.*, (2002) 1 SCC 234 that the interpretation of the provisions of section 138 will have to be made in the context, facts and circumstances of each case and accordingly it will have to be seen whether from the facts and circumstances of the case offence under section 138 is made out and whether the presumption which is raised under section 139 is rebutted or not. In the present case the accused has successfully rebutted the presumption which is raised under section 118 read with section 139 of the said Act. Cheque given by the accused is not meant to be deposited but referred a sort of collateral security which is clear from the evidence. It would not entail penal liability as contemplated in section 139 of the Negotiable Instruments Act. Cheque was not given for existing debt or legally enforceable liability.

***Gorantla Venkteshwara Rao* v. *Kolla Veera Raghava Rao*, 2006 (1) JCC (NI) 73 (AP)**

In this case the issue was that the cheque was given to discharge the debt borrowed on a promissory note but the said promissory note was not produced. It was held that mere loss of promissory demand note or its non-production is not sufficient to hold that there is no legally enforceable debt. Failure of accused to give reply to legal notice issued by the complainant drawee of cheque is one of strong circumstances to draw an inference that the accused borrowed amount in question and cheque was issued towards payment of legally enforceable debt.

See also *P. Venkatamma* v. *Dontham Sulochana,* 2006 (1) JCC (NI) 99 (AP).

***M. Chanderashekhar Rao* v. *Kutamba Rao,* 2006 (1) JCC (NI) 33 (AP)**

It is a case where the accused was acquitted on the ground that the legal notice is not in accordance with law and is invalid. The accused in entitled to benefit of doubt. Aggrieved by the said acquittal the complainant filed this appeal. The High Court considered the matter in the light of the civil suit which was decreed against the accused involving the amount borrowed by the accused from the complainant. It was found that the cheques were issued against discharge of a legally enforceable debt.

***Smt. Usha Suresh* v. *R.V. Shashidaran,* 2006 (2) JCC (NI) 131 (Kant)**

It was *held* that when the issue of cheque is admitted, the presumption under section 139 arises that the same was issued towards legally enforceable debt. Burden to rebut lies on the accused. Offering of mere explanation is not enough and the accused cannot get away from penal action therewith. Rebuttable evidence has to be placed before the court. In this case it was stressed that there was no relationship of creditor and debtor between the complainant and the accused which was negatived by the court on the basis of evidence produced.

***M.S. Narayana Menon@ Mani* v. *State of Kerala,* 2006 (2) JCC (NI) 198 (SC)**

In this case the Supreme Court spoke about the nature of rebuttal and said that it is not necessary for the defendant to disprove the existence of consideration by way of direct evidence. The standard of proof evidently is pre-ponderance of probabilities. Inference of pre-ponderance of probabilities can be drawn not only from the materials on record but also by reference to the circumstances upon which he relies. Presumption drawn under a statute has only an evidentiary value. Presumptions are raised in terms of the Evidence Act. Presumption drawn in respect of one fact may be an evidence even for the purpose of drawing presumption under another. Then it is held that the view of the appellant that the cheque was issued by way of security is probable. If it is accepted then the cheque cannot be held to be issued in discharge of debt. If cheque is issued for some other purpose, it will not fall under the ambit of section 138 of the Negotiable Instruments Act.

***Kairali Marketing & Processing Co-op Society Ltd.* v. *Pullengadi Service Co-op. Society Ltd.,* 2007 (1) JCC (NI) 95 (Ker)**

It is *held* that once execution and handing over the cheques are proved, presumption under section 139 of the Negotiable Instruments Act arises. Where undisputedly certain amount has been paid in partial discharge of liability in question, contention that cheques were not issued for due discharge of any legally enforceable debt/liability cannot also succeed. No worthwhile attempt was made to dislodge the presumption under section 139 of the Negotiable Instruments Act.

***Rajeev Gupta* v. *State,* 2007 (4) JCC (NI) 345**

In this case the Supreme Court referred to the provision of presumption under section 139 of the Negotiable Instruments Act and *held* that such a presumption mentioned in this section would operate not only against the drawer but against other persons who can be roped in by virtue of section 141 of the Negotiable Instruments Act.

Also refer:

Anil Hada v. *Indian Acrylic Ltd.*, 2000 Cr LJ 373; *Bimal Kumar Nopani* v. *State of Uttar Pradesh,* 2006 Cr LJ 2611.

***Ram Sethi* v. *M/s. BCC Properties Pvt. Ltd.*, 2007 (4) JCC (NI) 326 (Del)**

Case referred:

2003 SCC (Cri) 603.

Held, that it has to be presumed that a cheque is issued in discharge of any debt or other liability. The presumption can be rebutted by adducing evidence and the burden of proof is on the person who wants to rebut the presumption. Once a cheque is issued a presumption under section 139 of the Negotiable Instruments Act must follow and merely because the drawer issued notice to the drawee or to the Bank for stoppage of payment it will not preclude an action under section 139 by the drawee or the holder of the cheque in due course.

Also refer:

Tara Chand v. *State,* 2007 (4) JCC (NI) 318 (Del).

***S.N. Dhabolkar* v. *Duroplus India Private Ltd.*, 2007 (2) JCC (NI) 233 (Cal)**

It is a case where the accused admitted the liability in reply to the notice sent by the drawee. Case of the accused in the revisional petition being one of exaggerated bills towards goods supplied. Such plea never having been taken during trial through cross-examination of prosecution witness, presumption arising under section 139 of the Negotiable Instruments Act is found not negatived. Conviction and sentence under section 138 is held justified.

Refer also:

K. Bhaskarn v. *Sankaran Vaidhyan Baland,* 2006 (1) Bankmann 544 (SC); *Hiten P. Dalal* v. *Bratindranath Bannerjee,* 2001 DCR 47 (SC).

***K. Prakashan* v. *P.K. Surenderan*, 2007 (4) JCC (NI) 357 (SC)**

Cases referred:

2006 6 SCC 39; 2007 7 SCALE 137; 2007 5 SCC 264; 2003 3 SCC 232.

In this case, on the basis of material and circumstances of fact, the appellant was discharged but the finding of the trial Court were reversed by the High Court. The Supreme Court *held* that the judgment of acquittal ordinarily should not be disturbed when two views are possible. Trial Court asked the complainant to establish the transaction details whereas the High Court did not meet the reasons given by the Trial Court but proceeded on the premises under section 139 of the Act that appellant had not been able to discharge his burden of proof without posing further question as to how the said burden of proof can be discharged. Appeal is allowed

***Kamala S.* v. *Vidya Dharan M.J.*, 2007 (1) JCC (NI) 82 (SC)**

Cases referred:

(2006) 6 SCC 39; 2006 (14) SCALE 125.

The Supreme Court said that the presumption under section 139 of the Negotiable Instruments Act is rebuttable, whether the presumption stood rebutted or not would depend upon the facts and circumstances of each case. The standard of proof in discharge of the burden is terms of section 139 of the Act, being of pre-ponderance of probability, the inference, therefore, can be drawn not only from the material brought on record but also from the reference to the circumstances upon which the accused relies upon. The burden of proof on the accused is not as high as that of the prosecution.

***Birender Singh* v. *State*, 2008 (1) JCC (NI) 15 (Del)**

It is a case where the complainants/appellants could not explain as to why the respondent No. 2 issued cheques of more amount than the loan amount which created doubt about the truthfulness of the story of the complainant. Trial Court concluded that the defence beyond reasonable doubt and presumption created under section 139 of the Negotiable Instruments Act need not be rebutted by direct evidence to be adduced by the accused and the accused can rely upon the cross-examination of the complainant to rebut the presumption and his witnesses. The evidence of the complainant cannot be read to the extent it favours the complainant and overlook rest of the evidence which supports the case of the accused on the ground that it is the complainant's evidence. It is held that the complainant is a liar from his own case and there was no privity of contract and the cheques were not issued to the complainant against discharge of any liability.

Also refer:—(2001) BC 773 (SC)

***First E-learning Quest Pvt. Ltd.* v. *M/s. Tera Construction Pvt. Ltd.*, 2008 (1) JCC (NI) 30 (Del)**

It is a case of quashing of proceedings when the summoning order had been issued. The court held that *prima facie* the case stands clearly established and as laid down by the Supreme Court that under section 139 the court has to presume that the cheque had been issued against debt or liability. So it is not a case of interference at this stage. The petition is dismissed with costs.

Also refer:. *Ravi Chopra* v. *State*, 2008 (2) JCC (NI) 169 (Del).

***Latha K. Nair* v. *M/s. Gold Mohar Foods & Feeds Ltd.*, 2008 Cr LJ 1542 (Kant)**

Cases referred:

2006 Cr LJ 3140; ILR 2003 Kant 1730; AIR 1961 SC 1316.

Accused raised defence of having issued blank cheques as a security for sale and purchase transaction. Burden lies on the accused to prove that on the date of dishonour of cheque no amount was due from him to the complainant. Accused failed to rebut the presumption under section 139 of the Negotiable Instruments Act. Accused is guilty of offence.

***Rajendraprashad Gangabishen Parwal* v. *Santosh Kumar Parasmal Saklecha*, 2008 Cr LJ 2955 (Bom)**

It is a case where numerous authorities were cited. It is *held* that that rebuttal of the presumption by the accused need not always be by leading separate contrary evidence or by entering into witness box. He can successfully gather rebuttal material from evidence of the complainant which can sufficiently disprove the presumptive facts. In this case there was glaring discrepancies regarding the alleged loan as well as the financial adverse position of the complainant showing that he is not in a position to give such loan.

Refer also: 2008 Cr LJ 2405 (Bom).

***Binod Kumar Lall* v. *State of Jharkhand*, 2008 Cr LJ 3353 (Jhar)**

The accused was acquitted on the ground that the complainant was not having regular income nor any business and could not have advanced loan of Rs. 2,35,000 to the accused as claimed. Point of presumption under sections 118 and 139 of the Negotiable Instruments Act was also considered for acquittal. The High Court *held* that there is no material on record to differ from the order of acquittal.

***Yeshpal* v. *Vijya Kumar*, 2008 (3) JCC (NI) 321 (Mad)**

Case referred:

Krishan Janardhan Bhat v. *Dattatraya G. Hegde*, 2008 (1) JCC (NI) 50 (SC).

It is a case where the complainant could not prove the debt or liability and whereas the accused rebutted the presumption under section 139 of the Negotiable Instruments Act. It is *held* that degree of proof for the rebuttal of presumption under section 139 of the Negotiable Instruments Act is not comparable with that of the burden on the prosecution to prove the charge.

***Krishna Janardhan Bhat* v. *Dattatraya G. Hegde*, 2008 (1) JCC (NI) 50 (SC)**

It is *held* that state mandate raising presumption but does not say how presumption would be drawn and rebutted. Hence, balancing act indisputably would depend upon the factual matrix of each case under peculiar facts and circumstances of the case. Court below approached the case wholly from wrong angle. It is a wrong application of legal principle. High Court should have entertained the revision application. Appeal is allowed.

***M/s. Free India Concepts* v. *The State*, 2009 (1) JCC (NI) 33 (Del)**

It is a case where there is no material to show that the accused is connected in any manner with the accused company and as such no presumption can be raised under section 139 of the Negotiable Instruments Act against the petitioners and cannot be prosecuted under Sections 138, 139, 142 of the Negotiable Instruments Act.

***M/s. Kumar Exports* v. *M/s. Sharma Carpets*, AIR 2009 SC 1518: 2009 (1) JCC (NI) 34 (SC)**

It is said that the accused in a trial under section 138 has two options. He can either show that consideration and debt did not exist or that under the particular circumstances of the case the non-existence of consideration and debt is so probable that a prudent man ought to suppose that no consideration and debt existed. To rebut the statutory presumption an accused is not expected to prove his defence beyond reasonable doubt as is expected of the complainant in a criminal trial.

***P. Venugopal* v. *Madan P. Sarathi*, AIR 2009 SC 568**

Cases referred:

AIR 2008 SC 1325; 2005 Cr LJ 4184; ILR (2001) Kant 4127; AIR 1998 Kant 86.

It is *held* that the presumption raised in favour of the holder of the cheque must be kept confined to the matters covered thereby. The presumption raised does not extend to the extent that the cheque was issued for the discharge of any debt or liability which is required to be proved by the complainant. In case of this nature it is essentially a question of fact.

***Ashok Kumar* v. *Gulshan Kumar*, 2010 (1) Crimes 394 (Del)**

Cases referred:

Hiten P. Dalai v. *Bratindranath Banejee*, (2001) 6 SCC 16; *M.S. Narayana Menon* v. *State of Kerala*, (2006) 6 SCC 39; *Bharat Barrel & Drum MFg. Co.* v. *Amin Chand Pyarelal*, (1999) 3 SCC 35.

It is a case where the defence was that the cheque was stolen but no police report was lodged. No instructions were issued to the bank for stop payment. It was held that where cheque has been drawn and issued, statutory presumption is that it was issued for valuable consideration.

***Adarsh Gramin Sahakari Pat Sanstha Maryadit* v. *Shri Dattu Ramdasji Paithenkar*, 2010 (1) Crimes 714 Bom**

Cases referred:

Kusum Ingots and Alloys Ltd. v. *Pennar Peterson Securities Ltd.*, (2002) 2 SCC 745; *M/s Vijya Polymers (Pvt) Ltd.* v. *Vinnay Agarwal*, (2009) 4 Crimes 29 (Del); *Kamalaksha Laxman Prabhu* v. *S.G. Mayekar*, 2009 (1) Crimes 195 (Bom).

In this case it was held that while deciding criminal liability of the accused statutory presumption available under section 139 of the Negotiable Instruments Act in favour of holder cannot be ignored as also presumption under section 118 of the Act, apart from penal provisions contained in section 138 of the Negotiable Instruments Act.

CHAPTER III

MENS REA - NOT A DEFENCE

Section 140. Defence which may not be allowed in any prosecution under section 138.—It shall not be a defence in a prosecution for an offence under section 138 that the drawer had no reason to believe when he issued the cheque that the cheque may be dishonoured on presentment for the reasons stated in that section.

This section constitutes two doctrines:—

(1) *"non facit reum nisi mens sit rea"*

(2) Doctrine of strict liability.

Mens Rea

It is a general principle of criminal law that guilty intention is a necessary ingredient to every crime but the legislature may, by using express language or by implication, exclude an element of *mens rea* in any particular crime and unless such exclusion is deductible from the express language of the statute or by implication, *mens rea* forms a necessary ingredient of an offence. With the advent of Roman concepts of "dolus" and "culpa" into England, *mens rea* became such an inalienable part of criminal law that every crime committed is tested on the touchstone of *mens rea.* But, however, in India specific words are used to denote *mens rea,* such as "dishonestly", "fraudulently" "voluntarily", "intentionally" "deliberately" etc. However, use of *mens rea* was found visibile even in technical offences.

See:

(1) *Sriniwas Mull* v. *King Emperor,* AIR 1947 PC 135.

(2) *Hari Parshad Rao* v. *State,* AIR 1951 SC 204: 1951 SCR 322: (1951) 52 Cr LJ 768.

(3) *Nathu Lal* v. *State of Madhya Pradesh,* AIR 1966 SC 43: 1966 Cr LJ 71.

In the above stated cases it is said that *mens rea* is an essential ingredient of a criminal offence. Doubtless, a statute may exclude the element of *mens rea* but it is a sound rule of construction adopted in England and also accepted in India in construing a statutory provision creating an offence in conformity with the common law rather than against it. However, section 140 rules out the application of *mens rea.*

STRICT LIABILITY RULE

There are certain cases in which the liability of the defendant is strict and he can be made liable for the injury caused even though the act is unintentional and also without any negligence on his part. This form of liability was first formulated in the case of *Rylands* v. *Fletcher*, (1866) LR 1 Ex 265 by Blackburn, J. and approved by the House of Lords in (1868) LR 3 HL 30. The said rule of "Strict Liability" is brought by the Motor Vehicles (Amendment) Act, 1982 (w.e.f. 1-10-1982). Section 92A is added which is a beneficial and ameliorative legislation for an immediate aid to helpless victims of accident. It is based on the principle of "There is not to make reply, there is not to reason why" but to pay and satisfy the award what is fixed as minimum and if the claim is more than the minimum prescribed, it can be contested.

The exclusion of *"mens rea"* and inclusion of rule of "strict liability" can be seen very vividly in section 140 of the Negotiable Instruments Act, 1881 and Judicial decisions will illustrate this point more clearly.

JUDICIAL VIEW

***Mayuri Pulse Mills* v. *Union of India*, (1996) 86 Comp Cas 121: 1995 AIHC 5588: 1995 ISJ (Banking) 4: (1995) 1 Crimes 226 (Bom)**

Cases referred:

AIR 1977 SC 2279: (1977) 4 SCC 98: (1977) 40 STC 497; 1993 Mah LJ 1233; 1895 QBD 918.

Facts of the case.—In this case two cheques amounting to Rs. 1,11,780 were dishonoured and thereupon complying with the procedure laid down, a complaint was filed. The accused approached the higher courts for dropping the proceedings and finally a Criminal Writ Petition was filed in the Bombay High Court, raising an issue that the provisions of sections 138 and 140 of the Negotiable Instruments Act are unreasonable and, therefore, are violative of Article 14 of the Constitution of India. The High Court referred to sections 138 to 142 of the Negotiable Instruments Act and referred to various English cases and particularly *Sherras* v. *De Rutzen*, 1895 QBD 918 wherein Wright, J. has said:—

> "that there are three classes of cases where the legislature normally enacts absolute prohibition and one is a class of act which in the language of Lush J., in *Davies* v. *Harvey*, Law Rep 9 QB 433, are not criminal in any real sense, but are acts which in the public interest are prohibited under a penalty."

Then the High Court *held* that section 138 of the Negotiable Instruments Act can be said to be falling either in the class of Acts which are not criminal in real sense but are Acts which in the public interest are prohibited under the penalty or those were although the proceedings may be criminal in form, they are really only a summary made of enforcing a civil right. It is further *held* that this provision clearly rules out *"mens rea"* as a constituent part of the crime. The position of law is that section 138 brings into operation the rule of strict liability and, therefore, there is nothing unreasonable if it is provided in section 140 that certain defences may not be allowed in any proceedings under section 138. State of mind of accused person, his knowledge or reasonable belief are not the necessary ingredients of an offence under section 138 of the Negotiable Instruments Act, and, therefore, the provision contained in section 140 of the Act cannot be said to be unreasonable and violative of Article 14 of the Constitution of India.

***B. Mohan Krishna* v. *Union of India*, (1996) 86 Comp Cas 487: 1996 Cr LJ 636 (AP)**

Cases referred:

(1994) 1 Andh WR 73 (overruled); (1994) 5 SCC 410: 1994 SCC (Cri) 1433; AIR 1994 SC 2179: (1994) 5 SCC 54: 1994 SCC (Cri) 1325; AIR 1990 SC 1579: (1990) 2 SCC 203: 1990 SCC (Cri) 291; AIR 1989 SC 1671: (1989) 3 SCC 52: 1989 SCC (Cri) 509; AIR 1980 SC 1042: (1980) 2 SCC 478; (1979) 1 Andh LT 38; (1978) 19 Guj LR 1117; AIR 1974 SC 228: (1974) 1 SCC 167: 1974 Cr LJ 313; AIR 1972 SC 1061: (1971) 2 SCC 779; AIR 1971 SC 2346: (1970) 2 SCC 71: 1971 Cr LJ 1556; AIR 1971 SC 866; AIR 1970 SC 253; *Sweet* v. *Pansley*, (1969) 1 All ER 347; AIR 1966 SC 43: 1966 Cr LJ 71; AIR 1965 SC 722: (1965) 1 SCR 123: (1965) 1 Cr LJ 641; *Lim Chin Aik* v. *Queen*, 1963 AC 160; AIR 1962 SC 1052: 1962 Supp (3) SCR 235: (1962) 2 Cr LJ 215; AIR 1961 SC 1808: (1961) 2 Cr LJ 856: 64 Bom LR 240; AIR 1961 SC 1316: (1963) 1 MLJ (SC) 85; AIR 1958 SC 538: 1959 SCR 279: 61 Bom LR 192; *Handing* v. *Price*, (1948) 1 KB 695; *Brend* v. *Wood*, (1946) 62 TLR 462; AIR 1941 FC 47; AIR 1939 PC 53; AIR 1939 FC 1; *Sherras* v. *D. Rutzen*, (1895) 1 QBD 918; *Attorney-General for Canada* v. *Attorney-General for Ontario*, 37 AC 355.

Facts of the case.—There were six cheques in all. Three cheques amounted to Rs. 64345.28 and three other cheques amounted to Rs. 52214.79. All the six cheques were dishonoured for insufficiency of funds. The case was that without the consent of the Board for Industrial and Financial Reconstruction, no prosecution could be launched under section 17 of the Sick Industrial Companies (Special Provisions) Act and then no proceedings could be initiated against the petitioner and further the provisions of the Negotiable Instruments Act were challenged as violative of the Articles 14, 19(1), 20 and 21 of the Constitution of India.

The High Court *held* that the contention is aimed at invoking section 22 of the Sick Industrial Companies (Special Provisions) Act but its sphere of operation is confined to proceedings for the winding up of the company. It does not in any way bar prosecution of a company or any of its employees under the provisions of the Negotiable Instruments Act or any other Penal law.

Regarding constitutionality of the provisions of sections 138 to 142 of the Negotiable Instruments Act it was *held* that section 138 of the Act creates strict liability. When the two requirements constituting the offence, as specified in the section are fulfilled, then the drawer of the cheque shall be deemed to have committed the offence. Section 140 in clear terms excludes the defence that the drawer had no reason to believe, when he issued the cheque, that it may be dishonoured on presentation for the reasons stated in section 138. The exclusion of "*mens rea*" as a necessary ingredient of the offence under section 138 is thus clear and explicit. The exclusion of "*mens rea*" cannot be said to be arbitrary falling within the inhibition of Article 14 of the Constitution of India. The section has also provided many safeguards for an honest drawer of the cheque.

***Mahendra A. Dadia* v. *State of Maharashtra,* (1998) 4 All Mah LR 115: 1998 Cr LJ 4361 (Bom)**

Cases referred:

1998 AIR SCW 842; 1997 AIR SCW 4084; (1996) 6 SCC 369: 1996 SCC (Cri) 1340; 1996 Cr LJ 1692; (2000) 100 Comp Cas 274: 2000 Bank J 342: (1995) 1 Crimes 226 (relied on); 1992 Cr LJ 3779.

Facts of the case.—The point in issue is as to whether the complaint is maintainable in view of the fact that the applicants had called upon the Respondent No. 2 before the cheques were presented for encashment, not to present the cheques in question for encashment. In this regard sections 138, 139, 140 have been discussed and *held* that sections 138, 139 and 140 of the Act clearly rule out *mens rea* as an ingredient for the commission of an offence under section 138 of the Act and as such do not violate Articles 14 and 21 of the Constitution of India. State of mind of accused person, his knowledge or reasonable belief are not the necessary ingredients of an offence under section 138, the Negotiable Instruments Act.

***Rajinder Steels Ltd.* v. *Union of India,* (2000) 100 Comp Cas 274: 2000 Cr LJ 625 (Del)**

Cases referred:

AIR 1999 All 21; AIR 1998 SC 1057: (1998) 3 SCC 249: 1998 Cr LJ 1397: (1998) 1 KLT 582; (1995) 1 Crimes 226 Bom; (1993) 76 Comp Cas 105 (Ker); AIR 1988 SC 686: (1987) 4 SCC 431: 1987 SCC (214) 438; AIR 1980 SC 470: (1980) 2 SCC 360: (1980) 2 SCR 913: 1980 KLT 375; AIR 1966 SC 43: 1966 Cr LJ 71.

Facts of the case.—It is a Writ Petition under Article 226 of the Constitution of India for issuance of an order/directions thereby holding that Chapter XVII of the Negotiable Instruments Act as incorporated by section 4 of the Banking Public Financial Institutions and Negotiable Instruments Laws (Amendment) Act, 1988 (66 of 1988) is *ultra vires* the Constitution. Five issues were raised in the Writ Petition and one of the issue raised was:—

> "Whether *mens rea* is an essential ingredient for an offence under section 138 of the Negotiable Instruments Act."

The High Court, firstly reproduced sections 138 to 142. The arguments of the learned counsel for the petitioner was that sections 138 to 140 of the Act are *ultra vires* and violative of Article 21 of the Constitution of India. Section 140 takes away a very important and reasonable defence of the accused for an offence under section 138 of the Act and that by itself makes the provisions contained in sections 138 and 140 of the said Act as unconstitutional. That there must be mind at fault before there can be a crime, is a settled position of law. Instead of providing safeguards to the honest drawer, section 140 was enacted, which takes away a very valuable defence of law. By these provisions a person had to undergo the rigour of the criminal trial for a liability which is purely civil in nature. The petitioner raised many legal arguments like Article 51(c), Article 246(3), provisions of the C.P.C. and Article 11 of the International Covenants on Civil and Political Rights. Union of India in its reply relied upon

Entries 45 and 46 in List I of the 7th Schedule by which the Parliament has the competency to enact sections 138 to 142 and that suitable in-built safeguards are provided. The High Court *held* that exclusion of *mens rea* in a Penal statute is to curb the callous attitude of the drawers of cheques and to lend greater credibility to the commercial transactions. The High Court rejected the petition as being devoid of merit.

***G. Rukkumani* v. *K. Rajinderan*, (2001) MLJ (Cri) 777: 2001 Cr LJ 3120 (Mad)**

Facts of the case.—In this case it is said that offence under section 138 of the Negotiable Instruments Act is a statutory offence. The provision excludes *mens rea*, by creating strict liability. It does not say that there should be a direct nexus between the person who commits the act and the offence. But, from the words "such person shall be deemed to have committed an offence" giving room for a deeming provision would show that not only the principal or direct offender, an indirect offender, who has allowed room for perpetuation of the offence is also liable. Section 140 of the Negotiable Instruments Act in clear terms excludes the defence that the drawer had no reason to believe when he issued a cheque that it may be dishonoured on presentation for the reasons stated in section 138 of the Negotiable Instruments Act. The exclusion of *mens rea* as a necessary ingredient of an offence under section 138 of the Negotiable Instruments Act is very explicit.

***Sadhu Ram Singla* v. *State*, (2002) 2 BC 420: 2002 Bank J 251: (2002) 97 DLT 556: (2002) 62 DRJ 351: 2002 Cr LJ 2760 (Del)**

In this case it is said that assuming that *mens rea* is an ingredient of the offence under section 138 of the Act, it is for the petitioner who is Chairman-cum-Managing Director of the Company, to prove absence of *mens rea* on his part in all the complaints.

***Vijya Chowdhary* v. *Gian Chand Jain*, 2008 (3) JCC (NI) 291 (Del)**

Cases referred:

2008 (2) CCC 099 (Kar); 2008 (1) CCC 442 (Del); 2007 (4) CCC 387 (Kant); 1993 (1) Crimes 51; AIR 1998 SC 1057; 1999 Cr LJ 2883; 2007 (2) Crimes 467 (MP); 2002 (1) Crimes 104; 2007 (2) JCC (NI) 150; 130 (2006) DLT 534 SC; (1996) 2 SCC 739; 1993 Cr LJ 680; (2000) 2 SCC 745; 136 (2007) DLT 308.

There were many issues in this case and one of them pertained to section 140 of the Negotiable Instruments Act. It is said that offence under section 138 is not created in all cases of dishonour of cheque but only in such cases where the dishonour is for reasons stated in that section. As per section 140 of the Act it shall not be a defence in a prosecution for an offence under section 13 that the drawer had no reason to believe when he issued the cheque that the cheque may be dishonoured on presentation for the reasons stated in the section.

***Ramaswami Athappan* v. *Bharti Infotel Ltd.*, 2008 (1) JCC (NI) 102 (Del)**

Cases referred:

AIR 2007 SC 1682; 2001 (2) JCC (SC) 127.

It is said that presumption under section 138, 140 of the Negotiable Instruments Act is that the drawer of the cheque is presumed to have known that the cheque dawn when presented would be dishonoured under section 140 no defence for a person to urge that he was not aware on the date of cheque was drawn that when presented for payment such cheque would be dishonoured.

Note.—*These provisions depict an honest intention of the legislature to bring back the doctrine of "pious obligation" and doctrine of "locus poenitentia". In the view of Hindu lawyers repayment of debt is not merely a legal obligation, its non-payment is a sin, the consequences of which follow the debtor into the next world. Brihaspati (Dig. I. 228) goes to the extent of saying that "He, who, having received a sum lent or like, does not repay it to the owner, will be born hereafter in his creditor's house, a slave, a servant, a woman or a quadruped". Narda (I-9) says, "when a devotee, or a man who maintained a sacrificial fire, dies without having discharged his debt, the whole merit of his devotion, or of his perpetual fire belongs to his creditors". However, this debt should not be tarnished or tainted with immorality or illegality. This is why in section 138,* Explanation *it is stated. "For the purpose of this section, "debt or other liability" means a legally enforceable debt or other liability," and the person charged with the liability has the right to rebut the presumption as presumption under section 139 is a rebuttable presumption.*

Similarly, the legislature has introduced the "doctrine of locus poenitentia" by inserting three provisos (a), (b) and (c). Offence is not committed on mere dishonouring of the cheque but it is committed when the drawer of cheque fails to make the payment within 15 days of the receipt of notice issued by the payee. This period is a period of repentence and to show his bona fide *honesty by paying the dishonoured cheque amount to save himself from the rigour of criminal trial. Clauses (a), (b) and (c) of proviso to section 138 of the Act have been introduced to thwart the consequences of section 140 of the Act. Thus, these provisions are the outcome of deeply considered "checks and balances". Law has given the option to the person to get rid of his civil liability and if not, to face the criminal liability with all its consequences.*

CHAPTER IV

OFFENCE COMMITTED BY COMPANIES AND LIABILITY OF DIRECTORS

141. Offences by companies.—(1) If the person committing an offence under section 138 is a company, every person who, at the time the offence was committed, was incharge of, and was responsible to the company for the conduct of the business of the company, as well as the company, shall be deemed to be guilty of the offence and shall be liable to be proceeded against and punished accordingly:

Provided that nothing contained in this sub-section shall render any person liable to punishment if he proves that the offence was committed without his knowledge, or that he had exercised all due diligence to prevent the commission of such offence:

Provided further that where a person is nominated as a Director of a company by virtue of his holding any office or employment in the Central Government or State Government or a financial corporation owned or controlled by the Central Government or the State Government, as the case may be, he shall not be liable for prosecution under this Chapter.

(2) Notwithstanding anything contained in sub-section (1), where any offence under this Act has been committed by a company and it is proved that the offence has been committed with the consent or connivance of, or is attributable to, any neglect on the part of, any director, manager, secretary or other officer of the company, such director, manager, secretary or other officer shall also be deemed to be guilty of that offence and shall be liable to be proceeded against and punished accordingly.

Explanation.—For the purposes of this section,—

(a) "company" means any body corporate and includes a firm or other association of individuals; and

(b) "director", in relation to a firm, means a partner in the firm.

INTRODUCTION

Section 141(1) constitutes various components:—

(1) The offence committed satisfies section 138.

(2) It is committed by a company.

(3) The company shall be deemed to be guilty of the offence.

(4) Every person who, at the time of the offence committed, was incharge of, and was responsible to the company for the conduct of business of the company, shall also be deemed to be guilty.

So the first question arises is as to what is meant by the word "Company".

Company: According to section 2(10) of the Companies Act, 1956, "Company" means a company as defined in section 3. Section 3 says:—

> "'Company' means a company formed and registered under this Act or an existing company". 'Existing Company' means a company formed and registered under any of the previous company laws as specified in section 3(ii) of the Act."

However, section 141 itself has defined company under the *Explanation* as follows:—

> "'Company' means any body corporate and includes a firm or other association of individuals".

Body Corporate: It has been defined under section 2(7) of the Companies Act, 1956. "Body Corporate" or corporation includes a company incorporated outside India but does no include—(a) a corporation sole; (b) a Co-operative Society registered under any law relating to Co-operative Societies; and (c) any other body corporate (not being a company as defined in this Act) which the Central Government may, by notification in the Official Gazette, specify in this behalf.

Thus, body corporate means a body which has been or is incorporated under some statute and which has a perpetual succession and a common seal and is a legal entity apart from the members constituting it, will come within the definition of the term "body corporate" (See *Halsbury's Laws of England* and AIR 1963 SC 1811).

Firm: It has been defined under section 4 of the Indian Partnership Act, 1932 which says, "Persons who have entered into partnership with one and another all called individually "partners" and collectively "a firm" and the name under which their business is carried on is called the "firm name". In *Seth Hira Lal* v. *Sheikh Jamaluddin,* (1946) 224 IC 106 (FB) it was said that an important element in the definition of partnership is that it must be carried on by all or anyone of the partners acting for all. But firm is not a juristic person on a legal entity. It acts through its partner as agent of the firm.

Other Association of individuals: The Supreme Court defined partnership as merely an association of persons carry on the business of partnership and in law the firm name is compendious method of describing the partners while in the case of a company it stands as separate juristic entity from its shareholders (AIR 1955 SC 74). Thus 'person' includes an association of persons or a body of individuals, whether incorporated or not.

Thus, the term 'Company' under *Explanation* to section 141 is all inclusive and covers an individual, a firm, an association of individuals.

Now section 141, which deals with offence committed by the company (pertaining to dishonour of cheque) is to be analysed under three distinctive heads in the light of judicial pronouncements.

I. WHEN IS A PERSON CONSIDERED LIABLE FOR THE OFFENCE UNDER SECTION 138, COMMITTED BY THE COMPANY

***N. Dorai Swami* v. *Archana Enterprises*, 1995 Cr LJ 2306 (Mad)**

Cases referred:

1994 Mad LJ (Cri) 147; (1994) 2 Mad LJ (Cri) 663; 1991 Mad LW (Cri) 513; AIR 1988 SC 1128: (1987) 3 SCC 684: 1987 SCC (Cri) 632; AIR 1984 SC 1824: (1984) 4 SCC 352: 1984 SCC (Cri) 620; AIR 1979 SC 1977: (1980) 1 SCC 258: 1980 Cr LJ 834; AIR 1978 SC 1568: (1978) 4 SCC 58: 1978 Cr LJ 1687; AIR 1976 SC 1947: (1976) 3 SCC 736: 1976 Cr LJ 1533; AIR 1967 SC 1167: (1967) 2 SCR 423: 1967 Cr LJ 1081; AIR 1965 SC 1185: (1965) 1 SCR 269: (1965) 2 Cr LJ 250.

Facts of the case.—In this case two legal issues are raised:—

(1) The offence is committed by the company and not by the petitioner.

(2) The prosecution of the petitioner, without the company being made an accused is not sustainable in law.

The High Court discussed at length the various provisions of the Cr. P.C., various provisions of the Negotiable Instruments Act and referred to the cases cited above. Relying on AIR 1984 SC 1824: (1984) 4 SCC 352: 1984 SCC (Cri) 620, which says:—

> "Anyone or more or all of them may be prosecuted and punished. The company alone may be punished. The person incharge only may be prosecuted. The conniving officer may individually be prosecuted. One, some or all may be prosecuted. Each or any of them may be separately prosecuted or along with the company",

It was *held* that in an offence committed by the company under section 138, the Negotiable Instruments Act, persons incharge of the company and responsible to company for conduct of its business can alone be prosecuted. Even if specific averments in complaint as to person responsible to and incharge of company is not mentioned but certain officials of the company are arrayed as accused, it is sufficient. Absence of such averment in complaint is not material. Prosecution against companies and/or other individual officials named therein can be launched. The complaint could not be quashed.

***Visva Cement Products* v. *Karnataka State Financial Corporation Gadag,* (1997) 4 Kant LJ 23: 1997 Cr LJ 4598 (Karn)**

Cases referred:

1996 Cr LJ 408 (SC); 1996 Cr LJ 1354 (SC); ILR 1995 Karn 2667; 1994 Cr LJ 3115 (Karn); AIR 1976 SC 1672: (1976) 3 SCC 252: 1976 Cr LJ 1361; AIR 1972 SC 2639: (1973) 3 SCC 753: 1973 SCC (Cri) 521; (1971) 3 SCC 936: 1972 SCC (Cri) 184: 1971 CAR (SC) 66.

Facts of the case.—In this petition the petitioner had challenged the order of the lower court of taking cognizance on three grounds:—

(1) The Magistrate had not taken cognizance of the offence before taking sworn statement.

(2) That the list of witnesses was not furnished to the accused along with the summons.

(3) That the firm had not been arraigned as an accused.

The High Court after referring to various case laws, *held* that when the offence is committed by the company, either the company alone or the person incharge of the business of the company alone or both of them together can be prosecuted for the offence punishable under section 138, the Negotiable Instruments Act.

***R. Ramchandran* v. *Yerram Sesha Reddy,* (1997) 1 APLJ 329: (1997) 2 BC 252: 1997 Cr LJ 1595 (AP)**

Cases referred:

(1992) 3 Andh LT 468 (relied on); (1991) 2 MWN (Cri) HC (dissented).

Facts of the case.—It was a case where prosecution was initiated against the chairman alone and not against the company and the issue was whether prosecution against chairman is maintainable in view of non-prosecution of company. It was *held,* that in view of Supreme Court's decision in AIR 1984 SC 1824, that section 10 of the Essential Commodities Act and section 141 of the Negotiable Instruments Act are similar, that each or anyone of the persons mentioned may be separately prosecuted or prosecuted along with the company. Thus, prosecution initiated only against the chairman is maintainable.

***Suraj Theatre v. Kakarla Bhora,* (1997) 4 Crimes 496: (1998) 2 CCC 214: (1997) 5 Andh LD 778: 1998 Cr LJ 43 (AP)**

Cases referred:

(1996) 1 Crimes 412 (P&H); (1993) 1 Crimes 1145 (Del).

Facts of the case.—It is a case of dishonour of cheque where the notice was issued under section 138(b). According to section 138(b) the notice is to be issued to the drawer of the cheque only and not to others, which was done in this case. Cheque was issued by A2 on behalf of A1, the firm. A3 to A5 are also partners of A1. Notice was not needed to be issued to A3 to A5. The liability of the petitioners will arise if they are also incharge and responsible of the day-to-day business of the firm which could be established in the trial only. Hence, the petition failed.

***K.S. Subhraman* v. *Iyyammal*, 1998 Cr LJ 4758 (Mad)**

Cases referred:

1995 Cr LJ 2306 (Mad); (1994) 2 Crimes 72 (Ker); AIR 1984 SC 1824: (1984) 4 SCC 352: 1984 SCC (Cri) 620.

Facts of the case.—In this case the cheque was issued by the Managing Director of the Company on behalf of the company. Complaint was initiated against the Managing Director without prosecuting company. *Held,* that while the offence is committed by the company, either the company alone or the person incharge of the business of the company alone, or both of them together can be prosecuted for the offence under section 138.

***Krishna Murari Poddar* v. *State of Maharashtra*, (1999) 5 Bom CR 432: 1999 Bank J 514: (1999) 1 Mah LR 716: 1999 Cr LJ 1094 (Bom)**

Cases referred:

1998 Cr LJ 3287 (SC); 1983 Cr LJ 159; 1976 Cr LJ 1533.

Facts of the case.—Offence under section 138 of the Act was committed by the company. There is allegation that the cheque were post-dated and issued while the petitioners were directors of the company and were incharge of day-to-day affairs of the company at the relevant time. *Held,* that the essential ingredients to determine the liability of Directors is made out. Process issued to the petitioners could not be quashed.

***Girish K. Bhandari* v. *Lakshmi Finance and Industrial Corporation Ltd.*, (1999) 1 APLJ (Cri) 116: 1999 Bank J 907: (1999) 3 Civ LJ 810: 1999 Cr LJ 2718 (AP)**

Cases referred:

1998 Cr LJ 4521 (AP); 1998 Cr LJ 3287 (SC); 1983 Cr LJ 172 (SC).

Facts of the case.—In terms of section 141 of the Negotiable Instruments Act if an offence is committed by the company under section 138 of the Negotiable Instruments Act, every person who at the time of offence was responsible to the company for the conduct of the business of the company, shall be vicariously liable for the offence. It is sufficient to make an allegation in the complaint with regard to the liability of the accused company director as in the instant case to fasten liability on him. Whether he is actually liable or not will have to be considered through evidence. *Held,* that the complaint contains allegations against accused Nos. 2, 3 and 4, who are the directors of the company. So *prima facie* the allegations constitute an offence under section 138 of the Negotiable Instruments Act.

Note.—*Mere allegation is sufficient to implead the person along with the company as an accused.*

***Steel Authority of India Ltd.* v. *Harbhajan Singh*, 1999 All LJ 1420: (1999) 4 Civ LJ 892: (1999) 3 CCC 45: 1999 Cr LJ 3372 (All)**

Cases referred:

AIR 1983 SC 158: (1983) 1 SCC 9: 1983 SCC (Cri) 123; AIR 1972 SC 1607; 1974 Rajdhani LR 304; AIR 1948 All 46.

Facts of the case.—In this case the allegation was against Chairman-cum-Managing Director, Executive Director, General Manager, Purchase Officer that they were incharge of and responsible for conduct of company's business. The lower court dropped the proceedings against the opposite parties 1 to 5 on the plea that the complainant could not disclose as to what has been the constitution of the accused Nos. 1, 2, 3 and 6. The complainant filed revision against this order. *Held,* that there was sufficient material on record at the time of passing the impugned order. The Magistrate should have summoned the accused and not have given an escape route this way. The revision was allowed and case remanded back for consideration.

Note.—*At the stage of summoning the court has not to determine the correctness or improbability but only the existence of* prima facie *case.*

***Natesha Singh* v. *Klen and Marshalls of Manufacturers and Exporters Pvt. Ltd.,* (1999) 3 Civ LJ 757: (1999) 96 Comp Cas 538: (1999) 1 BC 398: 1999 Cr LJ 2693 (Mad)**

Cases referred:

(1997) 2 CTC 534 (Mad); 1997 Cr LJ 3616 (AP); (1996) 1 Crimes 148 (Raj); (1996) 1 Crimes 412 (P&H); (1993) 1 Mad WN (Cri) 33; (1983) 1 SCC 1: 1983 SCC (Cri) 115: AIR 1983 SC 67: 1983 Cr LJ 159 (SC).

Facts of the case.—It is case of dishonour of cheque wherein the company Mid East (India) Limited and its officials are the accused. Some of the officials moved the High Court on the ground that there are no specific averments against the petitioners with reference to their role in the conduct of the affairs of the company on whose behalf the cheques are issued. Some filed applications that they have not issued the cheque on behalf of the company and as such the complaint be quashed. *Held,* that there is specific mention that they are responsible for the non-payment of cheque after receipt of notice within the statutory period which alone would create the offence. The petitions are dismissed.

Note.—*The test is that taking the allegations and the complaint as they are, without adding or subtracting any thing, if no offence is made out then the High Court will be justified in quashing the proceedings in exercise of its powers under section 482 of the present Code.*

***Jairaj* v. *C. Aravinda,* (1999) 1 Bank LLR 165: (1999) 1 Crimes 512: (1999) 4 Rec (Cri) Mad 421: 1999 Cr LJ 229 (Mad)**

Case referred:

1995 Cr LJ 2306 (Mad).

Facts of the case.—The accused filed a petition under section 204, the Cr. P.C. to drop the proceedings. It was dismissed. This order of dismissal is challenged in this revision. It is a case where section 305, the Cr. P.C. was discussed which was the basis of the petition that the director cannot be made accused as representative of the company. However, the averments and the facts reveal that he has issued the cheque as Director of the Company and as such is covered under section 141, the Negotiable Instruments Act. *Held,* that in view of the special definition of "Company" given under *Explanation (a)* to section 141 of the Negotiable Instruments Act. Which is not akin to the definition given under section 305 of the Code, the case falls under the ambit of section 141 of the Negotiable Instruments Act. The petition stood dismissed.

***Raja Krishna Reddy* v. *Satwik Drugs Ltd.*, (1998) 2 Andh LT (Cri) AP 267: (1998) 2 Bank LLR 65: (1999) 96 Comp Cas 891: 1999 Cr LJ 4865 (AP)**

Cases referred:

AIR 1998 SC 1057: 1998 Cr LJ 1397: (1998) 3 SCC 249: (1998) 1 KLT 582; 1998 Cr LJ 419 AP; 1997 Cr LJ 1595; (1995) 1 BC 466 (Mad); 1992 Supp (1) SCC 335: 1992 SCC (Cri) 426: AIR 1992 SC 604: 1992 Cr LJ 527 (SC); (1992) 1 BC 361 (Mad).

Facts of the case.—It is a case where the company is not impleaded as an accused. *Held*, that if the offence is committed by the company, company as well as persons responsible for the conduct of business of the company can be prosecuted jointly or only one can be prosecuted.

Note.—*Refer 1992 Supp (1) SCC 335: 1992 SCC (Cri) 426: 1992 Cr LJ 527 (SC) wherein the Supreme Court has given various categories of cases in which the First Information Report and the criminal proceedings may be quashed as termination of proceedings at the initial stage would amount to killing of a "still born child". The process of criminal proceedings once set in motion has to end and culminate in enquiry and trial. The court should interfere in rarest of rare cases with a view to prevent the abuse of the process of any court or otherwise to meet the ends of justice.*

***Gummadi Industries Ltd.* v. *Khushroo F. Engineer*, (1999) 98 Comp Cas 296: 1999 Cr LJ 4246 (Mad)**

Cases referred:

(1999) 1 CTC 6; (1991) 2 Mad WN (Cri) 110.

Facts of the case.—It is a case where a promoter of the company issued 3 lakh equity shares to the complainant against a short-term investment of Rs. 30 lakh for 180 days. As per agreement after 180 days he can sell these shares in the market. If there is any shortfall it will be the liability of the promoter for which four post-dated cheques were issued to meet the shortfall liability. The cheques were dishonoured. The complaint was filed against the company and the promoter. It was *held* that only the promoter is liable to be prosecuted under section 138 of the Negotiable Instruments Act as the cheques are given by him in his individual capacity.

***Bharat Kumar Modi* v. *Pennar Peterson Securities Ltd.*, (1999) 3 Andh LT 595: 1999 Bank J 914: (1999) 97 Comp Cas 406: 1999 Cr LJ 3803 (AP)**

Cases referred:

(1) (1994) 80 Comp Cas 487 (Bom).

(2) 1992 Cr LJ 3779 SC.

Facts of the case.—In this case the plea taken was that the accused ceased to be the directors of the company subsequently but they were directors when the cheques were issued. Document, *i.e.*, Form No. 32 was also produced. The High

Court *held* that though the document is admissible but it has to be proved. Though a decision of the Supreme Court 1992 Cr LJ 3779 was cited but it was distinguished on the ground that if the complaint does not disclose the allegation, there is no bar for the Magistrate to discharge the accused but if there is allegation then the Magistrate cannot discharge the accused. *Held* that the accused cannot be discharged. They have to face the trial and prove the document on which they rely. The Revision Petition is dismissed.

***Saravanan* v. *G. Sampat,* (1998) 4 Crimes 561: 1999 Cr LJ 934 (Mad)**

Cases referred:

(1997) 2 MWN (Cri) 99. (distinguished); (1997) Cri O.P. No. 4601 of 1997 dated 19-9-1997 (Mad); (1996) 2 MWN (Cr) 10 (distinguished); (1995) 1 Mad LW (Cri) 132; 1995 Cr LJ 2306 (Mad) (relied on); 1994 Mad LJ (Cri) 147 (relied on).

Facts of the case.—In this case a cheque was issued by the partner of a firm. Complaint was filed against the partner and not against the firm. The plea taken before the High Court is that the complaint is not maintainable. The High Court relied on 1995 Cr LJ 2306 (Mad) and 1994 Mad LJ (Cri) 147 and *held* that the complaint is maintainable. The complainant need not include the firm as accused unless it is established that the firm alone was liable to discharge the liability.

***Sunil Sareen* v. *Government of N.C.T. of Delhi,* (2000) 83 DLT 830: (2000) 52 DRJ 319: 2000 Cr LJ 2087 (Del)**

Cases referred:

(1998) 5 SCC 749: AIR 1998 SC 128: 1998 Cr LJ 1 (SC); 1998 Cr LJ 4383 (Del); (1996) 2 AD 549 (Del); 1992 Cr LJ 3161 (SC); (1992) 2 CC Cases 145; (1983) 1 SCC 1: 1983 SCC (Cri) 115: 1983 Cr LJ 159 (SC); AIR 1977 SC 1754: 1977 Cr LJ 1146: (1977) 1 SCC 505; (1977) 1 FAC 163 (Del); 1976 Cr LJ 1533 (SC); (1962) 1 Cr LJ 770 (SC); AIR 1960 SC 1113: (1961) 1 SCR 1: 1960 Cr LJ 1499 (SC); AIR 1955 SC 216: 1955 Cr LJ 572 (SC).

Facts of the case.—In this case the complainant fastened the liability on the petitioner/accused in the capacity of his being director as well as being responsible for management of business of the company and the cheque issued to the complainant was not signed by the petitioner. Firstly the matter was discussed about the exercise of powers by the High Court under section 482, the Cr. P.C. and then secondly, the scope of sections 200 to 204, the Cr. P.C. was discussed. *Held* that the scope of section 202, the Cr. P.C. is very restricted only to finding out the truth or otherwise whether the process is to be issued under section 204, the Cr. P.C. or the complaint is to be dismissed under section 203, the Cr. P.C. So the process is issued on the basis of allegations contained in the complaint which alone are to be considered. The petition filed under section 482, the Cr. P.C. is dismissed.

***Orient Syntext Ltd.* v. *Besant Capital Tech Ltd.,* (1999) 3 Mah LJ 413: 2000 Cr LJ 210 (Bom)**

Cases referred:

1998 Cr LJ 3287 (SC); 1998 Cr LJ 4383 (Del); (1998) 2 Karn LJ 337; (1998) 3 Com Cas 186; (1996) 86 Com Cas 631 (P&H); 1995 Cr LJ 2306 (Mad); 1994 Mah LJ

677; AIR 1992 SC 1168: (1992) 2 SCC 552: 1999 Cr LJ 1523; AIR 1992 SC 1379: (1992) 3 SCC 317: 1992 Cr LJ 1956; AIR 1992 SC 1894: (1992) 2 SCC 213: 1992 SCC (Cri) 361; 1990 Cr LJ 1856 (MP); AIR 1988 SC 1128: (1987) 3 SCC 684: 1987 SCC (Cri) 632; AIR 1983 SC 67: (1983) 1 SCC 1: 1983 Cr LJ 159; (1978) 48 Com Cas 85 (Del); AIR 1976 SC 1947: (1976) 3 SCC 736: 1976 Cr LJ 1533.

Facts of the case.—In this case the trial court passed an order issuing process against the accused under section 138, the Negotiable Instruments Act. As the company and its directors failed to appear, Non-Bailable warrants were issued against accused Nos. 3 to 9. Against this order the matter came before the High Court. *Held,* that the averments in the complaint specifically state that the petitioners were incharge of and responsible for conduct of its business. Furthermore, non-payment of amount was attributed to and by negligence on the part of petitioners. Order rejecting the recalling of process issued by the lower court is proper. The case was discussed under the ambit of sections 204 and 482, the Cr. P.C.

***K.P.G. Nair v. Jindal Menthol India Limited,* (2000) 99 Comp Cas 519: 2000 CLC 576: 2000 Cr LJ 1213 (Del)**

Facts of the case.—On the basis of averments in the complaint that the accused at the relevant time was a director and was also incharge of and responsible for business of accused company, process was issued. It was challenged on the plea that the director has resigned before issuing of offending cheques and that the order of issuing process is illegal and prayed for quashing the proceedings. *Held,* that the question whether the director has resigned before the issuance of the cheques which are dishonoured, is a disputed question of fact and the High Court should not enter into the arena of a disputed question of fact. The learned Magistrate has not committed any illegality in taking cognizance of the case.

***M. Sivakami* v. *Bharat Ginning and Oil Mill Factory,* 2000 Bank J 636: (2001) 105 Comp Cas 125: 2000 Cr LJ 1043 (Guj)**

Cases referred:

1998 Cr LJ 4383 (Del); 1995 Cr LJ 2306 (Mad); 1992 Cr LJ 1442 (All).

Facts of the case.—In this case the process was issued against the company and accused Nos. 2 to 7 and this petition is filed by accused No. 5, challenging the order of issuance of process on the ground that there is no specific allegation against the petitioner's participation in business. This was challenged by the Respondent that there is a specific allegation that accused Nos. 2 to 7 are the authorised persons of the Mill. It is *held* that it is undisputed fact that the petitioner is a director of the company and, therefore, in the absence of any other material to show that the case falls into an exception provided for under proviso to section 141(1) of the Negotiable Instruments Act. The petition cannot be entertained and must fail.

***K. Pannir Selvam* v. *M.M.T.C. Ltd., New Delhi,* (2000) 99 Comp Cas 94: 2000 Bank Mann 958: 2000 Cr LJ 1002 (AP)**

Cases referred:

AIR 1999 SC 1216: (1999) 3 SCC 259: 1999 Cr LJ 1833; 1992 Supp (1) SCC 335: 1992 SCC (Cri) 426: AIR 1992 SC 604: 1992 Cr LJ 527 (SC).

Facts of the case.—Summoning order was issued to the accused Nos. 1 to 7. Notice was issued only to A1 and A2 for making the payments. Aggrieved by the order of issuance of process accused No. 6 challenged the order on the plea that firstly no notice was issued to him. Secondly, the petitioner is only a commercial Manager and not a director of the company. It is *held* that in view of AIR 1999 SC 1216: 1999 Cr LJ 1833, that it is not permissible in a petition under section 482, the Cr. P.C. to adopt a strictly hyper technical approach and serve the complainant through a cullender of finest gauzes for testing the ingredients of the offence alleged against the accused. As to whether the person in question was really incharge of the affairs of the company and was responsible to the affairs of the company or not and as to what functions he was assigned and what functions could be considered to hold that he was incharge of the company are matters which are to be gone into during the trial. The court relied on 1992 Cr LJ 527 and *held* that the criteria in the said case is not satisfied and hence the petition is dismissed.

***K. Janaki Manoharan* v. *Gayatri Sugar Complex Ltd.*, (2000) 4 Andh LT 325: (2000) 2 Andh WR 1: (2000) 4 Civ LJ 603: 2001 Cr LJ 52 (AP)**

Cases referred:

2000 CLC 1292 (AP); (2000) 3 Andh LT 271; (1998) 2 Bank CLR 442 (Karn); 1996 Cr LJ 1372 SC; AIR 1992 SC 604: 1992 Supp (1) SCC 335: 1992 Cr LJ 527; (1985) 2 SCC 370: 1985 SCC (Cri) 180: AIR 1985 SC 628: 1985 Cr LJ 817 (SC).

Facts of the case.—In this case, summoning order was issued to A1 to A5. A1 is the company. A2 is the Chairman-cum-Managing Director. A3 is the Joint Managing Director. A4 and A5 are the Directors. A4 and A5 approached the High Court against the order of the lower court. The complaint revealed that there are specific allegations against A1, A2 and A3 but no specific, clear and unambiguous allegation against A4 and A5 except that they are the Directors of the Company. *Held*, that issue of process against A1 to A3 is justified but against A4 and A5 it is not justified and be quashed.

***P.R. Shankar Rao* v. *Joseph and Joseph, Regis Kalingarayar*, 2001 Cr LJ 2392 (Mad)**

Cases referred:

2000 Cr LJ 1002 (AP); (1999) 80 Del LT 654; (1999) 3 SCC 259: 1999 SCC (Cri) 401: AIR 1999 SC 1216: 1999 Cr LJ 1833 (SC); 1999 Cr LJ 4606 (SC); 1999 Mad LJ (Cri) 107; 1998 Cr LJ 43 (AP); (1998) 2 Karn LJ 337; 1996 Cr LJ 1692 (SC); 1996 Cr LJ 180 (Mad); 1991 Mad LW (Cri) 513.

Facts of the case.—In this case many issues were raised but one of the issues was the impleadment of the Directors. The necessary averments made in the complaint was that A1, A2, A4 are the Directors of the A5 companies. The petitioner is the Director of A3 and A5 company and they were incharge of the affairs of the company. The High Court relying on (1998) 2 Karn LJ 337. *Held*, that the allegations against accused directors that they were incharge and responsible for conduct of business of company are sufficient to inculpate the Directors. The allegations need not be specific that the Commission of offence was with the knowledge and connivance of the Directors.

***Harsukhbhai Lakshmanbhai* v. *State of Gujarat*, (2001) 3 Guj LH 380: (2001) 3 Guj LR 2271: 2001 CR LJ 2623 (Guj)**

Cases referred:

(2000) 1 Guj LH (UJ) 2; (2000) 6 SCALE 578; 1998 Cr LJ 4348 (Del); 1998 Cr LJ 4521 (AP); AIR 1998 SC 2327: (1998) 5 SCC 343: 1998 SCC (Cri) 1315; 1997 Cr LJ 3616 (AP); (1994) 2 Crimes 259 (Bom); AIR 1992 SC 2206: (1992) 1 SCC 217: (1992) 1 KLT 1; 1992 Cr LJ 1442 (All); AIR 1989 SC 1982: (1989) 4 SCC 630: 1989 Cr LJ 2201; AIR 1983 SC 67: (1983) 1 SCC 1: 1983 SCC (Cri) 115: 1983 Cr LJ 159; AIR 1975 SC 1185: (1975) 1 SCC 774.

Facts of the case.—In this case the cheques were issued by accused No. A1 a partner, on behalf of partnership firm A3. A2 another partner assured that the said amount will be paid by the firm in this behalf. Accused No. A2 filed an application that he is not the drawer of the cheque and be acquitted. This application was rejected by the Magistrate. Being aggrieved by the order accused No. A2 filed this revision petiton. The High Court after discussing sections 138 and 141 of the Act and referring to various decisions and facts of the case *held* that there is clear and specific allegation against accused No. A2 that he was responsible to the firm in connection with carrying on business and that the offence has been committed with consent and connivance of accused A2. He is not a sleeping partner. He has not exercised due diligence to prevent such offence. The Revision petition is dismissed.

***Rajneesh Aggarwal* v. *Amit J. Bhalla*, (2001) 1 SCC 631: 2001 SCC (Cri) 229: AIR 2001 SC 518: 2001 Cr LJ 708 (SC)**

Cases referred:

AIR 1999 SC 2182: (1999) 5 SCC 693: 1999 Cr LJ 3498; AIR 1998 SC 1057: (1998) 3 SCC 249: (1998) 92 Comp Cas 88: (1988) 1 KLT 582.

Facts of the case.—In this case two issues were under consideration. Firstly the notice was issued to the Director of the company in his name who had signed the cheque on behalf of the company but no notice was issued to the company. The Supreme Court *held* that Notice cannot be construed in narrow technical way. It cannot be said that the drawer had no knowledge of the notice.

The second issue was that the whole amount covered by the cheque has been deposited by the drawer of the cheque. The Supreme Court *held* that it does not absolve the accused drawer of the liability of the offence. However, deposit can have some effect on sentence to be awarded. *Held,* that criminal proceedings cannot be quashed.

***Om Prakash Aggarwal* v. *State of Andhra Pradesh*, (2000) 2 Andh LT (Cri) AP 438: 2001 Cr LJ 253 (AP)**

Cases referred:

1998 Cr LJ 4521 (AP); AIR 1998 SC 128: (1998) 5 SCC 749: 1998 Cr LJ 1.

Facts of the case.—In this case A1 is the company. Accused 2 to 5 were incharge of the company for the conduct of business of A1. A5 was the Director of the company. This petition is filed by A5 under section 482, the Cr. P.C. for quashing the proceedings on the plea that A5 has nothing to do with the affairs of the company. There are no specific allegations against the petitioner A5 to implicate him. The High Court *held* that A5 is not only the Director of the Company but also along with other directors incharge of and responsible to the conduct of the business of the company and there is a specific allegation in this regard. *Held*, the criminal proceedings against A5 cannot be quashed.

***R.P. Balakrishna* v. *Muthoot Leasing and Finance Ltd.*, Bangalore, (2002) 3 BC 655: 2002 Bank J 750: (2002) 112 Comp Cas 191: 2002 Cr LJ 4444 (Karn)**

Case referred:

1992 Cr LJ 1442 (All).

Facts of the case.—The offence is committed by the company and proceedings are imitated against the employee of the company. The petition is filed under section 482, the Cr. P.C. on the ground that the petitioner is not a director of the company but only he is an employee of the company and that the complaint does not contain necessary averments to show that the petitioner was responsible for the conduct of the business of the company and that he has no role in the decision making process of the company. *Held*, that the material on record satisfies his involvement under section 141 of the Act and further the concept of strict rules of pleadings in a civil case cannot be imported in criminal proceedings and absence of details of evidentiary value in the complaint is neither necessary nor fatal to the case. The petition is dismissed.

***S.P. Subhramaniam* v. *Vasavi Cotton Traders*, (2002) 2 BC 330: (2002) 2 CCC 57: 2002 Cr LJ 4226 (AP)**

Cases referred:

(2001) 2 Andh LT (Cri) 440; 1999 Cr LJ 2718 (AP); 1998 Cr LJ 4521; AIR 1983 SC 158: (1983) 1 SCC 9: 1983 SCC (Cri) 123.

Facts of the case.—The issue involved is whether or not the petitioner is the Director of the company by date the cheques were issued. The petitioner is arrayed as A5 in the criminal complaint and whether is liable for the offence committed by the company. The High Court *held* that the facts reveal that A2 issued the cheque on behalf of the company A1 with the consent and knowledge of the petitioners herein who are the Directors of the company. It is for the petitioners to establish that they are not responsible for the day to day business of the company as mentioned in the proviso to section 141 of the Act. The petition is dismissed.

***Dev S/o Shankar Rao* v. *State of Andhra Pradesh*, (2002) 2 BC 260: (2002) 108 Comp Cas 607: (2002) 2 Crimes 122: 2002 Cr LJ 4770 (AP)**

Facts of the case.—In this case there were four accused. A1 is a private limited company. A2 is the Managing Director, A3 is the Director and father of A2, A4 is the accountant of the company. Cheques have been signed by A2. The allegation was that A2 to A4 were looking after the day-to-day business affairs of the company A1. On cheques being dishonoured the complainant got issued statutory legal notice to A1, A2, A3 and A4. The accountant of the company filed this petition under section 482, the Cr. P.C. on the ground that the petitioner herein is neither a director nor incharge of the company nor was responsible to the company for the conduct of the business of the company and that it cannot be said that he has committed an offence. The High Court discussed sections 138, 141(1) and 141(2) of the Act. *Held,* that in case of a company a person who is incharge of and was responsible to the company for the conduct of the business of the company need not be a Director, Manager, Secretary or other officer. As per section 138 read with section 141 every person incharge of and was responsible to the company for the conduct of the business of the company is liable. Hence, the petition is dismissed.

***Renewable Energy System Ltd.* v. *State,* (2002) 1 BC 729: (2002) 111 Comp Cas 786: 2002 Cr LJ NOC 172 (AP)**

Facts of the case.—This petition is filed under section 482, the Cr. P.C. on two grounds:

(1) That the Managing Director and Director have nothing to do with conduct of the business of the company.

(2) That memorandum of understanding had already reached into between the parties.

The High Court *held* that it cannot be accepted that the Managing Director and Director of the company have nothing to do with the company where there is allegation in the complaint that the Managing Director and Director of the company issued cheques with the intention of cheating the complainant. Further the Memorandum of understanding reached subsequently cannot be said to have superseded cheques issued earlier. Hence, the prosecution initiated against petitioners under sections 138, 141 cannot be quashed.

Note.—*See* also (2001) 1 SCC 631: 2001 SCC (Cri) 229: (2001) 104 Comp Cas 332: 2001 Cr LJ 708 (SC).

***Rajesh Kumar Jain* v. *Swaroop Chand Jain,* (2002) 3 BC 180: (2002) 2 MPLJ 322: (2002) 3 Rec Cri R 50: 2002 Cr LJ 2462 (MP)**

Cases referred:

2000 Cr LJ 1213 (Del); (2000) 4 MPHT 33 (NOC); 1999 Cr LJ 3803 MP.

Facts of the case.—In this case the accused took the plea that he has resigned from the directorship of the company. This plea was also taken earlier before the trial Magistrate which was rejected by the trial Magistrate. On revision the said plea was rejected. Thereupon the complainant moved the High Court. The High Court *held* that the complainant clearly averred in the complaint that the accused was Chairman and Director of company at relevant time and *prima facie* as Chairman and Director of the company was responsible for business of the company and moreover, it is a disputed fact that whether he resigned before the issue of cheque or after the issue of the cheque and the court cannot sit as a court of appeal to discuss the evidence on merit at the preliminary stage of the trial. Hence the revision succeeds and the impugned order is set aside.

***S.K. Real Estates* v. *S. Ahmed Meeran,* (2002) 1 BC 491: (2002) 111 Comp Cas 400: 2002 MLJ (Cri) 91: 2002 Cr LJ 1689 (Mad)**

Cases referred:

(1999) 1 Mad LW (Cri) 395; (1999) 1 Mad LW (Cri) 405; 1996 Cr LJ 3099 (Guj); (1994) 3 All Cr LR 381; 1992 Mad LW (Cri) 347 (followed).

Facts of the case.—In this case the complainant filed a complaint against a proprietorship concern as well as its proprietor as Accused No. 1 and Accused No. 2. According to section 11 of the I.P.C. and section 3(42) of the General Clauses Act, definition of person does not include proprietorship concern. *Held,* that complaint against proprietorship concern is dismissed as being withdrawn and the complaint against the proprietor is maintainable.

***B. Venkat Narindera Prasad* v. *State of Andhra Pradesh,* 2003 Cr LJ 2506 (AP)**

Cases referred:

(2002) 1 SCC 234: 2002 SCC (Cri) 121: AIR 2002 SC 182: 2002 Cr LJ 266 (SC); (2002) 7 SCC 655: 2003 SCC (Cri) 151; (2002) 1 Andh LT (Cri) 157; (2002) 1 Andh LT (Cri) 530; (2002) 2 Andh LT (Cri) 291; (2001) 10 SCC 218; AIR 1965 SC 1048; (2002) 2 Andh LT (Cri) 337.

Facts of the case.—In this case many points were raised: The first point was that the complaint is filed not by the proprietorship concern but by the proprietor in his individual capacity. The case title shows that it is Rampal Rajaram Bhati represented by Hansraj Bhati and there is mention that the complainant is the proprietor of his business under the name and style of Rampal Rajaram Bhati. In view of this the petition is rejected.

The second point raised is that they were not looking after the day-to-day affairs of the company and that there was no allegation in the complaint but this view put forth is contrary to what is stated in the complaint wherein it is clearly stated that A2 to A5 were taking active part in the conduct of the business of the company. In view of the specific allegation in terms of section 141 of the Act, they are deemed to have committed the offence.

The third point raised is that the filing of one complaint in respect of several cheques is bad in law (20 cheques). Since there is one single account in the ledger there is nothing wrong in filing a single complaint for several cheques.

The fourth point raised is that the petitioners resigned from A1 company on 19-4-2001 and by the date of commission of an offence they were not directors of the company and produced photocopy of Form No. 32. *Held,* that it is a matter to be decided in the trial and not at this stage. The petition filed by A3 and A4 is dismissed as there are no grounds to quash the proceedings.

***Poonam Mahajan* v. *Mohan Lal Swara,* (2003) 3 BC 589: (2003) 2 Crimes 445: 2003 Cr LJ 2442 (J&K)**

Facts of the case.—The issue raised is that the criminal proceedings cannot be taken against her as she is a sleeping partner and the cheques are issued by another partner. The court took the view that "Every person" mentioned in section 141 embraces also the sleeping partner. The petition was dismissed.

Note.—*The plea of being sleeping partner can be taken during trial as per proviso to section 141(1) of the Act.*

***Sunaina R. Mohant* v. *N.C.T. Delhi,* (2002) 2 Crimes 61: (2002) 95 DLT 362: 2003 Cr LJ NOC 8 (Del)**

Facts of the case.—In this case the issue raised was that whether the Director can be vicariously liable for the offence committed by the company after she has ceased to be a director.

Held: This issue can be looked into by the court in proceedings but not under section 482, the Cr. P.C. These questions are to be investigated by the trial court.

***Rohit Kumar Arora* v. *Indravadan R. Shaw,* (2003) 4 All Cri R 752: 2003 Cr LJ 3610 (Bom)**

Case Referred:

(2001) 10 SCC 218.

Facts of the case.—The issue raised is that there is no allegation in the complaint against the petitioners that either of them signed the cheque and that they are not liable to be punished in the capacity of being Directors of the company and that they are not responsible for the conduct of the business of the company. The High Court, *held* that if the accused wants to get exonerated or discharged, he has to bring such material before the court to convince it that he has no concern whatsoever with the issuance of cheque so dishonoured and in the present case the petitioners have neither annexed the copy of the complaint nor the reply given to the demand notice sent to them after the dishonour of the cheque. In the absence of that the trial court cannot arrive at the conclusion that the petitioners are entitled to be exonerated or discharged. The petition is dismissed.

***C.P. Srinivasa Rao* v. *S.S. Nagaraj,* (2004) 4 All Cri R 905: 2004 AIR Kant HCR 3023: 2004 Cr LJ 4389 (Karn)**

Cases referred:

2004 Cr LJ 672 (Karn); AIR 2004 Karn HCR 2669; 2003 SCC (Cri) 151: (2002) 7 SCC 655; AIR 2002 Bom 194; 2002 Cr LJ 3291; 2002 Cr LJ 374; 2001 Cr LJ 2945; (1998) 1 Andh LT (Cri) 426; (1996) 3 Crimes 85; 1981 Lab IC 538 (Karn); *Glossop* v. *Glossop,* (1907) 2 Ch D 370.

Facts of the case.—It is the case of the petitioner, accused No. 5 that he was not a Director of A1 Company on the date of issue of cheque and transaction as he has tendered his resignation long back on 28-2-1997 and that in the complaint there are no allegations against him except that he is a Director of the company, accused No. 1 and the cheque has been issued with his knowledge and consent. The contention raised was that there must be specific allegation that he was incharge of and responsible to the company (A1) for the conduct of business during the relevant period of transaction and issue of cheque which is not there and that he produced a Xerox copy of his resignation. *Held,* that the petition is dismissed and directed to file the petition before the Magistrate who can test the truth and the version of the complaint to establish what he has said. The case sent back to the Trial Court.

***Mahesh Jayalal Dadhia* v. *State of Maharashtra,* (2004) 1 All MR (Cri) 67: 2004 Cr LJ 169 (Bom)**

Facts of the case.—It is submitted that the applicant happens to be the Managing Director of the company and he has signed the cheque and as such his case squarely falls within the ambit of section 138 of the Act. None appeared for the petitioner. *Held,* that the Magistrate has to proceed with the matter by following the appropriate procedure. The application stands dismissed.

***Prudential Engineers/Builders and Developers, Bangalore* v. *Kuskoor Bharath Ram,* 2004 Bank J 715: (2004) 3 Rec Cri R 8: 2004 Cr LJ 672 (Karn)**

Cases referred:

(2003) 6 SCC 195: AIR 2003 SC 2612: 2003 SCC (Cri) 1314: 2003 Cr LJ 3117 (SC); 2003 SCC (Cri) 151: (2002) 7 SCC 655; 2002 Cr LJ 374; 2002 AIR Karn HCR 2932; ILR (2000) Karn 5000; 1997 Cr LJ 4208 (Karn); ILR 1997 Karn 3239; 1989 4 SCC 630: 1989 SCC (Cri) 783: 1989 Cr LJ 2201 (SC); 1988 Cr LJ 1112 (SC).

Facts of the case.—In this case the facts, more or less, are admitted facts. The question arises is that whether said admitted facts constitute an offence punishable under section 138 of the Negotiable Instruments Act, against all the partners or not. The complainant relies on section 25 of the Partnership Act and whereas accused relies on section 141 of the Act. Much stress is laid on the fact that while the notice of demand was issued, in the reply notice the liability is admitted by one of the partner. *Held,* in view of this the petition is dismissed and the petitioners are at liberty to file an application to this effect before the trial Magistrate.

***R. Sudha Madhuri Devi* v. *K. Sudha,* (2004) 4 BC 274: (2004) 4 ICC 409: 2004 Cr LJ 2167 (AP)**

Cases referred:

2003 Cr LJ 164; (2002) 2 Crimes 89; (1999) 3 SCC 259: AIR 1999 SC 1216: 1999 Cr LJ 1833 (SC); 1999 Cr LJ 4231; (1998) 3 Crimes 4 (AP); 1997 Cr LJ 3616 (AP); 1992 Supp (1) SCC 335: AIR 1992 SC 604: 1992 Cr LJ 527 (SC).

Facts of the case.—That the allegations in the complaint are vague and there are no specific allegations that the cheque was issued with the petitioner's consent. The issue raised is that whether the complaint satisfies the requirements of law. *Held,* that it is not necessary that a complainant should verbatim reproduce in the body of his complaint all the ingredients of the offence he is alleging. If factual foundation is laid in the complaint the court should not hasten to quash criminal proceedings. The complaint can be quashed in rare cases. In view of this the petition is dismissed.

***Rohit Chunnubhai Mehta* v. *Gujarat State Fertilizer Corporation Ltd.,* (2004) 3 Guj LR 1952: (2004) 4 ICC 460: 2004 Cr LJ 2298 (Guj)**

Cases referred:

2003 All LJ 2839: (2004) 1 SCC 438: AIR 2004 SC 115: 2003 Cr LJ 1249 (SC); AIR 2003 SC 511; AIR 2003 SC 1713: (2003) 3 SCC 485: (2003) 2 LLN 415; (2003) 10 SCALE 1000; 2003 Cr LJ 1161; (2003) 3 Rec Cri R 422; (2003) 1 Guj LR 424; 2002 Cr LJ 266; (2002) 7 SCC 655: 2003 SCC (Cri) 151; 2002 Cr LJ 3469; (2001) 6 SCC

463: (2001) 104 Comp Cas 472: (2001) 1 KLT 528: 2001 Cr LJ 972 SC; 2001 Cr LJ 3322 SC; 2001 Cr LJ 4765 SC; (2001) 10 SCC 218; (2000) 4 SCC 168: 2000 SCC (Cri) 786: AIR 2000 SC 2341: 2000 Cr LJ 2983 (SC); 1999 Cr LJ 4606 (SC); (1999) 1 SCC 113; AIR 1998 SC 2327: (1998) 5 SCC 343: (1998) 93 Comp Cas 329; (1997) 2 Guj LR 1191; (1996) 2 Guj LH 1121; (1992) 2 SCC 552: 1992 SCC (Cri) 412: 1992 Cr LJ 1523 (SC); 1992 Cr LJ 3779 (SC); 1991 Cr LJ 221 (SC); 1990 Supp SCC 607; 1986 Cr LJ 1116 (Guj); 1984 Tax LR 2133 (Del); (1983) 1 SCC 1: 1983 SCC (Cri) 115: 1983 Cr LJ 159 (SC); AIR 1981 SC 872: (1981) 2 SCC 335: (1981) 3 SCR 200; (1980) 2 Guj LR 341; (1976) 3 SCC 736: AIR 1976 SC 1947: 1976 Cr LJ 1533 (SC); (1975) 3 SCC 495: 1975 SCC (Cri) 87: 1975 Cr LJ 240 (SC); 1971 Cr LJ 1 (SC); 1956 SCR 247: AIR 1956 SC 379: 1956 Cr LJ 777 SC.

Facts of the case.—Many issues were raised and the main issue was that offence was committed by the company. There were clear allegations in the complaint suggesting knowledge and consent of petitioners as Directors of the company. The amount of transaction involved Rs. 5 crore. *Prima facie* it cannot be said that the cheques were issued without the knowledge or connivance of the Directors. Rather the complaint discloses that the complainant was induced to deliver goods on credit against the security of cheques. It indicates larger offence of cheating or abetment thereof. So the monetary transaction, issuance of cheques and their dishonouring can be examined in the trial. So the complaint cannot be quashed at initial stage.

Note.—*For territorial Jurisdiction, see also this case along with Supreme Court case 1999 Cr LJ 4606 (SC).*

***M. Moncharn* v. *C. Venktesh,* (2005) 1 Ker LJ 87: 2004 Cr LJ 4326 (Mad)**

Cases referred:

(2001) 2 Crimes 307 (Mad); 2000 Cr LJ 137 (Mad); (2000) 4 CTC 432 (Mad); 2000 Mad LJ (Cri) 14; 1998 Cr LJ 3287 SC; (1997) 2 CTC 534; (1989) 4 SCC 630: 1989 SCC (Cri) 783: 1989 Cr LJ 2201 (SC).

Facts of the case.—In this case the High Court *held* that under section 141(1) of the Act when the company is mandatorily made liable, no doubt need be entertained that the Director would automatically become one of the accused. However, he is given the liberty to prove that the offence was committed without his knowledge and inspite of exercising due diligence, to prevent the commission of such offence. Similar position is there in section 141(2) and this cannot be proved without conducting a trial. So the burden of proof lies on the accused to prove his innocence. It is not the duty of the High Court to cause any interference under any pretext even if *prima facie* on complaint anyone is made an accused being director or partner. Hence, the petition is dismissed at the admission stage itself.

***A.S. Pattabiraman* v. *Shalha S. Hadle,* (2004) 4 ICC 446: (2004) 3 All Cri LR 638: 2004 Cr LJ 2265 (Karn)**

Cases referred on behalf of petitioner:

(2004) 1 Crimes 197; 2003 SCC (Cri) 151; 2003 Cr LJ 3292 (Guj); 2002 Cr LJ 1353 (Karn); (2001) 1 DCLR 338 (Mad); ILR 2000 Karn 4773; ILR 1997 Karn 3239; 1983 Cr LJ 159: AIR 1983 SC 67: (1983) 1 SCC 1.

Cases referred on behalf of Respondent:

2004 Cr LJ 672; ILR 2003 Kant 5137; 2002 Cr LJ 4564 (All); 2002 Cr LJ 4226 (AP); 2002 Cr LJ 4444; ILR (2002) 1 Kant 2429; 2001 SCC (Cri) 1502: (2000) 10 SCC 529; AIR 1999 SC 1216: (1999) 3 SCC 259: 1999 Cr LJ 1833; 1997 Cr LJ 4598.

Facts of the case.—The petitioners filed various petitions for quashing the proceedings. There were eight accused. The grounds taken by the petitioners are:—

(i) There is no application of judicial mind.

(ii) There is no specific averment in the complaint to the effect that the petitioners had been incharge of the affairs of the company and had been responsible for conduct of business of the company.

(iii) That petitioner Nos. 1, 2, 4 ceased to be directors of the company.

All those grounds presented by the learned counsel of the petitioners on behalf of 1, 2, 3, 6 and 8 have been negatived. However, the respondent did not raise any objection against accused Nos. 4, 5 and 7. So the order against accused Nos. 4, 5 and 7 is set aside and the petitions filed by accused Nos. 1, 2, 3, 6 and 8 are dismissed.

***P. Ramchandra Reddy* v. *Sanghi Enterprises*, (2004) 4 BC 391: (2004) 4 ICC 416: 2004 Cr LJ 2171 (AP)**

Cases referred:

(2002) 3 SCC 98: 2002 SCC (Cri) 671: 2002 Cr LJ 998 (SC); AIR 2002 SC 477: (2002) 10 SCC 249: 2004 SCC (Cri) 527; (2002) 2 Crimes 89 (AP); AIR 1989 SC 1982: (1989) 4 SCC 630: 1989 Cr LJ 2201.

Facts of the case.—In this case the issue raised is that the complaint against the partners is not maintainable as they are not the partners of the said firm whereas in the complaint there is specific allegation against them. In this case section 28 of the Partnership Act was discussed. The High Court differentiated between company as a juristic person itself and whereas partnership firm is represented by the partners. It is only a name of the firm under which the partners are doing business and as such they are liable and come within the purview of section 141 of the Negotiable Instruments Act. The petition stands dismissed.

***S. Kumar* v. *Saptagiri Investments*, (2004) 3 All Cri R 661: 2004 Cr LJ 2150 (Mad)**

Cases referred:

2002 Cr LJ 4155 (Mad); (2000) 1 SCC 1: 2001 SCC (Cri) 174: 2000 Cr LJ 373: (2000) 1 KLT 141: AIR 2000 SC 145 (followed); (2000) 6 SCALE 578.

Facts of the case.—It is a case where the company is not impleaded as an accused but only the partners. The High Court relying on 2000 Cr LJ 373 (*Anil Hada* v. *Indian Acrylic Ltd.*) *held* that such persons cannot escape penal liability simply because the company is not prosecuted as a result of some legal impediments and all the criminal petitions filed, do not merit acceptance.

***K. Chander Shekhar* v. *Mac Charles India Ltd.*, 2005 Cr LJ 1120 (Karn)**

Must prove that the offence is committed without their knowledge and they exercised due diligence to prevent the commissioning of such offence.

***Target Overseas Export (P) Ltd.* v. *A.M. Iqbal*, 2005 Cr LJ 1931 (Ker)**

Notice issued to company—No separate notice to Director. *Held,* Director is liable.

***M.S. Ahamad Mohideen* v. *Salson*, 2005 Cr LJ 1353 (Mad)**

Partners are liable – They have to prove that they were not incharge of the firm.

***Rajesh Jain* v. *DCM Shriram Leasing and Financing*, 2005 Cr LJ 2239 (Del)**

Fixed Assets of the Company taken over by the State Financial Corporation under section 29 of the State Financial Corporation Act. Company existed – Not gone in liquidation. Other assets can be sold to pay. No quashing.

***Pentafour Products Ltd.* v. *Union of India*, 2005 Cr LJ 2071 (Mad)**

Sections 22(1) and 22A of the Sick Industrial Companies (Special Provisions) Act, has nothing to do with criminal proceedings. Magistrate is directed to proceed with the matter expeditiously.

***Rohit Parushram* v. *Dhiraj Riwal*, 2005 Cr LJ 4209 (AP)**

Proprietor firm is not made accused – only proprietor is made accused. It is not much of consequence.

***Polisetti Seetharamanjaneyulu* v. *Public Prosecutor High Court of Hyderabad*, 2005 Cr LJ 4297 (AP)**

If he is not a Managing Partner, he is a partner. Liability established. Plea that firm is not properly registered is not tenable. Partner is liable.

***Satya Parkash Aggarwal* v. *S.H. Aggarwal & Co.*, 2005 Cr LJ 3894 (Ori)**

Complaint cannot be quashed. Director can show at the trial that they are not liable. 2005 Cr LJ 2566 (SC) followed.

***Satya Prakash Aggarwal* v.*Utkal Steels Ltd.*, 2006 Cr LJ (NOC) 74 (Ori)**

Clear accusation of the responsibility of the Directors. Complaint cannot be quashed under section 482, the Cr. P.C.

***Chairman M.S. Zahed of H.M.T. Watches Ltd.* v. *Casmas Co-operative Bank Ltd.*, 2006 Cr LJ 1813 (Karn)**

Accused are incharge of day-to-day affair and business of the Company – *Prima facie* material exists against the accused/petitioner. Complaint cannot be quashed under section 482, the Cr. P.C.

***Dinesh Harakchand Sankla* v. *Kurlon Limited*, 2006 Cr LJ 261 (Karn)**

Person accused of offence is a partnership firm. The partner is involved in day-to-day work of business of firm – Can be held guilty of offence.

Alteration in date and drawer's signature. It is to be proved that the said alterations are not due to insufficiency of funds. The burden is on the accused.

***Mrs. Aruna Bansal* v. *State*, 2006 (2) JCC (NI) 150 (Del)**

Cases referred:

S.M.S. Pharmaceuticals Ltd. v. *Neeta Bhalla*, 2005 (6) Comp LJ 144 (SC); *S.V. Mazumdar* v. *Gujarat State Fertilizer Co. Ltd.*, 2005 (4) Comp LJ 493 (SC).

In this case three situations were described:—

(i) Person accused was incharge of or responsible for the conduct of business is essential

(ii) Merely being a director of the company is not sufficient to make the person liable

(iii) Managing Director/Joint-Director would admittedly be incharge of the company. Holder of such position in the company becomes liable under section 141 of the Negotiable Instruments Act. Signatory in the cheque dishonoured is clearly responsible for the incriminating act covered under section 141(2) of the Negotiable Instrument Act, 1881.

***Bimal Kumar Nopani* v. *State of Uttar Pradesh*, 2006 Cr LJ 2611**

Cases referred:

Anil Hada v. *Indian Acrylic Ltd.*, (2000) 1 SCC 1; *Ambesh Balwapuri* v. *M/s. Continental Carbon India Ltd.*, 2006 (1) ALJ 396; *S.M.S. Pharmaceuticals Ltd.* v. *Neeta Bhalla*, AIR 2005 SC 3512.

In this case three issues were agitated:—

(i) "Exceed arrangement" and "insufficiency of fund" have the same meaning.

(ii) The person responsible for the conduct or incharge of the business of the company can be prosecuted without prosecution of the company it self.

(iii) No new factual dispute can be allowed to be raised in this court under section 482, the Cr. P.C.

***Everest Advertising Pvt. Ltd.* v. *State (Govt. of NCT of Delhi)*, 2007 (2) JCC (NI) 141 (SC)**

In this case the learned Magistrate recalled the summoning order. High Court, for all intent and purpose upheld the order of the learned Magistrate and hence this appeal before the Supreme Court. The Supreme Court found that the respondent Nos. 2 and 3 took part in the meeting and hence cannot plead ignorance. Ingredients of section 141 are satisfied.

***Zenith Mining Pvt. Ltd.* v. *National Agriculture Co-operative Marketing Federation of India Ltd.*, 2007 (4) JCC (NI) 323 (Del)**

Case referred:

N. Rangachari v. *Bharat Sanchar Nigam Ltd.*, AIR 2007 SC 1682.

It is clear from the complaint that at the time of dishonour of cheque issued by the company petitioner No: 2 was director of the company and incharge of its affairs and hence the petition is dismissed which was for quashing the petition.

***A.K. Grenka* v. *M/s. Magma Leasing Limited,* 2007 (4) JCC (NI) 337 (Cal)**

From the reading of the complaint it appears that at the time of occurrence accused petitioner was not only director of the accused company but he was incharge and responsible to the company for its day-to-day business and regular affairs. So he is liable under section 141 of the Negotiable Instruments Act under vicarious liability.

Refer:

(2007) 2 SCC (Cri) 135; AIR 2006 SC 3086; (2007) 2 SCC (Ori) 192.

***Rama Swami Athappan* v. *Bharti Infotel Ltd.,* 2008 (1) JCC (NI) 102 (Del)**

Cases referred:

AIR 2007 SC 1682; 2001 (2) JCC SC 127.

Copy of Form 32 indicates that the petitioner had not resigned on the date of cheque in question was drawn and issued. Petition is dismissed.

***Manish Kant Agarwal* v. *M/s. National Agricultural Co-operative Marketing Federation of India Ltd.,* AIR 2009 (NOC) 1231 (Del)**

When there is offence committed by the company, for holding the director liable for criminal liability under vicarious liability, it is essential that a incriminating act is done by him. Director is neither the signatory of the cheque nor there is any averment to the effect that he is incharge of the affairs of the company. Complaint against the Director is not maintainable.

Refer also:

AIR 2009 (NOC) 952 Del; AIR 2009 (NOC) 406 (Mad); AIR 2009 (NOC) 403 (Ker); AIR 2009 (NOC) 132 (Ker).

II. PERSONS WHO ARE NOT LIABLE, THOUGH OFFENCE IS COMMITTED

***B. Lakshmi* v. *Trishul Coal Services & Transporters,* 1997 Cr LJ 3616 (AP)**

Cases referred:

(1) (1994) 2 ALT 7 (NRC).

(2) AIR 1992 SC 2206: (1992) 1 SCC 217: (1992) 1 KLT 1.

(3) 1992 ISJ (Banking) 129 (P&H).

Facts of the case.—Summoning orders were issued to a partnership (A1) its Managing partner (A2) and a partner wife of A2 (A3). A3 filed on application before the Magistrate pleading discharge on the ground that she is merely impleaded and that except this there is no allegation against her in the complaint. Her application is rejected on two grounds, *i.e.,* (i) That she is a partner in the company, and (ii) there is no provisions of discharging the accused after summoning order. Aggrieved by this order she approached the High Court. High Court after referring to sections 138 and 141 and referring to the decisions cited *held* that the offence is committed by the company and the only person incharge of and responsible for affairs and conduct of business of the company is liable. Cheque is issued by A2. There is no allegation against the petitioner

(A3) to be incharge and responsible for conduct of business of the firm. *Held*, that there can be no proceedings against her. The High Court also *held* that there is no provision in the Cr. P.C. that the Magistrate cannot discharge the accused after summoning. He can do so if there is no allegation against the accused.

Note.—*Now the position is that the Magistrate cannot discharge the accused after summoning. The accused has to go for revision of the recall of the summoning order and discharge.*

***Raj Kumar Mangla* v. *Indo Lowenbrau Breweries Ltd.*, (1997) 4 Crimes 180: (2001) 105 Comp Cas 787: 1998 Cr LJ 332 (P&H)**

Cases referred:

1992 Cr LJ 1442 All; (1992) 1 Rec Cri R 169.

Facts of the case.—This case is based only on one point. There is no averment in the complaint that the petitioner is incharge of and responsible to the company. This allegation is the essence of section 141 of the Act. The complaint and summoning orders issued against the petitioner is quashed. It may continue against the other accused.

***Mahendra Pratap Singh Ratra* v. *N.K. Metals*, (1998) 3 Chand Cri C 93: (1998) 31 CLA 325: 1998 Cr LJ 4383 (AP)**

Cases cited:

(1996) 4 Crimes 520 Del; 1995 Cr LJ 2306 Mad (Dissented from); AIR 1983 SC 67: (1983) 1 SCC 1.

Facts of the case.—It is a petition under section 482, the Cr. P.C. for setting aside the order of the Magistrate directing framing of charge against them under section 138 of the Negotiable Instruments Act. A cheque was issued by the Chairman-cum-Managing Director of the Company which got bounced. The complaint was filed against the company, Chairman-cum-Managing Director and two Directors of the Company. There was no averment or allegation with regard to responsibility of the petitioners/Directors *vis-à-vis* Company. There is no material showing alleged offence committed with the consent or attributable to any neglect on the part of the Directors. *Held*, the order for framing charges against the Directors under section 138 is liable to be quashed.

***Secunderabad Health Care Ltd.* v. *Secunderabad Hospitals (P) Ltd.*, (1998) 4 Crimes 74: (1998) 4 Andh LD 613: 1998 Cr LJ 4521 (AP)**

Cases referred:

(1998) 4 Supreme 364; (1997) 8 JT 705; (1994) 1 BC 648 (Mad); 1990 Cr LJ 2739 (AP); AIR 1983 SC 67: (1983) 1 SCC 1: 1983 Cr LJ 159.

Facts of the case.—It is a case where prosecution was launched against some of the Directors but no specific allegation however was made that they were incharge of and responsible for conduct of business of company. There is no averment that they have issued the cheque. Even sworn statement of the complainant does not reveal anything against them. The High Court quashed the proceedings under the inherent powers vested in it.

M. Inbarajan v. _Baladandapani_, (1999) 1 Civ LJ 799: (1999) 1 Bank LLR 629: (1998) 2 Mad LW (Cri) 631: 1999 Cr LJ 75 (Mad)

Facts of the case.—In this case prosecution was launched against 3 accused under section 138, the Negotiable Instruments Act wherein section 109, the I.P.C. was also invoked to rope in accused Nos. 2 and 3. Accused Nos. 2 and 3 were not holding any post in the company when the refund cheque was issued and got bounced. *Held* that the complaint against them is not maintainable.

M. Chokalingam v. _Sundram Finance Services Ltd._, 1999 Cr LJ 137 (Mad)

Cases referred:

1998 Cr LJ 3287; (1998) 3 Crimes 548; 1998 Cr LJ 3722 (Mad); (1996) 86 Com Cas 631 (P&H); (1995) 83 Com Cas 593 (Mad); (1994) 80 Com Cas 487 (Bom); (1994) 1 Mad LW (Cri) 278; 1992 Mad LW (Cri) 120; AIR 1989 SC 1982: (1989) 4 SCC 630: 1989 SCC (Cri) 783.

Facts of the case.—It is a petition under section 482, the Cr. P.C. for quashing of complaint against the accused. The cheque was issued by the company after the petitioner ceased to be the director of the company. There is no averment that the petitioner was Director of the company and was incharge of and responsible to the company at the time the offence was committed. *Held*, the complaint is liable to be quashed.

D. Chandra Reddy v. _Gowrisetti Prabhakar_, (2000) 99 Comp Cas 102: (2001) 107 Comp Cas 474: 2000 Cr LJ 2526 (AP)

Facts of the case.—In this case the cheques were drawn by the company, signed by the Managing Director arrayed as accused in his personal capacity and not as Managing Director of the company. There is no allegation in the complaint that the company has committed the offence. There is no allegation that the accused has issued the cheque from account maintained by him. Accused is not sought to be prosecuted as an officer of the company incharge of and responsible for the conduct of business of the company. *Held*, the complaint against the accused is liable to be quashed.

Jordan Engineers India v. _Nagarjuna Finance Ltd._, 2000 All LJ 1629: (2001) 1 Crimes 426: 2000 Cr LJ 4933 (AP)

Cases referred:

1998 Cr LJ 4521 (AP); (1998) 91 Com Cas 850 (Kant).

Facts of the case.—In this case there were five accused, *i.e.*, Company (A1), Managing Director representing the Company (A2), A director, an authorised signatory (A3), another director (A4), financial controller (A5). There is a bald averment that all the directors are responsible. The court looked to the position of each person which he is holding and came to the conclusion that there is nothing against A4 as no qualification is attached to him as to what role he has played in the commission of the offence under section 138, the Negotiable Instruments Act. However, (A5) has a definite role to play.

Held: Prosecution against A4 is not maintainable and other accused A1, A2, A3 and A5 have to face the trial.

***S.N. Bangur* v. *Klen and Marshalls Manufacturers and Exporters Pvt. Ltd.*, 2002 Cr LJ 4155: (2002) 3 BC 504: (2002) 3 Crimes 638: 2002 MLJ (Cri) 797 (Mad)**

Cases referred:

(2000) 6 Scale 578 (SC); 1999 Cr LJ 2693 (Mad).

Facts of the case.—In this case the petitioners A3, A4, A6 and A7 filed applications before the trial court praying for the dropping of the proceedings arising out of different private complaints filed by the respondent for the offence under section 138, the Negotiable Instruments Act. Since those petitions were dismissed the petitioners have filed this revision petition. The averments in the complaint are that the accused 3 to 7 failed to make payment and are guilty of the commission of offence under section 138 of the Act. The High Court *held* that mere words in the complaint that the accused Directors are responsible for the failure to make payment for the cheque amount without further material to prove consent or connivance are not sufficient to hold these directors guilty of the offence. Proceedings against them are liable to be dropped.

***H.N.D. Multa Feroze* v. *K.V.D. Parsad Rao*, (2002) 3 BC 221: 2002 Cr LJ NOC 236 (AP)**

Facts of the case.—The petitioner as owner of the Company borrowed loan from the respondent on behalf of the Company. The petitioner issued cheque for repayment from Company's account and not from his personal account. He is not the Director of the company nor person incharge of day-to-day affairs of the company. He cannot be proceeded against under section 138 of the Act. Respondents can proceed against the petitioner in civil court.

***Sonia Bhalla* v. *Rajnesh Aggarwal*, (2002) 3 BC 216: (2002) 4 Civ LJ 744: 2002 Cr LJ 3053 (HP)**

Cases referred:

(2000) 1 SCC 1: 2000 Cr LJ 373: (2000) 1 KLT 141: 2000 Cr LJ 373 (SC); (2000) 6 Scale 578; AIR 1998 SC 2327: (1998) 5 SCC 343: 1998 SCC (Cri) 1315: (1998) 93 Comp Cas 329; 1998 Cr LJ 332 (P&H); AIR 1989 SC 1982: (1989) 4 SCC 630: 1989 Cr LJ 2201; AIR 1971 SC 28.

Facts of the case.—Three petitioners filed the present petition under section 482, the Cr. P.C. for quashing the proceedings initiated against them.

The plea taken is that there are neither averments nor evidence that the three petitioners were in any manner responsible for day-to-day business of the company or that the offence was committed with their consent or connivance or that such offence is attributable to any neglect on their part. The High Court, in particular, referred to 2000 Cr LJ 373: AIR 2000 SC 145: (2000) 1 SCC 1, wherein it is stated that three categories of persons are brought within the purview of penal liability through the legal fiction envisaged under section 141 of the Act. They are:—

(i) the company which committed the offence,

(ii) Everyone who was incharge of and was responsible for the business of the company, and

(iii) any other person who is a director or officer of the Company with whose connivance or due to his negligence the company has committed the offence.

Held, that the proceedings against the petitioners and order summoning them are hereby quashed and proceedings against others shall continue.

***S.B. Shankar* v. *Amman Steel Corporation, Trichnapalli,* (2002) 2 BC 166: (2002) 3 CCC 76: (2002) 110 Comp Cas 50: 2002 Cr LJ 836 (Mad)**

Cases referred:

(2001) 2 Crimes 602; (2001) 2 CTC 78; 2002 Cr LJ 137; (1996) 9 SCC 766; (1995) 83 Comp Cas 593; (1994) 80 Comp Cas 487; 1977 TNLJ 11; 1975 TNLJ 287; AIR 1960 Mad 482; AIR 1932 Mad 497.

Facts of the case.—It is a case where cheques were issued by the accused company towards purchase of heavy melting scrap. The cheques returned unpaid. Petitioner resigned from chairmanship of accused company even before the credit purchase transaction between accused company and complainant. The petitioner was also not incharge of and responsible for affairs of the company when cause of action arose for non-payment of cheque amount on receipt of respective statutory notices. *Held* that proceedings against petitioner are liable to be quashed.

***Shakti Bhakoo* v. *Raj Laxmi Mills,* (2002) 1 BC 401: (2001) 3 CCC 447: 2002 Cr LJ 1994 (P&H)**

Cases referred:

(2000) 2 SCC 737: 2000 Cr LJ 1424 (SC); 1998 Cr LJ 332 (P&H); 1994 JSJ (Banking) 310; (1992) 1 Rec Cri R 169; 1992 Cr LJ 1442 (All).

Facts of the case.—In this case the petitioner prayed for quashing the criminal complaint and the order of summoning on the ground that the petitioner was only a sleeping partner and had nothing to do with the day-to-day affairs of the company and the cheques in question were lost by the other partner namely, Anoop Bhaku and that this complaint is a counter blast to the complaint lodged by Anoop Bhaku. *Held,* that the petitioner was a house wife and only a sleeping partner and was not responsible to conduct the business of the company and that prosecution launched against her is an abuse of the process of law and hence quashed.

***Sulochanna* v. *M. Kulasekarn,* 2003 Cr LJ 4373 (Mad)**

Cases referred:

2001 CLC 617; (2000) 2 SCC 636: 2000 SCC (Cri) 513: 2000 All LJ 496: 2000 Cr LJ 824 (SC); AIR 1977 SC 2185: (1977) 4 SCC 137: 1977 Cr LJ 1891.

Facts of the case.—The first accused is the firm represented by its Managing partner. The second accused is the Managing partner and accused Nos. 3 to 11 are the partners of the firm. The revision petition is filed by accused Nos. 3, 5, 7, 9 and 10 alleged to be the partners who are incharge of the conduct of the business and responsible for the day-to-day affairs of the firm. Except the averment in the complaint, there is no material to show that the petitioners are incharge and responsible for the day-to-day affairs of the company. Furthermore the petitioners denied the allegation at the earlier stage in the reply notice. There is no satisfying material to show that the cheques in question were issued with consent or connivance of the petitioners/accused. *Held,* the prosecution against them cannot be launched.

***A.C. Gupta* v. *Renu Gautam*, (2003) 3 BC 136: (2003) 2 Civ LJ 922: 2003 Cr LJ 1458 (HP)**

Cases referred:

(2002) Cr LJ 3053 (HP); (1999) Cr MMO No. 23 dated 9-9-1999 (HP); (1995) 2 Bank Case 265; (1994) 80 Comp Cas 750; (1992) 73 Comp Cas 434; AIR 1988 SC 1128: (1987) 3 SCC 684: 1987 SCC (Cri) 632.

Facts of the case.—The facts of the case are that cheque was issued by the firm signed by the appellant as partner. The appellant is impleaded in the complaint in his personal capacity and not as partner of the firm. There is no averment in the complaint that the appellant is the incharge and responsible to the business of the firm. Firm which is the drawer of the cheque is not impleaded as an accused. *Held,* the complaint is defective and there is non compliance of the provisions of the clauses (b) and (c) of proviso to section 138 of the Act and hence the acquitted order passed by the trial Magistrate is proper and there is no infirmity or illegality and does not call for any interference.

***Mukesh Gupta* v. *Kabson Gas Equipment Ltd.*, (2003) 114 Comp Cas 728: (2003) 1 Andh WR 216: (2003) 2 BC 322: 2003 Cr LJ NOC 164 (AP)**

Facts of the case.—The offence is committed by the company but complaint is filed against the petitioner who is one of the Directors of the Company. There is no averment or allegation that the petitioner was incharge and responsible to company for conduct of its business. *Held,* that the said complaint is not maintainable.

***P. Deeptha* v. *V.S. Chandra Sekaran*, (2003) 3 BC 479: (2003) 3 Crimes 470: (2003) 4 Cur CL 492: 2003 Cr LJ 4660 (Mad)**

Cases referred:

AIR 1971 AP 58; AIR 1960 SC 388.

Facts of the case.—Offence is committed by a company. Accused in question was neither incharge of nor responsible to the company for conduct of business of the company. It is also an admitted fact that she was minor at that time. *Held,* that proceedings against her are liable to be quashed.

***Chattan M. Maniar* v. *State of Maharashtra*, (2004) 4 BC 584: (2004) 2 Bom CR (Cri) 14: (2004) 3 Civ LJ 294: 2004 Cr LJ 2343 (Bom)**

Cases referred:

(2001) 10 SCC 218; 2001 Cr LJ 4819 (Bom); (1998) 4 LJ 830 (Bom); (1998) 91 Comp Cas 850.

Facts of the case.—The petitioner, advocate by profession, was one of the six directors of the company. The complainant sent a statutory notice only to the

Managing Director of the company who had signed the cheque and who was in sole management and incharge of the company. No notice was sent to the petitioner who was only a non-executive Director. He was not incharge of the company of its day-to-day affairs. Moreover, he has resigned from Board of Directors prior to issuance of cheque in question. *Held,* that the proceedings against the petitioner are liable to be quashed.

***Ramasita Finance and Investments Pvt. Ltd.* v. *Meenakshi Nagappa Halamanavar,* (2004) 2 Bank LLR 340: (2004) 3 BC 72: 2004 Cr LJ 1029 (Karn)**

Cases referred:

2002 Cr LJ 374; 2002 Cr LJ 3291; AIR 1998 SC 2327: (1998) 5 SCC 343: (1998) 93 Comp Cas 329; (1983) 1 SCC 1: 1983 Cr LJ 159: 1983 Cr LJ 159 SC.

Facts of the case.—Offence is committed by the company but Director of the company was prosecuted. There is no allegation that the accused was incharge and responsible to the company for conduct of its business. *Held,* that the order of the Fast-Track Court was right in holding that accused No. 4 was not liable to be prosecuted and hence the Revision Petition is dismissed at the admission stage itself.

***T.N. Devi* v. *A.C. Haridas,* (2004) 3 Ker 635: (2004) 2 Ker LJ 575: (2004) 3 Ker LT 355: 2004 Cr LJ 4710 (Ker)**

Case referred:

AIR 1992 SC 2206: (1992) 1 SCC 217: 1992 SCC (Cri) 88.

Facts of the case.—It is a case of Joint Account. Cheque was drawn from the said account being operated jointly by husband and wife. Cheque was issued by the accused husband to the complainant for discharge of his liability. *Held,* that merely because she happened to be the spouse of the accused and account can be operated by either of them, cannot make her culpably liable. More so, she cannot be *held* liable under section 141 of the Act too. She does not deserve to stand the trauma of this criminal proceedings. She is entitled to be relieved of the trauma which is unnecessary.

***Aseem Shabanali Merchant* v. *Brij Mehra,* (2004) 1 Bom CR (Cri) 529: (2004) 3 Rec Cri R 903: 2004 Cr LJ 1268 (Bom)**

Case referred:

2003 Bom CR (Cri) 146 SC (distinguished).

Facts of the case.—In this case there were three Directors of the complainant company and they were no more alive. The appellant was not Director of the company on date the complaint was made. Instead of bringing the legal heirs of the complainant on record, the appellant and his advocate remained absent and on date complaint was dismissed. *Held,* that the dismissal of complaint is proper. In this case 2003 Bom CR (Cri) 146 SC was distinguished. In the said case there was solitary instance of absence whereas in this case the advocate and the appellant were absent on three occasions.

***Monoben Ketanbhai Shah* v. *State of Gujarat*, (2004) 7 SCC 15: AIR 2004 SC 4274: 2004 Cr LJ 4249 (SC)**

Cases referred:

2003 SCC (Cri) 151: (2002) 7 SCC 655; 2002 SCC (Cri) 1038.

Facts of the case.—There is complaint against partners of a firm. There was no averment in the complaint that the accused at relevant time were incharge of and responsible to firm for conduct of its business. However, at a belated stage, partnership deed was filed to show that they are the partners of the firm. *Held*, that vicarious liability cannot be fastened on those partners who at the time of offence was committed, were not incharge of and responsible to firm for conduct of its business.

***S. Sultan & Co.* v. *Cement Corporation of India Ltd.*, 2005 Cr LJ 1134 (AP)**

Cheque issued in personal capacity. Firm is not liable.

***D.B. Mehta* v. *Ramesh Rikhabdas Shah*, (2004) 20 AIC 836: 2005 Cr LJ 403 (Bom)**

Produced Form No. 12 showing retirement before issue of cheque. It was the duty of the court to discharge.

***Merbane Financial Services Ltd.* v. *Chilipi Krish Garments (P). Ltd.*, 2005 Cr LJ 1823 (AP)**

The petitioner is neither signatory of cheque nor in charge of the undertaking. Order of acquittal is proper 2003 Cr LJ NOC 164 AP followed.

***S.M.S. Pharmaceuticals Ltd.* v. *Neeta Bhalla*, (2005) 8 SCC 89: 2005 SCC (Cri) 1975: (2005) 4 KLT 209: 2005 Cr LJ 4140 (SC)**

Director of Company is not vicariously liable by virtue of office he holds. Managing Director, Joint Managing Director, signatory of cheque liable.

***Balaji Trading Co.* v. *Kejriwal Paher Ltd.*, 2005 Cr LJ 3805 (AP)**

Company is liable even if there is no allegation against the Directors.

***Rachna Kapoor* v. *State of N.C.T. Delhi*, 2006 Cr LJ (NOC) 70 Del**

Bald accusation that the accused is the director of the Company is not sufficient. Complaint was quashed under section 482, the Cr. P.C.

Note.—(1) In case of individual, section 138 along with provisos read with section 142(b) of the Act must be satisfied.

(2) In case of company or firm or Association of persons ingredients of sections 141(1) and 142(2) are to be satisfied.

(3) The accused can seek shelter under Proviso to section 141(1) of the Act.

***M/s. Merbanc Financial Services Ltd.* v. *M/s. Chilipi Krish Garments*, 2006 (1) JCC (NI) 4 (AP)**

Cases referred:

2002 (1) ALD (Cri) 255 AP; 2003 (1) ALD (Cri) 261 AP; 2003 Cr LJ NOC 164.

Accused No. 4 had not issued any cheque. It is also not shown that the acquittal of the accused is either perverse or based on total misappreciation of the evidence available on record. Acquittal recorded by the Magistrate in hereby confirmed. Appeal is dismissed.

***Sabitha Ramamurthy* v. *R.B.S. Channabasavaradhya*, 2006 (JCC) (NI) 247 (SC)**

Cases referred:

(2004) 7 SCC 15; (2002) 7 SCC 655; (2001) 10 SCC 218; (2005) 8 SCC 89.

It is said that in terms of section 200, the Cr. P.C. the complainant is bound to make statements on oath as to how the offence has been committed and how the accused persons are responsible therefor. The complaint is found *mala fide* and frivolous. The court is directed to register a case against the complainant under the relevant provisions of the Code of Criminal Procedure.

***H.B. Chaturvedi* v. *State*, 2006 (1) JCC (NI) 3 (Del)**

In this case the chairman is accused No. 2. It is held that under the Companies Act, Chairman is not responsible for day-to-day business nor it can be inferred as a person consented or connived in the commission of the offence. Merely being a chairman, summoning order issued to him was not right. Order is quashed.

***Dr. Rajan Sanatkumar Joshi* v. *Rajnikant Govindlal Shah*, 2007 Cr LJ 2318 (Guj)**

Cases referred:

AIR 2007 SC 912; AIR 2006 SC 3086; AIR 2005 SC 3512; (2005) 13 SCC 540; AIR 1998 SC 128.

Additional Director of accused company resigned before cheque in question was dishonoured. There is no specific averment in the complaint as to how and in what manner the petitioner was responsible for conduct of the business of the company or otherwise responsible to it in regard to its functioning. Complaint against the petitioner is quashed.

***A.G. Gaggar* v. *The State*, 2007 (1) JCC (NI) 91 (Del)**

Cases referred:

(1992) 1 SCC 217; 2000 (1) JCC SC (1); (2004) 7 SCC 338; 2005 (3) JCC (NI) 203.

The complaint in this case is absolutely silent as to the role played by the petitioner. Simple status of a person as director of the company would be no justification to automatically to implead him in proceedings for violation of section 138, the Negotiable Instruments Act. The proceedings pending before ACMM are quashed.

Refer Also:

Ashok Newatia v. *State*, 2007 (2) JCC (NI) 202 (Del); *Sarla Jain* v. *Central Bank of India*, 2007 (4) JCC (NI) 313 (Del); *K.P.G. Nair* v. *State*, 2007 (4) JCC (NI) 363 (Del); *Harmeet Singh Paintal* v. *State*, 2007 (4) JCC (NI) 396 (Del); *J.C. Khandelwal* v. *State*, 2007 (4) JCC (NI) 413 (Del).

Note.—*More averment in the complaint that the petitioners are incharge and are responsible for the conduct of business will not do. There must be evidence to this effect because it is a case of vicarious liability.*

***Saraj Kumar Poddar* v. *State (NCT of Delhi)*, AIR 2007 SC 912**

Cases referred:

AIR 2006 SC 3086; AIR 2005 SC 3512.

It is obligatory on the part of the complainant to make specific allegations as are required by law to make the Director vicariously liable. Strict construction is necessary. Merely being described is not sufficient.

***N.K. Wahi* v. *Shekhar Singh*, AIR 2007 SC 1454**

Cases referred:

2007 AIR SCW 656; AIR 2006 SC 3086; AIR 2005 SC 3512.

Complaint must contain specific allegations against the Directors as to how the directors are incharge and responsible for the conduct of the business of the company. Mere allegations that the accused are the directors of the company and responsible officers of the company is not sufficient. Process issued against the directors is liable to be quashed.

***S.M.S. Pharmaceuticals Ltd.* v. *Neeta Bhalla*, 2007 (1) JCC (NI) 73 (SC)**

Cases referred:

(2001) 10 SCC 218; (2004) 7 SCC 15; 2006 (9) SCALE 212; 2007 (2) SCALE 36; (1990) 2 SCC 437; (2001) 8 SCC 522; (1975) 3 SCC 706.

In this case the Apex Court answered three questions:—

(i) It is necessary to specifically aver in a complaint under section 141 that at the time the offence was committed, the person accused was incharge of and responsible for the conduct of business of the company. This is the essential ingredient of section 141 of the Negotiable Instruments Act.

(ii) Merely being a director of the company is not sufficient to make the person liable under section 141 of the Act. A director is not the incharge of the company. It has to be shown as to how to be averred as a fact as there is no deemed liability of the director in such cases.

(iii) The Managing Director or Joint Managing Director are admittely in charge of the company and responsible to the company for the conduct of the business. They are covered under section 141 of the Act. The signatory of the cheque is clearly responsible for the incriminating act and will be covered under sub-section (2) of section 141 of the Act.

***Kapil Mehra* v. *Indusind Enterprises & Finance Ltd.*, 2008 Cr LJ 1134**

Cases referred:

AIR 2007 SC 912; AIR 2006 SC 3086; AIR 2004 SC 4274; (2002) 7 SCC 655; (2001) 10 SCC 218; AIR 1998 SC 128; 1994 Mah LJ 677 (Bom); 1991 Cr LJ 609 (Cal); AIR 1983 SC 67.

Held, that every person connected with the company shall not fall within the ambit of the provisions (section 141 of the Act). Only those persons who are incharge of and responsible for the conduct of business of the company at the time of the commission of the offence, will be liable for criminal action. Liability depends on the role one plays in the affairs of the company and not on designation or status which he holds in the company.

***B.B. Chowdhry* v. *Govinder Arora*, 2008 (1) JCC (NI) 88 (Del)**

Case referred:

AIR 2007 SC 1457.

Held, that it is not in dispute that in the complaint no reference whatsoever has been made to the petitioners. It is also not in dispute that in the pre-summoning evidence not a whisper has been made regarding the petitioners. Also there is no assertion specifying the part played by the petitioners in the transaction between the accused and the company. Complaint is quashed.

Refer also:

2008 (1) JCC (NI) 90 Del; 2008 (1) JCC (NI) 59 Del.

***Vinod Hingorani* v. *State of Maharashtra*, 2008 Cr LJ 2403 (Bom)**

Admittedly the applicant is not signatory of the cheque. It was not shown that he was incharge of and responsible for conduct of business of the accused company at the relevant time. Complaint against him is liable to be quashed.

Cases referred:

2007 All MB (Cri) 3314 (Bom); 2006 Cr LJ 1540; AIR 2005 SC 3512 (Rely. on); 2002 (7) SCC 655 (Rely. on); 2001 (10) SCC 218 (Rely. on).

***D.C.M. Financial Services Ltd.* v. *J.N. Sareen*, (2008) 2 JCC (NI) 233 (SC)**

Cases referred:

(2005) 8 SCC 89; (2007) 5 SCC 108; JT 2007 (9) SC 449; (2007) 9 SCC 481; (2007) 3 SCC 693; (2007) 5 SCC 103; (2004) 7 SCC 338.

A person who had resigned with the knowledge of the complainant in 1996 cannot be incharge of the company in 1998 when the cheque was dishonoured.

Appeal is dismissed.

***Vinay Kumar@ Vinay* v. *State*, 2009 (2) JCC (NI) 149 (Del)**

Cases referred:

(2005) 125 DLT 109; (2005) 8 SCC 89; (2007) 4 SCC 70; (2006) 10 SCC 581; (2007) 9 SCC 481; (2007) 3 SCC 693; (2008) 8 SCC 1.

Merely because a person is the chairman/vice-chairman of the company, it cannot be inferred that he has consented to or connived in the commission of the offence. Liability cannot be fastened on the petitioner. The petitioner is able to show that he had already resigned much prior to the commission of the alleged offence.

Also See

2009 (2) JCC (NI) 91 (Del); 2009 (2) JCC (NI) 98 (Del); 2009 (1) JCC (NI) 41 (Del).

***Ramraj Singh* v. *State of Madhya Pradesh*, 2009 (2) JCC (NI) 156 (SC)**

Cases referred:

2007 (4) SCC 70; 2007 (9) SCC 481.

Held:—Appellant who is General Manager of the company cannot be made vicariously liable as there was no specific role attributed to him in the complaint petition and also there was no evidence that he was incharge or responsible for the conduct of the business of the company.

***K.K. Ahuja* v. *V.K. Vora,* 2009 (3) JCC (NI) 194 (SC)**

Cases referred:

(2005) 8 SCC 89; (2006) 10 SCC 581; (2007) 3 SCC 693; (2007) 4 SCC 70; (2007) 5 SCC 54; (2007) 9 SCC 481; (2008) 8 SCC 1; 2009 (5) SCALE 670; (2007) 12 SCC 788; (1971) 3 SCC 189; (1981) 2 SCC 335; (2002) 7 SCC 655.

A Deputy General Manager is not a person who is responsible for the conduct of the business of the, company and also does not fall under any of the categories under section 85 of the Companies Act, 1956. He cannot fall under section 141(1) of the Act. In order to bring him under section 141(2), it has to be shown that he has consented or connived or negligence has been made by him. In the absence of such averment he cannot be made liable.

***Mama Chandra @ Mam Chand* v. *State of Jharkhand,* 2010 (1) Crimes 499 (Jhar)**

It is case where accused person sold a plot by way of cheating by forgery. They were arrested by the police. One of them, on release on bail, issued a cheque for Rs. 3,50,000 in favour of the complainant which got bounced. It was held that prosecution of offence under the Act could be launched only against, a person who has drawn the cheque. Cognizance of said offence against other accused persons was bad and is liable to be quashed.

Note.—*Section 138 of the Negotiable Instruments Act fastens liability only on the drawer of the cheque.*

Section 141 NI Act, Section 482, the Cr P.C. When issue is triable

Note.—*When a complaint is filed under Section 138/141 of the Act and is challenged under section 482, the Cr. P.C. for question, it is to be seen as to whether the fact stated is clease, cogent and convincing based on material evidence, if so the proceeding is liable to be quashed but if the issue is disputed and is triable to find its truthfulness, then the High Court will be reluctant to exercise power under section 482.*

***M/s. City Palace Electronic* v. *State,* 2006 (1) JCC (NI) 17 (Del)**

Cases referred:

1996 Cr LJ 638 (AP); 2002 Cr LJ 4392 (Ker); AIR 2000 SC 954; AIR 2001 SC 1161; 2005 (3) JCC (NI) 203 SC; (2005) 1 SCC 1583.

Held: That inherent power under section 482, the Cr. P.C. should not be exercised to stiffle a legitimate prosecution more so when the evidence has not been collected and produced before the court and issue involved either factual or legal not seen in their true perspective, it is better for the petitioner to defend themselves in the Trial Court and if they are so sure of their defence, they will get themselves discharged or acquitted, rather than rushing to the High Court. Petitions are *mala fide.*

***J.N. Bhatia* v. *State,* 2007 (2) JCC 171 (NI) 171 (Del)**

It is a case where numerous cases were referred. In this case the scope and ambit of section 482, the Cr. P.C. was discussed and held that the accused is entitled to approach High Court under section 482, the Cr. P.C. or under

Article 227 of the Constitution of India to have proceedings quashed against him when complainant does not make out any case against him, instead of having to undergo agony of a criminal trial.

Refer Also:

2007 (1) JCC (NI) 49 (Del); 2007 (4) JCC (NI) 402 (Del); 2007 (4) JCC (NI) 415 (Del); 2007 (4) JCC (NI) 333 (Del); 2007 (2) JCC (NI) 217 (Del).

***K. Uma Devi* v. *Manikandan, Proprietor Manisha Traders,* 2007 (1) JCC (NI) 88 (Mad)**

Cases referred:

2005 (4) Crimes 34; 2001 MLJ (Cri) 1082; 2001 (2) CTC 78; 2001 CC 518; 2003 CC 403; 2005 (3) CTC 380.

Held: It is to be seen during the trial Court and establish the contention that she as Director of the company resigned from the accused company and was no longer in charge and responsible for conduct of the business of the company. There is no ground to quash the proceedings.

***N. Rangachari* v. *Bharat Sanchar Nigam Ltd.,* 2007 (2) JCC (NI) 205 (SC)**

Cases referred:

(2005) 8 SCC 89; 2007 (2) SCALE 36; (2005) 4 SCC 173; (1998) 5 SCC 749; (1963) 1 SCR 253; (2004) 7 SCC 15; AIR 1999 SC 1216; AIR 1999 SC 2182; AIR 2001 SC 518.

The Apex Court held that section 141 of the Negotiable Instruments Act is to be read with section 291 of the Companies Act, 1956 and as such the contentions raised by the appellants can be dealt with after the conclusion of the trial. The Apex Court specially referred to *SMS Pharmaceutical* case, (2005) 8 SCC 89.

***V.C. Anthony* v. *M/s. City Financial Consumer Finance India Ltd.,* 2008 (1) JCC (NI) 76 Del**

Cases referred:

(2005) 8 SCC 89; (2007) DLT 783 (SC); 2006 (9) SCALE 212; JT 2007 (2) SC 233; AIR 2007 SC 1682; (1963) 1 SCR 253; (2004) 7 SCC 15; AIR 1999 SC 1216; AIR 1999 SC 2182; AIR 2001 SC 518.

Held: The question whether a person is a Director, incharge of the affairs of the company at the relevant time can only be judged during the course of the trial and the complaint cannot be quashed under section 482, the Cr. P.C. on this ground.

Refer Also

Shambu Kumar Aggarwal v. *Ved Parkash,* 2008 (3) JCC (NI) 284 (Del); *Nipam Kotwal* v. *M/s. Dominos Printech India Pvt. Ltd.,* 2008 (1) JCC (NI) 21 (Del).

***Budhmal Bansali* v. *The State of West Bengal,* 2008 (2) JCC (NI) 180 (Cal)**

Cases referred:

(2007) 1 C Cr LR (Ca) 793; 2007 (1) JCC (NI) 60 (SC); 2006 Cr LK 3076; 2002 Cr LK 836; 2000 C Cr LR (Ca) 363; (2005) 1 C Cr LR (Ca) 581; 2007 (2) E Cr

N 611; 1979 Cr LK 998; 1994 SCC (Cri) 1181; 2004 SC (Cri) 353; 2005 (1) KCC 109; 2007 (1) CHN 851 (Ca/DB); 1992 Supp (1) SCC 335; 2007 AIR SCW 7411.

The High Court *held* that at the stage of hearing an application under section 482, the Cr. P.C., relying on Form 32, petitioner cannot be discharged from the case. Form 32 is not a public document as not created by any public authority, whether the petitioner resigned from the company before issuance of cheque, still remains a disputed fact which is required to be proved or disproved at the stage of trial.

***Malwa Cotton and Spinning Mills Ltd.* v. *Virsa Singh Sidhu,* 2008 (3) JCC (NI) 353 (SC)**

Cases referred:

S.V. Mazumdar v. *Gujarat State Fertilizer Co. Ltd.*, 2005 (4) SCC 173; *N. Rangachari* v. *Bharat Sanchar Nigam Ltd.*, 2007 (5) SCC 108.

When factual disputes are involved as to the resignation of accused/ respondent from the Directorship of the company and delayed presentation before the Registrar of the Companies, which is essentially a matter of trial in respect of which evidence has to be led. The High Court could quash the proceedings in an application under section 482, the Cr. P.C.

***Paresh P. Rajda* v. *State of Maharashtra,* 2008 (3) JCC (NI) 249 SC**

Cases referred:

(2005) 8 SCC 89; (2007) 9 SCC 481; (2007) 4 SCC 70; (2007) 5 SCC 54; (2007) 5 SCC 108.

Notice was issued to the Company (A-1) and Chairman and Directors of the company (A2 to A4). A2 moved an application for discharge. It was rejected by the Magistrate and further by the High Court. The Apex Court held that it would be inappropriate to quash the proceedings at this stage where the trial has not yet started.

***Rajesh Kumar Gulati* v. *National Agricultural Co-operative Marketing Federation of India Ltd.,* 2009 (1) JCC (NI) 57 (Del)**

Cases referred:

(2005) 8 SCC 89; 2006 (9) SCALE 212; JT 2007 (2) SC 233; AIR 2007 SC 1682; (1963) 1 SCR 253; (2004) 7 SCC 15; AIR 1999 SC 1216; AIR 1999 SC 2182; AIR 2001 SC 518.

It was held that while replying to the notice the petitioner did not dispute the execution of the cheque. No plea was taken that he was neither incharge of and/ or responsible to the company for the conduct of the business of the company. Allegations in the complaint are sufficient to show that the accused were incharge of the affairs of the company at the relevant time. It is not a fit case for exercise of jurisdiction under section 482, the Cr. P.C.

Also Refer:

O.P. Aggarwal v. *State*, 2009 (1) JCC (NI) 68 (Del); *Dr. N.K. Sen Gupta* v. *State of NCT Delhi*, 2009 (2) JCC (NI) 106 (Del).

***Sudesh Jain* v. *State of NCT Delhi,* 2010 (1) JCC (NI) 1 Del**

Cases referred:

S.M.S. Pharmaceutical Ltd. v. *Neeta Bhalla,* (2005) 8 SCC 89; *T. Stanes & Co. Ltd.* v. *A. Jaffarullah,* (2000) 1 SCC 1174; *K.K. Ahuja* v. *V.K. Vora,* 2009 (9) SCALE 87; *Sabitha Ramamurthy* v. *R.B.S. Channavasavaradhya,* AIR 2006 SC 3086.

It is case under section 138 read with section 141 of the Negotiable Instruments Act where the issue is that of vicarious liability, for director of the company to make him vicarioiusly liable, it must be *prima facia* established by way of documents or by way of evidence which is led at the stage of preliminary evidence to show that he was actually holding such a position so as to conduct the day-to-day business. It is not merely holding of an office of a director which would be considered sufficient to bring a person within the ambit of vicarious liability for having committed an offence. In this case no such thing is shown that how he is incharge of day-to-day conduct of the business of the company at relevant time.

***Nitin Kumar* v. *NCT of Delhi through Its Standing Council,* 2010 (1) JCC (NI) 9 (Del)**

Cases referred:

Sameer Kamani v. *State,* 2009 (1) LRC 327 (Del); *S.M.S. Pharmaceuticals Ltd.* v. *Neeta Bhall,* (2005) 8 SCC 89; *Sabhitaramamurthy* v. *R.B.S. Channavasvaradhya,* (2005) 10 SCC 581; *N.K. Wahi* v. *Shekhar Singh,* (2007) 9 SCC 481; *K.K. Ahuja* v. *V.K. Vora,* 2009 (3) JCC (NI) 194; *Smt. Beena Sharma* v. *H.D.F.C. Bank Ltd.,* 2009 (4) JCC (NI) 257.

The court held as follows:—

(i) No distinction can be made between Director of a Public Limited Company and the Director of Private Limited Company

(ii) It cannot be said as a general rule that if there are two Directors in a company, both would be incharge of and responsible to the company for the conduct of the business of the company

(iii) Penal Statute of Criminal vicarious liability must be construed strictly. Merely attending of Board meetings would not attract criminal vicarious liability

(iv) It must he shown that the offence has been committed with the consent and connivance of the petitioner

(v) General allegation that the petitioner is actively involved in the offence of the company does not constitute necessary ingredient envisaged under Section 141 of the Negotiable Instruments Act.

***V.S. Gupta* v. *Punjab National Bank,* 2010 (1) JCC (NI) 17 (Del)**

Cases referred:

Dr (Mrs) Sarla Kumar v. *Sri International Finance Ltd.,* 2007 (2) NIJ 208 (Del); *O.P. Agarwal* v. *State,* 2009 (108) DRJ 494; *K.K. Ahuja* v. *V.K. Arora,* 2009 (3) JCC (NI) 194; *S.M.S. Pharmaceutical Ltd.* v. *Neeta Bhalla,* (2005) 8 SCC 89; *Saroj Kumar Poddar* v. *State (NCT of Delhi),* (2007) 3 SCC 693; *N.K. Wahi* v. *Shekhar Singh,* (2007) 9 SCC 481; *DCM Financial Services Ltd.* v. *J.N. Sareen,* (2008) 1 SCC 1; *Ram Raj Singh* v. *State of Madhya Pradesh,* 2009 (5) SCALE 670.

The Court held as follows:—

(i) When a certified copy of Form 32 is made available to the court, then it is a futile exercise of again go into the matter to find out as to whether the petitioner is a Director

(ii) A mere consultant to the company does not become a person in charge and responsible to the company for conduct of its business and the petitioner does not fall under the category (a) to (g) listed in section 5 of the Companies Act at the time of commission of offence and does not fall under the ambit of section 141(1) of the Negotiable Instruments Act.

III. NATURE OF COMPANY AND LIABILITY

Introduction: Word "Company" includes even firms and other associations. Sometimes, it so happens that the company has issued the cheques but its financial constraints become so acute that it cannot mobilize resources to meet the commitments or sometimes some legal impediments obstruct the flow of finance, making the company helpless to meet the requirements. When and if such situation arises, what can be the status of the criminal liability and whether the company can have some immunity to avoid the fastening of liability on it. Herein, certain peppery situations *vis-à-vis* criminal liability under sections 138, 141 of the Act are discussed.

SICK INDUSTRIAL COMPANIES (SPECIAL PROVISIONS) ACT (1 OF 1986), SECTION 22(1) AND SECTION 138 OF THE NEGOTIABLE INSTRUMENTS ACT, 1988

***BSI Ltd.* v. *Gift Holdings Pvt. Ltd.*, (2000) 2 SCC 737: 2000 SCC (Cri) 538: 2000 Cr LJ 1424 (SC)**

Cases referred:

AIR 2000 SC 145; (1993) 2 SCC 144.

Facts of the case.—Issue before the honourable Supreme Court was that when reconstruction efforts of a sick industrial company are pending under the provisions of the SICA, all other legal proceedings including any prosecution proceedings would stand suspended by the operation of the embargo contained in section 22(1) of the SICA.

Held, that if commission of the offence under section 138 of the Negotiable Instruments Act was completed before the commencement of proceedings under section 22(1) of the SICA, there is no hurdle in any of the provisions of the SICA against the maintainability and prosecution of a criminal complaint duly instituted under section 142 of the Negotiable Instruments Act. Appeals are accordingly dismissed.

***Kusum Ingots & Alloys Ltd.* v. *Pennax Peterson Securities Ltd.*, (2000) 2 SCC 745: AIR 2000 SC 954: 2000 SCC (Cri) 546: 2000 Cr LJ 1464 (SC)**

Cases referred:

2000 AIR SCW 521; AIR 1996 SC 2339: (1996) 2 SCC 739: 1996 SCC (Cri) 454.

Facts of the case.—In this case various provisions of the SICA, in particular, sections 22 and 22A were discussed and *held* that section 22, the SICA does not create any legal impediments for instituting and proceeding with a criminal case on the allegation of an offence under section 138 of the Negotiable Instruments Act against a Company or its Director. Section 22 only creates an embargo against disposal of assets of the company for recovery of its debts. The section does not bar payment of money by the company or its Directors to other persons for satisfaction of their legally enforceable dues.

***World Text Ltd.* v. *State of Rajasthan*, 2004 Bank J 102: 2004 Cr LJ 420 (Raj)**

Cases referred:

AIR 2000 SC 754: (2000) 2 SCC 636: 2000 Cr LJ 824; AIR 2000 SC 954: (2000) 2 SCC 745: 2000 Cr LJ 1464; AIR 1998 SC 128: (1998) 5 SCC 749: 1998 Cr LJ 1; AIR 1998 SC 2796 (1998) 7 SCC 698.

Facts of the case.—In this case various pleas were taken but the main plea was that the order of BIFR, clause (j) of Para. 10 prevents the company to dispose of or alienate any of its fixed deposits without specific prior approval of the charge holders and BIFR under section 22A of the Act and further stated that since the unit is operating the current assets may be utilized to the extent necessary for maintaining day-to-day operations.

Held that all the material facts have to be placed before the trial court so that the trial court may consider whether in the circumstances of the case section 138 of the Act 1881 is attracted or not. The petition is disposed of on the terms aforesaid.

***Montari Industries Ltd.* v. *State of Gujarat*, (1998) 1 Guj LR 35: (1998) 2 BC 125: 1998 Cr LJ 10 (Guj)**

Cases referred:

(1996) 6 SCC 369: 1996 SCC (Cri) 1340; AIR 1996 SC 2339: (1996) 2 SCC 739: 1996 SCC (Cri) 454; (1990) 1 Guj LR 557.

Facts of the case.—Besides, other contentions raised, one of the contention raised pertains to section 22 of the SICA. It is *held* that provision of section 22 apply only to winding up, execution, distress or like steps against any of the properties of the Sick Industrial Unit. Institution and continuation of other proceedings, are not vitiated by alleged bar under section 22, the SICA. *Held,* that initiation of proceedings is completely in accordance with law and cannot be termed as an abuse of the process of court.

***Avon Industries Ltd.* v. *Integrated Finance Company Ltd.*, (2002) 1 BC 88: 2001 Bank J 762: (2001) 2 Comp Cas 347: 2002 Cr LJ 4592 (AP)**

Cases referred:

2001 Cr LJ 522 (AP); 2001 Cr LJ 1586; AIR 2000 SC 145: (2000) 1 SCC 1: (2000) 1 KLT 141; AIR 2000 SC 954: (2000) 2 SCC 745: 2000 Cr LJ 1464; 2000 Cr LJ 1799; (2000) 6 Scale 578; 2000 Cr LJ 4117; 1998 Cr LJ 4521; (1998) 2 Andh LD (Cr) 201; 1997 Cr LJ 3616; 1988 Cr LJ 1112; (1985) 2 Andh LT 508; AIR 1984 SC 1824: (1984) 4 SCC 352: 1984 SCC (Cri) 620; 1983 Cr LJ 159; AIR 1983 SC 158: (1983) 1 SCC 9: 1983 SCC (Cri) 123; AIR 1971 SC 447.

Facts of the case.—In this case three points were raised:—

(i) Criminal proceedings should be quashed in view of initiation of liquidation proceedings against the company and that company law prevails over the Negotiable Instruments Act.

(ii) Section 22 of the SICA and section 138, the Negotiable Instruments Act.

(iii) That exact words as required under section 141, the Negotiable Instruments Act are not used in the complaint.

Held: The High Court negatived the contentions in view of the decisions of the Supreme Court on these issues and directed the appellant to file discharge petitions before respective courts if they so desire. The petitions were dismissed with aforesaid remarks.

***Shiva Paper Mills Ltd.* v. *United Alkalies & Acids Pvt. Ltd.*, 2008 (3) JCC (NI) 326 (Del)**

Cases referred:

M/s. Kusum Ingots & Alloys Ltd. v. *M/s. Pennar Peterson Securities Ltd.*, 2000 (2) RCR (Cri) 275; *Mr. Ajit Sarin* v. *M/s. Auto Tension Ltd.*, 2000 (2) JCC 480 (Del).

Company wad declared sick under section 22A, the Sick Industrial Company (Sp. Provisions) Act, 1985 and Board of Industrial and the Financial Reconstruction (BIFR). BIFR stayed/restrained all proceedings against the petitioner *vide* order dated 8-9-2003. Also cheque in question presented by R-1 on 29-10-2003 is after BIFR order dated 8-9-2003. As per decision cited as 2000 (2) RCR (Cri) 275 (SC), it would be unfair, unjust and against intent and purpose of Legislature to hold the petitioner to face trial. Petition is allowed and complaints are quashed.

***M/s. Hindustan Cables Ltd.* v. *The State Govt. of Nct of Delhi*, 2008 (2) JCC (NI) 141 (Del)**

Cases referred:

Adalat Prasad v. *Roop Lal Jindal*, 2004 (1) JCC 420 (SC); *Subhramaniam Sethuraman* v. *State of Maharashtra*, 2004 (4) Cri 78 (SC); *Kusum Ingots & Alloys Ltd.* v. *Pennar Peterson Securities Ltd.*, (2000) 2 SCC 745.

In this case though the company was declared sick but no restraint order was passed. BIFR passed directions to the petitioner company to make payment for the running of the day-to-day business of the company. Hence, the Magistrate has rightly taken cognizance under sections 138/141 of the Negotiable Instruments Act.

SECTION 138, THE NEGOTIABLE INSTRUMENT AND SECTION 536(2) OF THE COMPANIES ACT, 1956.

***Pankaj Mehra* v. *State of Maharashtra*, (2000) 2 SCC 756: 2000 SCC (Cri) 556: AIR 2000 SC 1953: 2000 Cr LJ 1781 SC**

Cases referred:

1987 (Supp) SCC 167; (1986) 59 Comp Cas 201 (Guj); (1984) 56 Comp Cas 19 (Bom); *Gray Inn Construction Company Ltd. (in re:)*, (1980) 1 All ER 814.

Facts of the case.—The issue raised was that after the commencement of winding up proceedings by the court under section 441(2) of the Companies Act, 1956, any disposition of the property after the commencement of winding-up proceedings, is void in terms of section 536(2) of the Act. The whole discussion was on the word "Void". *Held,* that the fact that petition for winding-up was presented prior to issuance of notice by payee to pay cheque amount would not extricate it from the offence under section 138 of the Negotiable Instruments Act. Word "void" in section 536 of the Companies Act does not mean void *ab initio* winding-up proceedings do not make company's debt unenforceable.

SECTION 138, THE NEGOTIABLE INSTRUMENTS ACT AND SECTION 28 OF PROVINCIAL INSOLVENCY ACT, 1920

***Srinivasa Trading Co.* v. *State of Andhra Pradesh,* (1997) 2 APLJ 418: (1997) 3 Civ LJ 752: 1998 Cr LJ 903 (AP)**

Cases referred:

(1994) 2 Andh LT 475; AIR 1960 Cal 469.

Facts of the case.—In this case the issue raised was that in view of section 446 of the Companies Act, 1956 and section 28 of the Provincial Insolvency Act, 1920, no suit or legal proceedings can be initiated with the leave of the court.

Held, that when the petitioners are not adjudicated as insolvents the question of taking permission from the court provided under section 28(2) of the Provincial Insolvency Act, 1920 does not arise. It does not apply to criminal proceedings and in proceedings initiated under section 138, the Negotiable Instruments Act.

***C.T. Thangaraj* v. *Marugesan,* (2000) 1 Civ LJ 79: (1999) 4 Rec Cri R 120: 1999 Cr LJ 3436 (Mad)**

Cases referred:

(1999) 2 Mad LW (Cri) 483; 1997 Cr LJ 717 (Cal); (1996) 1 Mad LW (Cri) 320; 1995 Cr LJ 1882 (Mad); 1994 Mad LJ (Cri) 706; AIR 1985 SC 582: (1985) 1 SCC 591; (1911) 35 Bom 63.

Facts of the case.—The issue raised is that once the Insolvency Petition filed covering the dishonoured cheque amount, is initiated, the complaint under section 138, the Negotiable Instruments Act is not maintainable. *Held,* that mere presentation or pendency of Insolvency petition would not disentitle complainant to seek for remedy by way of penal action. Hence proceedings initiated for dishonour of cheque cannot be quashed.

***Onkar Nath Goenka* v. *M/s. Gujarat Lease Finance Ltd.,* 2009 (2) JCC (NI) 109 (Del)**

In this case Bank accounts were frozen by an order of CBI wherein no operations were allowed and that the Debts Recovery Tribunal (Delhi) had already restrained the alienation of all movable and immovable assets of the petitioner and the accused company. Learned Metropolition Magistrate discharged the accused. Revision against discharge was also allowed. Hence the present petition. *Held,* that by the order of CBI as well as DRT, the petitioner is debarred from complying with the legal notice dated 13-7-1998, which led to the dishonour of cheques. The impugned complaint arraigning the petitioner for the offence under section 138 of the Negotiable Instruments Act is bad in law and is hereby quashed.

SECTION 138, THE NEGOTIABLE INSTRUMENTS ACT AND PARTNERSHIP ACT, 1932

***Anil Kumar Singh* v. *Kanak Prabha Datta,* 2003 All LJ 2015: (2003) 2 BC 557: (2003) 2 Crimes 427: 2003 Cr LJ 4078 (All)**

Facts of the case.—This case was discussed in the right of section 45 of the Partnership Act, 1932 along with sections 43, 63, 72 of the said Act which deal with dissolution of partnership. Section 45 of the said Act says that the liability of the partners continued even after dissolution of the partnership unless the public notice is given and mode of giving public notice is given under section 42 of the Act. Thus, when the retirement of the revisionist or dissolution of partnership has not been made in accordance with law nor any public notice is given, then the revisionist or any of the partners cannot be exonerated from the liability. The revision petition lacks merit and is dismissed.

***R. Raj Gopal* v. *S.S. Venkat,* (2001) 10 SCC 91: AIR 2001 SC 2432: 2001 Cr LJ 4936 (SC)**

Cases referred: AIR 2000 SC 145: (2001) 1 SCC 1.

Facts of the case.—It is a case in which the Partnership firm is not made the accused but only one of the partners. The Supreme Court in view of AIR 2000 SC 145 *held* that the law has been well-settled in the cited case. In the result the impugned order of the High Court is set aside and directed the trial court to proceed with the matter.

Note.—*The prosecution can be launched against the partners even without initiating prosecution against the firm.*

***B.N. Mehta* v. *Kapoor Agencies,* (2004) 1 BC 99: 2003 Cr LJ 2611 (HP)**

Cases referred:

AIR 2001 SC 2432: (2001) 10 SCC 91; AIR 2000 SC 145: (2000) 1 SCC 1: 2000 Cr LJ 373: (2000) 1 KLT 141; (2000) 6 Scale 578; (1999) 97 Comp Cas 922 (Mad) (dissented from); 1997 Cr LJ 1595 (AP); 1995 Cr LJ 1102 (Mad); 1992 Banking Cases 361 (Mad); AIR 1984 SC 1824: (1984) 4 SCC 352: 1984 SCC (Cri) 620; AIR 1971 SC 447: (1970) 3 SCC 491.

Facts of the case.—The cheque was issued by Super Bazar which is a Co-operative Society. The cheque was issued by accused in his capacity as General Manager of Super Bazar. Super Bazar/Co-operative Society, was not impleaded as co-accused. Relying on AIR 2001 SC 2432 (2001 Cr LJ 4936), *held* that if company is not prosecuted for any reason, the other persons can be prosecuted and cannot escape from the penal liability created through the legal fiction under section 141 of the Act. In result, the petitions fall and are dismissed.

***A.N. Nadarajan* v. *K.C. Nadarajan*, (1999) 3 Crimes 527: (1999) 1 Ker LJ 660: (1999) 2 KLT 512: 1999 Cr LJ 2472 (Ker)**

Cases referred:

(1994) 1 Ker LT 947; 1969 Ker LR 659; *Victorian Daylessford Syndicate Ltd.* v. *Dott.*, (1905) 2 Ch 624: 54 WR 231.

Facts of the case.—It was a case of Chit Fund transaction and the issue raised was under section 23 of the Contract Act, that the Private Chitti conducted by the respondent without obtaining permission from the Government or from the competent authority and without registering under the Chitties Act in contravention of the provisions of the Chitties Act is illegal and void and therefore, the consideration (cheques) is illegal under section 23 of the Contract Act and that the cheques are not issued to discharge a legally enforceable debt or other liability to attract the provisions of section 138 of the Act. The High Court referred to various other such similar Acts like Travancore Chitties Act, Cochin Kuries Act and Kerala Chitties Act, 1975. The High Court also referred to the legal position as stated by Anson in his *Law of Contract*, 19th Edn., page 206 and *held* the drawer of cheque liable under section 138 of the Act and also *held* that chitti transaction without obtaining permission from Government and without registering same is not void or immoral or opposed to Public Policy and as such the cheques issued and dishonoured fall within the ambit of section 138 of the Negotiable Instruments Act.

***Mohd. Isaq Gulsani* v. *J. Raja Mouli*, (2001) 2 BC 558: (2001) Bank J 734: 2001 Cr LJ 522 (AP)**

Cases referred:

AIR 2000 SC 145: (2000) 1 SCC 1: 2000 Cr LJ 373; AIR 1999 SC 2182: (1999) 5 SCC 693: 1999 Cr LJ 3498; 1999 Cr LJ 4865; 1997 Cr LJ 1595.

Facts of the case.—It is a case where the cheque was issued by the accused in the capacity of the President of the society. The society was not arrayed as party in the complaint as accused. *Held,* that the case falls under section 138 read with section 141 of the Act. The President of the Society is independently also liable. So omission to array the society cannot make the president to escape from the liability on that score. The criminal petition is dismissed.

***Amit Desai* v. *Shine Enterprises*, (2000) 3 CCC 60: (2000) 4 ICC 224: 2000 Cr LJ 2386 (AP)**

Cases referred:

(1999) 4 Crimes 98 (Ker) (dissented from); (1998) 8 SCC 559; AIR 1998 SC 3085; AIR 1989 SC 1769: (1989) 3 SCC 476; AIR 1975 Ker 144.

Facts of the case.—It is a case where section 69(2) of the Partnership Act, 1932 was discussed. The said partnership was not registered so by virtue of section 69(2), no suits to enforce a right arising from a contract shall be instituted in any court by or on behalf of a firm against any third party unless the firm is registered and the persons suing are or have been shown in the Register of Firms as partners in the firm. In this case the complainant is an unregistered firm. The contention raised was that the complainant is not maintainable because of the fact that the complainant firm is not registered under section 69(2) of the Partnership Act, 1932. *Held,* that the complaint is not maintainable.

***Gurcharan Singh* v. *State of Uttar Pradesh,* 2002 All LJ 1832: (2002) 3 BC 164: (2002) 4 Crimes 165: 2002 Cr LJ 3682 (All)**

Cases referred:

AIR 2000 SC 926: (2000) 2 SCC 737: 2000 Cr LJ 1424; 2000 Cr LJ 2386 (AP); (1999) 2 Ker LT 634; AIR 1975 Ker 144.

Facts of the case.—In this case three issues were raised:—

(i) The complaint so filed is not properly constituted.

(ii) The goods supplied were of sub-standard and hence not entitled to payment.

(iii) The firm being unregistered cannot file the complaint to recover the amount [section 69(2) of the Partnership Act].

Held, that even accepting the view of the learned counsel that the firm is not registered firm, yet the bar created by section 69 of the Partnership Act has no application for maintaining a complaint under section 138, the Negotiable Instruments Act. The petition is dismissed.

Note.—*The decision in 2000 Cr LJ 2386 (AP) was delivered by a Division Bench wherein it is held that complaint under section 138 is not maintainable in view of section 69(2) of the Partnership Act. But in the later decision of Allahabad High Court in 2002 Cr LJ 3682 (All) delivered by Single Bench Judge, it is held that the complaint is maintainable. The High Court relied upon the decision of the Supreme Court.*

***Madan Aggarwal* v. *State,* 2006 (3) JCC (NI) 193 (Del)**

Cases referred:

2005 (8) SCC 89; 121 (2005) DLT 431; 113 (2004) DLT 356; AIR 2004 SC 4274; 83 (2000) DLT 75; 80 (1999) DLT 654; 2006 (1) AD (Del) 457; 2006 (1) SCC 122; 2002 (8) SCC 236.

Held, that even a notice sent to one partner operates as notice to firm and other partners and ignorance as a plea of non-receipt of notice cannot be set up as a defence. Section 141 does not require each and every partner of the firm is to be issued with notice.

***Sri Vijyalaxmi Agencies, Nandyal, Kurnool District* v. *State of Andhra Pradesh,* 2006 (3) JCC (NI) 270 (AP)**

Case referred:

2005 (2) ALD (Cri) 595.

Cheque was issued on behalf of the partnership firm. There is mere averment that accused 2 to 5 who are partners, are actively involved in the day-to-day affairs of the firm. No specific role is attributed to accused Nos. 2, 4 and 5. *Held,* accused Nos. 2, 4 and 5 cannot be held liable and cannot be tried. The firm is liable because the cheques were issued by the managing partner on behalf of the firm.

***Major L.K. Toshkhani (Retd)* v. *Ravi Kumar*, 2007 (2) JCC (NI) 121 (Del)**

Cases referred

2004 (7) SCC 15; 2005 (8) SCC 89; 1994 Cr LJ 3115.

Held: The complaint ought to disclose specifically the role of the accused/ partner in order to fasten vicarious liability. In this case too the complaint had not disclosed to the petitioner, who was admittedly not a signatory to the cheque, was responsible to the firm or involved in the sense that he was in control of its affairs. Proceedings in the complaint are hereby quashed.

***Smt. Pratima Sharma* v. *M/s. Cartel Finance and Investments Pvt. Ltd.*, 2007 (4) JCC (NI) 392 (Del)**

Cases referred:

Monaben Katenbhai Shah v. *State of Gujarat*, (2004) 7 SCC 15; *K.P.G. Nair* v. *Jindal Menthol India Ltd.*, (2001) 10 SCC 218; *Katta Sujatha* v. *Fertilizers and Chemicals Travancore Ltd.*, (2002) 7 SCC 655.

Held: Position of Directors of a company is distinct from that of the partners of a partnership firm. A Director may or may not be liable for the conduct of the business of a company unless under the Article of Association of a Company it has been provided to the contra or by a Board Resolution a Director is made responsible for the conduct of business of a company but in a partnership firm the rule is to the contrary. Unless the partnership deed provides to the contrary every partner has a right in law to conduct the business of the partnership firm. Further under section 18 of the Partnership Act a partner is the agent of the firm for the purpose of the business of the firm. A director is not treated as an agent of the company. Section 141 speaks of vicarious liability and it has to be shown as to in what manner he was incharge and responsible for the conduct of business of the partnership firm.

***J.P.S. Sandhu* v. *M/s. Patiala Auto Enterprises*, 2008 (2) JCC (NI) 158 (P&H)**

Cases referred:

2000 (1) RCR (Criminal) 1 (SC); 2000 (1) RCR (Criminal) 565; 1999 (4) RCR (Criminal) 40; 2007 (1) Raj 205 SC; 2007 (2) Raj *** (SC): 2007 (1) JCC (NI) 112.

Respondent No. 3 posed himself as managing partner and took responsibility in all respect on behalf of everyone. The fact that the respondent No. 3 resigned would not be of any consequence. He cannot be permitted to escape from the responsibility arising out dishonour of the cheque.

Also refer:

Sunita Vijyakumar Deshpande v. *M/s. Mithan Lal Marketing Ltd.*, 2008 (2) JCC (NI) 124 Del; *M/s. Alfa Graphics* v. *Mr. Arjun Kohli*, 2008 (1) JCC (NI) 98 (Del).

***Shankar Lal Sharda* v. *The State NCT of Delhi*, 2008 (1) JCC (NI) 65 (Del)**

Case referred:

2000 (2) JCC 485.

In this case a winding-up order of the company was passed by the Punjab and Haryana High Court and all the disputed cheques were payable after that date.

So none of the accused could be held responsible for dishonour of cheques. *Held,* that a person incurs liability only under section 138 of the Negotiable Instruments Act if the act or omission is attributable to him.

***Southern Steel Ltd.* v. *Jindal Vijyanagar Steel Ltd.*, 2008 (2) JCC (NI) 231 (SC)**

Cases referred:

(2000) 2 SCC 737; (2000) 2 SCC 745.

Purchases were made after the appellant declared sick under the SICA. It is a case of *mala fide* intention of the company. It is not a case where the appellants are entitled to any indulgence of the Supreme Court under its extraordinary jurisdiction under Article 136 of the Constitution of India. The purchases were made holding out clear representation that the goods will be paid for.

***Aditya Goel* v. *State NCT of Delhi*, 2009 (2) JCC (NI) 117 (Del)**

Since the issue is of the maintainability of the complaint, the complaints should be heard at the pre-summoning stage and that no issue except maintainability shall be raised.

***R.L. Verma* v. *J.K. Verma*, 2007 (4) JCC (NI) 410 (Del).**

Cases referred:

JT 2007 (9) SCC 449; 2007 (2) SCALE 36; 139 (2007) DLT 361; 121 (2005) DLT 353; 121 (2005) DLT 431; AIR 2007 SC 1682.

Co-accused is H.U.F. against whom no basis was laid down in the complaint. Complaint is not maintainable against it.

***Standard Chartered Bank* v. *State*, 2007 (4) JCC (NI) 321 (Del)**

Banker's cheque was issued due to negligence as the account of the customer was lawfully attached by the competent authority. Summoning order on the basis of "Tort of negligence" is not maintainable.

***M.L. Gupta* v. *M/s. Ceat Financial Services Ltd.*, 2007 (1) JCC (NI) 18 Del**

Cases referred:

2000 Cr LJ 373; 2000 Cr LJ 1781 (SC); AIR 2003 SC 4172; (2000) 100 Comp Cas 755 (SC); (2001) 6 SCC 16.

The cheque was issued by the company *prior to its liquidation.*

Held, that on the date of presentation of cheque the company being in liquidation, the Managing Director and Director of the company are not being incharge of day-to-day affairs and conduct of business of the company. This case does not fall under the ambit of sections 138/141 of the Negotiable Instruments Act.

SECTION 138 OF THE NEGOTIABLE INSTRUMENTS ACT AND PROPRIETORSHIP CONCERN

***Raghu Luxminarayanan* v. *M/s. Fine Tubes*, 2007 (2) JCC (NI) 137 SC**

Cases referred:

(1998) 5 SCC 567; AIR 2005 SC 3512; AIR 2006 SC 3086; 2007 (3) SCALE 245.

It is held that a proprietorship concern is neither a partnership firm nor a company. The employee of the proprietorship concern cannot be held vicariously liable in view of section 141 of the Negotiable Instruments Act.

***Saheb Singh* v. *State (NCT of Delhi)*, 2008 (2) JCC (NI) 118 (Del)**

Cases referred:

2003 SCC (Cri) 603; 2002 Cr LJ 3935.

It is a case under section 482, the Cr. P.C., where the issue is a triable one that whether M/s. JEE is sole proprietorship concern or a partnership concern and it can be decided after recording evidence, the petition under section 482, the Cr. P.C. is not maintainable.

***Devendra Pundir* v. *Rajender Prasad Maurya*, 2008 Cr LJ 777**

Case referred:

2007 Cr LJ 2436 (rely. on).

First accused is admittedly a sole proprietrix of the concern who issued the cheque. Allegation that the husband of the first accused is actively participating and conducting the business is also vicariously liable. *Held,* that in a proprietorship, there is vicarious liability.

SECTION 141 AND MISCELLANEOUS ASPECTS

PUBLIC SERVANT

***K. Suresh* v. *M/s. Lloyds Finance Ltd.*, 2008 (2) JCC (NI) 145 (Del)**

Cheque was given by the Managing Director, Chief Account Officer, and Account Officer of M.P.S.R.T.C. The petitioner is the Managing Director having been appointed to that post in his capacity as I.A.S. officer. So he is a Public Servant under section 21, the IPC 1860. Prior sanction under section 197, the Cr. P.C. is mandatory before taking cognizance of the case under section 138, of the Negotiable Instruments Act. The order passed by the Ld. M.M. summoning the petitioner is set aside.

HINDU UNDIVIDED FAMILY

***Dada Saheb Rawal Co-op Bank of Dondoicha Ltd.* v. *Ramesh Jawarilal Jain*, AIR 2009 (NOC) 127 (Bom)**

Cheque issued by a firm of Hindu Undivided Family. Joint family business must be deemed a juristic person like company or firm and hence is covered under section 141 of the Negotiable Instruments Act. Term "Association of individuals" will include Hindu Undivided Family Business.

SOCIETY

***J.B. Garg* v. *State*, 2006 (3) JCC (NI) 245 (Del)**

Cases referred:

2005 (3) JCC (NI) 203 (SC); (2004) 7 SCC 15.

Petitioner No. 2 is the secretary of the society (Accused No. 1) which issued the cheque. Petitioner No. 2 is impleaded merely on the ground that he is the secretary of the society without specifying his role being incharge or responsible for conduct of the business of the society. The summoning order *qua* the petitioner is quashed.

SECTION 141 (PROVISO)

***V.K. Saxena* v. *State,* 2006 (3) JCC (NI) 251 (Del)**

It is a case under second proviso. Petitioner is accused No. 9 in the complaint. He is the General Manager of IDBI and since IDBI extended financial assistance to the accused company, the petitioner was nominated as Director of the accused company. He cannot be dragged by virtue of the proviso.

***Sham Sadashiv Wagh* v. *M/s. Muley Constructions Pvt. Ltd.,* AIR 2009 (NOC) 123 (Bom)**

It is a case of nominated Director, nominated by IDBI to oversee affairs of the company. He is not directly concerned with financial affairs of the company. He cannot be held vicariously liable.

Note.—*(1) Prosecution against a proprietary concern is not maintainable as it does not fall within the definition of "Person" but prosecution against the proprietor is maintainable.*

(2) The prosecution can be launched against a juristic person like a company, body corporate, etc.

(3) The prosecution proceedings can be initiated against the person incharge of and responsible to the company for the conduct of its business.

(4) The prosecution proceedings can be initiated against a person with whose consent or connivance of an act attributable to or due to any neglect on their part.

(5) The prosecution proceedings can be issued against the company or the persons incharge of and responsible for the conduct of the business of the company or both.

(6) Three categories of people are brought within the purview of the penal liability, i.e.,

(a) The company which committed the offence.

(b) Every one who was incharge of and was responsible for the business of the company.

(c) Any other person who is a Director, or a Manager a Secretary or other officer of the company with whose connivance or due to whose neglect the company has committed the offence.

(7) There is no need of issuing notice to each and every person involved. Notice to the company is enough to rope in other persons provided there is allegation in the complaint against that person.

(8) There is no need of detailed mention of the ingredients of the section but mere mention of the person incharge of and responsible to the company for its business is sufficient.

(9) Section 482, the Cr. P.C. is applicable only when the complaint is glaringly clear that the facts are vague and ambiguous but if there are disputed facts, the complaint is not maintainable.

(10) The person, accused, has an escape route if his case falls in the proviso to section 141 but it is to be established that he is not incharge of and not responsible to the company for its business.

(11) The second proviso to section 141 gives immunity to the nominated Directors. They shall not be liable to prosecution under this Chapter inserted by Act 55 of 2000 (w.e.f. 6-2-2003).

(12) Section 141 is all pervading and embraces in its grip all those deemed to be held liable either under sub-section (1) or sub-section (2).

CHAPTER V

COMPETENCY OF COURT – ITS POWERS AND COGNIZANCE OF OFFENCES

142. Cognizance of offences.—Notwithstanding anything contained in the Code of Criminal Procedure, 1973 (2 of 1974)—

(a) no court shall take cognizance of any offence punishable under section 138 except upon a complaint, in writing, made by the payee or, as the case may be, the holder in due course of the cheque;

(b) such complaint is made within one month of the date on which the cause-of-action arises under clause (c) of the proviso to section 138:

Provided that the cognizance of a complaint may be taken by the Court after the prescribed period, if the complainant satisfies the Court that he had sufficient cause for not making a complaint within such period.

(c) no court inferior to that of a Metropolitan Magistrate or a Judicial Magistrate of the first class shall try any offence punishable under section 138.

INTRODUCTION

Section 142 speaks of cognizance of offences—and the expression used there is "Notwithstanding anything contained in the Code of Criminal Procedure, 1973 (2 of 1974)".

Non Obstante Clause: This expression "Notwithstanding" means "*Non obstante* clause". It means that the provision given herein shall prevail over any other provision and that other provision shall not be of any consequence. Even if there is any inconsistency or departure in other provisions given in the same Act, the provision with "*Non obstante* clause" would prevail over the other provision.

In *Lalu Parshad* v. *State of Bihar*, AIR 1986 All 303, it is said that the effect of "*Non obstante* clause" is well-known. It overrides all other provisions in the same Act or in any other enactment.

In *Aswini Kumar Ghosh* v. *Arabinda Bose*, AIR 1952 SC 369: 1953 SCR 1, the Supreme Court said about "*Non Obstante* Clause" as follows:—

"It should first be ascertained what the enacting part of the section provides on a fair construction of the words used according to their natural and ordinary meaning and the *non obstante* Clause is to be understood as operating to set aside as no longer valid anything contained in relevant existing laws which is inconsistent with the new enactment. The *non obstante* Clause can reasonably be read as overriding "anything contained" in any relevant existing law which is inconsistent with the new enactment, although the draftsman appears to have had primarily in his mind a particular type of law as conflicting with the new Act."

In *Krishan Bhagwan* v. *State,* AIR 1989 Pat 217 (FB), it is said that the effect of a section having a *non obstante* Clause on the other provisions of the same Act is "of setting at naught and of obliterating" such other provisions.

The issue of section 142, the Negotiable Instruments Act particularly arose in *Plywood House* v. *Woodcraft Products Ltd.,* 1994 Cr LJ 543 (Ker) wherein section 4(2), the Cr. P.C. was referred. Section 4(2) of the Code requires that all offences under any law, other than the Indian Penal Code, shall also be enquired into or tried or otherwise dealt with according to the provisions of the Code, subject to any other enactments which require a different mode of trial for such offence. The *non obstante* Clause in section 142 of the Act is intended to make it clear that the three matters specified in the section have overriding effect on the provisions of the Code. The clause does not keep the provisions of the Code away from trial or enquiry into the offence under section 138 of the Act as for all other purposes. All that section 142 restricts is that in taking cognizance of the offence under section 138 a written complaint (made by either the payee or holder in due course) within one month of the cause-of-action envisaged in clause (c) of the section is *sine qua non,* whatever be the provisions of the Code. The contention that the *non obstante* Clause in section 142 is intended to sweep out all the provisions of the Code, bell, book and candle is, therefore, unsound and unsustainable.

Complaint: The other expression used is "Complaint in writing". Complaint has been defined in section 2(d), the Cr. P.C. which says:—"Complaint" means any allegation made orally or in writing to a Magistrate with a view to his taking action under this Code, that some person whether known, or unknown, has committed an offence but does not include a police report.

It is to be noted that the words used "allegation made orally" have been omitted in section 142(a) of the Negotiable Instruments Act. The word "Magistrate" used in the definition in the Code has been replaced in section 142(c) of the Act by "No court inferior to that of a Metropolitan Magistrate or a Judicial Magistrate of the first class" similarly the word "that some person, whether known or unknown" appears in the definition in the Code, does not find place in section 142(a) of the Act. Here the "person is known and called Drawer of the cheque" against whom the complaint is to be made. Thus the constituents of the complaint as per section 142 of the Act are:—

(1) A written allegation.

(2) Made by the Payee or the holder in due course, as the case may be.

(3) It is against the drawer of the cheque which is bounced.

(4) It is to be made to the Metropolitan Magistrate or a Judicial Magistrate of the first class, as the case may be.

(5) It must be made with the object that he should take action.

Payee: The complaint is to be made by the payee, and payee has been defined in section 7 of the Negotiable Instruments Act. A Negotiable Instrument is the off-spring of a unique type of contract which takes the shape of a "Tripartite Contract", a contract between three parties, a drawer, drawee and a payee. The person named in the cheque to whom the amount of cheque is payable is the "payee" or the "holder".

Holder in due course: It is defined in section 9 of the Negotiable Instruments Act. It has four constituents:

(i) He should be a holder for consideration.

(ii) He is a transferee in good faith.

(iii) The instrument must have been transferred to him before it becomes overdue.

(iv) The transferee should not have any reason to believe that there was any defect in the title of the transferor.

[*See* (1990) 3 CCC 402 (SC)].

CASE LAW

***P.K. Koya Moideen* v. *G. Hariharan*, (1996) 86 Comp Cas 399: 1996 Cr LJ 3153 (Ker)**

Section 9 of the Negotiable Instruments Act, *i.e.*, "Holder in due course" was discussed. The facts are that a cheque was drawn in the name of complainant's father. Subsequently the father died. The complainant claimed payment in capacity of executor of father's will. There is nothing to show that he paid any consideration to his father to claim payment. Genuineness of the Will is also to be adjudicated. The Judicial First Class Magistrate took cognizance of the case. Against this the matter was taken to the High Court and the issue was that the complainant is not a "holder in due course". The High Court referred to sections 7 and 9 of the Negotiable Instruments Act and found that the complainant is neither a "payee" nor a "holder in due course" as the Will made by the father of the respondent is not produced. *Held*, that the executor of the Will cannot be treated as the "holder in due course."

***Mahesh Goyal* v. *S.K. Sharma*, (1997) 2 CCC 522: (1997) 2 BC 273: 1997 Cr LJ 2868 (P&H): 1997 All LJ 1000**

Case referred:

(1995) 84 Comp Cas 782 (Kant)

Facts of the case.—It is a case under section 138, the Negotiable Instruments Act where in section 9 of the said Act was discussed. It is a case where the cheque was drawn by the drawer in his own name. So it is a self drawn cheque and as such section 138 is not attracted. The learned trial Magistrate took cognizance of the case and issued summoning order. Against this order the matter was taken to the High Court, wherein section 9 of the Act was discussed along with section 118(a) of the Act (Refer AIR 1961 SC 1316; AIR 1988 Cal 59). It was a self drawn cheque and the word "bearer" is not deleted. As per material on record shows that the said cheque was given for valid consideration and it was in possession of the respondent who complied with all the requirements as provided in proviso to section 138 and section 142(b) of the Act. *Held,* that the respondent is a "holder in due course" for valid consideration.

***D.M. Bhattav* v. *State Bank of Bikaner and Jaipur,* (2002) 2 BC 427: (2002) 5 Bom CR 280: (2002) 4 Crimes 354: 2002 Cr LJ 4851 (Bom)**

Cases referred:

AIR 1991 SC 441: (1991) 1 SCC 113: (1991) 70 Comp Cas 1; (1894) ILR 17 Mad 461; (1888) ILR 11 Mad 290.

Facts of the case.—In this case cheques were issued by a fictitious firm. Petitioner was shown as Director of the said firm. In all 11 fictitious firms were floated in order to cheat the bank. A criminal conspiracy was hatched out in collusion with some bank officials and a case was filed by CBI. The accused pleaded for discharge. The bank in its reply stated that the said cheques were purchased for consideration and the amount was credited to the account of the said firm and thus the complainant bank is a holder in due course. Section 9 of the Negotiable Instruments Act was discussed and the court came to the conclusion that the complainant Bank is holder in due course. This conclusion is based on the fact that case instituted by CBI pertains to opening of fictitious account in the Bank and does not pertain to 10 cheques which were dishonoured. These are the cheques that have been purchased by the Bank for consideration. This Bank is a holder in due course.

***Sangothu Narsimha Chary* v. *V. Raghunath,* 1 (2005) CCR 329**

The issue in this case is that the cheque was in the name of "Rachna Refrigeration". There is no indication in the complaint as to who Raghunath is who has filed the complaint. So Raghunath is neither the payee nor the holder in due course and thus the case militates against section 142 and Penal Statute has to be strictly construed. The petition is allowed and that the respondent is not entitled to prosecute the petitioner.

***Fragrant Leasing and Finance Company Ltd.* v. *Jagdish Katuria,* 2008 (1) JCC (NI) 67 (All)**

It is a case under sections 138 and 142 of the Negotiable Instruments Act. In this case three issues were agitated.

(i) Carbon Copy of notice was not filed and instead photo copy of the notice was filed. Accused admitted to have received the notice and had made a reply thereto. The complaint was dismissed on the ground of lack of proof of notice. The High Court found it not justified.

(ii) The complaint as filed by an employee of the company without filing letter authorizing him to file the complaint on behalf of the company. *Held;* such defect is curable and can be removed at a later stage by fining such letter.

(iii) Change of date in the dishonoured cheque is a material alteration. Burden lies on the complainant to prove that change of date was made with the consent of the accused which is missing here.

***K. Vasantha Kumari* v. *D. Devendra Reddy*, 2008 Cr LJ 1001 (Kant).**

In this case five issues were agitaled. They are:—

(i) The complaint is in the name of the payee only. Contents of the complaint are in relation to payee but complaint has been signed by deed of the power-of-attorney granted by the payee. Complaint is maintainable.

(ii) The issue is regarding non-registration of firm. *Held,* that the complaint is not liable to be dismissed for want of registration of the firm.

(iii) The fact of issue of cheques and execution of demand promissory note by the accused to sufficient to drawn the presumption under Section 139 of the Negotiable Instruments Act the burden of rebuttal is on the accused.

(iv) When the notice is sent on the correct address but not claimed by the accused, it is deemed to have been served.

(v) Compensation can be awarded with interest and costs also incurred by the complainant. Fine may extend to double the amount of the cheque.

***Roy Joseph Creado* v. *S.K. Tanisuddin*, 2008 Cr LJ 1509 (Bom)**

The complaint was filed by the power-of-attorney holder but the same is not verified. The deed of power-of-attorney is also defective and as such the complaint is incomplete. In the meantime the payee expired when the complaint was still defective. It cannot be verified by the legal heir. The court cannot take cognizance of the defective complaint

***M/s. Signaps* v. *M/s. Bumpy Udyog*, 2009 (1) JCC (NI) 54 (Del)**

It is a petition to quash the proceedings under section 482 of the Cr. P.C. cheque in question was offered as security in terms of an agreement which expressly states that the agreement is valid for one year and further extention can only be by the mutual written consent of the parties. Nothing has been brought on record to show that there was any such mutual consent. As such the security cheques are not enforceable beyond the period of agreement. *Held,* that it would be a matter of evidence whether the cheque which was presented for payment was a blank cheque which was subsequently filled up by the complainant or in fact issued by the accused after the expiry of the agreement. There were the disputed facts which cannot be resolved in proceedings under section 482 of the Cr. P.C. but will have to await trial.

***Suresh Sharma* v. *M/s. New Coolwell Industries*, 2009 (2) JCC (NI) 85 (Del)**

In this case the complaint was filed by the Manager of the firm in his personal capacity without filing the complaint for and on behalf of the payee or the holder in due course. Thus the appellant is not the payee of the cheque. The firm had not come forward either to file the complaint or to prove the authority of the Manager to file such complaint. Order to dismiss such a complaint is totally justified.

***Vijya Kapoor* v. *All Bank Finance Limited*, 2009 (2) JCC (NI) 97 (Del)**

This is a petition under section 482 of the Cr. P.C. for quashing of the proceedings. In this case the petitioner had resigned as Director of the company on 7-1-1993 and the Registrar of the Companies was informed on 25-9-1996. The cheques in question were post-dated cheques issued from March to August 2000. In view of the fact and the statement of respondent No. 1 that the appellant has been wrongly arrayed and has no objection if the complaint *qua* the petition is quashed. Complaint case *qua* the petition is quashed.

***National Small Industries Corporation Ltd.* v. *State (NCT Delhi)*, AIR 2009 SC 1284**

In this case the issue is whether the person who represents the company and is a public servant, has to examine in the criminal case before passing summoning order. The Apex Court held that where an incorporeal body is the payee and the employee who represents such incorporeal body in the complaint is a public servant, he being the *de facto* complainant. Clause (a) of proviso to Section 200 of the Code will be affected and consequently the Magistrate need not examine the complainant and the witnesses. The order of the High Court is set aside and the summoning order of the magistrate is restored case 2007 (1) JCC (NI) 69 is served.

Refer:

AIR 1998 SC 596. (Rely. on); AIR 1972 SC 2639; AIR 1970 SC 7. (Rely. on); AIR 1963 SC 1811.

***S.L. Construction* v. *Alapati Srinivasa Rao*, 2009 (1) JCC (NI) 12 (SC)**

In this case first notice was not served and the second notice had been withdrawn in terms of the reply issued by the learned advocate for the appellants themselves. Complainant cannot be said to have committed any illegality in presenting the cheque for the third time and issuing the third notice upon the defaulter. Issuance of a valid notice calling upon the drawer of the cheque to pay the amount in question and the appellant's failure to pay the amount in question within a period of 15 days from the date of receipt of a copy of the said notice upon them. A cause-of-action arose for filing a complaint petition. High Court cannot be said to have committed any error in passing the impugned order. Appeal is dismissed.

Section 142(a): It speaks that the court shall not take cognizance except upon a complaint, in writing, made by the payee or the holder in due course. The pertinent question arises is that the expression, "payee or the holder in due course", is to be interpreted and construed narrowly or in wider sense and thus a further question agitates the mind as to who can make a complaint for which we have to interpret this expression in the light of Judicial pronouncements.

***Prakash Chand* v. *State of Rajasthan*, 2010 (1) Crimes 430 (Raj)**

Cases referred:

Nalini Kumar Dey v. *State of Tripura*, AIR 1953 Tripura 4; *Rameshwar Lal* v. *Subhash Chandra*, 2006 (2) Cr LR 933; *Adalat Parshad* v. *Rooplal Jindal*, 2004 (7)

SCC 338; *N. Hariharan Iyer* v. *State of Kerala,* 2000 Cr LJ 1251; *Miriza Iqbal Hussain* v. *State of Uttar Pradesh,* AIR 1953 SC 60; *Pankajbhai Nagjibhai Patel* v. *State of Gujarat,* AIR 2001 SC 567.

In this case sections 161, 200, 202, 203, 204 of the Cr. P.C. and Sections 142 & 145 of the Negotiable Instruments Act were considered and held that section 200, the Cr. P.C. casts a duty on the Magistrate taking cognizance of an offence on complaint to examine upon oath the complainant and the witnesses present which is *sine qua non* for consideration of issue of process.

WHO CAN MAKE A COMPLAINT

***Manimekalai* v. *Chapaldas Kalyanji Sanghvi,* 1995 Cr LJ 1102 (Mad)**

In this case two issues were agitated:

(1) Power Agent cannot file a complaint.

(2) That the firm is not made the accused.

The High Court on the first point *held* that the payee represented by the Power Agent can very well file a complaint for offence under section 138 of the Act.

Note.—*See section 1A of the Power-of-Attorney Act, 1882 as inserted by the Powers-of-Attorney (Amendment) Act, 1982 (55 of 1982). See also section 2 of the said Act.*

***Satish Jayantilal Shaw* v. *Pankaj Mashruwala,* 1996 Cr LJ 3099 (Guj)**

The issue before the court was that the complainant is doing business in the name of proprietary concern "Asim Agencies" and the accused in the name of proprietary concern "Padmavati Sales Corporation". The cheques are issued by a proprietary concern to a proprietary concern and as such complaint cannot be filed in personal name as if any offence is committed. It is the proprietary concern which has committed the offence. So it is the proprietary concern who is the drawer of the cheque and it is the proprietary concern which is the payee.

The court rejected this contention stating that according to section 11 of the Indian Penal Code and section 3(42) of the General Clauses Act, any company or Association or body of persons is recognised as legal entity or juristic person. This definition does not include proprietor. Hence, a proprietary concern is not a legal entity or juristic person and thus, neither it can initiate any proceedings nor proceedings be initiated against it. In the case of proprietary concern it is the proprietor who can either indict or be indicted. As such in a proprietary concern, the proprietor is the payee or the accused as the case may be.

***S. Krishnamurthy* v. *A.R. Rajan,* (1996) 87 Comp Cas 212: 1996 Cr LJ 3552 (Mad)**

The issue before the court was that the cheque was in the name of the company but complaint was filed by the Managing Partner of the company who was authorised by the company to initiate the proceedings but the Managing Director is neither the payee nor a holder in due course. The contention raised is that the cheque is issued in the name of Mallur Jayalaxmi Finance and the complainant is A.R. Rajan. The High Court *held* that though the argument looks attractive at the first blush, a deep probe with reference to the oral and documentary evidence available in this case would expose that the contention raised is not correct. The Managing Partner is authorised to initiate proceedings on behalf of the company in the court of law. The contention raised has no merit.

***Mohan Lal Khemchand* v. *Pawan Kumar Mohanka*, 1996 Cr LJ 2927 (Cal)**

Cases referred:

1993 Cal Cri LR 225; AIR 1984 SC 718: (1984) 2 SCC 500: 1984 Cr LJ 647; AIR 1983 SC 67: (1983) 1 SCC 1: 1983 SCC (Cri) 115.

The issue was that "who can file the complaint". The cheque was in the name of Albert Devid Ltd., which was dishonoured. The complaint was filed by the Manager of the Company and the initiation of complaint by authorized agent is bad. It must be filed either by the payee or a holder in due course as the case may be. It is *held* that Albert Devid Ltd. is the holder in due course and is a juristic person and it must act through his officers.

***Payyati Savitri Devi* v. *Mali Reddy Damayantamma*, (1997) 4 Crimes 325: 1997 Cr LJ 3862 (AP)**

Cases referred:

1996 Cr LJ 3153 (Ker) (distinguished); 1995 Cr LJ 1102 (Mad); AIR 1914 Cal 429.

It is a revision against the order of the lower court whereby the lower court rejected the objection of the petitioner that the complaint is not maintainable being filed by a power-of-attorney holder. *Held*, that the complaint filed by the power-of-attorney holder is not maintainable and the decision of the Kerala High Court 1996 Cr LJ 3153 (Ker) was distinguished by referring to sections 198A and 199, the Cr. P.C.

***Swastika Coaters Pvt. Ltd.* v. *Deepak Brothers*, (1997) 89 Comp Cas 564: (1997) 2 BC 569: (1997) 2 Civ LJ 535: 1997 Cr LJ 1942 (AP)**

Cases referred:

Satish & Co. v. *S.R. Traders*, Criminal Appeal No. 180 of 1995 dated 28-11-1996 (AP).

The issue is that the cheque was in the name of the company but the complaint was filed by a Director of the company. A Director of a company cannot be a holder in due course and as such he cannot file a complaint. However, if he is properly authorised then he can file the complaint. In this case he admitted that there is no authorisation or resolution authorising him to file the complaint. *Held*, the complaint is not maintainable.

***Anil G. Shaw* v. *I.J. Chitranjan Co.*, (1998) 2 Crimes 374: (1998) 1 Guj LR 303: 1998 Cr LJ 3870 (Guj)**

Cases referred:

(1996) 2 BLLR 482 (P&H); (1995) 1 Guj LR 424; (1994) 1 BCLR 159; (1992) 3 Crimes 666 (followed); 1989 Cr LJ 1856 (J&K) (followed); 1984 Cr LJ 1326 (AP) (followed); 1984 Cr LJ 1 (SC); AIR 1956 SC 604: (1956) SCR 577: (1956) 30 ITR 163; AIR 1937 Nag 65; (1986) 35 Ch D 162, *Jackson & Co.* v. *Napper*; (1873) 8 QB 305, *Queen* v. *Justice of Kent*.

Facts of the case.—In this case the complaint is filed by power-of-attorney of payee, which was assailed as being hit by section 142(a) of the Negotiable Instruments Act. There was wide discussion on section 2 of the Power-of-Attorney Act (7 of 1882) and various authorities like Black's *Law Dictionary* and Broom's *Legal Maxims* were looked into and it was *Held,* that the complaint can be filed by the power-of-attorney of payee.

***Satish and Company* v. *S.R. Traders,* (1997) 2 Bank CLR 63: 1998 Bank J 400: 1998 Cr LJ 419 (AP)**

Cases referred:

(1984) 80 Comp Cas 558 (Mad); (1994) 1 Crimes 820 (Mad); (1994) 4 Cu Cri R 2374 (Mad); (1992) 1 Mad WN (Cri) 236 (dissented from); AIR 1991 Del 25; AIR 1991 (P&H) 185; AIR 1990 (Ker) 84.

Facts of the case.—The complaint was filed by Satish and Company represented by its Manager, Mr. N.K. Gupta on 20-7-1993 and his authorization letter was filed after one year and the authorisation letter was dated 17-6-1993. The issue was that what was the position of the Manager as on 20-7-1993 when the complaint was filed. The case was discussed in the light of sections 141, 142(a), 26, 27 of the Negotiable Instruments Act and Order XXIX, rule 1 of the CPC and *held* that a Manager of the company can file the complaint if properly authorised or vested with such power, otherwise not as he is neither a payee nor a holder in due course and any letter of authorisation filed after the cognizance of the complaint is taken, cannot cure the defect and hence the Criminal Appeal is dismissed.

***Credential Finance Ltd.* v. *State of Maharashtra,* (2001) 105 Comp Cas 864: 1999 Cr LJ 1032 (Bom)**

Cases referred:

1998 Cr LJ 700 (Guj) (Relied on); (1997) 4 APMR Journal 58 (distinguished); (1996) 86 Comp Cas 265 (P&H) (relied on); (1995) 1 Crimes 203 (Bom); (1994) 4 Bom CR 237; (1993) 77 Comp Cas 253 (Bom); (1991) 73 Comp Case 494 (Ker); (1974) 1 Crimes 820 (Mad); AIR 1960 SC 576: (1960) 2 SCR 739: 1960 Cr LJ 752 (SC).

Facts of the case.—The complaint was filed by the company through its Manager. No evidence was produced as to his authorisation to file the complaint along with complaint. The issue raised is that such a complaint is maintainable in the absence of authorisation of the Manager to file the complaint. It was *held* that a Manager or the Managing Director of the Company ordinarily by the nomenclature can be taken to be the person incharge of the affairs of the company for its day-to-day management and within that activity would certainly be calling the act of approaching the court either under civil law or criminal law for staying the trial in motion. It would be too technical and narrow a view to take that in the body of the complaint the authority is not elaborated upon and along with documents annexed to the complaint the authorisation is not produced and further *held* that neither the said Act nor the Companies Act, 1956 imposes a pre-condition that there has to be an authorisation as per statutory provisions. All that can be insisted upon is the existence of authorisation. In absence of it being a pre-condition, in the event of dispute, it will become a subject-matter of proof to be adduced at the time of trial and not at the time of taking cognizance of the case.

***A. Krishnan* v. *S.P. Kumar,* (2001) 106 Comp Cas 694: 2001 Cr LJ 3494 (Mad)**

Cases referred:

1998 Cr LJ 419 (AP) (dissented from); (1997) 2 Mad LW (Cr) 637; 1997 Cr LJ 1942 (AP); 1995 Cr LJ 254 (P&H); (1992) 1 Mad LW Notes (Cri) 236 (relied on); (1991) 1 Mad LW (Cri) 297.

Facts of the case.—In this case the complaint has been filed on behalf of the company, not only as a Manager, but also on the authorisation given by both the Managing Partner and the Partner of the company through the registered power-of-attorney. The High Court did not agree with the decision of Andhra Pradesh High Court in 1998 Cr LJ 419 (AP) and relied upon (1992) 1 Mad LW Notes (Cri) 236 and *held* that the complaint is maintainable.

***Pritama Reddy* v. *Charminar Co-operative Urban Bank Ltd.,* (2001) 105 Comp Cas 560: (2001) 2 CCC 318: (2001) 2 Crimes 365: 2001 Cr LJ 2178 (AP)**

Cases referred:

(2000) 4 ALD 544; (2000) 2 ALD (Cri) 458; (1999) 1 ALD (Cri) 745; (1997) 2 Crimes 115; (1995) 3 SCC 276: 1995 SCC (Cri) 503; 1993 Cr LJ 1974 (AP); AIR 1948 Mad 369; AIR 1914 Cal 479.

Facts of the case.—The complaint was filed by the Recovery Manager of the Bank who was authorised by the Managing Director of the Bank by executing special power-of-attorney. The issue was that whether Recovery Manager is authorised to file a complaint as being neither a payee nor a holder in due course. At the time of filing the complaint his power-of-attorney was filed but Board Resolution was made available at the time of the hearing. It was contended that the power-of-attorney given by the Managing Director is no authority without the Board Resolution and as such the complaint is not maintainable. *Held* that special power-of-attorney executed by the Managing Director in favour of the Recovery officer is sufficient and as such the complaint is maintainable.

***Ram Keshap Chits Pvt. Ltd.* v. *Chinnam Krishna Murty,* (2002) 2 BC 562: (2002) 1 Crimes 673: 2002 Cr LJ NOC 281 (AP)**

In this case the cheques were issued by accused in favour of Bank for payment to the complainant by way of Demand Draft. The cheques were dishonoured for want of funds. The issue involved was as to who is the payee, *i.e.,* the Bank or the complainant. It was contended that the complainant is not the payee but the Payee is the Bank alone and hence the court cannot take cognizance of offence under section 138. *Held,* that the plea is not tenable. Hence, the proceedings cannot be quashed.

***Eita India Ltd.* v. *N.C.T. of Delhi*, (2002) 3 BC 72: (2002) 3 Crimes 95: 2002 Cr LJ 4754 (Del)**

Cases referred:

(2002) 1 SCC 234: 2002 SCC (Cri) 121: AIR 2002 SC 182: 2002 Cr LJ 266 (SC); (2002) 2 SCC 406: 2002 SCC (Cri) 340: 2002 Cr LJ 996 (SC); 2002 Cr LJ 2601 (Del); 1998 Cr LJ 856 (SC); 1996 Cr LJ 3099 (Guj); (1995) 3 Cur Cri R 841 (Del); (1994) 3 SCC 440: AIR 1994 SC 1775: 1994 Cr LJ 2269 (SC); 1984 Cr LJ 1 (SC); (1983) 3 SCC 42: AIR 1983 SC 595: 1983 Cr LJ 1044 (SC); AIR 1963 SC 1430: (1963) 2 Cr LJ 397 (SC).

Facts of the case.—In this case the cheques in question were issued in the name of the sole proprietorship concern East India Transport Agency (EITA). The sole proprietorship concern could act only through its proprietor which happens to be the company. It is a *de jure* complainant and it had to act through some human Agency. Thus, the complaint could be filed by any person connected with the company, may be its director, or manager or any other person, so authorised by the company who can represent the company in legal matters. Any other view will defeat the purpose and object of the Act. The High Court referred to various case laws. *Held,* that the complaint is maintainable as Eita India Ltd. is the payee as being proprietor of East India Transport Agency and company acts through some human agency duly authorised to file the complaint.

***N.K. Ramaswami Iyengar* v. *Bangalore District and Bangalore Rural District Co-operative Bank Ltd.*, (2002) 3 BC 587: (2002) 6 Kant LJ 458: 2002 Cr LJ 3502 (Karn)**

Cases referred:

1999 Cr LJ 1032 (Bom); 1997 Cr LJ 4208 (Karn); (1994) 1 Mad LW (Cri) 34.

Facts of the case.—The complaint was filed on behalf of the Payee Bank by its Manager. By order dated 22-1-2000 process was issued against the accused/ petitioners. Against the order the matter was taken to the court of Session Judge and the Criminal Revision Petition was dismissed. Against this dismissal the accused approached the High Court under section 482, the Cr. P.C. raising an issue that the Bank is the payee but authorised its Managing Director to present the complaint but the complaint is presented by the Manager of the Payee Bank which is not authorised in view of section 142. In support of the contention of the respondent that Managing Director is authorised to file the complaint under the bye-laws of the Bank but the Manager has been authorised by a letter dated 9-11-1999 to file the complaint. The High Court upheld this view that the Manager authorised by the Managing Director can present the complaint.

***M.M.T.C. Ltd.* v. *Medchi Chemicals and Pharma (P) Ltd.*, (2002) 1 SCC 234: 2002 SCC (Cri) 121: AIR 2002 SC 182: 2002 Cr LJ 266 (SC)**

Cases referred:

(1998) 1 SCC 687: 1998 SCC (Cri) 475: 1998 Cr LJ 856 (SC); 1984 Cr LJ 1 (SC).

Facts of the case.—The complaint was filed by the senior Manager of the appellant company and then later on substituted by the Deputy General

Manager who had not been authorised by the Board of Directors to sign and file the complaint on behalf of the company or to prosecute the same. They are simply paid employees and hence the complaint is not maintainable. Against the order of the High Court the matter came up before the Supreme Court by way of SLP. The Supreme Court referred the above two cases and *held* that it is open to the *de jure* complainant company to seek permission of the court for sending another person to represent the company in the Court. Even presuming that initially there was no authority still the company can, at any stage, rectify that defect. At a subsequent stage the company can send a person who is competent to represent the company. *Held,* that the complaint is filed by the payee as the complaint is in the name and on behalf of the appellant company who is the payee of the cheque. Merely because the complaint is signed and presented by a person who is neither an authorised agent nor a person empowered under the Articles of Association or by Resolution of the Board to do so is no ground to quash the complaint. Thus, even presuming, that initially there was no authority, still the company can, at any stage, rectify that defect.

***S.P. Sampathy* v. *Manju Gupta,* (2002) 3 BC 77: (2002) 111 Comp Cas 492: 2002 Cr LJ 2621 (AP)**

Cases referred:

1997 Cr LJ 3862 AP (not good law); (1997) 1 Civil CC 81 (P&H) (dissented from); 1995 Cr LJ 1102 (Mad) (dissented from); (1994) 2 Civil CC 60 (Cal) (dissented from); AIR 1961 AP 208 (FB) (distinguished).

Facts of the case.—The High Court first referred to section 5 of the Cr. P.C. which lays down procedure for trial of all criminal cases except under any special or local law for the time being in force or any special form of procedure prescribed by any other law for the time being in force. The provisions of the Cr. P.C. to this effect are excluded by section 142 by virtue of *non obstante* clause. Section 142 prescribes two conditions:—

(1) That the complaint should be in writing.

(2) It should be made by the payee or a holder in due course.

In this case the complaint is made in the name of the complainant but signed by his power-of-attorney. Power-of-attorney has no entity in terms of section 142. There is no averment that the power-of-attorney is a holder in due course. *Held,* that complaint cannot be filed by a power-of-attorney holder on behalf of the payee under section 138, the Negotiable Instruments Act. The complaint can only be filed by the payee or a holder in due course.

Note.—*2002 Cr LJ 266 (SC) is not referred.*

***Indira* v. *Surgent Magarajan,* (2003) 3 BC 573: 2003 Cr LJ 2623 (Mad)**

Cases referred:

(1994) 4 Crimes 209 (Mad); (1998) 1 SCC 687: 1998 SCC (Cri) 596: (1998) 91 Comp Cas 361: 1998 Cr LJ 856 (SC).

Facts of the case.—In this case, the complainant, during the proceedings died leaving behind two daughters and two sons. The two daughters filed an application for substitution and to be represented by a power-of-attorney. The application was dismissed. Aggrieved by the order, the petitioner challenged the order of the lower court on the ground that the criminal case does not abate on the death of the complainant in a summons case in terms of section 256(2), the Cr. P.C. which says, "The provisions of section 1 shall, so far as may be, apply also to cases where the non-appearance of the complainant is due to his death." [Refer *Muniruddin Akand* v. *Kasamuddin Munshi*, (1947) 1 Cal 99; AIR 1967 SC 983; 1973 Cr LJ 492; 1970 KLT 545; AIR 1966 J&K 60]. *Held*, that the petitioners have right to get other person substituted as a complainant.

***K.M. Maregowda* v. *Seven Hills Export-Import Corporation, Bangalore*, 2004 Cr LJ 4119 (Karn)**

Cases referred:

2004 Cr LJ 1394 SC; 2004 Cri P. No. 4528 and 29 of 2003 D/26-7-2004 (Karn); (2002) 1 SCC 234: (2002) 108 Comp Cas 48: 2002 Cr LJ 266 SC; 2002 Cr LJ 2621 (AP); 2002 Cr LJ 2142 Karn HCR 1206 (Relied on); (2001) 105 Comp Cas 774; (2001) 6 Karn LJ 201; 2001 Cr LJ 3632 MP; (2000) 2 SCC 230: 2000 SCC (Cri) 379: 2000 Cr LJ 930 SC; 2000 Cr LJ 1251 (Ker); (1998) 1 SCC 687: 1998 SCC (Cri) 596: (1998) 91 Comp Cas 361: 1998 Cr LJ 856 SC; 1998 Cr LJ 1707 (Karn); (1981) 1 Karn LJ 564; AIR 1976 SC 1177: (1976) 1 SCC 719: (1976) 2 SCR 82.

Issues raised: (1) Whether a complaint for offence under section 138 of the Negotiable Instruments Act not signed by the complainant could be entertained?

(2) Whether a power-of-attorney holder of the complainant can file complaint in his capacity as power-of-attorney holder?

(3) Whether examination of power-of-attorney holder of complainant on oath satisfies the requirements of section 200 of the Cr. P.C.?

Issue No. (1): The High Court, in answer to this question referred to 2002 Cr LJ 266 SC which says, "the only eligibility criteria prescribed by section 142 is that the complaint must be by the payee or the holder in due course. This criteria is satisfied as the complaint is in the name and on behalf of the appellant company.

Issue No. 2: In answer of this issue, the High Court referred to 2002 Cr LJ 266 SC and 1998 Cr LJ 856 SC that the complainant has to be a corporeal person who is capable of making a physical appearance in the court. It has been *held* that if a complaint is made in the name of incorporeal person it is necessary that a natural person represents such a juristic person in the court. The court looks upon the natural person to be the complainant for all practical purposes. Thus section 142(a) has to be read with section 2 of the Powers-of-Attorney Act.

Issue No. 3: The High Court referred to AIR 1976 SC 1177 and 2000 Cr LJ 930 SC and section 200 of the Cr. P.C. and said that procedural law is not to be a tyrant but a servant, not an obstruction but an aid to justice. It has been wisely observed that procedural prescriptions are the handmaids and not the mistresses, a lubricant, not a resistant in the administration of justice. Where the non-compliance, the procedural will thwart fair hearing or prejudice doing of justice to parties, the rule is mandatory. But grammar apart, if the breach can be corrected without injury to a just disposal of the case, we should not enthrone a regulatory requirement into a dominant desideratum. After all courts are to do justice, not to wreck this end product on technicalities. Viewed in this perspective, even what is regarded as mandatory traditionally may perhaps have to be moderated into wholesome directions to be complied within time or in extended time. When the power-of-attorney holder who has stepped into the shoes of the complainant, was examined on oath and not the complainant as such who could not have been examined at any time in any manner, such a thing cannot be taken as vitiating the cognizance or complaint as the case may be. The High Court also referred to sections 462, 464 and 465 of the Cr. P.C. in this regard.

***G.J. Packing Private Ltd.* v. *S.S. Sales*, 2006 Cr LJ 214 (Bom)**

Complaint can be filed by power-of-attorney holder of Payee when power-of-attorney holder has full knowledge of transaction. His statement can be recorded by the Magistrate for verification of complaint.

He cannot depose on behalf of complainant. However, he can appear as a witness.

***Mahinder Kumar* v. *Armstrong*, 2005 (3) RCR (Criminal) 371 (MP)**

The High Court referred to various cases and in particular *Janki Vashdeo Bhojwani* v. *Indusind Bank Ltd.*, 2005 (1) MP LJ (SC) 421.

Wherein the Supreme Court has finally set at rest the controversy about filing of the complaint or plaint and examination of power-of-attorney as witness and ruled that, "a general power-of-attorney holder can appear, plead and act on behalf of the party but he cannot become a witness on behalf of the party. He can only appear in his own capacity. No one can delegate the power to appear in witness box on behalf of himself. To appear as a witness is altogether a different act. A general power-of-attorney holder or special power-of-attorney holder cannot be allowed to appear as a witness on behalf of the plaintiff/complainant in the capacity of plaintiff/complainant".

Refer also: *Ram Parshad* v. *Hari Narain*, AIR 1998 Raj 185.

***Janaki Vashdeo Bhojwani* v. *Indusind Bank Ltd.*, AIR 2005 SC 439**

It is said that Order III, Rules 1 and 2 empowers the holder of power-of-attorney to "act" on behalf of the principal. The word "acts" employed in Order III, Rules 1 and 2 confines only in respect of 'acts' done by the power-of-attorney holder in exercise of power granted by the instrument. The term "acts" would not include deposing in place and instead of the principal. If the power-of-attorney holder has rendered some "acts" in pursuance to power-of-attorney, he may depose for the principal in respect of such acts, but he cannot depose for the principal in respect of the matter which only the principal can have a personal knowledge and in respect of which the principal is entitled to the cross-examined.

***T. Muthu Karuppan etc.* v. *G. Raghavan*, 2006 Cr LJ 1076 (Mad)**

In this case the High Court spoke two things:—

(i) The power-of-attorney holder who was every authority to sign and act on behalf of the principal can lodge a complaint under section 138 of of the Negotiable Instruments Act. Further the affidavit of the complaint in proof of execution of the power-of-attorney is totally reduntant inasmuch as the deed to power-of-attorney is produced at the time of filing the complaint by the power-of-attorney holder. The sworn statement of the power-of-attorney can be recorded at the very inception.

(ii) But only during the course of trial the payee will have to come to the box and speak from his knowledge about the legal liability of the drawer, issuance of cheque, presentation of the cheque for payment, dishonour of cheque, issuance of statutory notice, etc.

***Prasanta Kumar Basu* v. *Narendra Kumar Anchalia*, 2007 (1) JCC (NI) 50 (Cal)**

In this case the issue is whether the person authorized by the proprietor (payee) can file the complaint. The High Court relied upon the decision of Andhra Pradesh High Court cited as 2006 (1) DCR p. 229 which says, "we hold that the power-of-attorney of a payee or a holder in due course of a dishonoured cheque can file a complaint for an offence under section 138 of the Negotiable Instruments Act after obtaining permission from the court, either before or after filing of the complaint." In the decision of Madhya Pradesh High Court cited as 2005 (2) DCR p. 439 it is said that the complaint could be presented by the GPA on behalf of the payee provided the complaint is signed by the payee himself and an affidavit in proof of his execution of G.P.A. is filed and other formalities are observed.

***Andavar Trading Company* v. *V. Senthilkumar & Co.*, 2008 (3) JCC (NI) 301 (Mad)**

In this case the document of power-of-attorney was not properly executed in accordance with law. It was attested by a Public Notary and is not a registered document. Though the power-of-attorney may not be needed to be registered but there are certain infirmities in the document. The power-of-attorney was prepared on 25-7-1993 and the attestation was done on 29-7-1993. Even the proprietrix was not put into witness box to depose that she has executed this power-of-attorney. In view of the legal infirmities in the power-of-attorney according to law, the complaint filed is not maintainable.

***M. Senthilkumar* v. *Seven Seas Shipping Services*, 2008 Cr LJ 1186 (Mad)**

This is a petition under section 482, the Cr. P.C. for quashing the proceedings wherein many issues were raised and one of the point pertained to power-of-attorney stating that:—

(i) The power-of-attorney was prepared at Bombay but the document has been endorsed by an advocate and Notary at Tirupar on 18-6-2005 where as it is prepared, signed, sealed and delivered at Bombay on 15-6-2005

(ii) The proprietor has given power-of-attorney whereas the complaint shows that the complainant is a firm.

(iii) The power-of-attorney is not in accordance with section 85 of the Evidence Act, 1872.

***M/s. Shankar Finance & Investments* v. *State of Andhra Pradesh*, 2008 (3) JCC (NI) 345 SC**

In this case the Supreme Court has stated three options when the payee is the proprietor:—

(i) The proprietor of the firm showing himself as proprietor of the firm.

(ii) The proprietary concern represented by its sole proprietor.

(iii) The proprietor(s) of the firm represented by the attorney holder under a power-of-attorney executed by the sole proprietor.

He can be examined under section 200, the Cr. P.C.

Note.—

(i) This issue only pertains to filing of complaint and not deposing on behalf of the proprietor.

(ii) The power-of-attorney must be having personal knowledge of the transaction.

***R.N. Sinha Proprietor Himalaya Overseas* v. *Nisha Jagtiani*, 2009 (2) JCC (NI) 160 (Del)**

It is *held* that in this case the complaint is filed by the SPA who is duly authorized and further more the complainant is herself appearing and can be cross-examined by the accused in relation to the statements made in the complaint and in the affidavit by way of pre-summoning evidence of SPA holder. The complaint is maintainable.

***Smt. Durgadevi* v. *Shalikram Vitthalrao Korde*, AIR 2009 (NOC) 1816 (Bom)**

It is *held* that complaint can be filed through holder of power-of-attorney. Such power-of-attorney holder can also be examined in place of complainant if he has personal knowledge of the transaction in question.

Also Refer: AIR 2009 SC 432.

Note.—*Catena of cases pertaining to "power-of-attorney" has well-settled the law that:—*

(i) A power-of-attorney can filed the complaint provided the document of power-of-attorney is executed according to law.

(ii) Power-of-attorney holder can depose about the transaction if happened during the power-of-attorney give to the person.

(iii) If the transaction happened before the power-of-attorney is given, he can appear as a witness only.

(iv) In no case he can depose on behalf of the complainant.

COGNIZANCE OF OFFENCES

***Chandrika (Smt) Through her Power-of-Attorney holder* v. *State of Rajasthan,* 2010 (1) Crimes 51 (Raj)**

Cases referred:

M/s. M.M.T.C. Ltd. v. *M/s. Medical Chemicals and Pharma (P) Ltd.*, AIR 2002 SC 182; *M/s. Shankar Finance and Investment* v. *State of Andhra Pradesh,* AIR 2008 SC 1017; *Hamsa* v. *Ibrahim,* ILR 1994 (1) Ker 622; *K. Gopal Krishnan* v. *Karnakaran rep by the Power-of-Attorney Holder,* 2007 (2) NIJ 258 (Mad) (DB); *Aashirwad Enterprises* v. *Sambhar Salts Ltd.*, 1997 (3) RCR (Cri) 221 (Raj); *Ajai Kumar Jain* v. *State of Rajasthan,* 2008 Western Law Cases (UC) (Raj) 229; *Mohil Fibers* v. *Shri Saai Agro Industries,* 2007 (1) NIJ 451 (HP); *Muthu Karuppan* v. *Raghavan,* 2007 (1) NIJ 68 (Mad); *Smt. Lalita Hundiya* v. *Govind Narayan Khuteta,* 2008 (1) RCC 410; *Jackson & Co.* v. *Napper,* 1986 (35) Ch D 162; *Queen* v. *Justice of Kant,* 1873 (8) QB 305; *Ravulu Subharao* v. *Income-tax Commissioner,* AIR 1956 SC 604; *Ramdeo* v. *Lalinatha,* AIR 1937 Nag 65; *Income-tax Commissioner* v. *Subha Rao,* AIR 1946 (33) Mad 411; *Vishwa Mitter* v. *O.P. Poddar,* (1983) 4 SCC 701.

In this case the complaint for offence under Section 138 of the Negotiable Instruments Act was filed in the name and on behalf of payee by Attorney-holder of payee. The complaint is valid and is maintainable.

Smt. Durgadevi v. *Shalikram Vitthalrao Korde,* 2010 (1) Crimes 566 (Bom).

Cases referred:

Roy Joseph v. *Sk. Tamisuddin,* 2008 (3) Mah LJ 705; *Mamtadevi P. Bhansali* v. *Pushpadevi K. Agarwal,* 2005 All MR (Cri) 3075; *Dr. Pradeep Mohanbay* v. *Mr. Minguel Carlos Dias,* 2000 Vol 102 (1) Bom LR 908; *Shanker Finance & Investments* v. *State of Andhra Pradesh,* 2008 (3) SCC (Cri) 558.

In this case it was held that complaint under Section 138 of the Negotiable Instruments Act can he filed through power-of-attorney holder and such attorney- holder can also be examined in place of complainant if he had personal knowledge of transaction in question.

This is the heading of section 142, the Negotiable Instruments Act. Section 190, the Cr. P.C. says, "subject to the provisions of this chapter, any Magistrate of the first class...........may take cognizance of any offence—In this section the word "may" is used. Whereas in section 142, the Negotiable Instruments Act the phrase used is—"shall take cognizance". Generally "shall" denotes "mandatory" and "may" denotes "discretionary". The word "may" used in section 190, the Cr. P.C. is shrouded with conflict of opinion. According to one view "may" signifies an option to take cognizance [AIR 1950 Cal 437, AIR 1951 SC 207, (30) Cr LJ 1056 Pat (FB), AIR 1961 SC 986, 1973 Cr LJ 886 (All)]. The other view is that "may" signifies "must" [AIR 1926 Cal 470 (FB), 1973 Cr LJ 503 (AP)]. In *Gopal Dass* v. *State of Assam,* AIR 1961 SC 986, it is said, "we are unable to construe the word "may" in section 190, the Cr. P.C. to mean "must". However, the Supreme Court in later decision of *A.C. Aggarwal* v. *Ram Kali,* AIR 1968 SC 1, has said, "the Magistrate is bound to take cognizance of any cognizable offence brought to the notice under section 190(1)(b) of the Cr. P.C. which means "must". In *State of*

Assam v. *Abdul Noor*, AIR 1970 SC 1367, the Supreme Court called "may" as judicial discretion.

But further question arises as to what is meant by "cognizance of offence". Das Gupta J. in *Superintendent and Legal Remembraner of Legal Affairs W.B.* v. *Ambani Kumar*, AIR 1950 Cal 437 has said—

> "It seems to me clear, however, before it can be said that any Magistrate has taken cognizance of any offence under section 190(1)(a), the Criminal P.C., he must have not only have applied his mind to the contents of the petition but he must have done so for the purpose of proceeding in a particular way as indicated in subsequent provisions of this chapter proceeding under section 200 and thereafter sending it for enquiry and report under section 202. When the Magistrate applies his mind not for the purpose of proceeding under the subsequent sections of this chapter but for taking action of some other kind, *e.g.*, ordering investigation under section 156(3) or issuing search warrant for the purpose of investigation, he cannot be said to have taken cognizance of the offence."

So cognizance is taken of an offence as soon as a court, competent for the purpose, applies its mind to the offence with the intention of initiating judicial proceedings against the offenders in respect of the offence. (AIR 1971 SC 2372, AIR 1963 SC 765). This question arose in—

***K.G. Sharma* v. *Pratap Auto Steels*, (2002) 4 Rec Cri R 814: (2002) 3 Raj LR 796: 2002 Cr LJ 3711 (Raj)**

Cases referred:

AIR 2000 SC 2946: (2000) 7 SCC 183: (2000) 3 KLT 605; AIR 1977 SC 2401: (1977) 4 SCC 459; AIR 1976 SC 1672: (1976) 3 SCC 252; AIR 1963 SC 765; AIR 1951 SC 207: (1951) 52 Cr LJ 775.

Facts of the case.—The complaint under section 138, the Negotiable Instruments Act was filed on 23-5-1998. The learned Magistrate ordered on 26-5-1998 that the case be registered and fixed on the date of 8-7-1998 for recording the statements of the complainant and its witnesses therefor. On 19-7-1999 an order was passed by the lower court that the accused be summoned through bailable warrants. In compliance of the order dated 19-7-1999 the accused appeared on 24-5-2000 and 20-7-2000. The issue raised was that the complaint was filed on 26-5-1998 and the cognizance was taken on 19-7-1999, so the cognizance was taken after the expiry of one year and hence it is time-barred.

The High Court referred to various case law, *held* that the court took cognizance on 26-5-1998 when it ordered for registration of case and ordered to record statements of the complainant and its witnesses. In particular a reference was made to AIR 1963 SC 765 which stated, "The word "cognizance" has no esoteric or mystic significance in criminal law or procedure. It merely means to become aware of or when used with reference to court or Judge, to take notice judicially. Taking cognizance does not involve any formal action or indeed action of any kind but occurs as soon as a Magistrate, as such, applies his mind to the suspected commission of offence.

The contra contention raised is that cognizance was taken on 19-7-1999 when an order was passed by the lower court that the accused be summoned through bailable warrants. Reliance was place on AIR 2000 SC 2946. The High Court found that the facts of that case are not applicable here, and moreover, in this case, the Supreme Court emphasised the same thing that, "Taking cognizance would mean the action taken by the court for initiating judicial proceedings against the offender in respect of the offence regarding which the complaint is filed." Thus the High Court found this contention untenable under law.

Originally, under the Banking, Public Financial Institutions and Negotiable Instruments Laws (Amendment) Act, 1988, clause (b) of section 142 is as follows:—

> "Such complaint is made within one month of the date on which the cause-of-action arises under clause (c) of the proviso to section 138".

In view of *"Non Obstante"* Clause, section 142(b) of the Negotiable Instruments Act, excludes section 468, the Cr. P.C. [AIR 1986 All 303; AIR 1952 SC 369; AIR 1989 Pat 217 (FB)]. So clause (b) of section 142 is the initiation of criminal proceeding when, "the drawer of such cheque fails to make the payment of the said amount of money to the payee, or as the case may be, to the holder in due course of the cheque within 15 days of the receipt of the said notice." If the payee or the holder in due course does not stick to the period of one month as stipulated or violates it, he will not have the assistance of the court to get redress of his grievance.

JUDICIAL VIEW

***Ancon Engineering Co. (P) Ltd.* v. *Amitava Goswami*, (1993) 1 CHN 298: 1994 Cr LJ 351 (Cal)**

Case referred:

(1992) 1 Crimes 23 (Ker) (relied on).

In this case a part payment was made towards dishonour of cheque. The Court *held* that the cause-of-action for prosecution for dishonouring of cheque does not arise by mere presentation of the cheque in bank and by its dishonour. Whenever any complaint is filed by any person under section 142, the Negotiable Instruments Act, it will have to be seen whether it has been filed within one month of the date on which cause-of-action arose under clause (c) of proviso to section 138. Any earlier abortive presentation of the cheque is to be kept out of consideration for the purpose of application of section 138.

***Poornasree Agencies* v. *Universal Enterprises*, (1995) 83 Comp Cas 66: 1995 Cr LJ 1858 (Ker)**

Cases referred:

Dodds v. *Walkar*, (1981) 1 WLR 1027; AIR 1958 Ker 326.

The facts of the case were as follows:—

(1) Cause-of-action arose on 24-6-1993 [proviso (c) to section 138].

(2) Complaint should be filed on or before 24-7-1993 [section 142(b)].

(3) Complaint filed on 26-7-1993.

Reasons for delay given was that on last day of filing, *i.e.*, 25-7-1993 it was holiday and that the last day of filing of complaint falls on 25-7-1993 and not 24-7-1993. The High Court referred to paragraph 143 of *Halsbury's Law of England*, Vol. 37, (3rd Edn.) where it is stated that "when the period prescribed is a calendar month running from any arbitrary date the period expires with the day in the succeeding month immediately preceding the day corresponding to the date upon which the period starts, save that, if the period starts at the end of a calendar month which contains more days than the next succeeding month, the period expires at the end of the later month". *Held*, the complaint is barred by limitation.

***Sardar Singh* v. *Karm Singh*, (1997) 4 Rec Cri R 671: 1997 Cr LJ 3751 (J&K)**

Facts of the case:

(1) The notice of demand of payment received on 16-9-1991.

(2) 15th day of the receipt of demand notice expired on 1-10-1991.

(3) Complaint was to be filed within one month from 2-10-1991 to 1-11-1991 within one month as per section 142(b).

Held: The complaint filed on 1-10-1991 is premature as the cause-of-action started only from 2-10-1991 onward and hence not maintainable.

***Mandhadi Ramachandra Reddy* v. *Gopuma Reddy Rama Reddy*, (1997) 4 Crimes 151: (1997) 2 LS AP 189: 1997 Cr LJ 4275 (AP)**

Facts of the case:

(1) Notice is assumed to be served on the drawer of cheque on 12-11-1994.

(2) The drawer of the cheque is required to make payment within 15 days, *i.e.*, 27-11-1994.

(3) Complaint is to be filed on or before one month, *i.e.*, 27-12-1994

(4) Complaint was lodged on 24-1-1995.

Held: Delay cannot be condoned. The court is barred from taking cognizance.

***Kunju Vishwanadhan* v. *Ramakrishnan Surendran*, (1998) 2 CCC 589: (1998) 1 KLJ 671: (1998) 1 KLT 694: 1998 Cr LJ 3553 (Ker)**

Cases referred:

(1994) 1 Ker LT SN 31, Case No. 28; (1993) 1 Ker LT 717; 1993 Cr LJ 771; 1990 Supp SCC 121: 1990 SCC (Cri) 646; AIR 1989 SC 630: (1989) 1 SCC 264; 1984 Cr LJ 647; AIR 1981 SC 1284; 1976 Cr LJ 1361; (1961) 2 Cr LJ 39.

Facts of the case:

(1) Cheque dishonoured on 2-5-1990

(2) Knowledge of dishonour of cheque by the appellant 8-5-1990

(3) Issue of Notice to the drawer on 14-5-1990

(4) Refused to take notice by the drawer of cheque as per endorsement on 26-5-1990

(5) Complaint was filed on 2-6-1990

(6) Cause-of-action took place on refusal after 15 days 10-6-1990.

Three issues were raised:—

(1) Whether date of issue of notice or date of refusal to take notice is material to the issue of limitation.

(2) Whether date of taking cognizance of the offence by the court is material to the issue of limitation.

(3) Whether complaint can be filed within one month on the refusal to take notice.

The High Court rejected all the issues with reference to various case laws and *held* that the complaint was filed before the cause-of-action arose and hence not maintainable. Acquittal of the accused by the lower court was proper.

***Nakoda Laminators* v. *State of Rajasthan*, 1998 Cr LJ 3525 (Raj)**

Facts of the case.—Cheque issued on 17-2-1994. First notice was issued to the accused on 9-3-1994. Second notice was sent on 15-3-1994. Both notices were sent within the period prescribed. So the drawer of cheque was to make the payment by 25-3-1994. He did not make the payment and thereby a complaint was filed on 25-4-1994, the last day of expiry of period of one month. *Held,* that the complaint was within Limitation.

***K. Murlidhar Rao* v. *State of Andhra Pradesh*, (1997) 6 Andh LT 79: (1997) 3 APLJ 399: 1998 Cr LJ 748 (AP)**

Case referred:

(1) 1994 Cr LJ 3115 (Karn).

Facts of the case.—A cheque was issued to discharge part of liability on 31-12-1996. The same when presented was dishonoured for want of sufficient funds. A notice was issued on 15-1-1997 demanding payment within 10 days, *i.e.*, 25-1-1997. The payment was not received. A complaint was filed on 1-3-1997. The objection was that time of 15 days was not given to the accused to make payment. This plea was rejected as the complaint was filed within one month of the expiry of fifteen days from the receipt of notice. The notice was received on 17-1-1997. The payment should have been made by 1-2-1997. The complaint was filed on the last day of the expiry of period of one month after the cause-of-action arises. The complaint filed was within time.

***Saketh India Ltd.* v. *India Securities Ltd.*, (1999) 3 SCC 1: 1999 SCC (Cri) 329: AIR 1999 SC 1090: 1999 Cr LJ 1822 (SC)**

Cases referred:

AIR 1972 SC 1293: (1972) 1 SCC 639; (1963) 1 All ER 11, *Cartwright* v. *Maccormack*, (1961) 2 QB 135; *Marren* v. *Dawson, Bentley & Co. Ltd.*, (1951) 2 All ER: (1951) 2 KB 792, *Stewart* v. *Chapman*, (1904) 1 KB 1: 89 LT 428; *Goldsmith's Company* v. *West Metropolitan Rail Company*, (1895) 2 QB 264: 64 LJ QB 694, *North Re Ex Parte was luck*.

The discussion centered around section 12 of the Limitation Act, 1963 and section 9 of the General Clauses Act, 1897 pertaining to calculation of time for the purpose of finding the applicability of limitation. The Supreme Court referred to various case law and the scope of section 12 of the Limitation Act, 1963 and section 9 of the General Clauses Act, 1897 and said that the rule is well-settled that where a particular time is given from a certain date within which the act is to be done, the day on that date is to be excluded and this rule is specifically provided in section 12 of the Limitation Act, 1963.

In this case the cheques dated 15th and 16th March, 1995 bounced when presented. Notices were served on the accused on 29-9-1995 within 15 days of the bouncing of cheques. The accused failed to make the payment. Thus the cause-of-action arose on 15-10-1995. The complaint was filed on 15-11-1995. It was contended that the complaint was filed beyond time. In terms of section 142(b) the complaint should be made within one month. A month is to be calculated according to the British Calendar as defined in the General Clauses Act, 1897. The issue raised was that whether the period had to be reckoned by excluding the date on which the cause-of-action arose. In this case the period of one month falls on 15-11-1995. Hence, the complaint was held to be filed in time.

***Josey Condody* v. *Chacko Thomas*, (1999) 4 Crimes 413: (1999) 2 Ker LJ 646: 1999 Cr LJ 4707 (Ker)**

Cases referred:

(1993) 3 SCC 1: 1999 SCC (Cri) 329: 1999 Cr LJ 1822 SC (relied on); (1999) 4 SCC 567: 1999 SCC (Cri) 600: (1999) 97 Comp Cas 575: 1999 Cr LJ 2276 (SC).

In this case the High Court discussed two points:—

(i) Computation of time (section 12 of the Limitation Act, 1963).

(ii) If there are two conflicting decisions of the Supreme Court consisting of same Judges, which decision is to be followed.

The High Court followed, 1999 Cr LJ 1822 SC and *held* that while computing period of one month for filing complaint is to be computed by excluding the day on which cause-of-action arose.

On the other point the High Court relied on the decision of Full Bench of the Allahabad High Court in *Ganga Saran* v. *Civil Judge, Hapur*, AIR 1991 All 114, after elaborate consideration of this aspect and the two lines of decision *viz.*, when there is a conflict in two Supreme Court decision of equal benches, the decision which is later in point of time will be binding on the High Courts and when there is conflict between judgments of the Supreme Court consisting of equal judges, incidence of time is not a relevant factor and the High Court must follow the judgment which appears to it to lay down law elaborately and accurately. On this propounded principle the High Court followed, 1999 Cr LJ 1822 SC.

***M.A. Abdul Khuthoss* v. *Ganesh & Co. Oil Mills*, (1999) 4 Civ LJ 889: (1999) 3 Crimes 83: (1999) 4 Rec Cri R 118: 1999 Cr LJ 3432 (Mad)**

Case referred:

(1) AIR 1967 Guj 15.

The facts of the case were that two cheques dated 29-9-1995 and 4-10-1995 bounced on presentation on 13-3-1996. After the issue of statutory demand notice no payment was received within the prescribed period of 15 days. Thereupon the complainant filed the complaint on 25-4-1996 for the offence under section 138 of the Negotiable Instruments Act, 1881. The complaint filed was without the signatures of the complainant and thus returned on the same day with endorsement. With due compliance the complaint was represented on 15-5-1996 and on the same day the sworn statement was taken and the case was taken on file.

The issue was that the complaint filed on 25-4-1996 was not a proper presentation and representation after due compliance on 15-5-1996 is barred by limitation under section 142(b) of the Act. As per section 142(b) of the Act the complaint should have been filed within one month of the cause of action.

(1) Cause-of-action arose on 6-4-1996.

(2) Complaint should have been filed on 6-5-1996.

(3) Complaint filed on 15-5-1996.

The High Court *held* that the complaint filed on 25-4-1996 was not a proper presentation and in view of section 2(d) of the Cr. P.C. and section 142(a) of the Negotiable Instruments Act, it is no complaint and presentation on 15-5-1996 was barred by limitation in view of section 142(b) of the Negotiable Instruments Act.

***Vinayagam* v. *Dr. Subhas Chandran,* (2001) 103 Comp Cas 569: 2000 Cr LJ 1597 (Mad)**

Cases referred:

(1995) 1 Mad LW (Cri) 300 (approved); (1995) 2 Mad Law (Cri) 405; AIR 1998 SC 1128; AIR 1966 SC 1631: (1964) 1 SCR 145.

In this case the issue before the Division Bench was that there were two conflicting decisions of the single Judges of this High Court. In (1995) 1 Mad LW (Cri) 300 it was *held* that initial presentation of the complaint within limitation period is a complaint validity presented and even if it is returned back to the complainant, still the complaint would be *held* to have been presented in time. In another case, Criminal R.C. No. 933 of 1993, it is *held* that if such complaint, which is filed in time, but returned to the party for representation, is represented after the period of limitation, then the court is precluded from taking cognizance on the ground of limitation provided under section 142 of the Negotiable Instruments Act. The Division Bench referred to section 2(d) of the Cr. P.C. and criminal rules of practice and *held* that Magistrate had no power to return the complaint for defects and if there were defects in complaint, then the complainant had to suffer. *Held,* that the subsequent complaint filed by the complainant after removing the defects has to be treated as filed within limitation and approved (1995) 1 Mad LW (Cri) 300 and overruled Cr. R.C. No. 933 of 1993 (Mad).

***Patel Dinnesh Kumar Shiv Ram Somdass* v. *Patel Keshav Lal Mohan Lal,* 2000 Cr LJ 3547: (2000) 4 Crimes 443: (2000) 3 CCC 7: (2000) 2 KLT 619 (Guj) (FB)**

Cases referred:

(1999) 3 SCC 1: 1999 SCC (Cri) 329: (1999) 96 Comp Cas 329: 1999 Cr LJ 1822 SC; (1999) 4 SCC 567: (1999) 97 Comp Cas 575: 1999 Cr LJ 2276 SC; 1998 Cr

LJ 559; 1997 Cr LJ 3691; 1996 Cr LJ 3409; 1995 Cr LJ 1904 (Karn); 1995 Cr LJ 1858 (Ker); 1993 Cr LJ 680 (Bom); (1991) 2 Guj LH 121; (1992) 2 Crimes 42 (Karn); (1990) 2 Guj LH 230; AIR 1982 NOC 650 (MP); AIR 1980 Ker 175; AIR 1972 SC 1293: (1972) 1 SCC 639: 1972 Cr LJ 872; AIR 1970 Tripura 71; AIR 1965 SC 229; AIR 1965 Ori 71; AIR 1938 Bom 447.

Facts of the case.—In this case the issue pertained to section 12 of the Limitation Act, 1963. The lower court acquitted the accused on the basis that the complaint filed was pre-mature. The matter came up before a single Judge of the High Court. There being conflicting decisions the matter was referred to the Full Bench.

The notice was issued on 6-2-1993. It was served on 9-2-1993. As no payment was made within 15 days the complaint was filed on 24-2-1993. The issue raised was whether the complaint filed was premature. The Full Bench referred to various case law and section 12 of the Limitation Act, 1963 and *held* as follows:—

(1) Notice was served on 9-2-1993.

(2) Period of 15 days was to be counted from 10-2-1993 which falls on 24-2-1993. Thus 24-2-1993 was the last day for the accused to make the payment and thereby the period of one month starts from 25-2-1993. The complaint filed on 24-2-1993 was pre-mature and without remanding it back to the learned single Judge, dismissed the petition there itself.

***Pruthvish B. Dave* v. *State of Gujarat,* 2000 Bank J 402: 2000 Bank J 629: (2000) 2 BC 141: (2000) 2 ICC 402: 2000 Cr LJ 122 (Guj)**

Cases referred:

1998 Cr LJ 4066 SC; (1995) 1 Guj LR 424.

Facts of the case.—It is a case of repeated presentation of cheque and limitation. A cheque was presented and was dishonoured for want of balance in the account. A notice was sent to this effect and served on him. There was no response from the respondent. Thereafter the cheque was again presented on 5-6-1997. It was again dishonoured with an endorsement of insufficient funds. Intimation was received on 6-6-1997. Thereafter the notice was served on the respondent. He did not pay the amount and therefore, a complaint was lodged on 9-7-1997.

The point agitated was, beside other points, that the complaint is time-barred. That on first presentation of the cheque, when it was dishonoured on 12-3-1997 a notice was issued and the time started running from the date of receipt of first notice and issuance of second notice could not extend the period of limitation/could not revive the cause-of-action. *Held,* complaint being not filed within the stipulated period after service of first notice, it was time-barred.

***Narinder Kumar* v. *Harnam Singh,* 2000 Bank J 622: (2000) 2 Civ LJ 224: (2000) 2 CCC 303: 2000 Cr LJ 257 (HP)**

Facts of the case.—The cheque is stated to have been presented to the bank on 5-1-1990. The notice of dishonour of cheque was issued on 16-1-1990 but posted on 17-1-1990. For non-payment the cause-of-action arises after the expiry of 15 days of the receipt of the said notice. The period of limitation will start running for lodging the complaint after the expiry of 15 days of receipt of notice and the complaint is to be filed within one month. The receipt of legal notice is 22-1-1990 and the period of 15 days expires on 6-2-1990 and cause-of-action starts from 7-2-1990 and the complaint is to be filed within one month from 7-2-1990. The complaint was filed on 21-2-1990. Thus the complaint is filed within time. But on another point "No subsisting debt or other liability" the acquittal of the accused was upheld.

***Harpreet Hosiery, Rehari* v. *Nitu Mahajan,* 2000 Cr LJ 3625 (J&K)**

Cases referred:

(1999) 4 SCC 567: 1999 SCC (Cri) 600: (1999) 97 Comp Cas 575: 1999 Cr LJ 2276 SC; 1998 Cr LJ 4066 SC; 1993 Cr LJ 1751 (Ori).

Facts of the case.—The appellant had issued 6 cheques of different amounts between 18-11-1991 and 23-12-1991. These cheques were dishonoured when presented. The first notice was issued on 25-2-1992 which could not be served. He again issued a notice on 7-3-1992 but met the same fate. A third notice was sent and finally the 4th notice was issued on 25-4-1992. Before issuing the last notice, *i.e.,* on 25-4-1992, the appellant represented the cheques on 20-4-1992 and that being dishonoured, issued the notice on 25-4-1992. The issue was whether each presentment of cheques gives a new cause-of-action or whether or not cause-of-action would arise once the cheque is dishonoured and its notice is received by the drawer. The High Court *held* that assuming the notice was issued on 25-4-1992, 15 days are to be given for making payment. So the time allowed was upto 10-5-1992. The complaint was filed on 9-5-1992, *i.e.,* on the 14th day itself. So the complaint filed was pre-mature.

***G. Hari* v. *John Promod Alexander,* (2000) 1 Ker 673: (2000) 4 Mah LJ 513: (2000) 2 Bom LR 323: 2000 Cr LJ 1653 (Ker)**

Facts of the case.—It is a case for quashing the complaint under the inherent powers of the High Court under section 482, the Cr. P.C. on the ground of barred by limitation. The facts are that the cheque was issued on 14-2-1996. On presentation it was dishonoured and returned back on 18-3-1996. Statutory notice was issued 28-3-1996 and was received by the drawer of the cheque on 29-3-1996. The complaint was filed on 3-6-1997. *Held,* that admittedly the complaint was filed after one month of the expiry of the statutory period of 15 days for making the payment and that the learned Magistrate had not applied his mind on this aspect while taking cognizance. The complaint was quashed.

***Mathias Packaging Ltd.* v. *Hindalco. Industries Ltd.,* 2000 Cr LJ 4836 (Mad)**

Cases referred:

1999 Cr LJ 2276; (1999) 1 Mad LW (Cri) 412 (followed); AIR 1998 SC 3043: (1998) 6 SCC 514: 1998 SCC (Cri) 1471: (1998) 2 KLT 765 (followed).

Facts of the case.—Two cheques were issued dated 2-4-1998 and 15-5-1998. The cheques, when presented, were dishonoured. Demand notice was issued on 27-7-1998. The petitioner sent the reply on 2-9-1998. The cheques were represented and were dishonoured on 21-9-1998. Another demand notice was sent on 24-9-1998. For not making payment the complaint was filed on 3-11-1998. High Court relied on AIR 1998 SC 3043: 1998 Cr LJ 4066 (SC) and *held* as under:

> "A cheque can be presented any number of times during the period of its validity by payee. On each presentation of cheque and its dishonour a fresh right and not cause-of-action accrues in his favour. He may, therefore, without taking pre-emptory, action in exercise of his such right under clause (b) of section 138, go on presenting the cheque so as to enable him to exercise such right at any point of time during the validity of the cheque. But, once he gives the notice under clause (b) of section 138, he forfeits such right, for, in case of failure of the drawer to pay the money within the stipulated period he would be liable for the offence and the cause-of-action for filing the complaint will arise."

The Supreme Court then *held* that the combined reading of section 138 and section 142 of the Negotiable Instruments Act leaves no room for doubt that cause-of-action within the meaning of section 142 arises and arises only once.

Note.—*Cause-of-action arises only once with the issuance of first notice. When limitation starts to run from the date of cause-of-action, it may not be intercepted and stopped by issuance of a second notice. (1998 Cr LJ 4046: AIR 1998 SC 3043).*

***Sudershan Khaitan* v. *Patheja Forgings Auto Parts and Manufacturing Ltd.*, (2001) 5 Bom CR 888: (2001) 3 Bom LR 565: (2001) 4 Mah LJ 62: 2001 Cr LJ 3872 (Bom)**

Case referred:

1998 Cr LJ 4066.

Facts of the case.—Cheque was issued on 14-4-1994. It was dishonoured on 17-9-1994. Again presented on 19-10-1994 and again it was dishonoured. A demand notice was sent on 28-10-1994. The payee again presented the cheque and got it dishonoured on 2-2-1995 and thereupon sent another notice dated 7-2-1993. The issue was whether after a cause-of-action had arisen on dishonour of cheque and demand notice sent on 28-10-1994, again a cause-of-action can be created by presenting the cheque and getting it dishonoured and issuing another notice. The High Court, followed the principle laid down by the Supreme Court in 1998 Cr LJ 4066 and *held* that for similar failure after service of fresh notice on subsequent dishonour, the drawer cannot be liable for any offence nor can the first offence be treated as "*non est*" so as to give the payee a right to file a complaint treating the second offence as the first one. It will not be a question of a waiver of right of the payee to prosecute the drawer but of absolution of the drawer of an offence, which stands already committed by him and which cannot be committed by him again.

***Pradyut Kumar Mohanty* v. *Dilip Singh Mehta*, (2001) 2 BC 453: (2001) 2 CCC 566: (2001) 3 Crimes 252: (2001) 78 DLT 378: 2001 Cr LJ 2322 (Ori)**

Cases referred:

2001 Cr LJ 972 (SC) (distinguished); 1998 Cr LJ 4066 (SC) (followed).

Facts of the case.—It was a case of presentation of cheque twice. Notice was also issued twice but complaint was filed within the stipulated period after the issue of second notice but barred by time as per first notice. The court applied the *ratio decidendi* of the case of *Sadanandan Bhadran* v. *Madhavan Sunil Kumar*, 1998 Cr LJ 4066 (SC) and *held* that issuance of second letter after the subsequent bouncing of the cheque does not give rise to a fresh or further cause of action. Complaint filed within 30 days after issuance of second notice would be barred by limitation.

***Dalmia Cement (Bharat) Ltd.* v. *Galaxy Traders and Agencies Ltd.*, (2001) 6 SCC 463: 2001 SCC (Cri) 1163: AIR 2001 SC 676: (2001) 1 KLT 528: 2001 Cr LJ 972 (SC)**

Cases referred:

AIR 1999 SC 1609; AIR 1999 SC 3762; 1998 Cr LJ 4066; AIR 1992 SC 1604; AIR 1981 SC 1284.

Facts of the case.—The cheque was presented and dishonoured. Notice was issued and acknowledgment received. However, the accused informed that he had received the cover without any contents and requested the complainant to mail its contents. Believing the accused but not admitting, by way of abundant caution he presented the cheque again and it was dishonoured again. Statutory notice was issued and complaint was filed within time after non-payment by the accused within a period of 15 days. The Supreme Court referred to section 27 of the General Clauses Act, regarding "presumption of service" and came to a conclusion that the first notice is "no notice". So the second notice was, in fact, a first notice and hence the complaint was *held* filed within time.

***V.V. Circuits Ltd.* v. *State of Uttar Pradesh*, (2001) 1 Bank LLR 64: (2000) 1 BC 499: 2001 Bank J 384: 2001 Cr LJ 1552 (AP)**

Case referred:

1998 Cr LJ 4066 (SC).

Held: Cause-of-action arises once notice is issued for demanding payment in lieu of dishonoured cheque but no prosecution initiated within prescribed time after cause-of-action arose. Holder of cheque cannot issue another notice demanding payment under guise of initiating prosecution. Proceedings would be liable to be quashed as being time-barred. The High Court relied on 1998 Cr LJ 4066 SC.

***Hemlata Gupta* v. *State of Uttar Pradesh*, 2002 All LJ 164: (2002) 2 BC 170: (2002) 1 Crimes 342: 2002 Cr LJ 1522 (All)**

Case referred:

(2000) 7 SCC 183: (2000) 3 KLT 605: AIR 2000 SC 2946 (followed).

Facts of the case.—The complainant received intimation from the bank on 11-6-1998 that the cheques were dishonoured as the drawer has closed the account. The complainant issued demand notice on 13-6-1998 and filed complaint on 26-6-1998. Summoning order was issued. The accused objected to the summoning order on the ground that the complaint is filed before expiry of 15 days. His objection is overruled. The learned Additional Sessions Judge *held* that the complained filed was pre-mature and not maintainable. The matter came before the High Court where distinction between "filing of complaint" and taking "cognizance of complaint" was discussed and *held* that section 142 speaks of "taking cognizance" and not "filing of complaint". In this case the complaint was filed on 26-6-1998 but cognizance was taken on 8-11-1998 which was much after 15 days of the notice dated 13-6-1998. Hence, the complaint was maintainable.

***Prashant Prabhakar Rao Gite* v. *S.K. Sarkar*, 2002 Bank J 159: (2002) 4 Crimes 311: (2002) 2 Mah LJ 125: 2002 Cr LJ 3001 (Bom)**

Cases referred:

(2001) 6 SCC 463: (2001) 1 KLT 528: 2001 Cr LJ 972 (SC); 2001 Cr LJ 4647 SC; 1999 Cr LJ 4571; 1999 Cr LJ 4606 SC; 1998 Cr LJ 4066 SC; (1992) 1 Crimes 743 (Ker).

Facts of the case.—The complaint issued four cheques dated 30-5-1998, 2-6-1998, 5-6-1998 and 7-6-1998 totalling Rs. 1,75,000. These cheques were presented on respective dates and were dishonoured. Cheques being drawn on outstation Bank, it took time for clearance and returned as dishonoured. They were again presented on 12-8-1998 and 14-8-1998 and were again dishonoured. On 12-10-1998 the complainant issued letter. This letter was not accepted by the other party. This was informed to the complainant on 16-11-1999. In the mean time on assurance by the other party the cheques were again presented on 28-10-1998. They were again dishonoured and intimation was received on 26-11-1998 from the Bank, statutory notice was issued on 3-12-1998. It was returned "not claimed" on 19-12-1998. The complaint was filed on 28-12-1998. Various decisions were cited from both sides. It was *held* that the provisions of the Act does not provide any form in which the notice or the communication is required to be sent except that the communication must be in writing. So the earlier communication of 12-10-1998 was also a statutory notice. Thus the complaint was filed beyond limitation.

***Ashok Kumar* v. *Kailash Chandra*, (2003) 2 Bank LLR 786: (2003) 1 BC 412: 2003 Bank J 333: (2003) 3 Raj LW 1944: 2003 Cr LJ 284 (Raj)**

Cases referred:

2002 Cr LJ 266 (SC); 2002 Cr LJ 1926; 2001 Cr LJ 972 (SC); 2001 Cr LJ 3326 (SC); 1999 Cr LJ 2276 (SC); 1998 Cr LJ 4066 (SC); 1998 AIR SCW 4112.

It was a case under section 482, the Cr. P.C. There was a dispute as to when the cheque was issued, facts relating to receipt, refusal or service of notice need to be decided which can be done only after recording evidence and then can be found out whether the matter falls within the ambit of limitation. Issue of applicability of section 258, the Cr. P.C. was also raised which was found unnecessary and not applicable. It was found that the petition under section 482, the Cr. P.C. was misconceived and was dismissed.

***Vinay Kumar Gupta* v. *P.K. Jain*, (2003) 3 Civ LJ 127: (2002) 100 DLT 463: (2003) 66 DRJ 483: 2003 Cr LJ 1122 (Del)**

Cases referred:

2001 Cr LJ 972 SC; AIR 1998 SC 3043; (2000) 1 SCC 397; (1996) 7 SCC 523; 1996 JCC 207.

Facts of the case.—Intimation about dishonour of cheque was received by the complainant on 26-4-2000. Notice of demand was sent on 4-5-2000. It was returned that the house was repeatedly found locked. It was received back on 8-6-2000. The complainant sent again a notice dated 12-6-2000 which was received on 29-6-2000. The complaint was filed on 29-7-2000. In this case section 27 of the General Clauses Act was also referred. Two questions arose in this case:

(1) What is the date on which demand notice was received by the drawer?

(2) What is the date of accrual of cause-of-action?

The High Court dismissed the petition on the plea that the limitation can be decided only after finding out whether it is to be counted from 4-5-2000 or from 8-6-2000, when it was received back. The matter could be decided only after the parties have led their respective evidence.

***Ramachandra Panigrahi* v. *State of Orissa*, (2003) 3 BC 576: (2003) 95 Cut LT 688: (2003) 1 Ori LR 615: 2003 Cr LJ 2921 (Ori)**

Facts of the case.—The cheque was dishonoured and as per intimation slip dated 17-10-2001. The notice should have been issued within 15 days of the receipt of intimation, *i.e.*, 1-11-2001. Notice of demand was issued on 3-11-2001. The notice was sent on wrong address. It remained undelivered and came back on 15-11-2001, without waiting for 15 days the complaint was filed on 27-11-2001, *i.e.*, on 13th day itself including 15-11-2001 and 12th day of 15-11-2001 is excluded. Accordingly the order of cognizance dated 10-12-2001 passed by S.D.J.M. was quashed and application under section 482 was allowed.

***Rayalasima Agro Enterprise* v. *Gujarat Agro Industries*, (2002) 3 BC 65: (2002) 3 Crimes 309: 2003 Cr LJ 1627 (AP)**

Cases referred:

(2000) 1 Ker LJ 610; 1999 Cr LJ 4606 SC; 1996 Cr LJ 604 (Mad).

Facts of the case.—In this case section 14 of the Limitation Act, 1963 and sections 201 and 470, the Cr. P.C. were referred. The complaint was filed at place 'A'. It was returned to be filed in proper court due to territorial jurisdiction. It was *held* that the period occupied from date of presentation of complaint in wrong forum till they were ordered to file in proper court shall have to be excluded. Section 473, the Cr. P.C. and section 5 of the Limitation Act, 1963 were also referred. It was *held* that section 142 of the Negotiable Instruments Act starts with "*Non Obstante* Clause" and as such no shelter can be taken under any other provision of any other Act and as such the provisions of section 142 are to be strictly construed. The complaint was barred by Limitation.

***N.G. Soma Shekhar* v. *S.V. Shivaprasad*, (2003) 1 BC 409: (2003) 115 Comp Cas 828: (2003) 1 Kant LJ 437: 2003 Cr LJ 351 (Karn)**

Cases referred:

AIR 1999 SC 1609: (1999) 4 SCC 567: 1999 Cr LJ 2276; 1998 Cr LJ 4066; (1998) 2 Karn LT 1.

Facts of the case.—Two cheques dated 5-7-1996 and 9-7-1996 were issued. On presentation they were dishonoured on 9-7-1996. Notice of demand was issued on 12-7-1996. Reply to notice dated 30-7-1996 was received by which the accused asked time for payment upto 7-11-1996. The payee again presented the cheques on 8-11-1996. On being dishonoured the payee issued demand notice on 11-11-1996. When there was no payment the complaint was filed. It was *held* that once the demand notice is issued, the limitation cannot stop running once the clock starts ticking even if the drawer of the cheque requests for some more time for payment.

***C.E.I. Consultancy* v. *Medi World Infotech*, (2002) 2 Andh LT (Cri) 242: 2003 Cr LJ NOC 159 (AP)**

It was *held* that merely because a complaint was presented well within time, was returned for rectification of some clerical or typographical errors or omissions and was represented after rectifying the defects, would not become time-barred merely because the representation of complaint was made after the prescribed period of limitation. The complaint cannot be said to be time-barred.

***Sou Surekha Sandip Hazare* v. *Instacomp*, (2004) 3 BC 33: (2004) 1 Bom CR (Cri) 374: (2004) 2 Rec Cri R 408: 2004 Cr LJ 1687 (Bom)**

Case referred:

1973 Cr LJ 159: AIR 1973 SC 55.

Facts of the case.—It was an appeal against the order of acquittal passed by the trial court. In this case the cheque was presented thrice but dishonoured. Two times, the drawer was informed on telephone and the third time notice was issued on 1-7-1996 and was received on 2-7-1996. The complaint was filed in the month of September, 1996 on the plea that after making enquiries from the postal department, *i.e.*, on 22-8-1996 the complainant came to know that the acknowledgment receipt was lost in handling and gave a certified copy of the said acknowledgment receipt. This plea was not accepted by the trial court and the High Court upheld the decision of the Trial Court that the complaint was time-barred.

***Santosh* v. *Gupta Brass Parts Co.*, (2004) 2 BC 542: (2004) 2 Crimes 582: (2004) 110 DLT 160: 2004 Cr LJ 2918 (Del)**

Facts: In this case the demand notice was issued on 20-7-2001. It was received on 23-7-2001. The drawer prepared the draft on 6-8-2001 and sent to the payee along with covering letter dated 13-8-2001 which was received on 17-8-2001. The lower court took the view that in section 138, the Negotiable Instruments Act, the expression used is, "within 15 days of the receipt of notice" and other expression is, "does not make the payment". This expression indicates that the payee must receive the payment within 15 days of the receipt of demand notice and as such in the order of the trial court there was no infirmity, perversity, impropriety, illegality or jurisdictional error.

Note.—*The High Court should have considered section 147 which is effective from 6-2-2003 as being a beneficial provision.*

***Bapulal B. Kachhi* v. *Krupa Chand Jain,* (2004) 1 BC 73: (2004) 1 Crimes 46: (2003) 3 MPLJ 66: 2004 Cr LJ 1140 (MP)**

Cases referred:

2002 Cr LJ 1522 (followed); AIR 2000 SC 2946 (followed); 1993 Cr LJ 680 (Bom).

Facts of the case.—In this case the complaint was filed before expiry of 15 days from the date of receipt of notice by the accused. However, cognizance of the complaint was taken after arising of cause of action. The order of the court refusing to register the complaint on ground that it was pre-mature, was not proper. It is worth noting that the expression used is "the court shall not take cognizance". There is no such expression, "the complaint shall not be filed".

***Veteran Co. Pvt. Ltd.* v. *State,* (2004) 4 BC 544: (2003) 4 CHN 525: (2004) 1 Cal LJ 134: 2004 Cr LJ 1258 (Cal)**

Cases referred:

(2002) 10 JT (SC) 134: (2002) 6 SCALE 169; (2002) 1 Cal LJ 586; 2001 Cr LJ 1586 (AP); (2000) 6 SCALE 578 (SC); 1999 Cr LJ 2693 (Mad); 1998 Cr LJ 4066 (SC); 1998 Cal Cr LR 287; AIR 1964 SC 538.

Facts of the case.—On dishonouring of cheque the complainant issued notice on 22-6-2001. The said notice was received by the drawer of cheque in June itself but suppressed this fact, issued the second notice to save limitation and on the basis of second notice initiated criminal proceedings. The complaint was filed on 7-9-2001. It was certainly beyond the period of limitation.

Note.—*For responsibility of the Directors for the offence under section 141 also see this case.*

***Srikanth P. Hutagee* v. *Gangadhar S. Hutagekar,* (2005) 1 BC 82: (2004) 4 Civ LJ 531: (2004) 5 Kant LJ 145: 2004 Cr LJ 3815 (Karn)**

Cases referred:

(1) 2000 Cr LJ 603 (AP).

(2) 1995 Cr LJ 350 (Mad).

Facts of the case.—The intimation of dishonour of cheque for reason, "stop payment", was received on 17-1-2000. Legal notice was issued on 2-2-2000. The notice should have been issued within 15 days, *i.e.,* on or before on 1-2-2000. The argument of the payee was:—

(1) That period of giving notice should be taken as 30 days as per amendment. (which only became effective from 6-2-2003).

(2) The cognizance should have been taken under section 420, the I.P.C. (There was no averment in the complaint to this effect).

Held: That the complaint could not be entertained. So taking cognizance of the offence and issuing process was bad in law.

***Ajai Gupta* v. *State of Maharashtra,* (2004) 2 Bom CR (Cri) 738: (2004) 4 ICC 641: (2004) 4 Mah LJ 132: 2004 Cr LJ 3648 (Bom)**

Case referred:

2001 Cr LJ 1250.

Facts of the case.—Intimation of dishonour of cheque was received from the bank on 30-4-2001. So limitation started from 1-4-2001. Notice of demand of payment was issued on 14-5-2001. It was received on 16-5-2001. The payee had to wait for 15 days which expired on 31-5-2001 and then within one month the complaint was to be filed within one month, *i.e.*, by 30-6-2001. The complaint was filed on 28-6-2001, which was within time.

***K.P. Chandrasan* v. *George Kollassani*, (2003) 3 BC 609: (2004) 1 CCC 291: (2003) 4 ICC 687: 2004 Cr LJ 2636 (Ker)**

Cases referred:

1999 Cr LJ 1822 SC (followed); 1999 Cr LJ 2276 SC (followed); AIR 1957 MP 114 (relied on); AIR 1929 Nag 96 (relied on).

Facts of the case.—The period of 15 days expired by 1-9-1996 and cause-of-action arose on 2-9-1996. For computing period of one month the first day, *i.e.*, 2-9-1996 was to be excluded and the last day, *i.e.*, 2-10-1996 is to be included. Since 2-10-1996 being holiday, the complaint was filed on 3-10-1996, which was within time. (Refer section 4 of the Limitation Act, 1963).

***Amravati Chits Investments* v. *T.M. Vaidyanathan*, 2005 Cr LJ 576 (Mad)**

Material alteration in the cheque from 25-2-1994 to 25-12-1994. It is done to save limitation. Dismissed.

***Vinayak* v. *Suhas Padmakar Asukar*, 2005 Cr LJ 218 (Karn)**

Complaint filed within time. Cognizance not barred by limitation.

***K. Krishna Kutty Nair* v. *Ashokan*, 2005 Cr LJ 1095 (Ker)**

Cheque dated 1-4-1993 dishonoured on 5-4-1993. 15 days expired on 20-4-1993. Cause-of-action arises on 6-5-1993, complaint filed on 5-6-1993. It is within time. Day of cause-of-action to be one day after expiry of 15 days

***V.R. Praveen* v. *Ismyll*, 2005 Cr LJ 1644 (Ker)**

Complaint filed beyond period of limitation. Acquittal cannot be set aside, AIR 2003 SC 2434 Distinguished.

***Gian Singh* v. *Oswal Steels, Chandigarh*, 2005 Cr LJ 2396 (P&H)**

Date of receipt of Notice is to be excluded. Period expired on 27-7-1990. Cause-of-action will arise from 28-7-1990. Complaint filed on 27-8-1990. It is within time.

***Mukesh Jain* v. *Balachander*, 2005 Cr LJ 3881 (Mad)**

Complaint and sworn statement should be read together. Dismissal not proper. Accused had no right of audience in revision against dismissal under section 203, the Cr. P.C.

***Narinder Nalwaya* v. *Ishwarlal*, 2005 Cr LJ 3610 (Raj)**

Cheque amount barred by limitation. Charges framed. Discharge not proper.

***Ganga Ram Singh* v. *State of Uttar Pradesh*, 2005 Cr LJ 3681 (All)**

Complaint filed premature – does not render liable to be dismissed. Court should wait for the period for cause-of-action.

Comments: By way of illustration, computation of period of limitation on hypothetical basis is as follows:—

(1) Cheque issued on 10-3-2005.

(2) Cheque presented for payment in the Bank. 11-3-2005.

(3) Intimation of dishonour of cheque as per cheque returning Memo. 13-3-2005.

(4) Notice of demand of payment in lieu of dishonoured cheque (within 30 days) to be made upto (30 days to be counted from 14-3-2005). 12-4-2005.

(5) Notice received on 15-4-2005.

(6) Payment to be received upto (within 15 days) starting from 16-4-2005. 30-4-2005.

(7) Date of filing of complaint if payment not received within 15 days [within one month of the date of cause-of-action arises under clause (c) of proviso to section 138, the Negotiable Instruments Act]. 31-5-2005.

***Chouradiya Trading Company* v. *Sushil Kumar*, 2010 (1) Crimes 166 (MP)**

Cases referred:

Bapulal v. *Krupa Chand Jain*, 2005 CLDC 18; *Rahul Builders* v. *Arihant Fertilizers and Chemicals*, 2008 (1) SCC (Cri) 703.

In this case complaint was filed under section 138 on 3.4.2002. Notice for dischonour of cheque for payment of money was sent on 26.3.2002 and received by the accused on 27.3.2002. Court took cognizance of the complaint on 28.9.2002. It was held that complaint cannot be dismissed because it was prematurely filed. Cognizance was taken after lapse of mandatory period prescribed under section 142(b) of the Negotiable Instruments Act. Complaint would be maintainable if the accused fails to pay the amount. Taking of cognizance of offence amounts to taking cognizance of the complaint.

***Gujarat Tours & Travels P. Ltd.* v. *Anup Gulati*, 2010 (1) JCC (NI) 38 (Del)**

Cases referred:

The State of Madhya Pradesh v. *Hiralal*, JT 1996 (1) SC 669; *Subhad S. Salaskar* v. *Jayaparkash M. Shah*, AIR 2008 SC 3086.

In this case the issue of Limitation was raised. Postal endorsement on the registered cover shown that the party has refused to accept it. It is a valid service. The cause-of-action to file the compliant arises when the fifteen days available to the respondent to make payment of the amount of the cheque expired. A fresh service of notice on a subsequent date would not give rise to a fresh cause-of-action as far as criminal liability under section 138 is concerned complaint filed beyond the period of one month of the date on which cause-of-action arose is not maintainable.

***Ramesh Sachdeva* v. *Shahhaz Khan*, 2010 (1) Crimes 400 (HP)**

Cases referred:

Subhod S. Salaskar v. *Jay Prakash, M. Shah*, (2008) 13 SCC 589; *C.C. Alavi Hazi* v. *Palpetty Muhammad*, (2007) 6 SCC 555; *D. Vinod Shivappa* v. *Nanda Belliappa*,

(2006) 6 SCC 456; *SIL Impart U.S.A.* v. *Exim Aids Silk Exporters, Bangalore,* (1999) 4 SCC 567.

It was held that where more then one notice is sent to the accused, date of receipt of former, notice by the drawer will give cause-of-action and other notices shall be inconsequential.

Note I.—*Day of 30-4-2005 is to be excluded and day of 31-5-2005 is to be included.*

Note II.—*Once notice is issued, law of Limitation cannot stop running once the clock starts ticking even if the drawer of cheque requests sometime more for payment.*

Note III.—*Issue of second notice will not save Limitation.*

Note IV.—*Section 5 of the Limitation Act, 1963 is available in view of proviso added to section 142(b) w.e.f. 6-2-2003. [See AIR 1984 All 334; AIR 1954 SC 411; AIR 1972 SC 749; AIR 1978 SC 5370; AIR 1981 SC 733; 2006 Cr LJ 193 (Bom);* R.K. Chawla *v.* Goa Antibiotic & Pharm. Ltd., *2006 Cr LJ 193 (Bom)]*

SECTION 142(b) PROVISO

***R.K. Chawla* v. *M/s. Goa Antibiotics & Pharmaceutical Ltd.,* 2006 (2) JCC (NI) 153 (Bom)**

Section 142(b) proviso was added by Amendment Act, 2002 w.e.f. 6-2-2003. Provisions of the Amending Act are applicable to pending complaints, but not applicable to cases which had already been disposed of. The Magistrate is empowered to condone delay in such cases on sufficient cause being made out for such delay. This amendment is not creating a new offence but it is merely regulating procedure for taking cognizance of offence by the Magistrate.

***O.P. Chirania* v. *The Director of Lotteries and Dy. Secretary to Govt. of Haryana,* 2008 (3) JCC (NI) 356 (Del)**

Cases referred:

(1995) DLT 284; 1996 (2) AIBLJ 44; 1993 Cr LJ 1751; (1998) 6 SCC 514; 1999 (1) JCC (NI) (SC) 256; (2005) 4 SCC 417; (2006) 1 SCC (Cri) 350; 1981 Supp SCC 87; 2008 Cr LJ 1386.

The issue was whether application of section 473, the Cr. P.C. and section 5 of the Limitation Act to be extended to an application under Sections 138/142 of the Negotiable Instruments Act. The court held as follows:—

1. Regarding Pre-Amendment Act, 2002, when Limitation starts to run then neither section 473, the Cr. P.C. nor section 5 of the Limitation Act can come to the rescue of the respondent.
2. Regarding post-amendment position in 2002, the cognizance can be taken by the court if the complainant satisfies the court that he had sufficient cause for not making the complaint within such period, but this amendment cannot operate retrospectively in view of *Anil Kumar Goel* case, 2008 Cr LJ 1386 and the expression in *Ram Richhpal Gupta,* 1995 (59) DLT 284 is held unsustainable.

***Guru Swarup Srivastava* v. *National Agricultural Co-operative Marketing Federation,* 2008 (3) JCC (NI) 254 (Del)**

Regarding insertion of proviso to section 142(b) of the Negotiable Instruments Act, if the complaint is not filed within the period and the payee is able to show sufficient cause why the complaint could not be made in time, to the satisfaction of the court, the Magistrate is empowered to condone the delay and take cognizance of the complaint.

***P.S. Aithala* v. *Ganapathy N. Hegde,* 2008 Cr LJ 1545**

In this case there was delay of 13 days in filing the complaint. Complaint was accompanied by application for condonation of delay and supporting document. Huge amount was involved. *Held,* that delay ought to be condoned.

Cases referred:

1998 Cr LJ 906 (AP); 1993 Cr LJ 1751 (Ori) (Rely. on).

***Smt. Minakshi Sharma* v. *Hitendra Kumar Sharma,* AIR 2009 (NOC) 1820 (Raj)**

It is a case under sections 138, 142(b) of the Negotiable Instruments Act and section 57(a) of the Evidence Act, 1872. Complaint was filed on 32nd day as earlier two days were gazetted holidays. Gazetted holidays are to be excluded while computing period of 30 days. The complaint is not barred by limitation.

***D. Babu* v. *M/s. Bhartia Industries Ltd.,* 2009 (3) JCC (NI) (Del)**

Cases referred:

1999 (2) JCC (Del) 418; 135 (2006) DLT 103; (2004) 13 SCC 492; (2001) 6 SCC 8.

In this case, the complaint was not filed within time. There is nothing on record to show that any application was made for condonation of delay or any attempt was made to satisfy the court that there was sufficient cause of not making the complaint within time. The complaint being filed beyond the period of limitation, it is quashed accordingly.

***Riga Sugar Co. Ltd.* v. *Kessels Engg. Works Pvt. Ltd.,* 2008 (2) JCC (NI) 149 (Del)**

Cases referred:

(1995) 1 SCC 42; (2004) 13 SCC 498; (1998) 6 SCC 514; (1999) 8 SCC 221; 135 (2006) DLT 103; AIR 2006 SCC 2179.

It is *held* that the notice sent by the complainant to the accused satisfies all the conditions of Section 138 of the Negotiable Instruments Act. There is delay in filing the petition. Ignorance of law is no excuse. The order framing notice against the petitioner is quashed. The petitioner is discharged.

Note.—*The contention was that delay cannot be condoned without notice to the accused.*

***Gangadhar* v. *Raghunathasa,* 2008 Cr LJ 1006 (Kant)**

It is said that cause-of-action for filing complaint does not commence merely on issuance of notice under section 138(b) proviso. But it commences from date of service of such notice on the drawer of cheque. If notice is not served cause-of-action shall not arise. The facts of the case are:—

(i) Cheque was presented on 28-3-1998.

(ii) No notice of dishonour of cheque was served on the drawer of the cheque.

(iii) Cheque was represented and dishnoured.

(iv) Notice was sent to this effect and the same was received by the drawer/accused on 25-4-1998.

(v) The complaint was presented on 12-5-1998 as no payment was received. The complaint presented was within time.

Refer:

AIR 2001 SC 676; 2001 (2) DCR 65; AIR 1999 SC 1609; AIR 1998 SC 3043.

***Anil Kumar Shukla* v. *State of Uttar Pradesh*, 2008 Cr LJ 2172 (All).**

In this case a truck was sold for Rs. 3 lakh, Rs. 75,000 was paid in cash and the balance was paid by 4 cheques, one cheque of Rs. 1.5 lakh and 3 cheques of Rs. 25,000 each.

In the case of cheque of Rs. 1.5 lakh, it was presented in the Bank on 10-6-2004 and was dishonoured. A notice was sent on 29-6-2004. The complaint was filed on 18-9-2004. Payment was to be made within 15 days and if not made, the complaint was to be filed within one month [Section 142(b)]: Thus the complaint filed on 18-9-2004 is barred by time.

In the case of cheque for Rs. 25,000 dated 5-8-2004 was also returned by the Bank unpaid on 27-8-2004. Notice was given on 3-9-2004. The said cheque is said to have been received on 6-9-2004 but the complaint was filed on 18-9-2004, before the expiry of the period of 15 days and thus the complaint being premature and without cause-of-action is liable to be quashed. The court distinguished between "taking cognizance" and "issue of summoning order" and held that cause-of-action accrues after expiry of 15 days from date of service of notice complaint filed before expiry of 15 days would be premature and cognizance taken thereon would be illegal and liable to be quashed.

Refer:—

AIR 2005 SC 4284; AIR 2001 SC 3372; AIR 2000 SC 2946; AIR 1998 SC 3043; 1977 Cr LJ 1420; AIR 1963 SC 765; AIR 1951 SC 207; AIR 1943 Pat 245; ILR (1910) 37 Cal 412.

SECTION 142(c)

INTRODUCTION

This provision is to be seen in the light of section 4(2), section 26(b) and sections 29(2) and 29(4) of the Criminal Procedure Code.

Section 4(2) stipulates "All offences under any other laws shall be investigated, inquired into, tried and otherwise dealt with according to the same provisions, but subject to any enactment for the time being in force regulating the manner or place of investigating, inquiring into, trying or otherwise dealing with such offences."

By virtue of section 4(2), the Cr. P.C. it is clear that a special law creating offences may also create special procedure for dealing with them and such procedure provided therein would not be invalid as being inconsistent with the provisions of the Cr. P.C. (*Refer* AIR 1958 Mad 544; AIR 1969 Ker 111; AIR 1958 Mys 143). However, if under a special law, no procedure is prescribed for dealing with the offence, then the procedure laid down in the Code is to be followed. [AIR 1936 All 830 (FB); AIR 1961 Cal 199; 1980 BLJR 464; 1978 Cr LJ 70; (1975) 79 Cal WN 129]. But where the procedure is prescribed, it is that procedure which is to be followed. [AIR 1973 SC 2204; AIR 1965 SC 1; 1976 Chand LR (Cri) 39 (FB); AIR 1970 AP 47; 1977 Cr LJ 1048].

Section 26(b) says, "Any offence under any other law shall, where any court is mentioned in this behalf in such law, be tried by such court and when no court...........".

This provision prescribes the courts by which offences under other laws can be tried. The prescribed court specified in the enactment shall only have the jurisdiction to try such offence. [AIR 1964 SC 1673; AIR 1971 Guj 1; AIR 1969 Ker 111; AIR 1967 MP 94; AIR 1949 Nag 137 (FB); AIR 1941 Lah 145 (FB)].

Sections 29(2) and 29(4), speak about the power vested in the court of a Magistrate of the First Class or that of a Metropolitan Magistrate to pass a sentence of imprisonment for a term not exceeding three years, or of fine not exceeding five thousand rupees, or of both. [Beng LR Supp 951 (FB); (1904) 1 Cr LJ 607 (Bom); 31 Cr LJ 175 (Rang)].

Section 142(c), the Negotiable Instruments Act, 1881: Now this provision stipulates that no court inferior to that of a Metropolitan Magistrate or a Judicial Magistrate of the first class shall try any offence punishable under section 138 and the punishment which may be inflicted is provided under section 138 itself. So jurisdiction of the court to try a particular offence is derived from the statute and the same is provided under section 142(c) of the Negotiable Instruments Act and trial by any court becomes without jurisdiction (1972 MPLJ 763; AIR 1960 Ker 234).

The jurisdiction of the court was challenged in *Pandian* v. *V. Sowrirayan,* 1999 Cr LJ 1364. In this case the issue raised was that though the cause-of-action arose at Thiruvarur, the complaint was filed before the Chief Judicial Magistrate, Kumbakonam who had no jurisdiction and the accused was entitled to be acquitted. In support of this contention reliance was placed on:—

(1) *Narang Industries Ltd.* v. *Ashok Leyland Finance Ltd.,* (1997) 2 Mad LW (Cri) 699.

(2) *Anjillath Mohammed Kunhi* v. *K.K. Abdul Kajeed,* 1996 Cr LJ 2395 (Ker).

It was *held* that the complaint was filed before the Chief Judicial Magistrate Kumbakonam who had got overall jurisdiction of the entire district of Thanjavur. The Chief Judicial Magistrate, received the complaint within time and made over to Judicial Magistrate, Thiruvarur who has got the territorial jurisdiction. Thus the case was tried by the Judicial Magistrate, Thiruvarur.

Place of Trial: No doubt, section 142 starts with "*Non Obstante* Clause" by virtue of which it overrides all other provisions in the same Act or in any other enactment [AIR 1967 Pat 137; AIR 1964 SC 207; AIR 1952 SC 369; AIR 1989 Pat 217 (FB)]. But there is no mention of place of trial for an offence under section 138, the Negotiable Instruments Act. So necessarily we have to resort to the provisions under Chapter XIII of the Criminal Procedure Code, 1973.

Section 177, the Cr. P.C. stipulates that "every offence shall ordinarily be inquired into and tried by a court within whose local jurisdiction it was committed."

It is a general principle of law that all crime is local [AIR 1930 Bom 490 (FB)] and thus the jurisdiction to try a person for an offence depends upon the crime having been committed within the area of such jurisdiction [(1975) 77 Punj LR 575; AIR 1959 All 67; 1978 BBCJ 313.]

Section 178, the Cr. P.C.: It deals with place of inquiry or trial and the section is:—

(a) when it is uncertain in which of several local areas an offence was committed, or

(b) where an offence is committed partly in one local area and partly in another, or

(c) where an offence is a continuing one, and continues to be committed in more areas than one, or

(d) where it consists of several acts done in different local areas, it may be inquired into or tried by a court having jurisdiction over any of such local areas.

This section is basically meant to resolve the difficulty that would arise where it is uncertain as to where the offence can be said to have taken place or it is a continuing offence or the offence constitutes many ingredients and each ingredient has taken place in different local area. [AIR 1957 SC 196; AIR 1934 All 499 (FB); 1980 Cr LJ 1171 (Mah); AIR 1966 SC 128; AIR 1973 SC 908; 1973 Cr LJ 908 (All)].

Section 179, the Cr. P.C.: It deals with offence triable where act is done or consequences ensue. It says, "when an act is an offence by reason of anything which has been done and of a consequence which has ensued, the offence may be inquired into or tried by a court within whose local jurisdiction such thing has been done or such consequence has ensued."

This section vests the jurisdiction in a court in whose local jurisdiction the act was done or the court in whose jurisdiction the consequence ensued [AIR 1960 SC 266; AIR 1965 SC 1921: 52 Cr LJ 1388 Assam (FB); AIR 1937 Sind 68 (FB); AIR 1934 All 499 (FB); AIR 1930 Bom 490 (FB)].

Section 142, the Negotiable Instruments Act, 1881: In dishonour of cheque, there are many factors that cumulatively constitute an offence falling under section 138, the Negotiable Instruments Act, 1881 and it becomes incumbent to analyse this provision through judicial pronouncements:

CASE LAW

***Pobathi Agencies* v. *State of Karnataka*, (1992) 73 Comp Cas 431: 1991 Cr LJ 2529 (Karn)**

The High Court considered sections 178 and 179, the Cr. P.C. and *held* that the place of jurisdiction can be:—

(1) The complaint can be filed in a court within the jurisdiction of which the cheque has been issued, or

(2) where the cheque was presented for collection, or

(3) the place where the cheque is not honoured.

***M.M. Malik, Managing Director, Dany Dairy and Food Engineers Ltd.* v. *Prem Kumar, Advisor, Haryana Milk Foods Ltd., Pehowa,* (1992) 73 Comp Cas 725: (1991) II BC 484: 1991 Cr LJ 2594 (P&H)**

It is *held* that dishonouring of the cheque was only a part of cause-of-action and the offence was completed only when the petitioner company failed to discharge its liability to the complainant herein. For discharging the debt the petitioners had to find out the creditors. Thus it is said, *"Debtor has to find the creditor"*.

***P.K. Murleedharan* v. *C.K. Pareed,* 1992 Bank J 655: (1992) 1 BC 315: (1993) 76 Comp Cas 615: 1992 Cr LJ 1965 (Ker)**

Cases referred:

(1991) 1 Ker LT 595; AIR 1965 Ker 295; AIR 1960 SC 1309; 1959 Cr LJ 1310 (Cal) (relied on); AIR 1957 MB 90; 1957 Cr LJ 322 (SC) (relied on).

In this case the High Court *held* that the venue of enquiry or trial has primarily to be determined by the averments contained in the complaint and then *held* that:—

(1) At the place where the drawer of the cheque fails to make payment of money.

(2) It can be the place where the bank to which the cheque was issued is located.

(3) It can be the place where the cheque was issued or delivered.

The court within whose jurisdiction any of the above mentioned places falls has, therefore, got jurisdiction to try the offence under section 138, the Negotiable Instruments Act.

***Ess Bee Food Specialities* v. *Kapoor Brothers,* (1993) 78 Comp Cas 570: 1992 Cr LJ 739 (P&H)**

The High Court *held* that the issuance of the cheques and their dishonouring are only a part of cause-of-action, the offence was complete only when the petitioners failed to discharge their liability to the respondent firm. For discharging a debt, it is the debtor who has to find out his creditor. (*Refer* 1991 Cr LJ 2594 P&H).

***Rakesh Nem Kumar Parwal* v. *Narayan Dhondu Joglekar,* (1993) 78 Comp Cas 822: 1993 Cr LJ 680 (Bom)**

Case referred:

1992 Cr LJ 1965 (Ker).

The High Court referring to sections 177 and 178, the Cr. P.C. and referring to 1992 Cr LJ 1965 (Ker) *held* that having defaulted in the first instance, the law casts a special obligation on the drawer of the cheque to make amends by tendering the payment to the payee and the correct approach in such a situation would be, to constitute the offence having been complete at the place where the payment ought to have been tendered to the drawee but was wrongfully not done.

***Gautam T.V. Centre* v. *Apex Agencies*, (1994) 79 Comp Cas 682: (1992) 3 Andh LT 441: 1993 Cr LJ 1004 (AP)**

The High Court referring to sections 177, 178 and 179, the Cr. P.C., *held* that cause-of-action is a bundle of facts. Issuance of cheque, presentation of the cheque, endorsement of dishonour, issuance of a statutory notice and location of the office of the person in whose favour the cheque was issued are all the factors which are to be taken into account for deciding the cause-of-action. It need not confine to particular transaction. Series of acts will result at different places. So the complaint can be filed in a court within the jurisdiction of which: (1) the cheque has been drawn, or (2) the place where the cheque is presented for collection and received an endorsement about the dishonour of the cheque, or (3) the place where the cheque is dishonoured.

Cases referred:

1992 Cr LJ 739 (relied on); 1991 Cr LJ 2529 (relied on); 1981 Cr LJ 1301; AIR 1930 Bom 490 (FB).

***Adapta Bhogi Raju* v. *S.G. Ramayya*, (1994) 2 BC 141: (1994) 1 Crimes 350: 1994 Cr LJ 411 (AP)**

In this case the transaction had taken place partly at two places, but the cheques issued at one place. The business was made at Rajamundhry. So a part of transaction took place there. The main settlement took place at Amalapuram and the cheques were issued at Amalapuram. So Amalapuram had the jurisdiction.

***Tarsem Lal Hans* v. *Prem Nath Palta*, 1995 Cr LJ 2408 (P&H)**

Cases referred:

Probhati Agencies v. *State of Karnataka*, (1991) 2 Rec Cri R 685; *T.K. Khungar* v. *Sanjay Ghai*, (1993) 3 Rec Cri R 612.

In this case the cheques were issued at Moga, were presented to a Bank at Moga for collection, but dishonoured by a Bank at Jalandhar but intimation of dishonour was received at Moga. Notices were sent by the respondent to make payment at Moga. So Moga Court had the jurisdiction to try the case.

Note.—*The basic point is that the offence under section 138, the Negotiable Instruments Act consists of several acts done in different local areas and as such, the offence may be inquired into or tried by a court having jurisdiction over any of such local areas.*

***Canbank Financial Services Ltd.* v. *Gitanjali Motors Ltd.*, (1996) 65 Comp Cas 485: 1995 Cr LJ 1222 (Del)**

Cases referred:

1992 CC 431 (Kant); (1992) 1 Crimes 973 (Ker) (distinguished); (1992) 2 Bank LJ 336 (Ker); (1988) 1 Crimes 514 (Del) (followed); AIR 1974 P&H 2.

In this case the complaint was returned to be filed in the proper court on the ground that it had no territorial jurisdiction to deal with the matter and hence the revision petition. The High Court *held* that dishonour of cheque *per se* is not an offence. To become an offence under section 138, the Negotiable Instruments Act, some further requirements have to be fulfilled and all those acts may be committed in different local areas and every such act constitutes a part of the cause-of-action. Place of payment will always retain its primacy as cheque is mere a mode of payment and the payment is to be made to the creditor at his place. Thus, the High Court heavily kept in mind sections 178 and 179, the Cr. P.C.

***Anjillath Mohammed Kunhi* v. *K.K. Abdul Kajeed*, (1999) 98 Comp Cas 607: 1996 Cr LJ 2395 (Ker)**

Cases referred:

1995 All HC 636 (P&H); (1994) Banking Cases 46 (Mad); 1992 Cr LJ 1965 (Ker); 1991 Cr LJ 2529 (Kant).

The issue was that the court in whose jurisdiction the cheque was issued, was only the competent court to entertain the complaint. The High Court while referring to the above cited case law *held* that the complaint could be filed at place where cheque was dishonoured and also where the cheque was issued.

***K.K. Ponnappan* v. *Sibi C.J.*, (1998) 2 CCC 659: (1998) 1 KLT 673: 1998 Cr LJ 2402 (Ker)**

Cases referred:

(1995) 2 Ker LT 900; 1992 Cr LJ 1965 (Ker); 1991 Cr LJ 2529 (Kant).

The High Court referring to sections 178 and 179, the Cr. P.C. and also referring to the cases cited *held* that provisions of section 138 are enacted by the Parliament in order to maintain the credibility of commercial transactions and to avoid bouncing of cheques which would impede commercial transactions. The place of filing the compliant cannot be restricted to the place where the cheque was issued or the place where the drawers failed to make the payment. *Held,* that the court within whose jurisdiction the cheque was presented had jurisdiction to entertain complaint.

***Varghese* v. *C.K. Ramani*, (1998) 3 Civ LJ 839: (1998) 94 Comp Cas 606: 1998 Cr LJ 2755 (Ker)**

Cases referred:

1991 Cr LJ 2594 (P&H); AIR 1977 SC 1101: (1977) 2 SCC 190: 1977 Cr LJ 940.

In this case there was discussion on sections 462 and 201, the Cr. P.C. regarding trial of the case in a court having no jurisdiction. The lower court acquitted the accused on the ground of non-jurisdiction. The High Court *held* that if the lower court came to the conclusion it would have taken action under section 201, the Cr. P.C. However, the High Court found that the court had the jurisdiction to entertain the complaint and also *held* that it was well-settled law that (1) the court has the jurisdiction over the area where the cheque was issued, or (2) delivered, or (3) where the drawer of the cheque failed to make payment of the money, or (4) the area where the payment was to be made.

***Sanjay Makkar* v. *Saraswati Industrial Syndicate Ltd.*, 1999 Cr LJ 1958 (All)**

Cases referred:

AIR 1998 SC 3043: (1998) 6 SCC 514: (1998) 2 KLT 765; (1993) 1 Crimes 723 (AP); (1992) 1 Crimes 973 (Cal); 1992 Cr LJ 1965 (Ker); 1981 Cr LJ 1667 (Ker); AIR 1957 MB 90; AIR 1952 PEPSU 5.

In this case the High Court referred to section 178, the Cr. P.C. and *held* that the question of jurisdiction has to be decided on the basis of the averments made in the complaint. So far as territorial jurisdiction is concerned, the cause-of-action arises:—

(1) where the cheque was drawn, or

(2) at a place where the cheque was presented, or

(3) a place where the payee made a demand for payment of the money by giving a notice in writing to the drawer within the stipulated period,

(4) and at a place where the drawer failed to make the payment within 15 days of the receipt of notice.

Therefore, the complaint may be filed in the Court within the jurisdiction of which

(1) the cheque has been drawn, or

(2) the place where the cheque was presented for collection and where an endorsement about dishonour was made, or

(3) the place where the cheque was dishonoured.

***K. Bhaskarn* v. *Sankaran Vaidhyan Balan*, (1999) 7 SCC 510: 1999 SCC (Cri) 1284: AIR 1999 SC 3762: 1999 Cr LJ 4606 (SC)**

Cases referred:

(1997) 2 Ker LT 539; AIR 1992 SC 1604: (1992) 1 SCC 647; AIR 1988 SC 2127: (1988) 4 SCC 551; AIR 1981 SC 1284.

This was an appeal against the order of conviction and sentence passed by the High Court of Kerala. The Kerala High Court converted the acquittal order passed by the lower order into conviction. The Supreme Court referred to sections 177, 178 and 179, the Cr. P.C. and said that these provisions in the Code should have been borne in mind when the question regarding territorial jurisdiction of the courts to try the offence was sought to be determined.

The Supreme Court further said that the offence under section 138 of the Act can be completed only with the combination of a number of acts. Following are the acts which are components of the said offence:—

(1) Drawing of the cheque.

(2) Presentation of the cheque to the bank.

(3) Returning the cheque unpaid by the drawee Bank.

(4) Giving notice in writing to the drawer of the cheque demanding payment of the cheque.

(5) Failure of the drawer to make payment within 15 days of the receipt of notice.

It is not necessary that all the five acts should have been perpetrated at the same locality. It is possible that each of those five acts could be done at five different localities. If the five different acts were done in five different localities, any one of the courts exercising jurisdiction in one of the five local areas can become the place of trial for the offence under section 138 of the Act. In other words, the complainant can choose any one of those courts having jurisdiction over any one of the local areas within the territorial limits of which anyone of those acts was done.

The Supreme Court further said that as the amplitude stands so widened and so expansive, it is an idle exercise to raise jurisdictional question regarding the offence under section 138 of the Act.

Note.—*It is a trend setter law propounded by the Supreme Court.*

***Naresh Chander* v. *State of Rajasthan*, (2000) 1 Raj Cri C 349: 2000 Cr LJ 5090 (Raj)**

Cases referred:

1997 Cr LJ 2122 (Mad); 1996 Cr LJ 2395 (Ker); 1993 Cr LJ 680 (Bom); 1993 Cr LJ 1008 (HP); 1991 Cr LJ 2594 (P&H).

In this case the issue was of territorial jurisdiction. The facts of the case were:—

(1) Cotton was purchased at Sri Ganganagar where the complainant deals in cotton.

(2) The purchaser lived in Kanpur.

(3) Cheques were issued in Abohar after arriving at settlement.

(4) Cheques were presented to the bank at Abohar.

(5) Cheques were payable at Kanpur as drawn on a bank at Kanpur.

(6) Cheques were dishonoured.

(7) Demand notice was issued from Abohar.

(8) Complaint was filed at Sri Ganganagar.

The High Court *held* that it is Sri Ganganagar where initially the accused was to make the payment because the initial cause-of-action arose at Sri Ganganagar which had the jurisdiction to entertain the complaint as the goods were supplied at Sri Ganganagar against which the payment was to be made.

***Krishan Kumar Menon* v. *Neoteric Informatique Pvt. Ltd.*, (2002) 1 BC 512: (2002) 1 Ker 51: (2001) 3 KLT 689: 2002 Cr LJ 706 (Ker)**

Cases referred:

(2001) 2 KLT 638: (2001) 2 KLT 57 (distinguished); 1980 KLT 411 (followed); 1970 KLT 45 (followed); AIR 2000 SC 2966: (2000) 7 SCC 640: 2001 SCC (Cri) 215; 1999 Cr LJ 4606 SC; AIR 1998 SC 128: (1998) 5 SCC 749; (1994) 4 SCC 711; AIR 1953 SC 210: 1953 SCR 1144.

It was a case pending under section 138, the Negotiable Instruments Act in a court outside the jurisdiction of Kerala High Court but the petition under section 482, the Cr. P.C. was filed in the Kerala High Court for quashing the complaint. It was *held* that the High Court under section 482, the Cr. P.C. could not exercise its inherent power to quash the complaint pending outside the jurisdiction of the High Court. However, the High Court under compelling circumstances could interfere under Article 226 of the Constitution of India and the petitioner could approach the High Court if he was advised so.

***Sunil Srivastava* v. *Ashok Kalra,* (2002) 101 DLT 245: 2003 Bank LJ 467: 2003 Cr LJ 1443 (Del)**

Cases referred:

1999 Cr LJ 4606 (SC); 1995 Cr LJ 1222 (Del); 1991 Cr LJ 2594 (P&H); (1988) 1 Crimes 514 (Del); AIR 1983 Karn 73; AIR 1977 Karn 204; AIR 1967 SC 1634: (1968) 38 Comp Cas 1.

In this case many issues were raised and one of the issues pertained to jurisdiction of the court. The High Court referred to the "trendsetter law" propounded by the Supreme Court in *K. Bhaskaran's* case (1999 Cr LJ 4606 SC) wherein the Supreme Court held as to what are the various causes of action in a case under section 138 of the Act to give territorial jurisdiction to a court.

***Partap Singh Yadav* v. *Atal Behari Pandey,* (2003) 2 Crimes 343: (2002) 100 DLT 673: (2003) 66 DRJ 101: 2003 Cr LJ 705 (Del)**

Cases referred:

1999 Cr LJ 4606 SC; 1995 Cr LJ 1222 (Del); 1991 Cr LJ 2594 (P&H).

In this case the facts disclosed that the respondent was residing at Delhi; the notice of demand was sent to the petitioner from Delhi, dishonouring of cheque was intimated to him at Delhi; and the payment was to be made at Delhi. So Delhi court had the jurisdiction. Now the guiding principle is, *"Where any part of cause-of-action has arisen within the territorial jurisdiction of that court and if so, that court has the jurisdiction to try the offence."*

***Mattathil Ouseph Ittira* v. *State of Kerala,* (2003) 2 Bank LR 814: 2003 Bank J 591: (2002) 2 Ker LJ 504: (2003) 2 Civ LJ 370: 2003 Cr LJ 514 (Ker)**

Case referred:

1999 Cr LJ 4606 (SC).

In this case the issue was that—(1) The cheque was issued in Sharjah, (2) Drawn on a bank at Sharjah, (3) Entire transaction took place in Sharjah. So the court at Thiruvalla had no Jurisdiction. At that place only the cheque was presented for collection. The High Court relied on the decision of the Supreme Court in *Bhaskarn's* case and *held* that the court at Thiruvalla has the territorial Jurisdiction to try the offence under section 138, the Negotiable Instruments Act.

[*Refer:* Para 11 of the decision of the Supreme Court in *Bhaskarn's* case 1999 Cr LJ 4606 (SC).]

"We fail to comprehend as to how the trial court could have found so regarding the jurisdiction question. Under section 177 of the Code 'every offence shall ordinarily be inquired into and tried in a court within whose jurisdiction it was committed'. The locality where the Bank (which dishonoured the cheque) is situated cannot be regarded as the sole criterion to determine the place of offence. It must be remembered that offence under section 138 would not be complete with the dishonour of cheque. It attains completion only with the failure of the drawer of the cheque to pay the cheque amount within the expiry of 15 days mentioned in clause (c) of proviso to section 138 of the Act. It is normally difficult to fix up a particular locality as the place of failure to pay the amount covered by the cheque. A place, for that purpose, would depend upon a variety of factors. It can either be at the place where the payee resides or at the place where either of them carries on business. Hence, the difficulty to fix up any particular locality as the place of occurrence for the offence under section 138 of the Act."

Note.—*Law is meant to punish the guilty but not to harass him through legally assumed notions. It is seen that in order to create hazardous compulsion and harassment to the drawer of the cheque, the payee presents the cheque to the bank for collection at a place thousands of kilometer away from the place where the transaction takes place and then issues the demand notice from that place and files the complaint there if the drawer of the cheque fails to make the payment. Law, in fact, did not contemplate such induced place of cause-of-action by self created intention of the Payee. By this, it is the payee that vests the jurisdiction in the court, which otherwise it would have not. This fact needs serious consideration by the Supreme Court.*

Bhaskaran's *case brought judicial uncertainty in the matter of territorial jurisdiction and section 177, the Cr PC was made almost nugatory. Even section 178, the Cr. P.C. was subjected to discretionary interpretation and now* Harman's *case (AIR 2009 SC 1168) has brought a new judicial surprise to unsettle the business norms. A further study of cases involving territorial jurisdiction are appended below.*

***Laxmi Travels Nagpur* v. *G.E. Countrywide Consumer*, 2006 Cr LJ 3704 (Bom)**

The facts are that:—

(i) Both parties are residing at Nagpur.

(ii) Basic transaction took place at Nagpur.

(iii) Cheque was presented and dishonoured at Nagpur.

(iv) Demand Notice was issued from Aurangabad, was received at Nagpur.

(v) Except issuance of demand notice from Aurangabad all transactions took place at Nagpur and not at Aurangabad.

Held: Mere issuance of notice from Aurangabad itself cannot give cause-of-action to file complaint at Aurangabad. Convenience of parties is also an important fact.

***Supra Enterprise* v. *Bygging India Ltd.*, 2006 (2) JCC (NI) 140 (Del)**

Though it is a civil suit but the question agitated was whether the court has the territorial jurisdiction. The points raised in support of Jurisdiction are:—

(i) That the defendant approached the plaintiff seeking to purchase cast iron pipes at Delhi.

(ii) The bills raised by the plaintiff against the defendant at Delhi.

(iii) The bills raised by the plaintiff are subject to the clause, "Subject to Delhi Jurisdiction".

The points raised against the territorial jurisdiction of the Court at Delhi are:—

1. The defendant has no office in Delhi. Its registered office is in Bombay.
2. The defendant does not carry on business in Delhi.
3. The bills were raised in Poona by the plaintiff and on the defendant at Bombay.
4. No cause-of-action has arisen at Delhi.
5. Mere the use of words, "Subject to Delhi Jurisdiction" cannot vest the jurisdiction in Delhi Court since it is not vested with such Jurisdiction.

It was held that it is not open to the parties to confer by their agreement, jurisdiction an a court which it does not possess under the Code. It has to be shown, firstly, that his court would in any event have had jurisdiction under the Code and further held that this court has no territorial jurisdiction.

Note.—*"Cause-of-action" where it happens decides the territorial jurisdiction.*

***Musaraf Hossain Khan* v. *Bhagheeratha Engg. Ltd.*, 2006 (2) JCC (NI) 113 (SC)**

In this case the bench of Hon'ble Mr. Justice S.B. Sinha and Hon'ble Mr. Justice P.K. Balasubramanyan discussed the concept of "cause-of-action" and said that "cause-of-action" within the meaning of clause (2) of Article 226 shall have the same meaning as is ordinarily understood. The expression "cause-of-action" has a definite connotation. It means a bundle of facts which would be required to be proved. The facts of the case are:—

1. Agreement giving rise to case entered into within the jurisdiction of the Calcutta High Court.
2. Project for which supply to stone chips and transportation was being carried out was also within state of West Bengal.
3. Payments were obviously required to be made within the jurisdiction of the Calcutta High Court.

The issue before the Supreme Court was whether Calcutta High Court or the Kerala High Court has the writ jurisdiction in this case. The Supreme Court referred to various cases and in particular the case cited as *Prem Chand Vijay Kumar* v. *Yashpal Singh*, (2005) 4 SCC 417 which speaks of the facts to he proved:—

(a) That the cheque was for payment of an amount of be money for discharge of a debt/liability and the same was dishonoured.

(b) That the cheque was presented within the prescribed period.

(c) That the complainant made a demand for payment of money by giving a notice in writing to the drawer within the stipulated period, and

(d) That the drawer failed to make the payment within 15 days of the receipt of notice. These are the facts to prove "cause-of-action" and it is to be read with section 142(b) of the Negotiable Instruments Act and held that Kerala High Court has no jurisdiction.

***Balraj Kumar* v. *Kuldeep Kaur,* 2007 (1) JCC (NI) 44 (P&H)**

In this case the High Court held that the relevant provisions of the Act would be satisfied by service of a notice under section 138 of the Act. The object of the notice is of giving chance to the drawer of the cheque to rectify his omission and if the payment is made within 15 days, the respondent would have been absolved of the liability.

Note.—*The object of notice is to give a chance to the accused to absolve himself of the criminal liability for the offence which he has committed when the cheque was dishonoured, but law cannot be set into motion till the second chance by sending a notice in writing is given.*

***M/s. Shri Krishna Polyester Ltd.* v. *State,* 2007 (4) JCC (NI) 381 (Del)**

The issue was of territorial jurisdiction and the facts are:—

1. Pay orders have been drawn at ANZ Grindlays Bank, Mumbai.
2. They have been delivered and received at Bombay.
3. Evidence pertaining to handing over and taking over is as per agreement executed at Bombay on 17-9-1999.

Held, Delhi Court has no jurisdiction and the learned ACMM is directed to return the complaint to be filed in the competent court at Bombay.

***Iqbal Ahmad Khan* v. *State of Uttar Pradesh,* 2008 Cr LJ 2177 (All)**

It is *held* that most of the acts such a drawing of cheque, presentation of cheque, return of cheque by drawer bank, etc., related to place "J" but only cheque was drawn on Lucknow Branch of Corporation Bank. Complaint filed at place *J* cannot be said to be not maintainable.

***Namita Ganwani* v. *State,* 2008 (1) JCC (NI) 8 (Del)**

In this case the issue of inconvenience and compensation thereof was raised. The High Court agreed with the issue of inconvenience/harassment and said that such practice of filing complaint at two places must be deprecated. However, the Court agreed with the issue of compensation stating that the act of the petitioner also caused inconvenience to the respondent. Law of Equity was invoked.

***Shamsad Begam* v. *B. Mohammed,* AIR 2009 SC 1355**

The Apex Court referred to the five acts as stated in the case cited as *K. Bhaskaran* v. *Sankaran Vaidhyan Balan,* 1999 (7) SCC 510 and said that in this case one of the components of the offence under section 138 was giving notice under section 138 of the Negotiable Instruments Act in writing to the drawer of the cheque demanding payment of the cheque amount. The said action took place within the jurisdiction of court at *"M"*. Therefore, court at *'M'* had jurisdiction to try the case.

Note.—*In* Bhaskaran's *case the expression "concatenation of all the five acts" is used. "Concatenation" means linked together. So all the five acts are to be considered as one homogeneous component and not heterogeneously.*

***M/s. Harman Electronics P. Ltd* v. *M/s. National Panasonic India Ltd.*, AIR 2009 SC 1168**

The issue before the Apex Court was the territorial jurisdiction of the court and the facts are:—

1. Appellant is a resident of Chandigarh.
2. He carries on business at Chandigarh.
3. The cheque in question was admittedly issued at Chandigarh.
4. Complainant has also branch at Chandigarh although its H.O. is said to be in Delhi.
5. The cheque was stated to be presented at Chandigarh.
6. The notice of demand was issued upon the appellant asking him to make the payment from New Delhi.
7. Admittedly the said notice was served upon the respondent at Chandigarh.
8. The payment was not made within 15 days of the receipt of notice.
9. The complaint was filed at Delhi and the issue of territorial jurisdiction arose.

The proceedings in the lower courts are as below:—

1. Cognizance of the offence was taken against the appellant by the learned Judge.
2. Additional Session Judge, relying upon *Bhaskaran's* case held that the court at Delhi has the jurisdiction
3. Aggrieved by the order, a Criminal Miscellaneous Petitioner was filed which was dismissed and hence this criminal appeal.

The issue before the Apex Court was, "whether" giving of notice" or "receiving of notice" is the criteria. The Apex Court held that "cause-of-action" arose when the notice was received and the court under whose jurisdiction the "cause-of-action arose" has only the jurisdiction and passed orders under Article 142 that the case he transferred from New Delhi to the District and Sessions Judge, Chandigarh who will assign the case to the court of competent jurisdiction. Delhi Court has no jurisdiction.

***Online JT Shoppe India Pvt. Ltd.* v. *State*, 2010 (1) JCC (NI) 27 (Del)**

Cases referred:

K. Bhaskarn v. *Sankaran Vaidhyan Balan*, (1999) 7 SCC 510; *Shamshad Begum* v. *B. Mohammed*, (2008) 13 SCC 510; *Prem Chand Vijay Kumar* v. *Yashpal Singh*, (2005) 4 SCC 417; *Hazman Electronics Private Limited* v. *National Panasonic India, Private Limited*, (2009) 1 SCC 720; *Shri Ishwar Alloy Steels Ltd.* v. *Jayaswals Neco Ltd.*, (2001) 3 SCC 609.

It is held that sending of notice from Delhi does not confer jurisdiction on Delhi Courts and the deposit of cheque with the banker of respondent in Delhi also does not confer jurisdiction on Delhi Courts when the cheque in presented to a bank outside Delhi and there is no other ground which would confer jurisdiction on Delhi Court.

***K.O. Issac* v. *State*, 2010 (1) CC Cases Del (HC) 207**

Cases referred:

K. Bhaskaran v. *Sankaran Vaidhyan Balan*, (1999) 7 SCC 510; *Shamshad Begum* v. *B. Muhammed*, (2008) 13 SCC 417; *Prem Chand Vijya Kumar* v. *Yashpal Singh*, (2005) 4 SCC 417; *Harman Electronics Private Limited* v. *National Panasonic India Private Limited*, (2009) 1 SCC 720; *Masarf Hussain Khan* v. *Bhagheertha Engg. Ltd.*, (2006) 3 SCC 658; *Delhi High Court Legal Services Committee* v. *Govt. of NCT Delhi*, 163 (2009) DLT 56.

It is a case where the office of the complainant is in Delhi 48 post-dated cheques were issued to Respondent No. 2 at Delhi. The transaction took place at Delhi. The cheques were presented at Delhi. *Held* that jurisdiction of Delhi Court to entertain complaints could not be disputed. Section 138 read with Section 178(b) & (d) Cr. P.C. clearly shown that the Jurisdiction is vested in courts at Delhi.

Note.—*This decision of the Apex Court has caused further ripples in the turbulent judicial ocean already created by the* Bhaskaran's *case. No doubt the decision of the Apex Court is binding but if it creates judicial inconvenience, it is right to express an opinion that the decision is not in the right perspective. Section 138 of the Negotiable Instruments Act is in two parts. First part deals with the offence and the second part (proviso) deals with "Cognizance of the offence" and the same is to be read with section 142(b) of the Negotiable Instruments Act.*

Part I specifically speaks "such person shall be deemed to have committed an offence." When the offence is said to have been committed, that situation is provided in the section itself and the components of that situation are:—

(i) The cheque is drawn by a person.

(ii) On an account maintained by him with a banker.

(iii) The cheque is issued for payment of any amount of money to another person out of that account.

(iv) For the discharge, in whole or in part, of any debt or other liability. (debt or other liability finds its reflection in the *Explanation*).

(v) The said cheque is returned by the bank unpaid.

(vi) Reasons for returning the chaque unpaid are given in the Section. (The scope of the reasons has been judicially enlarged).

So if these ingredients are satisfied the offence is said to have been committed.

Part II of section 138 of the Negotiable Instruments Act (provisos) is introduced with a clear motive that the dishonest evader is to be punished and the honest person who could not arrange payment when the cheque is presented, be given a chance to show his honesty. Thus non-payment within 15 days of the receipt of notice is not that the offence is completed but it means that cognizance of the complaint is to be taken.

Furthermore, section 142(b) makes the matter more clear. It refers to (i), within period of one month of the date on which the cause-of-action arises and (ii) it refers to clause (c) of proviso to section 138. The expression "cause-of-action" must be construed "cause-of-action to file the complaint". It has nothing to do with the territorial jurisdiction.

It will be appropriate to refer to the doctrine of "Proper Law of Contract." When there is ambiguity as to the court of Jurisdiction, then the tilting tendency of the contract is to be taken into consideration and this principle of civil law can be incorporated very conveniently into the Negotiable Instruments Act on the basis of law of equity, justice and good conscience.

Now the filing of new cases under Negotiable Instruments Act is causing deviation from the doctrine of "forum non-convenients" (see *Mayar (H.K.) Ltd* v. *Owners & Parties Vessel M.V. Fortune Express*, 2006 (2) SCALE 30.

See 1. *Achintya Mandal* v. *M/s. Haitanya Agro Products*, 2009 (2) JCC (NI) 94 (Del).

This case was decided on the basis of *Harman Electronics'* case, AIR 2009 SC 1168.

CHAPTER VI

DISHONOUR OF CHEQUE – SUMMARY TRIAL IF REQUIRED

143. Power of Court to try cases summarily.—(1) Notwithstanding anything contained in the Code of Criminal Procedure, 1973 (2 of 1974), all offences under this Chapter shall be tried by a Judicial Magistrate of the first class or by a Metropolitan Magistrate and the provisions of sections 262 to 265 (both inclusive) of the said Code shall, as far as may be, apply to such trials:

Provided that in the case of any conviction in a summary trial under this section, it shall be lawful for the Magistrate to pass a sentence of imprisonment for a term not exceeding one year and an amount of fine exceeding five thousand rupees:

Provided further that when at the commencement of, or in the course of, a summary trial under this section, it appears to the Magistrate that the nature of the case is such that a sentence of imprisonment for a term exceeding one year may have to be passed or that it is, for any other reason, undesirable to try the case summarily, the Magistrate shall after hearing the parties, record an order to that effect and thereafter recall any witness who may have been examined and proceed to hear or rehear the case in the manner provided by the said Code.

(2) The trial of a case under this section shall, so far as practicable, consistently with the interests of justice, be continued from day to day until its conclusion, unless the Court finds the adjournment of the trial beyond the following day to be necessary for reasons to be recorded in writing.

(3) Every trial under this section shall be conducted as expeditiously as possible and an endeavour shall be made to conclude the trial within six months from the date of filing of the complaint.

INTRODUCTION

Section 143 deals with summary trial. Though there is "*Non Obstante* Clause" the provisions of sections 262 to 265, the Cr. P.C. shall, as far as may be, apply to such trials. To understand this section more vividly, a reference is to be made to various other provisions.

Section 138 of the Negotiable Instruments Act: "Such person shall be deemed to have committed an offence and shall, without prejudice to any other provisions of this Act, be punished with imprisonment for a term which may be extended to two years or with fine which may extend to twice the amount of the cheque or with both".

Section 142(c) of the Negotiable Instruments Act: "no court inferior to that of a Metropolitan Magistrate or a Judicial Magistrate of the first class shall try any offence punishable under section 138."

Section 29(2), the Cr. P.C.: "The Court of a Magistrate of the first class may pass a sentence of imprisonment for a term not exceeding three years or of fine not exceeding five thousand rupees or of both."

Section 262, the Cr. P. C.: (1) In trials under this chapter, the procedure specified in this Code for the trial of summary case shall be followed except as hereinafter mentioned.

(2) No sentence of imprisonment for a term exceeding three months shall be passed in the case of any conviction under this chapter.

Order XXXVII, Rule 1 sub-rule (2)(a): "This Order shall apply to suits upon bills of exchange, hundis and promissory notes".

So if the case is tried under summary trial then clause (2) of section 262, the Cr. P.C. shall stand applicable but instead section 143(1) proviso shall apply also if the Magistrate so desires such sentence of imprisonment and fine can also be imposed as stipulated herein and infliction of such punishment shall be lawful. In other words, sentence provided under section 262(2), the Cr. P.C. can be ignored by the Magistrate.

Along with these provisions it is worthwhile to mention *section 357, the Cr. P.C.* which speaks of order to pay compensation. *Section 357(1(b) says:* "in the payment to any person of compensation for any loss or injury caused by the offence, when compensation is, in the opinion of the court, recoverable by such person in a civil court."

It is to be noted that section 143 is inserted by the Negotiable Instruments (Amendment and Miscellaneous Provisions) Act, 2002 (55 of 2002), section 10 (w.e.f. 6-2-2003). Since all these provisions deal with punishment for the offence, it is desirable to have a judicial view as to how the judiciary perceives it in its different aspects.

JUDICIAL VIEW

SENTENCE OF FINE

***Selvaraj* v. *P. Vishwanathan*, 1999 MLJ (Cri) 738: (1994) 4 Rec Cri R 276: (1999) 2 MLW (Cri) 489: 1999 Cr LJ 4766 (Mad) (FB)**

Cases referred:

(1998) Cri RC No. 512/93/D/29-1-1998 (Mad) (overruled); 1996 Cr LJ 636 (AP); 1996 Cr LJ 1223 (Ker) (followed); (1995) 3 SCALE 72; (1995) 83 Comp Cas 191 (Mad); AIR 1994 SC 1343: (1994) SCC 323: (1994) 1 CLR 544; 1994 Cr LJ

3452 (Ker) (followed); AIR 1992 SC 81: (1992) 1 SCC 335; (1991) Cri O.P. Nos. 1856, 1857 of 1991 D/12-6-1991 (Mad); AIR 1987 SC 117: (1986) 4 SCC 447; AIR 1984 SC 718: (1984) 2 SCC 500: 1984 Cr LJ 647 (distinguished); AIR 1984 SC 1022; AIR 1980 SC 962: 1980 Supp SCC 92: 1980 Cr LJ 690; AIR 1966 SC 1931: (1966) 3 SCR 663; AIR 1964 SC 207: (1964) 4 SCR 280; AIR 1963 SC 1241; AIR 1963 SC 1561; AIR 1960 SC 905; AIR 1957 SC 444: 1957 SCR 370; AIR 1957 SC 657; AIR 1955 SC 435; AIR 1954 SC 92: 1954 SCR 587; AIR 1954 SC 202: 1954 SCR 913; AIR 1952 SC 369 (distinguished); *Rex* v. *Grant*, (1951) 1 All ER 28; AIR 1950 SC 188: 1950 SCR 459; *Nokes* v. *Doncaster Amalgamated Collieries*, 1940 AC 1014: (1940) 3 All ER 549; AIR 1933 PC 218; *London County Council* v. *Aylesbury Dairy Co. Ltd.*, (1898) 1 QB 106.

MAJORITY VIEW

Facts of the case.—In this case sections 29, 325, the Cr. P.C. were discussed. The **Majority view** – Sirpurka, J. (P. Thangavel, J. concurring): A Metropolitan Magistrate or a Judicial Magistrate of the first class trying an offence punishable under section 138 would have the power to award punishment more than five thousand rupees which is a limit provided by section 29 of the Cr. P.C., owing to the express language of section 142(c) read with section 138 of the Act.

Minority view (A. Raman, J.): The Magistrate has no power to impose a fine of more than Rs. 5000. In case where the offence under section 138 of the Act has been made out, it is his duty to follow the procedure under section 325, the Cr. P.C. when he feels that a case is made out for imposing fine of more than Rs. 5000.

Note.—*So far as punishment is concerned, the provisions are not happily worded. No doubt, special law overrides general law, but when there is conflict of higher magnitude leading to the provisions of general law becoming nugatory, then a harmonious interpretation has to be read in the provisions to clear the legal controversy and for that purpose section 357 can be incorporated in section 138. The punishment portion may be read as follows:—*

> *"be punished with imprisonment for a term which may be extended to two years AND fine which may extend to five thousand rupees and appropriate and adequate compensation commensurate with the cheque amount which is dishonoured."*

***Jonnadula Mallikarjuna Rao* v. *Dodda Venkata Subhareddy*, (2000) 2 Andh LT (Cri) 6: (2000) 2 Andh WR 19: 2001 Cr LJ 2008 (AP)**

Case referred:

AIR 1999 SC 3762.

Facts of the case.—In this case the accused is sentenced to undergo six months simple imprisonment and a fine of Rs. 66038. In criminal petition filed under section 482, the Cr. P.C. the issue of award of fine as part of sentence was agitated and section 29(2), the Cr. P.C. was discussed. It is *held* that the powers of the Magistrated to impose fine is restricted to Rs. 5000 under section 29(2), the Cr. P.C. Imposition of fine higher than Rs. 5000 as part of sentence is not sustainable. However, the High Court observed that no pecuniary limit is contemplated under section 357, the Cr. P.C.

***Pankajbhai Nagjibhai* v. *State of Gujarat,* (2001) 2 SCC 595: 2001 SCC (Cri) 369: (2001) 104 Comp Cas 418: 2001 Cr LJ 950 (SC)**

Cases referred:

AIR 1999 SC 3762; 1996 Cr LJ 1223 (Ker) (distinguished); 1994 Mad LJ (Cri) 91 (distinguished).

Facts of the case.—In this case the Trial Magistrate convicted the accused and sentenced him to imprisonment for six months and a fine of Rs. 83,000. The conviction and sentence were confirmed by the Sessions Judge in appeal and the Revision filed by the convicted person was dismissed by the High Court and hence this S.L.P. (Cri) was filed.

Held, that the Judicial Magistrate first class cannot impose sentence of fine beyond Rs. 5000 in view of limitation contained in section 29(2) of the Cr. P.C. The *Non Obstante* Clause contained in section 142 of the Negotiable Instruments Act does not expand powers of the Magistrate as far as fine is concerned. The Supreme Court further *held* that if a Magistrate of first class thinks that the fact situation in a particular case warrants imposition of a sentence more severe than the limit fixed under section 29(2) of the Code, he can as per section 325 of the Code forward the accused to the Chief Judicial Magistrate. Even that apart, a Magistrate who thinks it fit that the complainant must be compensated with his loss he can resort to the course indicated in section 357 of the Code. No limit is prescribed in section 357 of the Code as regards award of compensation.

COMPENSATION/INADEQUACY OF SENTENCE

***Bhavani* v. *D.C. Dodda Xangaiah,* 2000 Cr LJ 3814 (Karn)**

Facts of the case.—A cheque for Rs. 1,50,000 was dishonoured. The Trial Court has levied punishment of fine only to the extent of Rs. 15,000 and not the amount which represents the cheque value or double of it. Being aggrieved by the inadequate fine amount levied, the present revision is filed, relying upon the decision in *B. Hari Krishna* v. *Macro Links Pvt. Ltd.,* ILR 2000 (Ker) 2855. The High Court *held* that it would be almost obligatory on the part of the trial Court when the case has ended in conviction to award a compensation that would be commensurate with the legal principles of fair-play and this in our view, having regard to the provisions of section 117 of the Negotiable Instruments Act, which should not be less than the face value of the cheque, the interest computed at 18% per annum and the costs that may be computed by the court. The High Court modified the fine to Rs. 3 lakh, out of which Rs. 2,95,000 shall be payable to the complainant as compensation and Rs. 5000 to be appropriated to the State. Accordingly the petition is allowed.

***Suganthi Suresh Kumar* v. *Jagdeeshan,* (2002) 2 SCC 420: 2002 SCC (Cri) 344: 2002 Cr LJ 1003: (2002) 1 KLJ 444: (2002) 1 CCR 88 (SC)**

Cases referred:

(2001) 2 SCC 595: AIR 2001 SC 567: (2001) 104 Comp Cas 418; (1999) 7 SCC 510: 1999 SCC (Cri) 1284; (1988) 4 SCC 551 (referred, relied & approved);

(2001) 3 Ker LT 431 (not approved); AIR 1995 SC 1935: (1994) 4 SCC 29; AIR 1988 SC 1353: (1988) 4 SCC 551 (relied).

Facts of the case.—In this case the amount involved was Rs. 4,50,000. The trial Magistrate convicted the accused and sentenced to undergo imprisonment till rising of the court and fine of Rs. 5000. Amount remained unpaid during the pendency of the case. The plea taken by the respondent is that the petitioner has filed a civil suit and all the properties of the respondent are attached. The Supreme Court *held* that no drawer of cheque can be allowed to take dishonour of cheque issued by him light heartedly. The case is remitted back with the directions to hear both sides again in matter of sentence and pass sentence which is condign. The sentence passed by the Magistrate is set aside in view of rehearing of the case on sentence.

***Dr. B.N. Suryanarayana Rao* v. *B.C. Seshadri*, (2003) 2 BC 226: (2003) 114 Comp Cas 333: (2003) 3 Kant LJ 134: 2003 Cr LJ 1421 (Karn)**

Facts of the case.—In this case the cheque amount was Rs. 1,52,000. The trial court imposed a fine of Rs. 20,000 and in default to undergo simple imprisonment for four months. The High Court *held* that the sentence should have been adequate and no lenient view should have been taken because the same case was pending in the Consumer Forum. The High Court found the sentence imposed as inadequate and set aside. The respondent is directed to pay a fine twice the cheque amount and in default to undergo simple imprisonment for one year. Out of the fine Rs. 10,000 to be defrayed by the State towards prosecution expenses and balance to be paid as compensation to the complainant.

Note.—*The order of the High Court is erroneous to the extent that Rs. 10,000 to be defrayed by the State towards prosecution expenses for two reasons:—*

(1) *It is hit by section 29(2), the Cr. P.C.*

(2) *It is the duty of the court to try the case to impart justice and to punish the guilty for which no cost is to be recovered from the accused and there is no such provision in criminal jurisprudence.*

***Nagaraj* v. *Gowramma*, (2004) 4 BC 44: (2004) 4 Kant LJ 262: (2004) 3 Crimes 562: 2004 Cr LJ 2947 (Karn)**

Case referred:

(2001) 2 Mad WN (Cri) DCC 72.

Facts of the case.—The cheque amount was Rs. 60,000 which is dishonoured. The trial Magistrate imposed a fine of Rs. 10,000. The complainant, aggrieved by this inadequate fine, filed revision before the Sessions Judge, Bangalore, where the fine was modified to Rs. 65,000. The High Court, relying upon the decision in *Rajinderan* v. *Usha Rani*, (2001) 2 Mad WN (Cri) DCC 72 *held* that the petition under section 482 is not maintainable and further *held* that there is no good reason to interfere with the orders by both the trial court as well as the learned Sessions Judge.

***N. Krishna Shetty* v. *N. Mruthyunjaya Rao,* 2004 AIR Kant HCR 3126: (2005) 1 All MR (Cri) 21: 2004 Cr LJ 4792 (Kant)**

Cases referred:

AIR 2004 SC 3978; AIR 2001 SC 567: (2001) 2 SCC 595: 2001 SCC (Cri) 369; ILR (2000) Kant 2855 (followed); (1988) SCC (Cri) 984: (1988) 4 SCC 551: AIR 1998 SC 2127.

Facts of the case.—The cheque amount was Rs. 75,000. It was decreed for a sum of Rs. 85,000 in the Lok Adalat and thus a fine of Rs. 5000 imposed by the trial Magistrate does not call for revision and relied upon *Anil Kumar* v. *Alka Gupta,* AIR 2004 SC 3978. It is *held* that the fine of Rs. 5000 imposed by the Magistrate is illegal and incorrect. The High Court modified the sentence and imposed a fine of Rs. 80,000 in default of payment a simple imprisonment was prescribed. Out of the fine amount a sum of Rs. 75,000 shall be paid to the revision-petitioner and Rs. 5000 shall be credited to the State.

Note.—*The High Court should have considered that the matter has already been decided in a Civil Forum and the effect of the civil suit should have been visible in the criminal case and should have been considered as one falling under section 147 of the Negotiable Instruments Act. If the order of the High Court is not illegal but then positively it is harsh and excessive.*

***Thomas* v. *State of Kerala,* (2004) 2 All Cri R 878: (2004) 3 BC 128: 2004 Cr LJ 1273 (Ker)**

Facts of the case.—The petitioner was found guilty under section 138, the Negotiable Instruments Act and sentenced to undergo simple imprisonment for six months and also to pay a fine of Rs. 20,000. The Sessions Judge upheld the sentence but set aside fine of Rs. 20,000 and modified it to pay Rs. 15,000 as compensation under section 357(3), the Cr. P.C. to the complainant. The amount of compensation was not paid. Now the contention was that the impugned order cannot be executed by arrest warrant and if the judgment is not complied with the amount of compensation cannot be realised by following revenue recovery proceedings. The High Court found the order of the appellate court not correct and *suo motu* order was passed for revision of the appellate Judgment.

***Kurutti Venkata Appa Rao* v. *Kaki Uma Shankar Rao,* (2003) 3 BC 326: (2004) 3 Civ LJ 149: (2004) 2 CCC 272: 2004 Cr LJ 1126 (AP)**

Facts of the case.—The cheque amount of Rs. 70,000 was dishonoured. The trial court found the respondent guilty but only imposed a fine of Rs. 3000 by taking into consideration that the respondent is unemployed and is blessed with a daughter. The High Court *held* that the said sentence does not conform to letter and spirit of provisions of the Cr. P.C. or the Negotiable Instruments Act, and therefore is not proper. *Held,* that the court ought to have either imposed the sentence of imprisonment or ordered payment of compensation. The order of the court regarding sentence is set aside and remanded back for passing fresh orders as to sentence, duly giving an opportunity to the respondent.

***Magan Lal Jain* v. *Abhijeet Kumar Dash,* (2002) 4 BC 317: (2004) 3 Civ LJ 373: (2004) 28 OCR 137: (2004) 1 Ori LR 554: 2004 Cr LJ 2415 (Ori)**

Cases referred:

AIR 2002 SC 281; AIR 2001 SC 567: (2001) 2 SCC 595: 2001 SCC (Cri) 369: (2001) 1 KLT 517; 2001 Cr LJ 008 (AP).

Facts of the case.—The cheque amount was Rs. one lakh. The trial court found the respondent guilty and awarded compensation of Rs. 3000 out of a fine of Rs. 5000. Two pleas were raised:

(1) The trial court has power to award compensation under section 357(3), the Cr. P.C. as the Court cannot impose fine more than Rs. 5000 in terms of section 29(2), the Cr. P.C.

(2) The contention of the other side was that the complainant can recover amount by filing civil suit. However, this plea is found untenable.

On the point of compensation, the High Court remitted back the case to the trial court to reconsider the question of grant of compensation with reference to the decisions referred above and pass necessary orders.

NON-DEPOSIT OF FINE MONEY

***Ram Nath* v. *Jagdish Parshad Garg,* (1999) 3 Civ LJ 456: (1999) 3 Crimes 114: (1999) 3 WLR 157: 1999 Cr LJ 2136 (Raj)**

Case referred:

1998 Cr LJ 1397.

Facts of the case.—Two cheques amounting to Rs. 75,000 and Rs. 60,000 were dishonoured when presented. The accused was found guilty and convicted and sentenced him to undergo three months S.I. with fine of Rs. One lakh and in default to further undergo S.I. for another 10 days. It was further directed that the amount if realised, Rs. 75,000 shall be given to the complainant by way of compensation. The Appellate Court upheld the decision of the lower court.

In this revision petition it is submitted that the petitioner has already undergone 3 months imprisonment imposed by the trial court but has not been in a position to pay or deposit the fine of Rs. One lakh. The High Court *held* that there can be no interference by the High Court under section 401, the Cr. P.C. The only alternative is to file a civil suit for the recovery of the said amount and the civil suit be filed within 4 months and the court is directed to decide the matter expediously within a period of 4 months.

SUSPENSION OF SENTENCE

***Stanny Felix Pinto* v. *Jangid Builders Pvt. Ltd.,* (2001) 2 SCC 416: 2001 SCC (Cri) 345: AIR 2001 SC 659: 2001 Cr LJ 1039 (SC)**

Facts of the case.—It is a case where a fine imposed was Rs. 20 lakh and the High Court directed to deposit a sum of Rs. 4 lakh for suspension of sentence. The Supreme Court *held* that the direction of the High Court is not unjust or unconscionable when the fine is very heavy. Appeal is accordingly dismissed.

SECTION 138 AND ORDER XXXVII, RULE 2, C.P.C.

***Avneet Food Products* v. *Government of N.C.T. Delhi,* (2003) 114 Comp Cas 798: (2003) 66 DRJ 121: 2003 Cr LJ (NOC) 238 (Del)**

The point missed in the criminal Petition is that the complainant can recover the cheque amount by way of summary suit under Order XXXVII, rule 2, the CPC. *Held,* that the fine under section 138 cannot be equated as allowing complainant to receive double amount of the cheque as in default the accused can always be sent to imprisonment. Proceedings under section 138 are independent in nature and cannot be quashed on the premise that the complainant can recover the amount by way of a summary suit under Order XXXVII, the CPC.

***Basant India Ltd.* v. *Vibgyor Infotech,* 2006 (1) JCC (NI) 68 (Del)**

The facts of the case are that the complaint under section 138 of the Negotiable Instruments Act was filed on 6-10-2005 and it was adjourned to 9-12-2005, when summoning order was passed. The matter has now been posted to 1-2-2007, whereas under section 143 of the Act, the matter should be disposed of as expediously as possible preferably within six months. *Held,* the petitioner should move application before the concerned Magistrate for preparing the date and the date be preponed. Efforts be made to dispose of the matter within six months from the date of receipt of this order.

***Shri Pankaj Narang* v. *State,* 2006 (1) JCC (NI) 69 (Del)**

In this case the issue was that the petitioner was not incharge or responsible to the company for conduct of the business and, therefore, the mere allegation whatsoever in the complaint cassies no weight and held that there matters have to be dealt within as summary cases and there matters of defence should be raised in the trial court instead of challenging every interlocutary order passed by the Metropolitan Magistrate. The amendments have been made to bring these cases on fast track primarily to create confidence and credibility in the people *qua* the transactions based on cheques.

***M/s. Hora Sales Agencies* v. *M/s. Quest Components P. Ltd.,* 2006 (1) JCC (NI) 22 (Del)**

A petition was filed under section 482 of the Cr. P.C for quashing the complaint filed under sections 138, 142 of the Negotiable Instruments Act. *Held,* trial under section 138 is to be tried summarily by virtue of section 143 of the Negotiable Instruments Act as amended by Act 55 of 2002 and sections 262 to 265, of the Cr. P.C. and endeavour shall be made to conclude the trial within 6 months from the date of filing the complaint. If this court entertains such petition it has to examine oral as well as documentary evidence which is yet to come on record of Trial Court and has to face the test of cross-examination which is not envisaged under section 482 of the Cr. P.C. No interference in the trial under section 482, of the Cr. P.C.

***Vinay Kumar* v. *State of Uttar Pradesh,* 3161 All 2009**

In this case the complainant did not appear before the Magistrate on the date fixed for his appearance. Magistrate had no option but to dismiss the complaint and acquit the accused.

Refer:

1987 All LJ 1008; AIR 1986 SC 1440; AIR 1958 Punj 317; AIR 1948 Mad 45; AIR 1936 All 658; Section 256 Cr. P.C.

***Mrs. Jain Babu* v. *K.J. Joseph,* AIR 2009 (NOC) 404 (Kant)**

In this case under Section 138 of the Negotiable Instruments Act, various provisions like sections 205, 313, 313(b), 353(6), 389(3) were discussed along with section 143 of the Negotiable Instruments Act and held as follows:—

(i) Plea of accused exempted under section 205, the Cr. P.C. can be recorded through his counsel.

(ii) Examination of the accused under Section 313(B), the Cr. P.C. can also be dispensed with.

(iii) Personal appearance of the accused for receiving judgment can be directed if sentence is one of substantive imprisonment.

(iv) It is mandatory for the court to direct the accused to remain present on the specified day for execution of sentence.

REMISSION OF SENTENCE

***N.A. Ravi Kumar* v. *S. Suresh Kumar,* (2003) 1 BC 20: (2002) 3 Crimes 542: 2002 Cr LJ 3820 (Mad)**

Cases referred:

AIR 2001 SC 3703; AIR 2000 SC 890: (2000) 3 SCC 394; AIR 2000 SC 1179; (2000) 1 Mad WN (Cri) 78 (SC); (2000) 1 Mad WN (Cri) 72; (2000) 1 CTC 206 (Mad); AIR 1996 SC 2512: (1996) 5 SCC 495; 1996 Mad LJ (Cri) 261; AIR 1987 SC 2225: (1987) 4 SCC 296; AIR 1974 SC 31: (1974) 3 SCC 531: 1974 Cr LJ 150; AIR 1961 SC 600: (1961) 3 SCR 440.

Facts of the case.—It is a case where sections 432 and 433 of the Cr. P.C. were discussed. Section 432 deals with remission of sentence and section 433 deals with "appropriate Government". In the light of these two sections the High Court *held* that the offence under section 138 of the Negotiable Instruments Act is a legislation relating to the cheques as contained in Entry 46 in List I of the Seventh Schedule of the Constitution of India. Therefore, this legislation would definitely fall under the exclusive competence of the Union Government. Hence, any remission of sentence of an offence under the Negotiable Instruments Act can be granted only by the Central Government as it would relate to the matters concerned with List I of the Seventh Schedule. As such the G.O. issued by the State Government granting remission to some offences would not apply to the offence under the Negotiable Instruments Act.

***State of Kerala* v. *Soma Thomas,* (2004) 19 All Ind Cas 956: (2004) 3 BC 421: (2004) 2 Ker 498: 2004 Cr LJ 2222 (Ker)**

Facts of the case.—In this case the High Court discussed section 432(7), the Cr. P.C. and Articles 73 and 246 of the Constitution of India and *held* that a person who is convicted and sentenced for an offence under section 138 of the Negotiable Instruments Act, the appropriate Government for the purpose of section 432 of the Code is the Central Government and not the State Government.

Note.—*It is to be noted that remission of sentence should not be confused with set off as is covered by section 428, the Cr. P.C.*

Summary Trial: Section 143 has been inserted in the Negotiable Instruments Act by the Negotiable Instruments (Amendment and Miscellaneous Provisions) Act, 2002 (55 of 2002), section 10 (w.e.f. 6-2-2003). This provision is taken from the Code of Criminal Procedure, 1973 on pick and choose method. Clause (1) has been taken from section 260, Cr. P.C. and proviso to clause (1) is taken from section 260(2), the Cr. P.C. The other proviso to clause (1) is taken from section 262(2) duly modified in terms of sentence.

Now with the introduction of section 143, there can be two types of trials. Regular trial or Summary trial.

But it is not made clear as to under what circumstances there will be summary trial. Is it the prerogative of the Magistrate of first class or it is on the application of the complainant/accused? Furthermore, the punishment prescribed is "imprisonment for a term not exceeding one year and an amount of fine exceeding five thousand rupees" so there will be both imprisonment and fine which shall be more than Rs. 5000. It is a pity that the drafting is not happily worded. Section 29(2) and section 325(1), the Cr. P.C. have been heterogeneously mixed, and it is not understood as to why provision of section 357, the Cr. P.C. is not inserted in suitable form so that the concept of punishment becomes very clear.

CHAPTER VII

SUMMONS - HOW AND WHEN PRESUMED SERVED

144. Mode of service of summons.—(1) Notwithstanding anything contained in the Code of Criminal Procedure, 1973 (2 of 1974), and for the purposes of this Chapter, a Magistrate issuing a summons to an accused or a witness may direct a copy of summons to be served at the place where such accused or witness ordinarily resides or carries on business or personally works; for gain, by speed post or by such courier services as are approved by a Court of Session.

(2) Where an acknowledgment purporting to be signed by the accused or the witness or an endorsement purported to be made by any person authorised by the postal department or the courier services that the accused or the witness refused to take delivery of summons has been received, the Court issuing the summons may declare that the summons has been duly served.

INTRODUCTION

This section starts with "*Non Obstante* Clause". "Notwithstanding" means that this provision shall prevail over any provision governing mode of service of summons as contained in the Code of Criminal Procedure, 1973 (2 of 1974) and that other provision shall not be of any consequence. Full Bench of Patna High Court in *Krishna Bhagwan* v. *State,* AIR 1989 Pat 217 (FB) has said that "*Non-obstante* clause" has the effect of setting at naught and of obliterating such other provisions. Clause (1) of section 144 has been further qualified by the use of expression "and for the purpose of this section". It means that this mode of service of summons is exclusively meant for Chapter XVI of the Negotiable Instruments Act, 1881 and not applicable to other chapters of the Act.

Now a reference is to be made to the provisions contained in the Code of Criminal Procedure, 1973 (2 of 1974) governing "mode of service of summons" in the light of section 144 of the Negotiable Instruments Act.

Section 69, the Cr. P.C.: Section 144 is inserted with some modification of section 69, the Cr. P.C. which says:—

"(1) a Court issuing a summons to a witness may, in addition to and simultaneously with the issue of such summons, direct a copy of the summons to be served by registered post addressed to the witness at the place where he ordinarily resides or carries on business or personally works for gain.

(2) When an acknowledgment purporting to be signed by the witness or an endorsement purporting to be made by a postal employee that the witness refused to take delivery of the summons has been received, the court issuing the summons may declare that the summons has been duly served."

So clause (1) of section 69, the Cr. P.C. speaks of two ways of serving the summons:—

(i) By serving personally. (Section 62, the Cr. P. C.)

(ii) By Registered Post.

But under section 144, the Negotiable Instruments Act, the service of summons is as follows:—

(i) By serving personally (Section 62, the Cr. P.C.)

(ii) By Speed Post, or

(iii) By such courier services as are approved by a Court of Session.

Now section 144 speaks of summons to be served both on the accused and witness whereas section 69, the Cr. P.C. speaks of service of summons on witness only. Section 144 of the Negotiable Instruments Act is a new provision. It intends to avoid delay in the service of summons and section 144, the Negotiable Instruments Act, by inserting service of summons by speed post or approved courier is intended to make the process faster.

Clause (2) of section 144 is almost similar to that of clause (2) of section 69, the Cr. P.C. except in place of "witness", it is now "accused or witness". Clause (2) of section 144 is a clear authority to the effect that, notwithstanding the absence of the evidence of the Postman, the endorsement made by him is admissible in Evidence.

CASE LAWS

(1) In *Bapayya* v. *Venkataratnam,* (1991) 1 CCC 254 *it has been laid down* unequivocally that the admissibility of the endorsement of refusal made by the Postman does not depend upon the oral testimony of the person making the endorsement. It is in the discharge of his official duties that the Postman makes the endorsement of "refusal".

(2) In the case of *K.V. Subbayya* v. *P.R.R.T. Co.,* AIR 1972 AP 72, it was *held* that the endorsement, made by Postman even without producing the Postman concerned in the court, on the ground that it is in the discharge of his official duties that the Postman makes his endorsement in his official capacity in the proper exercise of the official function.

(3) In a case (1968) 9 Guj LR 116 this issue was raised where there was no endorsement that person refused to accept service. It cannot be *held* that that person refused it.

***M/s. MacCharles (I) Ltd.* v. *Chandershekhar,* 2006 (1) JCC (NI) 51 (Kant)**

This case was placed before the Division Bench by way of reference. It was *held* that offences punishable under section 138 of the Negotiable Instruments

Act, or under the Indian Penal Code, substituted service an accused by way of affixation of one of duplicates of summons on a conspicous part of the house of the accused where he ordinarily resides or such part of place where he carries on business or works for gain, is permissible as prescribed by section 65 of the Cr. P.C., if service cannot by exercise of due diligence be effected as provided under section 62, 63 or 64 of the Cr. P.C. Similar is the position under the Negotiable Instruments Act, as envisaged under section 144 thereof. Substituted mode of service to an accused is recognized in a criminal trial whether it be an offence under the I.P.C. or the Negotiable Instruments Act.

Note. Also Refer

Bhimrao, AIR 1963 Mys 239; *Hemendra Nath* v. *Arehana*, 1971 Cr LJ 817.

CHAPTER VIII

EVIDENCE ON AFFIDAVIT - A NEW PROVISION IN CRIMINAL JUSTICE

145. Evidence on affidavit.—(1) Notwithstanding anything contained in the Code of Criminal Procedure, 1973 (2 of 1974), the evidence of the complainant may be given by him on affidavit and may, subject to all just exceptions be read in evidence in any enquiry, trial or other proceeding under the said Code.

(2) The Court may, if it thinks fit, and shall, on the application of the prosecution or the accused, summon and examine any person giving evidence on affidavit as to the facts contained therein.

INTRODUCTION

This section also starts with "*Non Obstante* Clause" which can be reasonably read as overriding "anything contained" in any relevant existing law which is inconsistent with the new enactment, although the legislature appears to have had primarily in mind a particular type of law as conflicting with the new provision.

Section 273, the Cr. P.C. says, "Except as otherwise expressly provided, all evidence taken in the course of the trial or other proceedings shall be taken in the presence of the accused, or, when his personal attendance is dispensed with, in the presence of his pleader". It is not sufficient to read out to the accused the deposition of the complainant taken in the absence of the accused. So also merely recording a statement that what the witness has to say is contained in a document which is filed as an Exhibit is not enough. It, in fact, amounts to evidence taken in proxy, but the procedure laid down is to be followed. Now this section 145 speaks of the evidence to be given by way of Affidavit.

Clause (2) of section 145 speaks of cross-examination of the witness whose evidence by way of Affidavit is filed. The object of cross-examination is two-fold: (i) to bring out desirable facts of the case modifying the examination-in-chief or establishing the cross-examiner's own case (ii) to impeach the credit of the witness. This is covered by section 137 of the Evidence Act, 1872.

In the Civil Procedure Code, there is a provision under Order XIX, rule 1 which says:

> "Any court may at any time for sufficient reason order that any particular fact or facts may be proved by Affidavit, or that the affidavit or any witness

may be read at the hearing, on such conditions as the court thinks reasonable:

Provided that where it appears that either party *bona fide* desires the production of witness for cross-examination and that such witness can be produced, an order shall not be made authorising the evidence of such witness to be given by affidavit.

Order XIX, rule 2 empowers the court to order attendance of deponent for cross-examination. But now by the amendment of the Civil Procedure Code, the evidence by way of Affidavit has become procedural.

Section 145 is, in fact, a combination of the Cr. P.C. and the C.P.C. and is inserted to ensure a speedy trial. Judicial pronouncements in this regard speak favourably. (*See* section 296, the Cr. P.C.)

CASE LAW

***K.S.L. & Industries Ltd., Mumbai* v. *Munna Lal Khandelwal,* 2005 Cr LJ 1201 (Bom)**

Case referred:

AIR 2004 SC 355.

Facts of the case.—In this case two issues were raised:—

(1) Whether the complaint under section 138 of the Act, according to legislative mandate, requires to be adjudicated expeditiously and in any event within six months from the date of summons or warrant as the case may be.

(2) Whether inspite of mandate of section 145(1) of the Act, the court is obliged to examine the complaint even in respect of matters which have been stated on affidavit. The court *held* that affidavit is allowed and if required it is subject to cross-examination.

***K. Srinivasa* v. *Kashi Nath,* 2004 AIR Karn HCR 342: 2004 Cr LJ 4566 (Karn)**

Case referred:

AIR 2001 SC 3955.

Facts of the case.—It is a case under section 138 wherein section 145 was discussed. It is *held* that the Magistrate can dispense with the sworn statement of the complainant and his witnesses by accepting their affidavit. No prejudice is caused to the accused if process is issued on the basis of Affidavit. The High Court referred to the case of *State of Punjab* v. *Naibuddin,* AIR 2001 SC 3955: 2001 Cr LJ 4656 in which section 296, the Cr. P.C. was discussed.

***Vinod Singh Negi* v. *State of Uttaranchal,* 2005 Cr LJ 3827 (Uttaranchal)**

Facts of the case.—It is a case at an enquiry level under sections 200, 202, the Cr. P.C. by which the Magistrate taking cognizance of an offence on complaint shall examine upon oath the complainant and the witnesses present. Similarly section 202, the Cr. P.C. is an enquiry by any Magistrate to whom the complaint is made over to him under section 192, the Cr. P.C., may enquire himself or direct an investigation by the Police Officer or any such other person, for the purpose of deciding whether or not there is sufficient ground for proceeding. So it is an enquiry under section 200 or 202, the Cr. P.C. and the Complainant is entitled to file affidavit under section 145 of the Negotiable Instruments Act.

It is an Inquiry under sections 200, 202, the Cr. P.C. Complainant is entitled to file affidavit under section 145, the Negotiable Instruments Act.

***K.S.L. Industries Ltd., Mumbai* v. *Munnalal Khandelwal*, 2005 Cr LJ 1201 (Bom)**

Affidavit allowed. If required it is subject to cross-examination.

***Indo International Ltd., Chennai* v. *State of Maharashtra*, 2006 Cr LJ 208 (Bom)**

If the affidavit is submitted there is no need to again record examination-in-chief of the complainant.

***Indraprastha Holdings Ltd.* v. *Vijya J. Shah*, (2006) 1 Mah LJ 101: 2006 Cr LJ 574 (Bom)**

This provision for recording evidence by way of affidavit is purely procedural in nature. It is retrospective in nature and is applicable to complaints pending on 6-2-2003.

***M/s. Indraprastha Holdings Ltd.* v. *Vijya J Shah*, 2006 (2) JCC (NI) 230 (Bom)**

Held: Section 145 is purely a rule of procedure which merely affects the procedure will have to be presumed to be retrospective in its operation and will apply to all complaints pending on the date on which the Amending Act came into force.

***Magma Leasing Ltd.* v. *State of West Bengal*, 2007 (4) JCC (NI) 367 (Cal)**

The abject behind introduction of section 145 is to make the procedure more easy and to make it loss cumbersome so that in matter of big companies, or big firms or his partnership concerns either the directors or the partners can place their evidence before the court by Affidavit. This procedure does not take away the right of accused to cross-examine such witnesses. Cross-examination is the most effective weapon in the armoury of the accused. The accused is at liberty to submit before the court expressing his intention whom he wants to cross examine whose evidence was taken on affidavit and if and when such application is made the Magistrate would summon such witnesses to appear in the court for cross-examination. The effect of the section is retrospective.

***Ranvir Singh Kharab* v. *Smt. Santosh*, 2007 (1) JCC (NI) 65 (Del)**

It is *held* that it is permissible for the court to receive the affidavit filed under section 145 of the Negotiable Instruments Act at the stage of section 200, the Cr. P.C. and to act upon the same. *Vasudevan* v. *State of Kerala*, 2005 (5) CRJ 740 was followed.

***Radhey Shyam Garg* v. *Sh. Naresh Kumar Gupta*, 2008 (3) JCC (NI) 311 (Del)**

It is said that the purpose behind enacting section 145 of the Negotiable Instruments Act appears to be to expedite the disposal of the complaint made under section 138 of of the Negotiable Instruments Act and to save the time of the court and the witnesses as also to save costs and inconvenience being caused to one or the other party. Evidence led on affidavit by the complainant, by virtue of Section 145 of the Act, is good evidence in any enquiry, trial and other proceedings under the code. Pre-summoning stage in akin to the stage of enquiry. Such evidence, however, can be read even at the stage of trial and other proceedings. The court referred to the decision of the Supreme Court in *State of Punjab* v. *Naib Din*, 2002 SCC (Cri) 33 and relied upon the same.

Note.—Refer:

(i) *KSL and Industries Ltd.* v. *Mannalal Khandelwal*, 2005 (2) JCC (NI) 125 (Bom).

(ii) *Peacock Industries Ltd.* v. *Budhrani Finance Ltd.*, IV (2006) BC 302 (Bom).

(iii) *State of Jharkhand* v. *Govind Singh*, 2005 (10) SCC 437.

(iv) *Maharaja Developers* v. *Udaysingh Partapsinghrao Bhonsle*, 2007 Cr LJ 2207.

***Delhi Finance Company* v. *Renu Aggarwal*, 2008 (1) JCC (NI) 92 (Del)**

It is a case where the complainant's witness who was partly examined, did not appear for cross-examination in spite of repeated adjournments. Thereupon the learned Metropolitan Magistrate closed the C.E. and thus this appeal. The court *held* that the complainant should have been more vigilant in leading evidence. Frequent adjournments sought on one ground or the other and granting the same by the learned courts disreputes the entire judicial system. The exemptions were sought without disclosing the circumstances and the court could not exercise the discretion. The complainant was found negligent in producing evidence before the trial court and the respondent has been compelled to contest there appeals for no fault of her. The High Court allowed the appeals subject to cost of Rs. 15,000 in each case. The order of the learned Metropolitan Magistrate is set aside and the complaint is restored to its original number and the cost he paid to the respondent.

Note.—*Even non production of evidence inspite of repeated exemptions falls under Section 145 of the Negotiable Instruments Act as it retards the progress of the proceedings.*

***Trimurti Associates Private Ltd.* v. *The State of West Bengal*, 2009 (3) JCC (NI) 215 (Cal)**

It is a case where the Metropolitan Magistrate granted adjournment for 4 months in one go simply for the purpose of hearing regarding acceptance of the affidavit in spite of the fact that the court was directed to dispose of the case within six months. Law is very clear in this respect. Section 145 of the Act provides that notwithstanding any thing contained in the Code of Criminal Procedure, the evidence of the complainant may be given by him on affidavit. The case has entered 14 years of his existence. The Magistrate is directed to immediately dispose of this case without granting any adjournment.

Note.—*Delay in disposing of the case expeditiously is against the spirit of section 143 of the Negotiable Instruments Act and affects the economic equilibrium of the country.*

***Radhey Shyam Garg* v. *Naresh Kumar Gupta,* 2008 (3) JCC (NI) 311**

In this case the word "Examine" used in section 145(2) of of the Negotiable Instruments Act was discussed as to what it means. The Apex Court discussed section 145(2) of the Negotiable Instruments Act in the light of section 296(2), the Cr. P.C. and held that "to examine" means "cross-examination" However, since there is dissimilarity in the signatures on the affidavit, an enquiry may he held in this regard in terms of section 340, the Cr. P.C.

***Geeta Marine Services Pvt. Ltd.* v. *State,* AIR 2009 (NOC) 951 (Bom)**

In this case the affidavit of complainant in lieu of examination-in-chief was given. It is held that the complainant has to enter the witness Box and formally depose as to the contents of the affidavit. Only thereafter the affidavit can be read as examination-in-chief.

***Subramanian M.B.* v. *Krishna Kumar P.,* AIR 2009 (NOC) 724 (Ker)**

Evidence was given by way of affidavit. *Held,* that it is a desirable practice and not mandatory. It saves judicial time and promotes speedy justice. However, refusal for same does not amount to denial of justice. Court cannot compel the complainant to file proof affidavit in lieu of examination in chief. Acquittal of accused on account of refusal of complainant to file proof affidavit is not proper.

***Pushp Holdings Ltd.* v. *State of Maharashtra,* AIR 2009 (NOC) 126 (Bom)**

Affidavit in lieu of examination-in-chief was filed. No verification clause was appended to the affidavit. It is held that such defect is curable. Court can permit complainant to insert verification clause in the affidavit.

***Jayawant Gadekar* v. *Prakash Raut,* AIR 2009 (NOC) 125 (Bom)**

It is *held* that the defence evidence can be led by filing affidavit. Defence evidence includes evidence of the accused also which can be filed by way of affidavit. So there is no bar for the accused to file his evidence by way of evidence. Order of Magistrate refusing permission to the accused to tender evidence on affidavit is liable to be set aside.

***Abdul Aziz Lokhundwala* v. *Nasir Ali,* 2010 (1) Crimes 694 (Bom)**

Cases referred:

Varkey Joseph v. *State of Kerala,* AIR 1993 SC 1982; *Ashok Marketing Ltd.* v. *PNB,* AIR 1991 SC 855; *J.K. Cotton, Spinning & Wearing Mills Co. Ltd.* v. *The State of Uttar Pradesh,* AIR 1961 SC 1170; *Ameer Trading Corporation Ltd.* v. *Shahpurjee Data Processing Ltd.,* AIR 2004 SC 355; *KSL & Industries Ltd.* v. *Mannalal Khandelwal,* 2005 (2) All MR 581 (Bom); *Peacock Industries Ltd. Udaipur* v. *Budhrani Finance Ltd., Bombay,* 2006 (5) Mah LJ 162.

It is case where the provision of Section 145 of the Negotiable Instruments Act was challenged as *ultra vires* of he Constitution violating Article 21. It was held that it cannot be said that the provision cantained in Section 145 of the Negotiable Instruments Act are in any way violate the fundamental rights of the accused in any manner or that it violates the rights of the accused to have a fair trial.

***M/s. Mandvi Co-op Bank Ltd.* v. *Nimesh S. Thakore*, 2010 (1) JCC (NI) 42 (Del)**

Cases referred:

Dental Council of India v. *Hari Prakash*, (2001) 8 SCC 61; *Nathi Devi* v. *Radha Devi*, (2005) 2 SCC 271; *Raghunath Rai Bareja* v. *Punjab National Bank*, (2007) 2 SCC 230; *State of Punjab* v. *Naib Din*, (2001) 8 SCC 578; *Union of India* v. *Deoki Nandan Aggarwal*, 1992 Supp (1) SCC 323; *Duport Steels Ltd.* v. *Sirs*, (1980) 1 All ER 529.

The court discussed Section 145(2) of the Negotiable Instruments Act in detail and held as follows:—

(i) Any affidavit filed by the complainant or any of his witness is subject to cross-examination as to the facts stated in the Affidavit.

(ii) If any documents are submitted along with the affidavit, they are subject to the objection regarding validity and or sufficiency of proof and if such objection is raised the deponent has to appear before the court.

(iii) Section 145(2) of the Negotiable Instruments Act and Section 256(2) of the Cr. P.C. stand differently and it would be completely wrong to interpret the true scope and meaning of one in the light of other.

(iv) Objections raised by the accused on the statements made by the complainant are to the considered by the court

(v) Sections 143 to 147 are having retrospective effect as these provisions are procedural in nature.

(vi) The court has not to fill up the self-perceived blank

(vii) The court has not to draw an analogy between the evidence of the complainant and the accused in a case of dishonoured cheque.

CHAPTER IX

BANK'S CHEQUE RETURNING MEMO – MANDATORY PRESUMPTION OF DISHONOUR OF CHEQUE BUT REBUTTABLE

146. Bank's slip *prima facie* evidence of certain facts.—The Court shall, in respect of every proceeding under this Chapter, on production of bank's slip or memo having thereon the official mark denoting that the cheque has been dishonoured, presume the fact of dishonour of such cheque, unless and until such fact is disproved.

INTRODUCTION

This section speaks of "shall presume". Section 4 of the Evidence Act, 1872 has defined *"shall presume"*—"whenever it is directed by this Act, that the court shall presume a fact, it shall regard such fact as proved, unless and until it is disproved." *"Disproved"* is also defined under section 3 of the Evidence Act, 1872— "A fact is said to be disproved when, after considering the matter before it, the court either believes that it does not exist or considers its non-existence so probable that a prudent man ought, under the circumstances of the particular case, to act upon the supposition that it does not exist.

Now "Dishonour of cheque" is covered by section 92 of the Negotiable Instruments Act, 1881 which is to be read along with sections 30 and 31 of the Act.

Section 30: It speaks of drawer's liability. Drawer is liable to holder, in case the cheque is dishonoured by the Drawee or the acceptor, but before the liability could be enforced a due notice has to be given to or served upon the drawer.

Section 31: This section lays down a general liability on the Banks (Drawee of cheques that all cheques be paid normally) when there is sufficient money in the account of the drawer and his signature does not differ, the Drawee Bank has no right to refuse payment of the cheque on unfair excuse particularly when there was no restraint order of any court (AIR 1988 Cal 265). But as a general rule the Drawee (Bank) is not liable to the Payee (Holder) but it is liable to the drawer thereof only (AIR 1954 SC 554). Now by an exception the liability of payment of cheque towards its payee can be fixed towards Drawee Bank under general principles of law as for money had and received for the payee of the cheque's use but subject to the limitation that the recipient bank should have received money from the drawer to meet the amount of that cheque. So section 31 makes obligatory for the banks as drawee of cheques to honour those cheques normally when presented or when required to do so except for certain reasons which due to developed law and banking practice have become in vogue.

Thus under section 92, a promissory note, bill of exchange or cheque is said to be dishonoured by non-payment when the maker of the note, acceptor of the bill or drawee of the cheque makes default in payment upon being duly required to pay the same.

There are various reasons by which the drawee Bank can return the cheque unpaid. Section 138 has considered two reasons for returning the cheque unpaid. They are:—

(1) Insufficient funds in the account.

(2) Exceeds arrangement.

Judicial pronouncements have added another reason for returning of cheque unpaid, *i.e.*, Refer to drawer, Payment stopped, Account closed which amount to be deemed to lead to shortage of funds, *i.e.*, no funds to meet the payment of the cheque amount. Thus, the area is enlarged judicially and these reasons are to be read now in section 138, the Negotiable Instruments Act.

The cheque is returned unpaid by the bank with a cheque returning memo or bank's slip which indicates the reason for returning the cheque unpaid and section 146 shall presume the dishonouring of cheque as a fact unless and until it is disproved.

CASE LAWS

The Supreme Court in *Kusum Ingots & Alloys Ltd.* v. *Pennar Peterson Securities Ltd.*, AIR 2000 SC 954 has said that the object of bringing section 138 on statute is to inculcate faith in the efficacy of banking operations and credibility in transacting business on Negotiable Instruments. But for establishing the requirements in section 138 no burden on the part of the complainant is placed to prove before Court the entire details of the transaction resulting in the issuance of the cheque.

Note.—*see* also *Joseph Jose* v. *J. Baby Puthuval Puravidom Poothoppu*, 2002 Cr LJ 4392 (Ker).

***P.K. Thankamma* v. *Sundaresan T.S.*, 2006 Cr LJ 843 (Ker)**

Section 114 of the Evidence Act is applicable that all official acts are presumed to be done regularly and properly.

Section 138 is fortified with sections 139, 140 and 146 by which the burden of disproving the case has fallen on the shoulders of the accused like section 105 of the Evidence Act, 1872. Rebuttable presumption means shifting of burden of proof on to the accused which is the underlying rigour of these provisions. The complainant after filing the complaint starts almost sitting like a mere *idle* spectator and it is the accused who is tormented with the rigours of the case due to the provisions of sections 139, 140 and 146.

***A.K. Chowdhary* v. *Ashok Kumar Malhotra*, 2007 (2) JCC (NI) (Del)**

Case referred:

S.I.L. Impart, USA v. *M/s. Exim Aides Silk Exporters*, 1999 Cr LJ 2296.

It was a case for quashing of proceedings where two expressions "Notice" and "information" were clarified. The word "Notice" is qualified by further words "in writing" and whereas the words "information" which is a broader term, is left without any controlling term. In this case the "Return Memo" bore remarks "Account closed". It is a valid return Memo Criminal Complaint is maintainable.

Note.—*Section 138 of the Negotiable Instruments Act speaks of "returned by the bank unpaid," giving reasons for dishonour shown in the "cheque returning Memo" and section 146 of the Negotiable Instruments Act speaks about "cheque returning memo" as mandator presumption of dishonour of cheque but rebuttable.*

CHAPTER X

DISHONOUR OF CHEQUE – A COMPOUNDABLE OFFENCE

147. Offences to be compoundable.—Notwithstanding anything contained in the Code of Criminal Procedure, 1973 (2 of 1974), every offence punishable under this Act shall be compoundable.

INTRODUCTION

Section 147 has been inserted by the Negotiable Instruments (Amendment and Miscellaneous Provisions) Act, 2002 (55 of 2002) with effect from 6-2-2003. It starts with "*Non Obstante* Clause" whereby it means that no section in the Criminal Procedure Code, contrary to section 147, the Negotiable Instruments Act shall apply.

Section 320, the Cr. P.C.: Speaks of compounding of offences, sub-sections (1) and (2) of section 320, the Cr. P.C. speak about specified offences covered under the Indian Penal Code that can be compounded by a person by whom offence may be compounded or by a person by whom offence may be compounded but with the permission of the court. Sub-section (9) says, "No offence shall be compounded except as provided by this section.

Section 482, the Cr. P.C.: This section is to be read in the light of section 320(9), Cr. P.C. Section 482, the Cr. P.C. says, "Nothing in this Code shall be deemed to limit or affect the inherent powers of the High Court to make such order as may be necessary to give effect to any order under this Code, or to prevent abuse of the process of any court or otherwise to secure the ends of justice."

This section is based on the principle, embodied in the maxim, "*quando lex aliquid alicui concedit, concedere videture id sine quo res ipsa esse non potest.*" (*See* 1977 Cr LJ 1458; AIR 1930 Lah 465). However, the judicial view is conflicting in spite of the fact that Supreme Court has given specified principles that would govern the exercise of the inherent jurisdiction of a High Court given by section 482. [AIR 1978 SC 47; AIR 1977 SC 2185; 1983 Cr LJ 1501 (SC)].

JUDICIAL VIEW-I

SECTIONS 320 AND 482, THE CR. P.C.

***Emperor* v. *Sukh Dev*, AIR 1929 Lah 705**

It is said, "The inherent jurisdiction of the court which received recognition in section 561A, the Criminal Procedure Code (Old Code) cannot be invoked for the purpose of doing an act which would conflict with any of the provisions of the law or general principles of criminal jurisprudence. The rule of law is firmly established that, when a statute confers on the court a specific power, the court cannot by relying upon its inherent jurisdiction, extend the scope of that power."

***Kumar Singh Chhajor* v. *Emperor,* AIR 1946 PC 169**

It is a case by virtue of which the High Court's power of revision is taken away under special Criminal Courts Ordinance (2 of 1942). By this the High Court under section 561A, the Cr. P.C. can claim inherent jurisdiction to exercise powers expressly taken away by legislation.

***Khushi Ram* v. *Hashim,* AIR 1959 SC 542: 1959 Cr LJ 658**

It is a case pertaining to commitment proceedings. The Magistrate found that a *prima facie* case has been made out and on this passed an order committing the accused persons to trial before the Court of sessions. So in this case section 561A and section 215 (Old Code) were discussed by the Supreme Court. It is said that the inherent powers of High Court under section 561A, the Cr. P.C. cannot be invoked in regard to matters which are directly covered by special provisions of the Code and hence the High Court is clearly in error in invoking that section in quashing a commitment proceedings which is a matter directly covered by section 215, the Cr. P.C. (Old Code).

***R.P. Kapoor* v. *State of Punjab,* AIR 1960 SC 866: (1960) 3 SCR 388: 1960 Cr LJ 1239**

In this case the Supreme Court discussed the nature and scope of the inherent powers of the High Court under section 561A of the Code. The apex Court observed that section 561A of the Code saves the inherent powers of the High Court to make such orders as may be necessary to give effect to any order under this Code or to prevent abuse of the process of any court or otherwise to secure the ends of justice. There is no doubt that this inherent power cannot be exercised in regard to matters specifically covered by the other provisions of the Code.

***Ramesh Chandera J. Thakar* v. *A.P. Jhaveri,* AIR 1973 SC 84: (1973) 3 SCC 884: 1973 Cr LJ 201**

It is a case under section 420, the I.P.C. and section 13 of the Maharashtra Act. Section 420, the I.P.C. is compoundable with the permission of the court and section 13 of the Maharashtra Act is non-compoundable. The apex Court *held* that on indivisible permission given to withdraw a compoundable and non-compoundable offence is invalid in its entirety.

***State of Karnataka* v. *L. Munaswami,* 1977 SCC (Cri) 404: AIR 1977 SC 1489: 1977 Cr LJ 1125: (1977) 2 SCC 699**

In this case the Supreme Court adopted a middle course stating, "considerations justifying the exercise of inherent powers for securing the ends of justice naturally vary from case to case and a jurisdiction as wholesome as the one conferred by section 482 ought not to be encased within the strait-jacket of a rigid formula. The ends of justice are higher than the ends of mere law though justice has got to be administered according to laws made by the legislature.

***Madhu Limaye* v. *State of Maharashtra*, AIR 1978 SC 47: (1977) 4 SCC 551: 1978 Cr LJ 165**

In this case section 397(2) and section 482, the Cr. P.C. were discussed. The Supreme Court propounded three principles pertaining to the inherent powers of the High Court:—

(i) That the power is not to be resorted to if there is specific provision in the Code for the redress of the grievance of the aggrieved party;

(ii) That it should be exercised very sparingly to prevent abuse of process of any court or otherwise to secure the ends of justice;

(iii) That it should not be exercised as against the express bar of law engrafted in any other provision of the Code.

***State of Haryana* v. *Bhajan Lal*, 1992 SCC (Cri) 426: AIR 1992 SC 604: 1992 Cr LJ 527: 1992 Supp (1) SCC 335**

In this case sections 482, 154 and 157, the Cr. P.C. were discussed, wherein First Information Report was quashed by the High Court under section 482, the Cr. P.C. and that order was challenged. The Supreme Court observed that it may not be possible to lay down any precise, clearly defined and sufficiently canalized and inflexible guidelines or rigid formula and to give exhaustive list of myriad kinds of cases wherein such power should be exercised. However, by way of illustration the Supreme Court gave seven situations to be kept in mind.

The above stated judicial view has more tilting tendency towards section 320(9), the Cr. P.C. which says, "No offence shall be compounded except as provided by this section." The Supreme Court has adopted a *via* media approach. It has given legal sanctity to section 482, the Cr. P.C. and also has not ignored section 320(9), the Cr. P.C. But there is another judicial view which needs a look.

JUDICIAL VIEW-II

SECTIONS 320 AND 482, THE CR. P.C.

***State of Bombay* v. *Nilkanth Shripad Bhave*, AIR 1954 Bom 65 (FB)**

In this case the court referred to various decisions, in particular, *Emperor* v. *Nazir Ahmed*, AIR 1945 PC 18 and *Jairamdas* v. *Emperor*, AIR 1945 PC 94 and opined that section 561A (*See* 482 of the New Code) was enacted to emphasise the fact that the High Court has the widest jurisdiction to pass orders to secure the ends of justice. Section 561A must give the power to this court to entertain applications which are not contemplated by Criminal Procedure Code. Therefore, if the High Court feels that ends of Justice require that an order should be made in an application, although the application is not contemplated by the Code, the High Court will entertain the application and make the necessary orders to secure the ends of justice.

***R.P. Patel* v. *State of Gujarat*, 1978 Cr LJ 1192 (Guj)**

It is a case under section 125, the Cr. P.C. wherein the learned Magistrate tried to effect reconciliation in the light of section 23(2) of the Hindu Marriage

Act, 1955. The Sessions Judge while dealing with a transfer application, pertaining to the matter passed strictures against the Magistrate for trying to effect reconciliation. Against the order of passing strictures, the High Court observed that the court deserves commendation and not condemnation. The Judge should have a pat on the back and not slap on the cheek. This observation impliedly speaks of compounding.

***Hindu Singh* v. *State of Uttar Pradesh*, 1983 SCC (Cri) 49 (2): (1982) 3 SCC 368 (11)**

It is a case under sections 324 and 325, the I.P.C. Supreme Court under Article 136 allowed compounding of the offences in view of the fact that the parties are closely related and set aside the order of conviction and sentence.

***Ramji Lal* v. *State of Haryana*, (1983) 1 SCC 368: 1983 SCC (Cri) 189**

It is a case under sections 323, 324 and 325 read with section 34, the I.P.C. Looking to the victim voluntarily entering into composition to restore friendly and good neighbourly relations with the accused and rejecting compensation, the Supreme Court lauded the chartered attitude of the accused and commendable attitude of the victim in order to restore harmony in society and accepted the composition under section 320, the Cr. P.C.

***State of Karnataka* v. *Basavaraju*, (1990) 2 Crimes 196 (Karn)**

It is a case under section 498A, the I.P.C. and sections 3 and 4 of the Dowry Prohibition Act, 1961. The trial court effected the compromise. The High Court observed that the trial court did not commit any error in according permission to compound the offence keeping in its view the welfare of the parties in the matrimonial case, the larger interest of the couple and its impact on the society.

Cases referred:

Mahesh Chand v. *State of Rajasthan*, AIR 1988 SC 2111: 1990 Supp SCC 681: 1991 SCC (Cri) 159; *Suresh Babu* v. *State of Andhra Pradesh*, (1987) 2 JT 361.

***Thalhapadi Venkatalakshmi* v. *State of Andhra Pradesh*, 1991 Cr LJ 49 (AP)**

It is a case under section 498A, the I.P.C. Court took cognizance of the offence under section 498A, the I.P.C. against the husband. A reconciliation took place by which both agreed to lead harmonious matrimonial life. Permission was sought by parties to compound offence. The High Court *held* that keeping in view larger interest of parties and to secure ends of justice, the parties could be allowed to compound offence by court in exercise of powers under section 482, the Cr. P.C.

***State of Rajasthan* v. *Gopal Lal*, (1991) 3 Crimes 74: (1992) 1 Rec CR 589: 1992 Cr LJ 273 (Raj)**

In this case the parties had entered into a compromise and had prayed for acquittal of the accused persons. The trial court refused to entertain the application in view of section 320, the Cr. P.C. Hence, this petition for leave to appeal. For advance of the cause of Justice the High Court permitted the parties to compound the offence. The High Court directed that a copy of the judgment be sent to the Home Secretary for taking such action as is deemed proper with regard to amendment of section 320, the Cr. P.C.

***Suresh Nath Mal Rathi* v. *State of Maharashtra*, 1991 Mah LJ 1106: 1992 Cr LJ 2106 (Bom)**

In this case numerous case laws were discussed and finally the High Court *held* that considering the peculiar and special circumstances permission is accorded to compound the offence. The High Court even recommended to the Government for amendment of section 320, the Cr. P.C. and section 498A, the I.P.C.

***Daggupati Jayalakshmi* v. *State*, 1993 Cr LJ 3162 (AP)**

It is a case under section 498A, the I.P.C. There was a compromise between husband and wife. The court *held* that though non-compoundable but permissible only by the High Court under section 482, the Cr. P.C. in exceptional cases.

***Pepsi Foods Ltd.* v. *Special Judicial Magistrate*, 1998 SCC (Cri) 1400: 1998 Cr LJ 1: (1998) 5 SCC 749**

Held that the power conferred on the High Court under Articles 226 and 227 of the Constitution and under section 482, the Cr. P.C. have no limit, but more the power more due care and caution is to be exercised while invoking these powers. It may not, however, be lost sight of provisions that exist in the code of revision and appeal but sometime for immediate relief. Section 482 of the Code or Article 227 may have to be resorted to.

***G.V. Rao* v. *L.H.V. Parsad*, (2000) 3 SCC 693: 2000 SCC (Cri) 733: 2000 Cr LJ 3487**

The case is under sections 415, 419, 420 read with section 34, the I.P.C. The Supreme Court observed that the complaint having arisen out of matrimonial dispute, the court would not encourage such disputes. Though the High Court quashed the complaint on an erroneous view, still the court would not interfere with High Court's order. The Supreme Court also by way of advice, told that marriage is a sacred ceremony, the main purpose of which is to enable the young couple to settle down in life and live peacefully.

***B.S. Joshi* v. *State of Haryana*, (2003) 4 SCC 675: 2003 SCC (Cri) 848: AIR 2003 SC 1386: (2003) 2 KLT 1062**

The Supreme Court *held* that section 320, the Cr. P.C. does not limit or affect the powers under section 482, the Cr. P.C. and that if for the purpose of securing the ends of justice, quashing of FIR becomes necessary, section 320 would not be a bar to the exercise of power of quashing. It would be improper to decline to exercise power of quashing on the ground that it would be permitting the parties to compound non-compoundable offences.

The above cited case laws do show that judicial mind has neither disturbed the sanctity of section 320, the Cr. P.C. nor ignored the supremacy of section 482, the Cr. P.C. In between these two sections an essential element of "securing the ends of the justice" is introduced as the courts are to dispense justice according to law. Keeping in view these citations, we have to see their application pertaining to dishonour of cheque and its consequences.

JUDICIAL VIEW-III

BEFORE THE INSERTION OF SECTION 147 IN THE NEGOTIABLE INSTRUMENTS ACT, 1881

***K.V. Antony* v. *J. Sherafudin*, 1996 Cr LJ 135 (Ker)**

In this case the court *held* that having initiated criminal proceedings under section 138, the offence cannot be compounded under the inherent powers of the High Court. As permission to compound the offence under section 320(2), the Cr. P.C. cannot be granted by the High Court in exercise of its inherent powers, there cannot be any doubt that offence under section 138 of the Negotiable Instruments Act can be compounded under section 482, the Cr. P.C. The view taken was that any offence coming under a special enactment *cannot be compounded* under the provisions of the Code.

***M. Mohan Reddy* v. *Jairaj D. Bhale Rao*, 1996 Cr LJ 1010 (AP)**

Cases referred:

Daggupati Jayalakshmi v. *State*, (1993) 2 ALT (Cri) 159 (Rel. on); *Annamdevula Srinivasa Rao* v. *State of Andhra Pradesh*, (1995) 3 ALT 349 (Dissented from).

In this case the argument was that compounding of offences is provided in section 345 of the Code of Criminal Procedure of 1898. The old Cr. P.C. was repealed by the new Cr. P.C. of 1974. Section 320 of the new Cr. P.C. deals with the compounding of offences mentioned therein. The new Cr. P.C. dealt with compounding of offences punishable under the Indian Penal Code only, but not dealt with the offences under other penal laws. The Negotiable Instruments Act, is silent about the compounding of the offence punishable under section 138 of the said Act. The High Court agreed with this view and *allowed compounding of the offence.*

***Voruganti Chinna Gapaiah* v. *Godavari Fertilizers and Chemicals Ltd.*, 2000 Bankmen 513: 1999 Cr LJ 1184 (AP)**

It is a case of dishonour of cheque (section 138, the Negotiable Instruments Act). Though the cheque was issued towards discharge of payment of outstanding dues, there was a subsequent agreement by which complainant agreed to receive the amount in instalments. In such a case payment to be made in lump sum for which the cheque is issued, is wiped out and in its terms new agreement is substituted. The High Court set aside the judgment and sentence passed by the law court.

Note.—*It appears that the High Court followed the doctrine of Novation (section 62 of the Contract Act, 1872). The principle of Novation constitutes (i) a contract in existence, (ii) some new contract has been substituted for it, resulting in discharge of the old contract. Substitution of a new contract is the core of Novation. Its essential feature is that a right under the original contract is relinquished and new rights referable to a new contract are created. (Refer AIR 1960 Pat 400; AIR 1966 Ker 303; AIR 1956 Raj 12).*

***M. Rangaswamaiah* v. *R. Shettappa*, 2001 Bank J 510: (2000) 1 Crimes 359: (2000) 6 Kant LJ 585: 2002 Cr LJ 4792 (Karn)**

Cases referred:

1996 Cr LJ 1010 (AP); 1998 Cr LJ 4424 (Guj); (2000) 1 SCC 762: 2000 SCC (Cri) 310.

In this case the High Court laid emphasis on section 4(2), the Cr. P.C. and not on section 320, the Cr. P.C. The spirit behind section 4(2), the Cr. P.C. is to be looked which speaks of, "offences under any other law." There is no prohibition in the Negotiable Instruments Act against compounding of an offence punishable under section 138 of the said Act. On this basis the High Court permitted the compounding of offence.

JUDICIAL VIEW-IV

AFTER THE INSERTION OF SECTION 147 OF THE NEGOTIABLE INSTRUMENTS ACT

***Kirpal Singh Partap Singh* v. *Balvinder Kaur Hardip Singh Lobana*, 2004 Cr LJ 3786 (Guj)**

Cases referred:

1998 Cr LJ 4424 (Guj); AIR 1997 SC 987: (1997) 4 SCC 241: 1997 SCC (Cri) 544: 1997 Cr LJ 1519; (1994) 1 Guj LR 415; (1990) Supp SCC 63; AIR 1977 SC 308: (1976) 4 SCC 622; AIR 1964 SC 260: (1964) 1 Cr LJ 152.

In this case section 41, the I.P.C., section 320(6), the Cr. P.C. section 482, the Cr. P.C. and section 147, the Negotiable Instruments Act were discussed and *held* that merely because the litigation has reached to a revisional stage or that even beyond that stage, the nature and character of the offence would not change automatically and it would be wrong to hold that at revisional stage, the nature of offence under section 138, the Negotiable Instruments Act should be treated as if the same is falling under Table II of section 320, the Cr. P.C. and that the offence can be compounded at any stage, even when the convict is undergoing imprisonment with the liability to pay as directed in the sentence.

***Sudha Beevi* v. *State of Kerala*, (2004) 4 BC 71: (2004) 3 ICC 526: (2004) 2 Ker LJ 138: 2004 Cr LJ 3418 (Ker)**

Cases referred:

AIR 2003 P&H 98; AIR 1981 SC 1274: (1981) 2 SCC 585: 1981 ALJ 467; AIR 1966 SC 1178: (1966) 2 SCR 828; AIR 1933 Lah 470.

It is a peculiar case where the issue involved is:—Is the hirer of a motor vehicle liable to be prosecuted under section 138 of the Negotiable Instruments Act after the vehicle is seized and has been repossessed by the owner and the higher purchase agreement is terminated? The High Court discussed sections 43 and 138 of the Negotiable Instruments Act and according to section 43, the Negotiable Instruments Act, "a negotiable instrument creates no obligation of payment if it is accepted or endorsed without consideration." (Refer AIR 1952 Punj 226) In view of section 43, if the vehicle is seized, the owner has other legal remedies to recover the amount but not resorting to criminal proceedings under section 138 of the Negotiable Instruments Act.

Note.—*This case is pregnant with the spirit of section 147 of the Negotiable Instruments Act.*

***Nijjer Agra Foods Ltd.* v. *Nasib Chand,* (2004) 1 All Cri R 104: 2004 Cr LJ 529 (Del)**

It is a case where the petitioner gave two post-dated cheques in favour of the respondent in lieu of Bank guarantee. Payment against said cheques was made by way of demand drafts as per agreement. Therefore, the liability of said cheques ceased to exist. Hence, respondent was not entitled to present said cheques even if some amount was due from the petitioner as offence under the Act 1881 ceases to exist. It was *held* that there was no occasion for the learned court to reject the application for dropping the proceedings.

Note.—*This case is based on the doctrine of "Novation", "Accord and satisfaction", "ceasing of liability" and "spirit of section 147, the Negotiable Instruments Act."*

***Venktesh Dutt* v. *M.S. Shoes East Ltd.,* (2004) 2 BC 19: (2004) 109 DLT 480: (2004) 2 Rec Cri R 24: 2004 Cr LJ 1695 (Del)**

It is a case where the agreement was entered into between the parties during the pendency of complaint. The complainant accepted the cheques given by the accused. By virtue of this acceptance cause of action pertaining to initial cheques ceases to be available to the complainant as fresh cause-of-action becomes available in respect of cheques issued pursuant to agreement between parties. *Held,* proceedings arising out of original complaint are liable to be quashed.

Note.—*"Doctrine of Novation" is applied.*

***Employees State Insurance Corporation* v. *A.P. Heavy Machinery and Engineering Ltd.,* 2005 Cr LJ 1080 (AP)**

Cases referred:

2002 Cr LJ 4792 (Karn); AIR 2000 SC 3543; AIR 2000 SC 3145; (2000) 1 SCC 762.

In this case the High Court discussed various provisions of Employees' State Insurance Act (34 of 1948) and sections 138 and 147 of the Negotiable Instruments Act. A cheque was issued towards statutory obligation being the liability to pay ESI contribution by the employer. The said cheque was dishonoured for the reason "exceeds arrangements" subsequently the amount was paid by Demand Draft and the matter was settled between the parties. The issue raised was, "whether the offence stands compounded." The High Court *held* that the facts and circumstances recording of acquittal is not proper. The settlement between the parties can only be recorded. However, the High Court said that the settlement between the parties is hereby recorded and the criminal appeal is disposed of.

***Rameshbhai Somabhai Patel* v. *Dineshbhai Achalanand Rathi,* 2005 Cr LJ 431 (Guj)**

Case referred:

O.P. Dhalokia v. *State of Haryana,* 2000 SCC (Cri) 310.

The High Court *held* that the offence of dishonour of cheque is compoundable even at revisional stage. In view of amendment inserting section 147 which came into force on 6-2-2003, parties can compound offence without any further qualification or embargo. Date of offence or first conviction is not relevant. Offence is made straightway compoundable like the case described under section 320(1), the Cr. P.C. section 320(9), the Cr. P.C. has no role to play because of "*Non Obstante* Clause" in section 147, the Negotiable Instruments Act. The High Court particularly referred to the pragmatic approach of the Honourable Supreme Court in the case of *O.P. Dholokia,* (2000) 1 SCC 762 under Article 136 of the Constitution of India. As per the settled legal position the effect of compounding of the offence is that of acquittal.

***Rameshbhai Somabhai Patel* v. *Dineshbhai Achalanand Rathi,* 2005 Cr LJ 431 (Guj)**

Matter can be compounded even at the Revision stage under section 320(1), the Cr. P.C. Refer (2001) 1 SCC 762.

***Employees' State Insurance Corporation* v. *A.P. Heavy Industries and Engg. Ltd.,* 2005 Cr LJ 1080 (AP)**

Acquittal is improper. Settlement can be recorded.

Refer 2002 Cr LJ 4792 (Kant); AIR 2000 SC 3543; AIR 2000 SC 3145; (2000) 1 SCC 762.

***K. Gyansagar* v. *Ganesh Gupta,* (2005) 7 SCC 54: 2005 SCC (Cri) 1593: 2006 Cr LJ 948 (SC)**

Compounding of offence was done even when the case had gone to the Supreme Court. Amount paid and affidavits are filed by the complainant and the accused.

***Usha Badri Poonawalla* v. *Kurien Babu,* 2006 Cr LJ 618 (Bom)**

When MoU is signed and amount received – To continue with the proceedings amounts to abuse of process of law.

***Kan Singh* v. *Bhim Singh,* 2006 (3) JCC 273 (Raj)**

In this case conviction and sentence was passed by the trial Court and affirmed by the court of ASJ. The accused went in revision. It is held that:—

(i) The complainant is the person competent to compound the offence.

(ii) The complainant in the compromise has stated that he has received the cheque amount and nothing is due to he recovered from the petitioner.

(iii) That the complainant has made the compromise voluntarily with the petitioner.

The complainant is permitted to compound the offence and the offence being compounded, the petitioner is acquitted of the charge.

***Employees' State Insurance Corporation* v. *A.P. Heavy Machinery and Engg. Ltd.,* 2006 (1) JCC 25 (AP)**

In this case the accused paid the cheque amount subsequent to the filing of the complaint by way of demand draft. The issue was "whether in such a case the acquittal recorded by the learned Magistrate is in accordance with the law."

It is *held* that the matter in relation to which the cheque has been issued, had been settled between the parties and in as much as such settlement may have to be given effect to, keeping in mind the object of introducing the relevant provisions of the Act, the court can note the same and record the said settlement between the parties. Though the deposit by way of demand draft is made, it is only a subsequent event. Hence, recording of acquittal cannot be said to be in accordance with law and settlement alone could have been recorded.

Note.—*Refer Section 320(8) Cr. P.C. in this regard.*

***A. Sreekantan Nair* v. *P. Valsarajan*, 2007 (2) JCC 237 (Mad)**

In this case the dispute is settled. A sum of Rs. 30,000 was paid and for a balance of Rs. 50,000 a post-dated cheque was issued on 3-4-1998. On 8-10-1998 the cheque was presented in the Bank for collection and bounced. The accused was already acquitted in terms of settlement. Complaint was filed but dismissed and hence this appeal.

The High Court referred to the case *Sayeed Ishaque Memon* v. *Ansari Nazeer Ahamed*, (2006) 1 SCC (Cr) 533, which says:—"In the present case, both the parties have filed joint petitions for compromise is lawful, as such one accord permission to compromise the same."

In view of this decision of the Supreme Court, the compromise between the parties that full amount of Rs. 50,000 has been paid, the compromise is recorded and the criminal appeal is dismissed.

***Sabu Georgel* v. *Home Secretary, Department of Home Affairs New Delhi*, 2008 (2) JCC 189 (NI) (Ker)**

In this case the High Court *held* that section 147 of the Negotiable Instruments Act falls under section 320(1), the Cr. P.C. and not under section 320(2), the Cr. P.C. It is said that section 147 of the Negotiable Instruments Act and section 320, the Cr. P.C. read along with sections 4 and 5, the Cr. P.C. can lead only to the conclusion that the offence under section 138 is compoundable without the permission of the court and in the event of such compromise, the procedure under section 320, the Cr. P.C. has got to be followed.

The issue before the High Court was:—

(i) Can composition of an offence under Section 138 of the Negotiable Instruments Act even after the conviction and sentence have become final after the judgment of the trial court, appellate and revisional courts be accepted.

The High Court held that it is vested with the power under section 482, the Cr. P.C. and of course Articles 226/227 of the Constitution in a fit case and found this case falling under the category of "Fit Case".

***M/s. Gowri Containers* v. *S.C. Shetty*, 2008 Cr LJ 498 (Kant)**

In this case the High Court took a lenient view as full and final settlement was made between the parties and the settlement amount is paid. The accused is sentenced to pay a fine of Rs. 1000 in default the accused No. 1 shall undergo simple imprisonment for one month in each case. The respondent is granted one month time to pay the fine.

***Rajan K. Moorthy* v. *M. Vijayan*, 2008 Cr LJ 1254 (Mad)**

The High Court *held* that offence of dishonour of cheque is compoundable at any stage, be it revision or final stage. The Negotiable Instruments Act being special Act prevails over provisions of Criminal P.C. which is general law. Plenary powers under Article 226 of the Constitution and section 482 of the Criminal P.C. can be exercised by the High Court to relieve the accused of sentence by compounding the offence.

***Sisi Baha Topno* v. *State of Jharkhand*, 2008 Cr LJ 3346 (Jhar)**

In this case the accused was convicted and sentenced to simple imprisonment of 6 months and compensation of Rs. one lakh payable to the complainant. A compromise petition was filed under section 320(6), the Cr. P.C. duly signed by both the parties by which the complainant had waived compensation of Rs. one lakh. The respondent had already paid Rs. 1,50,000 to the complainant and balance would be paid in next six months. The High Court, in view of the compromise, set aside the sentence of imprisonment and acquitted the petitioner under section 320(8), the Cr. P.C. with exemption to surrender.

***Satya Chit Funds (P) Ltd.* v. *Prakash Khattar*, 2008 (1) JCC (NI) 5 (Del)**

It is a case where there was an oral agreement out of court. According to the complainant the accused agreed to pay Rs. 1,50,000 out of which Rs. 60,000 was paid. According to the accused the agreed amount was Rs. 1,00,000 and the balance payable is Rs. 40,000 The Metropolitan Magistrate then directed the complainant to return Rs. 60,000 to the accused which the complainant declined to return. The Metropolitan Magistrate disposed of the four complaints by a common order as the matter having been compounded relying upon a judgment of this court reported as 2004 (1) JCC (NI) 44, and hence there is appeal on the basis of "Non-Consensus" between the parties.

The High Court set aside the impugned order on the ground that:—

(i) The learned court could have not taken note of any compromise which is oral and out of court.

(ii) That the learned court could not have asked the complainant to return the part money received by him.

(iii) That the provision for compounding the offence was not there in the Act. (The case appears to be before the amendment Act effective from 6-2-2003).

The Trial Court was directed to proceed further in the cases from the stage at which they stood at the time of passing the impugned order.

***Vinay Devanna Nayak* v. *Ryot Seva Sahakari Bank Ltd.*, 2008 (1) JCC (NI) 94 SC**

It was *held* that compromise arrived at between the parties even after conviction and sentence rendered by the trial Court and after made by appellate and revisional court, taking into consideration the provision of section 147 of the Negotiable Instruments Act and primary object underlying section 138. The Supreme Court disposed of the appeal on the basis of settlement arrived at between the parties and acquitted the accused-appellant of the charge levelled against him.

***R. Rajeshwari* v. *H.N. Jagadish*, 2008 (2) JCC (NI) 113 (SC)**

In this case the Supreme Court held that indisputably provisions of section 320, the Cr. P.C. would be applicable to pending proceedings before the Court. Table under section 320, the Cr. P.C. is not attracted since the table is only for the I.P.C. Settlement is permissible under law and *ex-facie* is not violative of public policy.

***Phool Chand Saraogi* v. *State of Rajasthan*, AIR 2009 (NOC) 959 (Raj)**

It is held no doubt that the offence under section 138 of the Negotiable Instruments Act is compoundable under section 147 of the Act but a compromise requires an agreement between the litigating parties and if one party is not agreeable then there can be no compromise. In the present case the complainant is not willing and ready to compromise and in such case there cannot be a compromise and proceedings cannot be quashed even if the amount is deposited in the court once an offence is committed under section 138 of the Negotiable Instruments Act any payment made subsequently thereto will not absolve the accused of the criminal offence though in the matte of awarding of sentence it may have some effect on the court trying the case.

***Thakur Arora* v. *State (NCT of Delhi)*, 2009 (2) (NI) JCC 113 (Del)**

In this case the complaint was filed. Subsequently, there was a compromise and petition was filed under section 147 of the Negotiable Instruments Act read with section 320(8)/255, the Cr. P.C. The accused was acquitted as matter was compromised. The cheque issued in terms of settlement bounced when presented. The issue before the court was, "whether such cheque issued in terms of compromise will create liability towards accused." The High Court referred to *Lalit Kumar Sharma* v. *State of Uttar Pradesh*, 2008 (2) JCC (NI) 219 which says, "second cheque issued in terms of compromise did not create a new liability. The same cannot be said to have been issued towards payment of debt". If the complainant cannot be permitted to file fresh complaint an account of dishonour of cheque issued pursuant to compromise, then original complaint must be permitted to revive as the compromise (MoU) is specific in nature. Learned ACMM is directed to assign the case to the concerned MM for proceeding according to law.

***Ritesh Gupta* v. *State of Punjab*, 2010 (1) CC Cases (HC) 79 (P&H)**

Cases referred:

G. Sivarajan v. *Little Flower Kuries and Enterprises Ltd.*, 2005 (2) DCR 408; *Rameshbhai Somabhai Patel* v. *Dineshbhai Achalanand Rathi*, 2005 Cr LJ 431; *O.P. Dholakia* v. *State of Haryana*, (2000) 1 SCC 762.

An application for compounding was filed along with the Affidavit. The court was satisfied that the matter can be compounded and allowed the petition. The Sentence imposed by the two courts below is set aside and the petitioner is acquitted of the offence for which be was convicted and sentenced.

***Sudarshan Paddar* v. *State of Jharkhand*, 2010 (1) Crimes 175 (Jhar)**

Cases referred:

Anil Kumar v. *State of Jharkhand*, 2008 (1) East Cr C 201 (Jhar).

It is held that conviction of the accused can be set aside and he can be acquitted under Section 320(8), the Cr. P.C. if the parties have compromised the dispute amicably out of the court.

ESSENCE OF SECTION 147 OF THE NEGOTIABLE INSTRUMENTS ACT

The Negotiable Instruments Act, 1881 was amended by the Banking Public Financial Institutions and Negotiable Instruments Laws (Amendment) Act, 1988 wherein a new Chapter XVII containing of five sections 138 to 142, with an object to enhance the acceptability of cheque in settlement of liabilities by making the drawer liable for penalties in case of bouncing of cheques due to insufficiency of funds in the account or for the reason that it exceeds arrangements by the drawer, with adequate safeguards to prevent harassment of honest drawers.

The country is under the process and progress towards globalization. So the intention of the legislature and object of enacting this Amendment Act was, not in fact, to punish the drawer of the cheque, but to see that he realizes the sanctity of the issue of cheque and that it is honoured. It is a piece of Legislation "in terrorism". But it is found that the fear of punishment could not deter or frighten the people and large number of cases are reported to be pending in the courts under sections 138, 142 of the Negotiable Instruments Act. To achieve the objective a Working Group was constituted to review section 138 of the Negotiable Instruments Act and make recommendation as to what changes were needed to effectively achieve the purpose of that section.

So various recommendations were made and also sections 143 to 147 were inserted by the Negotiable Instruments (Amendment and Miscellaneous Provisions) Act, 2002 (55 of 2002). Whereas the sentence was increased from, "a term which may be extended to one year" to "a term which may be extended to two years", there also a provision of "compoundable of offences" under section 147 was provided. The object behind this section is to give sanctity to the doctrine of "locus penitentiae".

Note.—*To achieve the object of economic loftiness on the strength of which the country can flourish with prosperity. Its other object is, to a great extent, to avoid the rigours of sentence. The object is to realise the amount and not punish the drawer for his disobedience to law. This is why these new provisions from sections 138 to 147 were introduced in the Negotiable Instruments Act which is basically a Civil Act. If the Legislative intention has been to make it a criminal Act, it would have enacted a separate Act for "Dishonour of cheque". Thus, it is on the honourable courts to look to the spirit behind section 147 and endeavour should be made by the courts to effectively persuade the parties to compound the offence.*

CHAPTER XI

DISHONOUR OF CHEQUE AND OTHER ASPECTS

HOLDER IN DUE COURSE

Section 9 of the Negotiable Instruments Act defines this phrase thus: "Holder in due course" means any person who for consideration became the possessor of a promissory note, bill of exchange or cheque payable to bearer, or the payee or indorsee thereof if payable to order before the amount mentioned in it became payable, and without having sufficient cause to believe that any defect existed in the title of the person from whom he derived his title.

CASE LAW

Braja Kishore Dixit **v.** ***Purna Chandra Panda*****, AIR 1957 Ori 153**

It is said that under section 9, a holder in due course has to satisfy three necessary conditions, *i.e.*,

(i) an indorsee becomes a holder in due course for consideration,

(ii) he can become an indorsee before the amount mentioned in the promissory note became payable, and

(iii) he should have no sufficient cause to believe that any defect existed in the title of the person from whom he was to derive the title.

V. Ponnappa Mootham Sons **v.** ***Catholic Syrian Bank Ltd.*****, (1991) 1 SCC 113: AIR 1991 SC 441: (1991) 70 Comp Cas 1: (1990) 3 CCC 402 (SC)**

The Supreme Court has spoken that to be a holder in due course a person must be:—

(i) a holder for consideration,

(ii) a transferee in good faith,

(iii) the instrument must have been transferred to him before it became overdue, and

(iv) the transferee, namely the person who for consideration became the possessor of the cheque, should not have any reason to believe that there was any defect in the title of the transferor.

CASE LAW AFTER THE AMENDMENT OF 1988

P.K. Koya Moideen **v.** ***G. Hariharan*****, (1986) 86 Comp Cas 399: 1996 Cr LJ 3153 (Ker)**

Facts of the case.—The cheque in question was drawn in favour of the father of the complainant. He died on 19-5-1993. It is stated that the father of the complainant executed a Will and that the complainant and his brother were made the executor of the Will. In the complaint it is averred that he has filed the complaint in the capacity of an executor of the Will. The cheques were presented for collection on 18-10-1993 and after complying with requirements a complaint was filed. It is contended that the complainant is neither a 'payee' nor is a 'holder in due course' in terms of sections 7 and 9 of the Negotiable Instruments Act. The "Will" in question is not produced in the court. *It is* held *that the complaints should have not been taken cognizance of by the court as the complainant is neither the payee nor the holder in due course. The complaints are quashed.*

***Mahesh Goyal* v. *S.K. Sharma,* 1997 All LJ 1000: 1997 Cr LJ 2868 (P&H)**

Case referred: (1995) 84 Comp Cas 782 (Karn).

Facts of the case.—In this case the issue was that the cheque was drawn to self and in such case when it was not addressed to any third person whom the payment is due, section 138 is not attracted. The High Court *held* that section 138 requires that the cheque should be drawn by the person from the account maintained by him. It can be drawn in his own name as self or in the name of third person. It should be payment of the debt. The complainant is a holder in due course in terms of section 9 of the Act. The High Court relied on *Praveen Metal Industries* v. *M. Bala Subhramanayam,* (1995) 84 Comp Case 782 Karnataka where the question of "Holder in due course" was raised. *Held,* that the complainant is "holder in due course" and the complaint is maintainable.

***Devassia Joseph* v. *Joseph George,* (1997) 3 Ker 197: 1997 Cr LJ 3410 (Ker)**

Facts of the case.—It was a case falling under section 9 and section 118(g) of the Negotiable Instruments Act. It is an appeal against the judgment and decree passed in a civil case. The issue raised is that whether the plaintiff is a "holder in due course". The suit was filed for realization of amount due on three pronotes which were later endorsed in favour of the plaintiff. Section 9 was the subject of discussion, that the plaintiff filed the suit as "Holder in due course". The High Court *held* that the plaintiff is entitled to get the amount due under those pronotes as a "Holder in due course".

***Swastik Coaters Pvt. Ltd.* v. *Deepak Brothers,* (1997) 89 Comp Cas 564: 1997 Cr LJ 1942 (AP)**

Case referred:

Satish & Co. v. *S.R. Traders,* 1998 Cr LJ 419 (AP)

Facts of the case.—In this case the complaint was filed by one of the Directors in his name when the company is a drawee itself. Company being a legal person would be the holder in due course. Director of the Company would not be the "holder in due course". Complaint without proper authorization is not maintainable in terms of section 142(a) of the Negotiable Instruments Act.

***D.M. Bhattar* v. *State Bank of Bikaner,* (2002) 4 Crimes 354: (2002) 2 BC 427: 2002 Cr LJ 4851 (Bom)**

Cases referred:

AIR 1991 SC 441: (1991) 1 SCC 113: (1991) 70 Comp Cas 1; (1894) ILR 17 Mad 461; (1888) ILR 11 Mad 290.

Facts of the case.—In this case there is dishonour of cheque. The cheques were issued by a fictitious firm. Petitioner was shown as Director of the said firm. Bank is holder in due course of the said cheques. Prosecution was pending against the petitioner before special Judge by CIB in regard to opening of fictitious accounts in fictitious name and not related to the cheques. Complaint was lodged against the petitioner by the purchaser of the cheque. It is not necessary that in favour of the purchaser there should be an endorsement also. Purchaser of cheque is a "Holder in due course" in terms of section 9 of the Act.

***Sangothu Narsimha Chary* v. *V. Raghu Nath,* 1 (2005) CCR 329**

Facts of the case.—It is a case under sections 138 and 142 of the Negotiable Instruments Act. A cheque of Rs. 10,000 drawn in favour of the complainant by the petitioner towards part satisfaction of the debt due to him. It was dishonoured for want of sufficient funds. In this case 'Rachna Refrigeration' was the payee but the complaint is filed by one V. Raghu Nath even without mentioning as to how he is connected with 'Rachna Refrigeration'. It cannot be said that the first respondent is either Payee or "Holder in due course" and as such does not fall under the ambit of section 142(b) of the Negotiable Instruments Act. The petition is accordingly allowed.

RECALL OF PROCESS

INTRODUCTION

Section 142(a) says, "no court shall take cognizance of any offence punishable under section 138 except upon a complaint, in writing, made by the payee or, as the case may be, the holder in due course of the cheque."

Section 142(c) says, "no court inferior to that of a Metropolitan Magistrate or a Judicial Magistrate of the first class shall try any offence punishable under section 138."

However, the complaint in writing is to be made under *section 200, the Cr. P.C.* The Magistrate shall examine the complainant though the facts are fully set out in the written complaint, to find out whether the complaint is justifiable or whether it is frivolous or vexatious.

Section 202, *the Cr. P.C.* speaks of postponement of issue of process. The scope of enquiry, either by the Magistrate himself or to be made by a public officer or by some other person as he thinks fit, is only to ascertain the truth or falsehood of the allegations made in the complaint and the accused has got absolutely no *locus standi* and is not entitled to be heard on the question whether the process should be issued against him or not (AIR 1963 SC 1430; 1976 Cr LJ 1533).

Sections 203 *and* 204, *the Cr. P.C.* If the Magistrate comes to the conclusion that there is no sufficient ground for proceeding, he shall dismiss the complaint under section 203, Cr. P.C. However, if the Magistrate finds sufficient ground for proceeding and the case appears to be a summons case (section 138, the Negotiable Instruments Act), he shall issue summons for the attendance of the accused under section 204, the Cr. P.C. At the time of issue of process, the Magistrate is not to go into the adequacy of the evidence or the probability of the accused being guilty. [AIR 1967 SC 1947; 1979 Cr LJ 974 (Bom)].

Now the question arises as to whether the accused can file a petition for discharge after the issue of process. In trial before a court of session, the accused can file a petition under section 227, the Cr. P.C. for discharge and he can be discharged if there is no ground whatsoever to sustain the charge against the accused. [(1970) 72 Bom LR 585]. In trial of warrant cases the accused can file a petition under section 239 the Cr. P.C. or section 245, the Cr. P.C. as the case may be for his discharge (AIR 1972 SC 545; 1969 Cr LJ 1120; AIR 1960 SC 810; AIR 1967 (Guj) 263; 1977 Cr LJ 1370 (Kant); (1986) 2 SCC 756; (1973) 76 Bom LR 270]. But there is no such provision in trial of summons cases by Magistrate. So a reference has to be made to case laws.

CASE LAW

***K.M. Mathew* v. *State of Kerala,* AIR 1992 SC 2206: (1992) 1 SCC 217: (1992) 1 KLT 1**

In this case the Supreme Curt *held* that the Magistrate is empowered to recall the summoning order and the Magistrate has jurisdiction to recall the process.

***Swarn Munjal* v. *State of Uttar Pradesh,* 2000 DCR 651 (All)**

It is *held* that in a case of dishonour of cheque under section 138, the Negotiable Instruments Act, the Magistrate has the power to recall the summoning order.

***S.C. Rastogi* v. *Renu Kalra,* Cur Cri R (2000) 2 (Del) 575**

It is *held* that the accused is entitled to hearing at the stage of notice. Power to drop proceedings against the accused is vested in the court.

***Adalat Parshad* v. *Roop Lal Jindal,* AIR 2004 SC 4674: (2004) 7 SCC 338: (2004) 3 KLT 382: (2004) 2 KLJ 727**

Cases referred:

(1) *K.M. Mathew* v. *State of Kerala,* AIR 1992 SC 2206.

(2) *Nilamony Routray* v. *Bennett Coleman & Co. Ltd.,* (1998) 8 SCC 594.

Facts of the case.—In this case reference was made to sections 203 and 204, the Cr. P.C. and *held* that once the cognizance is taken by the Magistrate in summons cases and process is issued, the Magistrate has no jurisdiction to recall the summoning order. AIR 1992 SC 2206 is overruled.

***Sanjeev Rai* v. *State of Uttar Pradesh,* 2005 Cr LJ 1977 (All)**

Facts of the case.—The High Court *held* that summons case falls under Chapter XX of the Cr. P.C. The application for discharge under section 245(2), the Cr. P.C. pertains to cases of trial of warrant cases under Chapter XIX, Cr. P.C. whereas summons case falls under Chapter XX, the Cr. P.C. where there is no provision for recall of summoning order.

SECTION 140

***Krishan Gupta* v. *State of West Bengal,* 2007 Cr LJ 2502**

Reading sections 138 and 140 together, it would be clear that dishonour of the cheque by a bank on the ground that the account is closed would be covered by the pharase "The amount of money standing to the credit of that account is insufficient to honour the cheque."

In this case the remarks is "account closed" means "not sufficient funds" comes within the ambit of section 138 of the Negotiable Instruments Act.

***M/s. Sumat Pershad & Sons* v. *M/s. Headstart Advertising and Marketing Pvt. Ltd.*, 2006 (3) JCC (NI) 265**

Cases referred:

2004 (7) SCC 338; 2001 (6) SCC 16; 1999 (1) SCC 113; 2002 (1) SCC 234; 2003 (3) SCC 232.

The case was under section 138 of the Negotiable Instruments Act where presumption was raised under section 139 of the Act. The court relying upon *Adalat Prasad*, 2004 (3) JCC 1347 held that no order can be passed for recalling the summoning order and secondly the presumption under section had been rightly raised. The presumption can be rebutted by adducing evidence and the burden of proof is an the person who rebuts the presumption and that can be done during the course of the trial. This cannot be done at the stage of summoning or at the stage of issuance of notice under section 251, the Cr. P.C.

***M/s. Penarama Overseas Pvt. Ltd.* v. *M/s. Grasim Industries*, 2007 (2) JCC (NI) 199 (Del)**

It is a case under section 138 of the Negotiable Instruments Act and section 482, the Cr. P.C. for recall of summoning order. The issues raised are triable issues and can be raised during the course of trial and not under section 482, the Cr. P.C. *Held*, that neither the complaint nor the summoning order has led to failure of justice and needs no interference under inherent jurisdiction.

Note.—*Now recall petition has to be filed in the High Court.*

SECTION 138 AND SECTION 420, THE I.P.C.

This subject falls under section 142(a) of the Negotiable Instruments Act which says, "No court shall take cognizance of any offence punishable under section 138 except upon a complaint, in writing made by the Payee or, as the case may be, the holder in due course." Now the question is whether it is a simple case of dishonour of cheque or it also contains ingredients of section 420, the Cr. P.C. A simple case under section 138 falls exclusively within the jurisdiction of the Metropolitan Magistrate or Judicial Magistrate of first class and can be initiated by filing a complaint in writing, whereas also the case involving both section 138, of Negotiable Instruments Act and section 420, the I.P.C. can also be filed before such Magistrate and then what is the role of the Police in such cases. Various case laws throw much light on this aspect.

CASE LAW

***H. Mohan* v. *State of Karnataka*, (1992) 73 Comp Cas 560: 1991 Cr LJ 1866 (Karn)**

Facts of the case.—In this case the cheque was dishonoured and the complainant issued notice to the drawer of the cheque. Sometimes after the payee filed a complaint before the Sub-Inspector of Police for taking necessary action. On this basis the complaint was registered as crime No. 62/90 and after investigation the police filed the charge sheet on which the Magistrate took cognizance of the case. It is *held* that in view of section 142 of the Negotiable Instruments Act and section 4(2) and section 5, the Cr. P.C. the entire proceedings are quashed. Section 4(2) and section 5, the Cr. P.C. are not attracted in view of section 142 of the Negotiable Instruments Act and as such Police is not empowered to investigate the case under section 138, the Negotiable Instruments Act.

***Central Bank of India* v. *Saxons Farms*, (1999) 8 SCC 221: AIR 1999 SC 3607: (1999) 35 CLA 199: 1999 Cr LJ 4571 (SC)**

It is *held* that under section 142, court can take cognizance of an offence punishable under section 138 only on a complaint in writing made by the payee. Therefore, the Police cannot start investigation under section 138. But if a cheque is dishonoured drawer may expose himself to prosecution under various sections of the Indian Penal Code which are cognizable and Police can take up investigation.

***OPTS Mark Pvt. Ltd.* v. *State of Andhra Pradesh*, (2001) 2 BC 622: (2001) 3 Civ J 249: (2001) 2 BC 622: 2001 Cr LJ 1489 (AP) (FB)**

It is said that even after introduction of section 138 of the Negotiable Instruments Act, prosecution under section 420, the I.P Code is maintainable in case of dishonour of cheuqes or post-dated cheques issued towards payment of price of the goods purchased or hand loan taken or in discharge of antecedent debt or towards payment of goods supplied earlier, if the charge sheet contains an allegation that the accused had dishonest intention not to pay even at the time of issuance of the cheque, and the act of issuing the cheque which was dishonoured and caused damage to his mind, body or reputation.

Cases referred:

AIR 2001 SC 383; AIR 2000 SC 754: (2000) 2 SCC 636: 2000 Cr LJ 824: 2000 All LJ 496; AIR 2000 SC 1869: (2000) 3 SCC 269: 2000 Cr LJ 1487; AIR 1999 SC 3499; 1997 SCC (Cri) 1073; (1997) 5 Andh LT 509 (FB); (1997) 1 Andh LT (Cri) 92; AIR 1996 SC 977: (1996) 2 SCC 37: 1996 SCC (Cri) 210; (1996) Cri P. No. 6180 of 1995 D/15-10-1996 (overruled); (1995) Cri P. No. 3731 of 1994 D/11-12-1995 (overruled); AIR 1944 SC 1183; 1992 Cr LJ 2991; 1992 Cr LJ 3080 (Ker); (1988) 1 Crimes 812; 1987 Cr LJ 1485 (Cal); 1986 Cr LJ 207 (AP); 1983 Cr LJ 106 (Ker); *Reg* v. *Gilmartin*, (1983) 1 All ER 829: 1982 Cr LJ 1482 (Del); *Reg* v. *Charles*, 1977 AC 177; AIR 1973 SC 1143: (1973) 1 SCC 287; AIR 1968 SC 1767; 1967 Ker LT 804; AIR 1965 SC 1767: (1965) 3 SCR 218; AIR 1957 All 246; AIR 1955 Andh 87 (FB); AIR 1955 Andh 221 (FB); AIR 1953 Mad 351; AIR 1938 Mad 129; AIR 1930 Bom 179; *Queen* v. *Hazelton*, 23 WR 139.

***G. Sri Hari* v. *Nand Kishore Lahoti*, (2002) 2 ALD (Cri) 646: (2003) 1 BC 538: (2003) 2 Civ LJ 737: 2003 Cr LJ 643 (AP)**

Cases referred:

2001 Cr LJ 1489 (AP) (FB); (1996) 3 Crimes 402 (Bom); (1995) 4 Crimes 457 (Mad); 1993 Cr LT 1974; (1990) 2 Andh LJ 675.

Facts of the case.—It is a case of dishonour of cheque but two cases are filed, one case for the offence under section 420, the I.P.C. and the other under section 138 the Negotiable Instruments Act. In this case section 210, the Cr. P.C. was discussed which speaks of procedure to be followed when there is complaint case and Police investigation in respect of the same offence.

The High Court instead of giving any finding directed the lower court to club both the matters and hold a common trial. This direction seems to have been passed in view of the decision in 2001 Cr LJ 1489 (FB) where it is said that bouncing of cheque can also be an offence under section 420, the I.P.C.

***S. Jayaswami* v. *State of Orissa*, 2005 Cr LJ 2896 (Ori)**

Cases referred:

AIR 2000 SC 27; AIR 2002 SC 754 (relied on).

Facts of the case.—This is an application under section 482, the Cr. P.C. arising out of the case No. 896/2004 and 144/2004 under section 420/34, the I.P.C. and section 138, the Negotiable Instruments Act for quashing the case under sections 420/34. The High Court *held*, referring to the above cited cases that it is a case of parallel proceedings which is not permitted under law as virtually both the cases are based on the same allegation of bouncing of cheque. It is a case of abuse of the process of court and law. The proceedings in G.R. Case No. 896/2004 is quashed.

***Rakesh Jain* v. *State of Jharkhand*, 2005 Cr LJ 2124 (Jharkhand)**

Prima facie case under section 420, the I.P.C. is made out.

***M/s. Morgan Tectronics P Ltd* v. *State*, 2007 (1) JCC (NI) 69 (Del)**

Cases referred:

1970 Cr LJ 1; 1981 Cr LJ 422; 1981 Cr LJ 175; 1989 Cr LJ 1888; 1992 JCC 461.

It is a case under sections 138, 141, 142 of the Negotiable Instruments Act and section 420/406, the IPC in this case the complaint is field by a Public Servant. Summoning order was issued without examining the complainant under section 200, the Cr. P.C. This issue was challenged. *Held* that as the company does not come within the ambit of "Public Servant", the examination under section 200, the Cr. P.C. cannot be dispensed with. So the summoning order is quashed. It was challenged. The court applied the maxim, *"qui per alium facit per seipsum faeere videtur"*.

***M/s. Surya Lakshmi Cotton Mills Ltd.* v. *M/s. Rajvir Industries Ltd.*, 2008 (1) JCC (NI) 42 SC**

Cases referred:

1992 Supp (1) SCC 335; (1992) 4 SCC 305; (1995) 6 SCC 194; (2006) 6 SCC 736; 2007 (12) SCALE 364; 2007 (12) SCALE 391.

It is a case under section 138, of the Negotiable Instruments Act and sections 405/406, the IPC. It is a case of fraudulently use of blank signed cheques which is a criminal breach of trust. It is found that case under section 406, the IPC is made out and the officer incharge of the police station shall confine to the charge under section 406, the IPC.

***Desh Deepak Sharma* v. *State of Delhi,* 2008 (2) JCC (NI) 222 (Del)**

Cases referred:

AIR 1999 SC 1028; 1992 Supp (1) SCC 3356; 2005 (1) SCC 122.

It is a case pertaining to section 138 of the Negotiable Instruments Act and sections 420/406, the I.P.C. Metropolitan Magistrate declined to summon the accused under sections 420/406, IPC. Revision was filed before AS. and it was dismissed. High Court was moved in this regard. It was *held* that section 420, IPC is different from section 138 of the Negotiable Instruments Act. The case shall proceed under sections 420/34, the IPC.

***R.P. Mathur, Prop Radhika Leather Fashions* v. *S.R.P. Industries Ltd.,* 2009 (2) JCC (NI) 73 (Del)**

Cases referred:

2001 (1) JCC (SC) 158; 2008 (16) SCALE 240; (1998) 4 SCC 655; (1983) 1 SCC 1.

In this case the complaint is under section 138 of the Negotiable Instruments Act and sections 420, 477A, 120B, the IPC. It is *held* that when the offences are separate and distinct, it is not a case of "Double Jeopardy".

***Punit Pruti* v. *State Govt. of N.C.T. of Delhi,* 2010 (1) Crimes 439 (Del)**

Cases referred:

Sagar Suri v. *State of Uttar Pradesh,* (2000) 11 SCC 636; *Vir Parkash Sharma* v. *Anil Kumar Agarwal,* (2007) 7 SCC 373; *V.Y. Jose* v. *State of Gujarat,* (2009) 1 SCC (Crl) 996; *Bhala Nath Arora* v. *State,* 1982 Cr LJ 1492; *Mubark Ali Ahmed* v. *The State of Bombay,* AIR 1957 SC 857; *M.M. Monga* v. *Union of India,* 1996 JCC 590; *R.P. Mathur Prop RLF* v. *S.R.P. Industries Ltd.,* 2009 (2) JCC (NI) 73.

It is a case under Section 138 of Negotiable Instrument Act and Sections 420, 468, 471, 120B, the I.P.C. The Court held that if from circumstances it is established that the failure to meet a cheque was not accidental but was the consequence expected by the accused the presumption would be that the accused intended to cheat.

SECTION 138 AND CIVIL SUIT

Earlier Dishonour of cheque by non-payment was covered by section 92 of the Act and section 93 covers giving of notice by the holder about the dishonour of cheque and section 117 contains the rules governing payment of compensation by any party liable to the holder and special rules of evidence are covered by section 118 and the special rule in section 118 cannot affect the rule under section 114 of the Evidence Act, 1872 (AIR 1965 SC 920).

But with the introduction of chapter XVII by the Banking Public Financial Institutions and Negotiable Instruments Laws (Amendment) Act, 1988 (66 of 1988), section 4 (w.e.f. 1-4-1989) bouncing of cheque due to insufficiency of funds in the accounts of the drawer of the cheque or for the reason that it exceeds the arrangements made by the drawer, has made the drawer liable for penalties which shall be imprisonment for a term which may be extended to one year

(Now two years) or with fine which may extend to twice the amount of the cheque or with both.

Note.—*"Two years" is substituted by the Negotiable Instruments (Amendment and Miscellaneous Provisions) Act, 2002 (55 of 2002) section 7 (w.e.f. 6-2-2003). The scheme of the provisions contained in the new Chapter would indicate that it is primarily to provide an additional criminal liability over and above the civil remedies available under the Act to the Payee or holder in due course. This remedy under section 138 is optional. The Payee or holder in due course may, for his own reasons, waive or renounce his right and omit to file a complaint against the offender within the time specified by section 142(b) for filing a complaint [1995 Cr LJ 1384 (Ker) (FB)]. The case laws illustrate this point very clearly.*

CASE LAW

***Pawan Kumar* v. *Asish Enterprises, Regd. Partnership Firm by its Partner,* (1993) 78 Comp Cas 346: 1992 Cr LJ 1619 (Bom)**

Cases referred:

1991 Cr LJ 963 (Bom); 1991 Cr LJ 609 (Cal); (1991) 1 Crimes 226 (Kant); 1991 Cr LJ 1771 (Ker); (1991) 1 Ker LT 269; (1991) 1 Ker LT 40; AIR 1990 SC 494: 1990 Supp SCC 686: 1990 Cr LJ 320; 1989 Cr LJ 559 (All); 1989 Cr LJ (NOC) 74 (Karn); AIR 1988 SC 709; AIR 1983 SC 158; AIR 1979 SC 850; AIR 1977 SC 1754: (1977) 1 SCC 505: 1977 Cr LJ 1146; 1977 Mah LJ 715; AIR 1961 SC 1494: (1961) 2 Cr LJ 696.

Facts of the case.—In this case two issues were agitated:

(1) Whether the complaint constitutes ingredients of sections 138 and 420, the I.P.C.?

(2) Whether a civil suit instituted can be a ground for dismissal of complaint?

The High Court referred to various case laws on these two issues. Regarding issue No. 2 the High Court *held* that there is nothing in law to prevent the criminal Courts from taking cognizance, provided the elements of an offence are made out on the face of the complaint/petition itself, merely because on the same facts, the person concerned might be also subjected to civil liability. If the allegations disclose a criminal offence, the complaint ought not to be dismissed even if civil remedy is obtainable. It is not the function of the Criminal Courts to have anything to do with disputes relating to property. It is the function of Civil Court to decide the case involving the right of property. Where the complaint shows only a civil dispute as to title or as to other civil liability, the Magistrate ought not to deal with the matter but should dismiss the complaint. The criminal courts are not to entertain matters which are properly within the jurisdiction of Civil Courts. However, in this case the elements of criminality are present and hence the petitions are dismissed.

***Kuchil Kumar Nandi* v. *Modi Cement Ltd.,* (1997) 1 Cal LJ 427: (1997) 2 All Cri R 10: 1997 Cr LJ 805**

Cases referred:

AIR 1996 SC 2339: (1996) 2 SCC 739 (distinguished); 1994 Cr LJ 674 (Ker) (relied on); 1993 Cr LJ 2486 (Ker); 1993 Cr LJ 744 (P&H); 1992 Supp (1) SCC

335: 1992 Cr LJ 527: AIR 1992 SC 604 (relied on); AIR 1977 SC 1754: (1977) 1 SCC 505: 1977 Cr LJ 1146.

Facts of the case.—In this case under section 138 of the Negotiable Instruments Act, many averments made, show that many civil disputes are pending between the parties and also a criminal case is pending which has been stayed by a bench of this court. It is found that this case has no ingredients satisfying section 138 of the Act. The subject-matter of this complaint is also there in the earlier suits. Hence, the complaints are quashed.

***Deepa Finance Corporation* v. *A.K. Mohammad*, (2001) 3 CCC 382: (2001) 4 Rec Cri R 206: 2001 Cr LJ 3582 (Karn)**

Facts of the case.—It is a case where 8 post-dated cheques were issued and the said cheques when presented, were dishonoured for the reason. "Exceeds arrangement" The trial court found various discrepancies in the cheques and found that section 138 is not attracted. The trial court also found that in respect of the same loan account the appellant has filed a civil suit and obtained an order of attachment before judgment in respect of a sum of Rs. 1,65,532 payable from the department of PWD and, therefore, came to the conclusion that there is no subsisting loan and acquitted the accused. The High Court upheld the judgment of acquittal on the following grounds:—

(i) It is not clear that from which account the cheques have been drawn by the respondent as the cheques do not bear any account number.

(ii) *That the petitioner has already got the attachment before judgment in a civil suit pertaining to same transaction and thus no liability subsists.*

***G.N. Raju* v. *B.S. Jayaprakash* , 2006 Cr LJ 820 (Karn)**

Filing of complaint under section 138 is no hindrance in filing a civil suit for recovery of amount which is legally recoverable.

Mere filing of complaint does not mean "taking cognizance of case". It means application of mind of court.

DISHONOUR OF CHEQUE AND OTHER ASPECTS

***Anju Trading Co.* v. *Electrolux Kelvinator Ltd.*, 2007 (2) JCC (NI) 221 (Del)**

Cases referred:

AIR 1926 Nag 315; 98 (2002) DLT 832; (2005) 10 SCC 626; AIR 2000 Del 38; I (1992) BC 205.

It is alleged that the respondent/defendant filed a case under section 138 of the Negotiable Instruments Act in respect of Ch. No. 804340 against the appellant. The appellant instituted a civil suit under the Specific Relief Act for 5 reliefs with a specific prayer that the respondent/dependant be restrained from proceeding with the complaint filed under sections 138/141 of the Negotiable Instruments Act before a Single Judge. Appeal was preferred. *Held,* that no restraint order could have been passed by the learned Single Judge staying the proceedings initiated against the appellant under section 138 of the Negotiable Instruments Act as that would amount to an order passed in violation of the law. The court relied on I (1992) BC 205 *M/s. Aristo Printers Pvt. Ltd.* v. *M/s. Perbanchal Trade Centre Guwahati.*

***M/s. Sri Krishna Agencies* v. *State of Andhra Pradesh,* AIR 2009 SC 1011**

Case referred:

AIR 1999 SC 3499 (followed).

It is a case under section 138 of the Negotiable Instruments Act. Criminal Appeal is filed under section 482, the Cr. P.C. for quashing the complaint filed for dishonour of cheque on the ground that complainant had already taken recourse to Arbitration proceedings. The Apex Court followed the case of *Rajesh Agarwal,* AIR 1999 SC 3499 where the same issue was raised and it was held that merely because arbitration proceedings have been undertaken, the criminal proceedings could not be thwarted. The appeal is allowed and the order of the High Court was set aside and restored the complaint before the learned DCMM, Hyderabad to be proceeded with in accordance with law.

***M/s. Sri Krishna Agencies* v. *State of Andhra Pradesh,* 2009 (1) JCC (NI) 31 (SC)**

Case referred:

(1999) 8 SCC 686.

It is a case under section 482, the Cr. P.C. on the ground that the appellant has already taken recourse to Arbitration proceedings so the case is basically of a civil nature and the criminal complaint cannot be proceeded with. *Held,* that there is no bar to the simultaneous continuance of a criminal proceeding and civil proceeding if the two arises from separate cause-of-action.

SINGLE COMPLAINT AND DISHONOURING OF CHEQUES MORE THAN ONCE

Section 219, *the Cr. P.C.* says that, "when a person is accused more than one offence of the same kind within the space of twelve months from the first to the last of such offences whether in respect of the same person or not, he may be charged with and tried at one trial for, any number of them not exceeding three. The section further says that the offences are of the same kind when they are punishable with the same amount of punishment under the same section of the Indian Penal Code (45 of 1860) or of any special or local law. So this section constitutes three essentials.

(1) This section by its terms refers to the case of a single accused. [(1905) 33 Cal 292; (1916) PR No. 17 of 1917)].

(2) The accused must be charged with not more than three offences of the same kind [(1951) 53 Bom LR 928 (FB)].

(3) That offences must be committed within a year [(1926) 49 All 312].

CASE LAW

***Y. Sharma* v. *Surya Fin Cap Ltd.,* (2002) 1 BC 588: (2001) 93 DLT 693: (2001) 60 DRJ 292: 2002 Cr LJ 807 (Del)**

Facts of the case.—In this case two cheques were dishonoured. Cause-of-action accrued to respondent with a gap of only one day. For the first dishonoured cheque the notice was made on 7-1-1997 and for the second cheque notice was made on 8-1-997. The issue was that two different cheques covered by two different notices cannot be covered by a single complaint. The High Court referred to section 219, the Cr. P.C. and *held* that a single complaint is maintainable.

***Pinto Stick* v. *M.L. Oswal*, 1997 Cr LJ 2122 (Mad)**

Case referred:

(1994) 1 Mad LW (Cri) 34.

Facts of the case.—It is a case where there is a single transaction amounting to Rs. 45816.12 against which 4 cheques have been issued. The issue was that more than three instances have been clubbed together and thereby section 219, the Cr. P.C. has been violated and referred to the case of *Ruby Leather Export* v. *K. Venu of Vandhana Chemicals etc.*, (1994) 1 Mad LW (Cri) 34, wherein it is said that there is patent violation of section 219, the Cr. P.C. and directed that the complaint can choose on which of these cheques he can have the prosecution maintained. The case is remanded back to put a fresh question on section 219, the Cr. P.C.

***Shree Lalit Fabrics* v. *Linkers Associates Ltd.*, (1996) 62 DLT 507**

It is a case where a composite notice was issued instead of issuing notice for each dishonoured cheques. It is *held* that such a requirement cannot be read into section 138 of the Negotiable Instruments Act as a mandatory requirement.

***M/s. Printo Stick* v. *M.L. Aswal*, 1997 Cr LJ 2122 (Mad)**

Case referred:

1994 (1) Mad LW (Cri) 34.

It is a case where four cheques relating to four instances were clubbed together in a single case. The court relied upon the case of *Ruby Leather Exports Rep by its Proprietor, Bhaskar* v. *K. Venu, Rep. Vandhana Chemicals*, 1994 (1) Mad LW (Cr) 34, where the true spirit of section 219 was discussed and accordingly held that the order of the Trial Court is bad. Matter was remanded bank to the Trial Court to put fresh question to the complainant to choose one of the cheques to maintain prosecution.

***Kershi Pirozshah Bhagvagar* v. *State of Gujarat*, 2007 Cr LJ 3958 (Guj)**

It is a case of dishonour of four cheques. It constitutes four distinct offences. So the provisions of Section 219 of the Cr. P.C. cannot be invoked clubbing two alleged offences in one complaint on the ground that all cheques were given as part of same transaction is not sufficient to bring the case within the ambit of section 219.

Cases referred:

2005 (2) Guj LR 1451; 1999 DCR 329 (Guj) (Overruled); 1991 (1) Guj LR 111 (held *per incuriam*); 1999 DCR 339 (Kar); 1984 Cr LJ 334. (SC); AIR 1983 SC 60; AIR 1981 SC 1068; AIR 1962 Guj 128 (FB); AIR 1960 Guj 40 (FB); AIR 1952 Bom 177 (FB) (Followed); (1908) 10 Bom LR 973.

***Sanjay Kumar Ghai* v. *State*, 2008 (1) JCC (NI) 84 (Del)**

Cases referred:

(2004) 13 SCC 527; (2005) 10 SCC 80; (2000) 10 SCC 596.

It is a case of five complaints and a joint trial. The petitioner filed an application under sections 219, 220, the Cr. P.C. The application was dismissed and hence this petition under section 482, the Cr. P.C. for quashing the impugned order of the learned Magistrate. The court *held* that the complainants in these complaints are in these cases are different and the bank accounts where the cheques were presented by these complainants are also different. Under these circumstances there is no illegality or infirmity in the impugned order passed by the trial Court. Moreover all these complaints are at the different states so it cannot be said that any prejudice has been caused to the petitioner by not consolidating all these complaint cases. There is no illegality in the order. The petition is dismissed.

Note.—*Composite notice for more than one cheque and more than 3 offences in one trial are two different concepts. There cannot be violation of section 219, the Cr. P.C.*

NON-PRESENCE OF COMPLAINANT

***Travel Agents Association of India (TAAI) Chennai* v. *Eastman Travel and Tours (M) Pvt. Ltd.*, (2004) 4 Cur Cri R 310: 2004 MLJ (Cri) 417: 2004 Cr LJ 2766 (Mad)**

Cases referred:

2004 Cr LJ 143 (Bom); (2002) 8 Scale 331 (SC).

Facts of the case.—Complainant closed his evidence. Accused did not want to examine any witness. So the matter was posted for arguments. On that day the complainant was not present. Court dismissed the complaint for non-appearance of the complainant and the accused was acquitted. This is an appeal against the order of acquittal. The High Court referred to section 314, the Cr. P.C. and *held* that it being a summon case, the court would have passed the order on the basis of the evidence adduced by the complainant. Dismissal of complaint is legally not sustainable. The matter is remitted back for passing order on the basis of the evidence. Both parties can put forth their case if they so desire.

***Lakshmi Steel Industries* v. *State*, 2005 Cr LJ 1197 (Raj)**

Complainant not appearing before trial Court. Failed to adduce evidence. Accused acquitted. High Court agreed with the order of acquittal .

Refer:

(2003) Cri LR 211 SC; AIR 1998 SC 596.

***M/s. Plaza Cables Electric Pvt Ltd.* v. *Mr. Kamal Khurana*, 2006 (3) JCC (NI) 267 (Del)**

Complaint filed under section 138 of the Negotiable Instruments Act was dismissed in default of non-prosecution. The case was in Tis Hazari Court and posted on 13-5-2005. It was transferred to Rohini Court and was to be taken up for hearing on 13-1-2006. The complaint was dismissed on 13-1-2006 for non-appearance of the appellant. The appellant could explain the reason for non-appearance. *Held,* that technicalities should not block the road for Justice. There is no adjudication or rights and liabilities of the parties on merits. No prejudice shall be caused to the respondent in case the parties are heard on merits of the grievance failed by the appellant in his complaint. The case is remanded back to the concerned trial Court for decision on merits in accordance with law.

***M/s. Ankita Overseas Pvt. Ltd.* v. *Shakeel Ahmed*, 2006 (3) JCC (NI) 286 (Del)**

Complaint under section 138 of the Negotiable Instruments Act was dismissed in default for non-prosecution. On that day none was present even on behalf of the respondents before the court below though they had already been served with the notice of the complaint prior to the said date. The court *held* that there is no reason to disbelieve the reasons given by the appellant. No prejudice shall be caused to the respondents in case the instant appeal is allowed. The case is remanded back for disposal on merits according to law.

Refer Also:

M/s. Digitronics Infosys Pvt. Ltd. v. *Mr. Davinder Sahani*, 2007 (1) JCC (NI) 15 (Del); *Joginder Kapil* v. *Sanjay Gupta*, 2007 (1) JCC (NI) 5 (Del); *Danvanti Mutual Benefits Ltd.* v. *State of Haryana*, 2008 (2) JCC (NI) 167 (P&H).

***S. Anand* v. *Vasumathi Chandera Sekhar*, 2008 (2) JCC (NI) 127 (SC)**

Cases referred:

AIR 1998 SC 536; (2004) 12 SCC 509.

In this case the complaint was dismissed in default and the accused/appellant was acquitted, in terms of section 256(1), the Cr. P.C. It was reversed by the High Court and hence appeal before the Supreme Court. The Supreme Court did not approve the manner in which the appeal is disposed of by the High Court. The Trial Court is directed to proceed with the matter according to law and dispose of the case expeditiously. Both the parties are directed to appear before the trial Court.

***S. Rama Krishna* v. *S. Rani Reddy (D) by his LRs*, 2008 (2) JCC (NI) 215 (SC)**

It is a case of acquitted of the accused. Record revealed that the accused was always present. 15 days were given for inclusion of LRs, but no steps were taken. The respondents did not seriously press their application. The case cannot be allowed to remain pending and thus the judgment of acquittal is in order. The Apex Court relied on the fundamental right of "Speedy Trial".

***M/s. Becton Dickinson India Ltd.* v. *M/s. Shika Pharma (P) Ltd.*, 2009 (2) JCC (NI) 121 (Del)**

Cases referred:

AIR 1990 SC 2134; 1981 Cr LJ 422.

The complaint filed under sections 138, 141 and 142 was dismissed in default and the respondent/accused were discharged. It was upheld by the ASJ. Now the Criminal Appeal is under section 482, the Cr. P.C. It was held that despite knowing the date after inspection of file, taking a plea of noting wrong date and not attending the court does not smell justified. The order passed by the learned Magistrate has no infirmity.

***Jagdish Bagri* v. *Rajindera Kumar Luhariwala*, 2009 (1) JCC (NI) 71 (SC)**

It is *held* that the High Court took the matter *ex-parte*. It was found that the cheque was given as security in terms of the agreement of payments to be made.

Since the agreement was not complied with, the cheque issued does not remain a security. However, the issue of non-appearance was considered by the Apex Court favourably, the matter was remanded to the High Court for fresh consideration.

***Ravi Sharma* v. *The State (NCT of Delhi)*, 2010 (1) JCC (NI) 3 (Del)**

Cases referred:

M/s. Digitronics Infosys Pvt. Ltd. v. *Devender Sahni*, 2007 Cr LJ (NOC) 187; *Kalpana Tyagi* v. *Sneh Lata Sharma*, 2003 (2) JCC (NI) 129; *T. Azizur Rehman & Co.* v. *Super Supplies*, 2007 (3) JCC 302 (NI); *R.P.G. Transmission Ltd.* v. *Sakura Seimitsu (I) Ltd.*, 2005 (119) DLT 393.

The complinant under section 138 of the Negotiable Instruments Act was dismissed on the ground of non-appearance of the complainant, which means acquittal of the accused under section 256, the Cr. P.C. So the only remedy is to file an appeal against acquittal and not an application for restoration.

SECTION 204, Cr. P.C. AND INTERLOCUTORY ORDER

***Shri Niwas Mulchand Ladniya* v. *Laxmi Narayana Jainarayan Rathi*, (2003) 2 Mah LJ 813: (2003) 4 Rec Cri R 460: 2003 Cr LJ 3795 (Bom)**

Cases referred:

(1999) 3 SCC 134: 1999 Cr LJ 1620: AIR 1999 SC 1028 (followed); AIR 1980 SC 962: 1980 Supp SCC 92: 1980 Cr LJ 690; AIR 1978 SC 47; AIR 1977 SC 2185: (1977) 4 SCC 137: 1997 Cr LJ 1891.

Facts of the case.—In this case the main issue was whether a Revision is maintainable against order passed under section 204, the Cr. P.C. in a case of dishonour of cheque. Section 397(2), Cr. P.C. was referred which says, "the powers of Revision conferred by sub-section (1) shall not be exercised in relation to any interlocutory order passed in any appeal, enquiry, trial or other proceedings". On plain reading of the section it is clear that order passed under section 204 taking cognizance and issue of process is not an interlocutory order. The High Court followed AIR 1999 SC 1028 wherein it is said that section 397(2) has been used in a very restricted sense and not in a broad or artistic sense and merely denotes orders of purely interim or temporary nature and any order passed which substantially affects the right of the parties cannot be an "interlocutory order". *Held* order passed under section 204, the Cr. P.C. is not an interlocutory order.

SECTION 205, THE Cr. P.C. AND OFFENCE UNDER SECTION 138

***Devasis Samantaray v. State of Orissa*, (2003) 25 OCR 594: (2003) 2 Cri LR 219: (2003) 4 All Cri R 769: 2003 Cr LJ 3774 (Ori)**

Cases referred:

(2002) 94 Cut LT 726; (1999) 2 Ori LR 191 (followed); 1995 Cr LJ 224; (1999) 2 Ori LR 361.

Facts of the case.—The issue was to quash the order rejecting the prayer for extending the benefit available under section 205, the Cr. P.C. The court referred to various decisions and *held* that it is not mandatory for the accused to personally appear in court before filing the application under section 205(1), the Cr. P.C. The *ratio decidendi* of the various decisions is that power under section 205(1), the Cr. P.C. can be exercised by a Magistrate at the stage of issuance of summons but also at subsequent stage even after issuance of Non-bailable Warrant.

***Rohit S. Ved* v. *State of Kerala,* 2009(3) Crimes 122 (Ker)**

Cases referred:

ILR 2008 (4) Ker 88; 1999 (3) KLT 714.

Held, that if personal appearance is not required and can be exempted under section 205, the Cr. P.C., the application for exemption can be allowed without personal presence whether such personal appearance is requested/mandated by issue of Summons or Warrant.

***M/s. East India Produce Ltd.* v. *Nirmal Khandelwal,* 2010 (1) JCC (NI) 5 (Cal)**

Cases referred:

Bhaskar Industries Ltd. v. *Bhiwani Denim & Apprels Ltd.*, 2001 (3) CHN (SC Suppl) 63; *V.K. Jain* v. *Union of India,* 2000 SCC (Cri) 302.

It is case where the Metropolitan Magistrate dismissed the application filed under Section 205, the Cr. P.C. praying for dispensing with personal appearance. It was held that in view of the case of *Bhaskar Industries,* exemption may he granted from personal appearance. Order of Metropolitan Magistrate and Assistant Sessions Judge are set aside. The case is remanded back who will despose of the application without insisting an appearance of the accused.

Note.—*The Supreme Court in AIR 1973 SC 262 has said that in trivial cases, technical cases where no moral turpitude is involved, where the accused are ladies, old and sickly persons, factory workers, labourers, busy business people, the courts should exempt from personal appearance.*

SECTION 45 OF THE EVIDENCE ACT

***T. Madhava Rao* v. *M. Guman Reddy,* (2003) 1 Crimes 581: (2003) 2 BC 190: 2003 Cr LJ 1043 (AP)**

Case referred:

(1997) 2 Bank LJ 58 Ker.

Facts of the case.—The point arisen was as to when the opinion of the hand writing expert can be solicited. The respondent denied the existence of chit fund transaction between him and the petitioner for which he wanted the pass book to be sent to handwriting expert to establish the existence of chit fund transaction. The permission sought was denied as the signatures of the respondent in pass book has no relevance with the issue of cheque by the petitioner that the cheque was given as a collateral security. Relied on the case law cited will not help the petitioner as in the cited case the accused denied his signatures on the cheque for which the opinion of the handwriting expert was sought.

DISMISSAL OF COMPLAINT

***Mohammed Ilyas Ahamad* v. *Abdul Subhan*, (2001) 3 CCC 32: (2001) 3 Rec Cri R 458: 2001 Cr LJ 2821 (Kant)**

Facts of the case.—These are criminal petitions filed under section 482, the Cr. P.C. wherein sections 200, 203, the Cr. P.C. were discussed. It is a case where the complaint was dismissed for default. However, the proceedings of the order sheet disclose that immediately after the dismissal the counsel appearing for the petitioner appeared requesting the recall of the order and exempting the complainant's presence. The court allowed the restoration. This order of restoration was challenged and the Sessions Judge set aside the restoration Order and hence this petition under section 482, the Cr. P.C. The High Court did not find any illegality in the order passed by the Magistrate and the order passed by the Sessions Judge but the High Court *held* that an offence under section 138, the Negotiable Instruments Act and offence under the I.P.C. provisions largely differ as there is no remedy under section 138 to file a second complaint when the first complaint is dismissed for default. Therefore, in order to secure the ends of justice, the case is remitted back to the court of Magistrate for trial in accordance with law.

WITHDRAWAL OF COMPLAINT

***Biju Thomas* v. *Devakiamma*, (2001) 2 BC 53: (2001) 2 Crimes 472: (2001) 3 ICC 113: (2001) 1 Ker 449: 2001 Cr LJ 790 (Ker)**

Case referred:

(1986) 2 Crimes 393.

Facts of the case.—It is a case where the petitioner filed an application for withdrawal of the complaint as the matter has been settled but on the date of consideration of the application the complainant was absent. The only option for the Magistrate was either to grant permission to withdraw or acquit the accused but the Magistrate issued N.B.W. and initiated steps under sections 82 and 83, the Cr. P.C. against the accused which is highly improper.

NO VICARIOUS LIABILITY

***Partap Singh Yadav* v. *Atal Behari Pande*, (2003) 2 Civ LJ 461: (2002) 100 DLT 673: (2003) 66 DRJ 101: 2003 Cr LJ 705 (Del)**

Cases referred:

AIR 1999 SC 3762; 1995 Cr LJ 1222 (Del); 1991 Cr LJ 2594 (P&H); (1988) 1 Crimes 514 (Del).

Facts of the case.—In this case the cheque was drawn by the petitioner's son for payment of debt of his father. The cheque was dishonoured and no payment was made even after receipt of notice in terms of clause (c) of proviso to section 138. The complaint is filed against both the father and the son. It was *held* that the

Magistrate should have not taken cognizance against the father as there is no principle of vicarious liability. The person who has issued the cheque, can be *held* liable if found guilty.

SECTION 204, THE Cr. P.C. AND PROCEDURE

***Ashok Ambalal Shah* v. *Gurubachan*, 1992 Cr LJ 893 (MP)**

Cases referred:

AIR 1986 SC 833: (1986) 3 SCC 67: 1986 Cr LJ 917; 1986 Cr LJ 207 (AP); 1986 Cr LJ 483 (Mad); 1980 Guj LT 103; AIR 1976 SC 1947: (1976) 3 SCC 736: 1976 Cr LJ 1533; AIR 1963 SC 1430; AIR 1960 SC 1113: (1961) 1 SCR 1: 1960 Cr LJ 1499.

Facts of the case.—It is a case of dishonour of cheque but the complaint is filed under section 420, the I.P.C. No procedure required under dishonour of cheque as specified under proviso (a)(b) to section 138 and section 142(b) is followed. Even the ingredients of section 420, the I.P.C. are not satisfied. The High Court found the complaint is fit to be quashed under section 482, the Cr. P.C.

TRANSFER PETITION

***Ayyanar Agencies* v. *Sri Vishnu Cement Ltd.*, (2000) 10 SCC 596: 2001 SCC (Cri) 1511: (2000) 3 Crimes 31: 2000 Cr LJ 2472 (SC)**

Facts of the case.—The facts are that the respondents filed five complaints under section 138, the Negotiable Instruments Act before the Metropolitan Magistrate court Chennai and thereafter one complaint filed at Hyderabad in respect of two cheques also under section 138, the Negotiable Instruments Act. This petition is for transferring the complaint from Hyderabad to Chennai as parties in all the cases are the same and the offence is of the same nature though sprouted from different cheques. It would be advantageous to all the parties to have all the cases before the same court. The Supreme Court looking to the convenience of the parties and their interest ordered the transfer of the case from Hyderabad to Chennai court where other complaints are pending.

EXAMINATION OF WITNESSES

***B.M. Arif* v. *Boston Tea (India) Ltd.*, (2005) 1 CCR 124 (Kant)**

Facts of the case.—It is a case wherein sections 254 and 315, the Cr. P.C. were discussed. In this case the accused wanted to examine a witness and asked for issue of summons. The Magistrate ordered that the application of the accused be kept in abeyance until the evidence of the accused. This order was challenged. The High Court referred to section 315, the Cr. P.C. which says that the accused is a competent witness but no adverse inference can be drawn for his non-examination similarly the High Court referred to section 254, the Cr. P.C. and concluded that the order of the Magistrate keeping the application of the accused in abeyance be quashed and the trial be initiated in terms of section 254(1), the Cr. P.C.

Note.—*For section 315, the Cr. P.C. refer AIR 1968 SC 110; AIR 1968 SC 20; 1973 Cr LJ 262. For section 254(1), the Cr. P.C. refer 1 WR (Cri) 77.*

FIXING TIME LIMIT FOR RECORDING PRELIMINARY EVIDENCE

***Jindal Photo Films Ltd.* v. *State,* (2001) 91 DLT 34: (2001) 58 DRJ 584: 2001 Cr LJ 2790 (Del)**

Cases referred:

AIR 2001 SC 567; AIR 2001 SC 676; (2001) 2 Crimes 45 (Del); (1997) 3 Rec. Cri R 520 (Del); (1996) 64 DLT 815; (1991) 1 WTR 1351; *Mungroo* v. *R.*

Facts of the case.—In this case the question arose, was that whether dispute relating to dishonouring of cheque under section 138, the Negotiable Instruments Act should be subject to time limit for recording the preliminary evidence. The order given to the Metropolitan Magistrate was that the preliminary evidence should be recorded as early as possible but in no case recording of such evidence shall be deferred beyond two months from the date of receipt of complaint by the Magistrate. The High Court (DB) *held* that fixing a time limit for recording preliminary evidence is impermissible. But courts dealing with matters have to keep in view the objective behind enactment of the Act and desirability of early disposal. Justice cannot be made to move at snail's pace.

LONG ADJOURNMENT

***Khanna Hotel (P) Ltd.* v. *State,* 2004 Bank LJ 344: (2003) 4 Crimes 198: (2003) 106 DLT 158: 2004 Cr LJ 180 (Del)**

Facts of the case.—It is a case where a long date of one year was given for first appearance in a case under section 138, the Negotiable Instruments Act which is violative of section 143(2) and (3) of the Negotiable Instruments Act. The learned justice felt a great agony in expressing his views for the insurmounting backlogs and suggested remedial measure to give sanctity to section 143 of the Act. He called Government and Judiciary as two masters and a house with two masters can never be strong.

CUSTODY OF CHEQUES

***Chetanbhai Vasantbhai Mistary* v. *State of Gujarat,* 1 (2005) CCR 50 (Guj)**

Cases referred:

1977 Cr LJ 575 (relied on); AIR 1954 Mad 214 (relied); 1991 Cr LJ (not applicable); 1990 Cr LJ (not applicable); 1985 GLH 61 (not applicable); 2002 CCR 345 SC (not applicable).

Facts of the case.—It is a case of 48 cheques recovered in connection with the complaint lodged under sections 384, 385, 386 and 506(2) of the I.P.C. The accused filed an application for handing over the property under section 451, the Cr. P.C. The learned Magistrate passed the order accordingly which was set aside by the Sessions Judge and hence the petition against the order of the Sessions Judge. The High Court referred to various provisions of the Negotiable Instruments Act and also provisions of the Criminal Procedure Code like sections 451, 457, the Cr. P.C. and restored the order of the Magistrate ordering delivery of the cheques to the petitioner subject to conditions mentioned therein.

WHO IS THE DRAWER OF CHEQUE

***Navin Chandra Dharmshiv Bhai Doshi* v. *Natvarlal & Co. Ahmedabad,* (2001) 3 Guj LH 399: (2001) 4 Rec Cri R 82: 2001 Cr LJ 3105 (Guj)**

Cases referred:

(1994) 35 (1) Guj LR 886; (1994) 2 Crimes 259 (Bom); (1993) 1 Bank Case 8 (Mad); (1991) 1 Guj LH 342.

Facts of the case.—The wife of the accused husband is running the business. The contention was that accused No. 2 signed the cheque on the authority of accused No. 1. So accused No. 1 should be *held* responsible for the bouncing of the cheque. It is to be seen that the cheque is issued by a proprietary concern of accused No. 1 and thus accused No. 2 is not the drawer of the cheque. In this case sections 397 and 401, the Cr. P.C. were discussed to say that the revisional court does not interfere unless the judgment of the lower court is based on misreading of the evidence, perversity, or manifestly miscarriage of justice or error of law. It is *held* that the fact has to be proved, under what authority accused No. 2 has signed the cheque and how he is not the drawer of the cheque which can be done in the trial. Hence, the petition is dismissed.

JURISDICTION

***Hong Kong and Shanghai Banking Corporation* v. *Manas Satpati,* (2005) 1 AD (Del) 601**

Facts of the case.—It is a case based on sections 177, 178, the Cr. P.C. Both parties live in New Delhi but the complaint is filed in Karkardoma Court on the plea that the notice was posted from the Head Post Office. Krishna Nagar which falls in the jurisdiction of Karkardoma Courts. *Held,* that a person who puts the law into motion cannot choose jurisdiction as per his own convenience. Cause-of-action and ordinary place of residence of parties is a guiding factor for ascertaining the aspect of territorial jurisdiction. *Merely posting a letter could not give right to the petitioner to file the complaint in that area.* However, the High Court, in the interest of justice, instead of quashing the judgment, directed that the complaint be sent to the court of competent jurisdiction.

INTIMATION RECEIVED IS RELEVANT

***Amina* v. *Baby,* 1 (2005) CCR 233 (Ker)**

Facts of the case.—The issue is, which date is relevant, *i.e.,* date of receipt of intimation or date of letter of intimation for the purpose of section 138 (proviso) (b). The facts are that the cheque is bounced on 25-1-1997 as informed to the accused by a letter. The notice is dated 11-2-1997 and posted on 13-2-1997. Notice should have been sent within 15 days, but notice was sent after 15 days. But *held* that date of receipt of intimation is relevant and not the date of letter of intimation. So the notice sent is within time.

NON-OBSTANTE CLAUSE

Cases referred:

AIR 1978 SC 1568 (followed); 1972 Ker LT 728 (followed); AIR 1967 SC (followed).

Facts of the case.—Section 4(2), *the Cr. P.C.* says, "All offences under any other law shall be investigated, inquired into, tried or otherwise dealt with according to the same provisions, but subject to any enactment for the time being in force regulating the manner or place of investigating, inquiring into, trying or otherwise dealing with such offences."

It is a case where there is impleadment of parties subsequent to taking cognizance of offence. It was pleaded that due to *non-obstante* clause in section 142, provision of section 319(4), the Cr. P.C. will not apply. *Held,* that *non-obstante* clause in section 142, no doubt has overriding effect but does not bar other provisions of the Code of Criminal Procedure Code. *Non-obstante* clause does not affect section 319(4), the Cr. P.C.

SECTION 138 OF THE NEGOTIABLE INSTRUMENTS ACT AND SECTION 482, THE CR. P.C.

***Pritam Singh* v. *Tawi Education Trust,* 2005 Cr LJ 277 (J&K)**

Held: High Court will not interfere in exercise of its inherent power at initial stage of issue of Process.

SECTION 138 OF THE NEGOTIABLE INSTRUMENTS ACT AND SECTION 357, THE CR. P.C

***Maheshwar Duttatraya Kale* v. *Capt. Atul Wasudeo Divekar,* 2006 (3) JCC (NI) 235 (Bom)**

Cases referred:

Hari Singh v. *Sukhbir Singh,* 1988 SCC (Cri) 984; *Dalmiya Cement (Bharat) Ltd.* v. *Galaxy Traders and Agencies Ltd.,* 2001 (6) SCC 463; *Suganti Suresh Kumar* v. *Jagdeeshan,* 2002 (2) SCC 420; *Stanny Felix Pinto* v. *Jangid Builders, Pvt. Ltd.,* 2001 (2) SCC 416.

It is a case under section 138 of the Negotiable Instruments Act wherein compensation of Rs. 13 lakh was ordered. Appeal was filed before the Session Court. Sentence was suspended till final decision of the appeal. Subject to the deposit of half of the amount of cheque (Rs. 6,25,000) within 15 days. The condition imposed was challenged. Time was extended till 20-1-2006. NBW will not be executed till 20-1-2006. Notwithstanding time extended by the court, appellate court will proceed hearing the appeal if ready in all respects. Order accordingly.

***Ajai Bansal* v. *Smt. Nirmal Jain,* 2006 (1) JCC (NI) 107 (P&H)**

Cases referred:

AIR 1988 SC 2127; AIR 1999 SC 3762.

It is a case where the trial Court convicted the accused sentenced to 6 months rigorous imprisonment and a fine of Rs. 5000, but no compensation was ordered to be paid. There was an appeal against this order which was dismissed by the Additional Sessions Judge and hence this instant petition. The court modified the order and allowed Rs. 75,000 as compensation under Section 357(3) and in case of default the respondent shall undergo rigorous imprisonment for a period of 3 months.

***M/s. Sasi Poly Colours* v. *M/s. Lakshmi Polymers,* 2006 (3) JCC (NI) 255 (Mad)**

Cases referred:

2001 SCC (Cri) 369; 2002 Cr LJ 1003; AIR 1988 SC 217; 2002 (1) MWN (Cri) DCC (Mad) 68.

In this case the learned Magistrate has found the respondents accused guilty for an offence under section 138 of the Negotiable Instruments Act, convicted and sentenced them to undergo simple imprisonment till the rising of the court and to pay fine of Rs. 5000 in each case. The complainant filed the revision petitions which were allowed. In addition to the sentence of imprisonment or fine as ordered by the trial Court, respondent/accused Nos. 2 and 3 are further directed to pay compensation of twice the cheque amount of each cheque in view of the powers conferred under section 357(4), the Cr. P.C.

***Dilip S. Dhanukar* v. *Kotak Mahindra Co Ltd.,* 2007 (2) JCC (NI) 153 SC**

Cases referred:

AIR 1957 SC 540; 1971 (3) SCC 337; 1970 (1) SCC 547; 2003 (8) SCC 50; 1978 (3) SCC 552; 2004 (4) SCC 311; 2000 (8) SCC 437; 2002 (6) SCC 462; 2002 (6) SCC 663; 1988 (4) SCC 551; 2006 (3) SCC 178; 1978 (4) SCC 111; 2007 (4) SCALE 143; 1995 Cr LJ 3217; 2006 (10) SCALE 21; 2006 (9) SCALE 194; 2005 (2) SCC 638; 2004 (9) SCC 772; 2001 (2) SCC 416; (2006) 3 All ER 428; (1970) 2 All ER 871; (2000) 2 All ER 109.

The Supreme Court in this case laid down certain guidelines as follows:—

(i) In a case of this nature section 357(2) would be attracted even when the appellant was directed to pay compensation.

(ii) The appellate court, however, while suspending the sentence was entitled to put the appellant on terms but no such term could be put as a condition precedent for entertaining the appeal which is a constitutional and statutory right.

(iii) The amount of compensation must be a reasonable sum.

(iv) The court, while fixing such amount, must have regard to all relevant factors including the one referred to in sub-section (5) of section 357, the Cr. P.C.

(v) No unreasonable amount of compensation can be directed to be paid. In this case the Apex Court reduced the compensation from Rs. 15 lakh to Rs. one lakh.

***D. Purshotam Reddy* v. *K. Sateesh,* 2008 (3) JCC (NI) 341 SC**

Cases referred:

2007 (6) SCC 528; JT 2008 (7) SC 643; 2007 (14) SCALE 556.

Held, that when there are two cases arising out of the same cause-of-action, one a civil case and the other section 138 of the Negotiable Instruments Act, a compensation allowed under the Negotiable Instruments Act must be taken into account by the civil Court under the maxim, "*Actus curiae neminem gravilit.*"

***M/s. Indocount Finance Ltd.* v. *Mrs. Sushma Kapoor*, 2009 (1) JCC (NI) 8 (Del)**

Cases referred:

(1988) 4 SCC 551; 2002 (1) Crimes 265 (SC); AIR 1999 SC 3762; 2005 (2) JCC 1178; 2005 (2) JCC 1182; (2007) 6 SCC 528.

In this case the matter was settled in Lok Adalat wherein the complainant agreed to receive the amount of the cheque. After agreeing the petitioner wants to continue the litigation demanding compensation. Even the cheque has been withdrawn from Magistrate's Court. No merit in the petition.

NON-MARKING OF COMPLAINT

***V. Satyanarayana* v. *Sandeep Enterprises*, 2005 Cr LJ 12 (Kant)**

Held: Non-marking of complaint not fatal to complainant's case.

DRAWER—A GUARANTOR

***Noble T. Francis* v. *Saleena Jos*, 2005 Cr LJ 640 (Ker)**

Cheque issued by wife on behalf of the husband. Acquittal by the Court. Order reversed by High Court; 2002 Cr LJ 3935 relied on.

ISSUE OF NON-BAILABLE WARRANT

***Mohd. Inam Ahmad* v. *State of Uttar Pradesh*, 2005 Cr LJ 4187 (All)**

Issuance of N.B.W. – Compelling appearance through coercive method – Not appreciate – High Court gave 30 days' time to appear.

SUBSTITUTED SUMMONS

***Mac Charles (I) Ltd.* v. *Chandrashekar*, 2005 Cr LJ 3700**

Held: Substituted summons permissible—whether offence is under section 138, the Negotiable Instruments Act or under the I.P.C. If accused is not coming under rule 2 of the Criminal Rule of Practice, case can be split up. No. *Ex parte* decision.

SEPARATE COMPLAINT FOR FORGERY

***M. Ravi* v. *Elumalai Chettiar*, 2006 Cr LJ 1059 (Mad)**

Separate complaint by the accused that cheque has been forged as the cheque was issued for another transaction. Separate complaint is not maintainable. Court will take notice while disposing of the complaint filed by the payee.

STAY OF PROCEEDINGS

***Gurcharan Singh* v. *Allied Motors Ltd.*, (2005) 10 SCC 626: 2005 SCC (Cri) 1653: 2006 Cr LJ 360 (SC)**

Dishonour of Cheque – Stay of Proceedings – For pendency of civil proceedings (Arbitration) – Cause-of-action in two proceedings are different – Award passed can be defence in criminal proceedings – Cannot be ground to stay complaint under section 138.

***Constellation Enterprises Ltd.* v. *P.E.C Ltd.*, (2006) (1) JCC (NI) 59 (Del)**

Cases referred:

2003 (3) JCC 304; *Daljit Singh Chandok* v. *State*, Cri MC No. 2764/2005 decided on 9-1-2006.

Held, that in terms of Cri M.C. No. 2764/2005 *Daljeet Singh Chandok* v. *State,* decided on 9-1-2006, whatever defences are being raised should be raised before the trial Court and the court under section 482, the Cr. P.C. cannot examine the documentary and oral evidence which may have to be led before the trial Court which has to be tested by cross-examination. Under such circumstances there is no justification for interference under section 482, the Cr. P.C. The petition is dismissed.

***M. Ramesh* v. *Vankadara Sunil Kumar,* 2006 (1) JCC (NI) 31 (AP)**

Case referred:

(1999) 7 SCC 510.

It is *held* that while considering a petition under section 482, the Cr. P.C. this court has to consider the averments in the complaint only but not the defence of the accused. The question of ownership and authorizing to issue the cheque can only be decided after the trial.

***Ramji Lal* v. *Amit Ved (Since deceased),* 2007 (4) JCC (NI) 364 (Del)**

This petition is under section 482 the Cr. P.C. read with Article 227 of the Constitution of India. The court observed that the plea taken by the petitioner is an after thought taken after a lapse of 5 years and furthermore it is a plea of defence which could have been taken before the trial Court. It is an abuse of the process of law and is dismissed with heavy costs.

***Raj Kumar Khurana* v. *State (GNCT of Delhi),* 2008 (1) JCC (NI) 62 (Del)**

Cases referred:

1990 (2) RCR 335; 1993 (3) RCR 507; 2004 (Vol 119) Comp Cas 18.

It is a petition filed after a lapse of 6 years. This plea should have been taken before the trial Court. Furthermore, the benefit of section 462, the Cr. P.C. cannot be extended to persons who do not approach the court at the earliest possible opportunity. The petition is dismissed.

***Dhanjit Singh Nanda* v. *State,* 2009 (2) JCC (NI) 99 (Del)**

Cases referred:

(1998) 5 SCC 749; AIR 1982 SC 1238; (1988) 4 SCC 655; (1983) 1 SCC 1; (2005) 2 SCC 571.

The petition is on the ground that respondent was debarred from recovering the loan amount being not a registered money lender. It is *held* that proceedings under section 138 of the Negotiable Instruments Act are not recovery proceedings and are meant to punish the person who after issuing a cheque to honour the same and also commits a default in paying the said amount on receipt of a notice.

EXEMPTION FROM PERSONAL APPEARANCE

***Shrikant Somani* v. *Ram Kumar Agarwal,* 2006 (1) JCC (NI) 90 Del**

Cases referred:

2002 IV AD (Del) 242; (2001) 7 SCC 401.

It is a petition seeking exemption from personal appearance. The petitioner is normally a resident of Delhi and has set up the execuse of his being a resident of Pune only to avade the process of the court. The summons issued by the court was served upon the petitioner in Delhi. There is no substance in the petition.

***Sushil Suri* v. *State*, 2006 (3) JCC (NI) 274 (Del)**

Case referred:

2004 (3) JCC NI 180 (relied on).

The petition for exemption was dismissed. He had not sought exemption till the conclusion of the trial but till the evidence of the complainant is recorded. He further stated that he would not dispute his identity and shall be bound by the statements made by his advocate. There is substance in the petition. The Metropolitan Magistrate is directed to hear the petition afresh.

CHEQUE ISSUED NOT OUT OF ACCOUNT

***Pramod* v. *C.K. Velayudhan*, 2006 (1) JCC (NI) 63 (Ker)**

Cases referred:

2004 Cr LJ 4249 (SC); 2004 Cr LJ 4079 (AP); 2002 (112) Comp Cas 204 (AP).

Joint reading of section 138 and section 141 shows that an offence under section 138 can be committed by a person, a company, a firm or an association of individuals. In case of juristic persons also, it must be established that cheque in respect of which offence under section 138 is committed in drawn by such juristic person from the account maintained by him in a bank. If not the society is not liable.

***Jugesh Sehgal* v. *Shamsher Singh Gogi*, 2009 (3) JCC (NI) 210 (SC)**

Cases referred:

(1992) 4 SCC 305; (1977) 4 SCC 451; 1992 Supp (1) SCC 335; (2008) 3 SCC 574.

The dishonoured cheque was issued from an account which is non-existent on the day it was issued or that the account from where the cheque was issued pertained to some one else. So the necessary ingredient is not satisfied and the result being the criminal liability cannot be fastened.

CONTEMPT PROCEEDINGS

***Vikas Vij* v. *Rajiv Marwah*, 2008 (2) JCC (NI) 201 (Del)**

There was a compromise in court proceedings under sections 138, 142 of the Negotiable Instruments Act. Respondent No. 1 disobeyed the compromise effected in court proceeding. *Held*, that contempt proceedings cannot be resorted to as a weapon of offence as it is a matter between the court and the contemnor. Unless a compromise results in a undertaking to the court and is accepted by the court, breach thereof would not be actionable under contempt proceedings.

CHEQUE LOST

***Raj Kumar Khurana* v. *State of (NCT of Delhi)*, 2009 (3) JCC (NI) 181 SC**

Cases referred:

(2005) 13 SCC 161; (2009) 1 SCC 516; (2008) 8 SCC 1.

Cheque was returned by the bank on the ground that it was reported lost by the drawer. Court while exercising its jurisdiction for taking cognizance of offence under section 138 was required to consider only the allegations made in the complaint petition and the evidence of the complainant and his witnesses, if any. It could have not taken into consideration the result of complaint petition or closure report in respect of FIR lodged by the appellant for lost of the said cheque. Refusal of the bank of honour the cheque would not bring the matter within the mischief of the provision of section 138. The bank has to say whether the appellant had sufficient funds in his bank account or not.

DRAWER'S BANK

***Shroff Publishers & Distributors Pvt. Ltd.* v. *M/s. Springes India Pvt. Ltd.*, 2007 (4) JCC (NI) 329 (Del)**

Cases referred:

AIR 1998 SC 3043; (1997) 3 Cri 433; (1999) 3 Cri 252; (1999) 3 Cri 97; AIR 2001 SC 1161.

Held, that a cheque must in order to charge the drawer be presented at the bank upon which it is drawn before the relations between the drawer and his banker has been altered to the prejudice of the drawer. So the cheque must be presented in the drawer's bank to attract criminal liability.

NON-CONSIDERATION OF WHOLE MATTER BY THE HIGH COURT

***M/s. V.G. Saraf and Sons* v. *H. Ranjith*, 2009 (2) JCC (NI) 142 SC**

The accused was acquitted by the High Court that the bill represents only for Rs. 1,61,000 and whereas the cheque was for Rs. 1,86,606.95. The complainant has explained the difference which represents the cheque amount. The Supreme Court remitted the case back to the High Court to consider the matter afresh taking into consideration the various aspects highlighted.

HAND-WRITING EXPERT

***Mamtadevi* v. *Vijay Kumar Agarwal*, 2008 Cr LJ 970**

Cases referred:

2007 Cr LJ 1897; 2006 (13) SCALE 459; 2003 All MR (Cri) 639; AIR 2001 SC 2120; AIR 1966 SC 529; AIR 1965 SC 1887; AIR 1953 Cal 773.

It is a case for referring the document to hand-writing expert. The accused did not file any such application during trial and even in the appellate stage filed an application after two years. The object of the appellant is to fill the lacunae. The order of the appellate court is proper.

***Manda Syam Sunder* v. *Kurella Anjaneyachari*, AIR 2009 (NOC) 122 (AP)**

The cheque was returned dishonoured with endorsement "insufficient funds" and not on the ground of that the signature was not tallying. No purpose will be served in sending the document to hand-writing expert. Refusal to send the cheque to hand-writing expert is not illegal.

SECTION 138, THE NEGOTIABLE INSTRUMENTS ACT AND SECTIONS 82/83, THE CR. P.C.

***Sanjay Chaturvedi* v. *State*, 2006 (3) JCC (NI) 241**

Cases referred:

118 (2005) DLT 28; 2004 (3) JCC (NI) 180; 2003 (2) JCC 661; 2004 (1) JCC 308; 2003 (3) JCC 1485.

Case is under the Negotiable Instruments Act. Petitioner was summoned for 14th July, 2006. He appeared through counsel. He moved an application for exemption from his personal appearance. It was dismissed by ACMM and issued Non-bailable warrants for 26th August, 2006 N.B.W.S could not be executed for 26th August as the premises were locked. ACMM issued process under sections 82/83, the Cr. P.C. Both these orders was challenged. Both these orders were set aside in view of cases 2004 (1) JCC 308 and 2003 (3) JCC 1485.

SECTION 138, THE NEGOTIABLE INSTRUMENTS ACT AND SECTION 91, THE CR. P.C.

***G.S. Majawala* v. *Om Prakash Mittal*, 2007 (4) JCC (NI) 408 (Del)**

Cases referred:

1999 (II) AD (Del) 639; 2001 (V) AD (Del) 657.

It is a case under section 138 the Negotiable Instruments Act in which application under section 91, the Cr. P.C. was filed directing the respondent to produce the balance sheets, Income-tax Returns for Assessment Years 1997-98, 1998-99, 1999-2000 and also all account books.

The said application was dismissed. The High Court found that such application for filing documents is not relevant for the purpose of this controversy and as such the petition under section 482, the Cr. P.C. is not maintainable.

SECTION 138, THE NEGOTIABLE INSTRUMENTS ACT AND SECTION 243, THE CR. P.C.

***Kalyani Bhaskar* v. *M.S. Sampuranam*, 2007 (1) JCC (NI) 1 SC**

During trial the appellant filed an application under section 243, the Cr. P.C. requesting the Magistrate to send the cheques for expert opinion in order to ascertain the correctness and genuineness of the signatures. The application was dismissed. Revision petition was filed. It was dismissed. *Held,* that the applicant is entitled to rebut the case of the respondent (complainant) and if the cheque on which the respondent has relied upon for initiating criminal proceeding against the appellant would furnish good material for rebutting that case. The banker of the appellant during cross-examination deposed that he had not verified the signature before returning the cheque. The Apex Court allowed the criminal appeal considering the order of the High Court erroneous and unsustainable.

***T. Nagappa* v. *Y.R. Murlidhar*, 2008 (2) JCC (NI) 211 SC**

Case referred:

(2007) 2 SCC 258.

In this case there is allegation of misuse of the cheque for which application was moved under section 243, the Cr. P.C. for expert opinion for determining the age of the signature of the drawer of the cheque. The accused knows how to prove his case. He has a right to defend himself. What should be the matter, is not the discretion of the court. The application is allowed as being *bona fide*.

SECTION 138, OF THE NEGOTIABLE INSTRUMENTS ACT AND SECTION 245, THE CR. P.C.

***Tarini Polytext Pvt. Ltd.* v. *M/s. Gopal and Co.*, 2009 (3) Cri 106 (Ori)**

The court *held* that criminal court in a summons trial cannot entertain an application under section 245, the Cr. P.C and drop proceedings in the midst of the hearing.

***M/s. Saint-Gobain Diamant Winter Ltd.* v. *Jagdamba Marbles*, 2008 (1) JCC (NI) 14 (Del)**

Case referred:

JT 2004 (7) SC 243.

The Magistrate passed order under section 245, the Cr. P.C. without recording evidence as required under section 244, the Cr. P.C. The order is, therefore, not sustainable in the eyes of law.

Note.—*Section 245, the Cr. P.C. has to be read with section 244, the Cr. P.C.*

SECTION 138, NEGOTIABLE INSTRUMENTS ACT AND SECTION 251, THE CR. P.C.

***Shri G.S. Sabuja* v. *M/s. Ifei Venture Capital Funds Ltd.*, 2006 (1) JCC (NI) 71 (Del)**

Cases referred:

(2005) 7 SCC 69; (2002) 8 SCC 236; (1999) SCC 209.

Held, that application under sections 251/482, the Cr. P.C. can be made only when there is illegality on the face of the complaint or the summoning order which is not evident in this case.

***M/s. Asia Metal Corporation (HDF)* v. *State*, 2006 (2) JCC (NI) 170 (Del)**

Cases referred:

2005 Cr LJ 2862; 2005 SCC (Cr) 242.

In this case all the accused persons except one were discharged. Revision petition was filed. The court *held* that there is no provision of discharge at the stage of section 251, the Cr. P.C. but only at the stage of section 258, the Cr. P.C. The impugned order of the trial Court is set aside and the discharged persons are directed to appear before Metropolitan Magistrate on the date fixed.

***Jaipal Singh Rana* v. *Swaraj Pal Singh*, 2008 (2) JCC (NI) 130 (Del)**

Cases referred:

2007 (2) SCC 258; 2003 (2) DCR 610.

In this case the Metropolitan Magistrate dismissed the application under section 251, the Cr. P.C. On revision it was also dismissed by A.S.J. Thus the order become final. Later on the case was transferred to another court of Metropolitan Magistrate, who allowed such application against which the High Court *held* that the order sending the cheque for CSFL opinion was not sustainable as the order of the earlier Metropolitan Magistrate had already become final.

SECTION 138, THE NEGOTIABLE INSTRUMENTS AND SECTION 258, THE CR. P.C.

***Balaji Trading Company* v. *Kejriwal Paper Ltd.*, 2006 (1) JCC (NI) 91 (AP)**

Cases referred:

(2001) 10 SCC 218; (2002) 7 SCC 655; (2004) 7 SCC 15; 2002 (1) ALD (Cri) 225 (AP); 1998 (4) Cri 74 (AP); AIR 1984 SC 1824; AIR 2004 SC 408; 2005 (1) ALD (Cri) 124 (SC); AIR 1992 SC 2206.

Application was moved by the accused for discharge wrongly mentioning sections 239, 245, the Cr. P.C. Court can treat such application as one under section 258, the Cr. P.C. Such application cannot be dismissed for mentioning wrong provisions of law. If the complaint on the face of it does not disclose any offence, there is no base to drop proceedings.

Note.—*"Recall of Summoning" order and "drop of proceeding" are two different proceedings.*

SECTION 138, THE NEGOTIABLE INSTRUMENTS ACT AND SECTION 311, THE CR. P.C.

***Manoj Sharma* v. *Naresh Gupta*, 2008 (1) JCC (NI) 19 (Del)**

Case referred:

AIR 1991 SC 1346.

It is an application under section 311 for recall of the complainant. Looking to the conduct of the accused, it is *held* that the application is filed to delay the matter and is an abuse of the process of law. The petition is dismissed.

***M/s. Kriplex Chits Pvt. Ltd.* v. *State*, 2008 (1) JCC (NI) 40 Del**

It is a case under sections 311/482, the Cr. P.C. The application for recalling the complainant was dismissed. It is found that the accused is filing one application or the other to delay the matter. Time of the witnesses is equally important as that of the accused. The accused has already been examined under section 313, the Cr. P.C. *Held,* that there is no illegality in dismissing the application filed under Section 311, the Cr. P.C.

***Madanmohan Chandak Kundan Lal* v. *State of Maharashtra*, 2008 Cr LJ 968 (Bom)**

Case referred:

AIR 1991 SC 1346.

Application was made by the accused under section 311, the Cr. P.C. seeking examination of the witness and recall of the complainant. Obviously the intention of the accused was to prolong the trial. His earlier application for such purpose was already rejected. *Held,* that the accused cannot repeatedly move the same application once any order assumes finality.

SECTION 138, THE NEGOTIABLE INSTRUMENTS ACT AND SECTION 313, THE CR. P.C.

***Smt. Keya Mukherjee* v. *Magma Leasing Limited*, 2008 (2) JCC (NI) 204 SC**

Cases referred:

AIR 1988 SC 2163; AIR 1969 SC 381; AIR 1953 SC 468; 1993 (3) SCC 208; 1973 (2) SCC 793; AIR 1963 SC 612; 2000 (8) SCC 740.

It is a case where the petition filed under section 313(1)(b), the Cr. P.C. was rejected. This rejection of petition was challenged in revision and finally the matter reached the Supreme Court by way of Criminal Appeal. It is *held* as follows:—

(i) The court can exempt the accused of personal appearance provided to submit the questions arise given by the court within the due time.

(ii) If the court does not put any question to the accused on the incriminating material against him such incriminating material cannot be used against the accused.

SECTION 138, THE NEGOTIABLE INSTRUMENTS ACT AND SECTION 315, THE CR. P.C.

***Manoj Sharma* v. *Naresh Gupta*, 2008 (1) JCC (NI) 11 (Del)**

In this case an application was made under section 315, the Cr. P.C after the case was posted for orders. The petition was rejected and thereafter the Revision Petition was also rejected and hence this criminal Misc. Petition. It is *held* that the present petition is a dilatory tactic adopted by the Revisionist since he remained unsuccessful in protracting the trial before the trial Court. It is a false, bogus and frivolous application and hence is dismissed.

SECTION 138, THE NEGOTIABLE INSTRUMENTS ACT AND SECTION 378(4), THE CR. P.C

***M/s. Goyal Enterprises* v. *State of Jharkhand*, 2008 (2) JCC (NI) 156 SC**

Cases referred:

2001 (1) SCC 607; 1981 (4) SCC 129; 1987 (2) SCC 222; 2003 (11) SCC 519; 1971 (1) All ER 1148; 1974 ICR 120 (NIRC); 2004 (1) SCC 547.

Respondent No. 2 was convicted under section 138, the Negotiable Instruments Act. In revision ADJ set aside the order of conviction. An application was made before the High Court for grant of leave under section 378(4), the Cr. P.C. It was summarily dismissed without giving any reasons. It was held that it is denial of justice. The order of the High Court, being unsustainable, is set aside.

SECTION 138, THE NEGOTIABLE INSTRUMENTS ACT AND SECTION 482, REAL WITH SECTION 427, THE CR. P.C.

***State of Punjab* v. *Madan Lal*, 2009 (2) JCC (NI) 129 (SC)**

Cases referred:

AIR 1988 SC 2143; 2001 (6) SCC 311.

In this case the convictions were in respect of three dishonoured cheques under three different complaints. The High Court *held* that the sentences awarded by the lower courts were to run concurrently. According to the State, the order of the High Court is erroneous. The Apex Court held that:—

(i) Period of sentence undergone by the accused is to be set off against the sentence of imprisonment in connection with the same case.

(ii) Quantum of punishment is to run concurrently.

SECTION 138, THE NEGOTIABLE INSTRUMENTS ACT AND SECTION 436, THE CR. P.C.

***Sushil Suri* v. *State*, 2006 (2) JCC (NI) 124 (Del)**

Cases referred:

2000 (1) JCC 2006 (Del); 1984 (2) Crimes 413; 49 Cr LJ 1948; AIR 1942 Mad 740; AIR 1965 AP 444; 1957 (2) Andh W.R. 383; 2003 (3) JCC 1485; 1958 SCR 1226; 2001 (58) DRJ 113.

In this case the trial Court imposed conditions while granting bail and the same is challenged. The court *held* as follows:—

(i) That the imposition of personal bond of Rs. two lakh and a surety of the like amount is not unreasonable.

(ii) The condition with regard to the petitioner's seeking permission of the court prior to his going abroad is set aside.

(iii) Regarding date of departure, tentative date of return, places where he would be staying abroad, is not a condition of bail.

SECTION 138 AND AUTHORITY OF THE DIRECTOR TO DEPOSE

In this case the complainant is a company. Authority of the Director to depose was the issue. There was no evidence (documentary) to show that he is the Director of the Company and that he has been authorized to depose on behalf of the company. Resolution of the company was not produced and he had pleaded his ignorance in cross-examination about the resolution passed by the Board of Directors. *Held,* acquittal of the accused is proper.

PAYMENT MADE AFTER THE EXPIRY OF PERIOD

***Col. S.S. Chaudhri* v. *State*, 2009 (2) JCC (NI) 132 (Del).**

It is *held* that any payment made after the expiry of statutory period does not exonerate the accused from the offence committed for under Section 138. Neither the accused has paid original cheque amount within the prescribed time nor honoured the cheque as compromised. There is no circumstance to alter the sentence by reversing the order awarding compensation, altering the S.I. into R.I.

TAKING COGNIZANCE MEANS APPLICATION OF JUDICIOUS MIND

***Smt. Patchiammal* v. *K.C. Sriramulu*, AIR 2009 (NOC) 132 (Kant)**

The court simply put its signatures on the printed form of order sheet contains words, "Cognizance is taken." It does not amount to taking cognizance as the trial Court has not applied its mind. Complaint is not pre-mature warranting acquittal of the accused.

SECTION 138 AND REDUCTION IN SENTENCE

***Basavaraj* v. *M/s Dhanlaxmi Finance Co. (R) Terdal*, (2010) 1 SCC 1**

In this case the accused was convicted for dishonour of cheque. The appeal only related to the sentence awarded. The Supreme Court held that where appellant had paid hefty amount of compensation as a penalty for dishonour of cheque issued by him and no materials was placed on record that the appellant had earlier committed any such similar offence or then the sentence of imprisonment can be remitted. The Supreme Court remitted that sentence of imprisonment, but the fine and compensation levied was kept in tact

SECTION 138 AND ARTICLES 226 AND 227 READ WITH SECTION 482, THE CR. P.C.

Cases referred:

R.P. Kapoor v. *State of Punjab*, AIR 1960 SC 866; *State of Haryana* v. *Bhajan Lal*, 1992 Suppl (1) SCC 335; *Smt. Nagawwa* v. *Veeranna Shivalingappa Konjalgi*, (1976) 3 SCC 736.

It is held that petitioner under Articles 226 and 227 of the Constitution of India read with Section 482, the Cr. P.C. for quashing the complaint for dishonour of cheque is not maintainable since allegations made in the complaint, if taken on their face value and as true in its entirety do *prima facie* speaks of commission of an offence. The court has to see the allegations and not the defence which the accused may have. If there is dispute whether the document is genuine or, has to be decided in the trial after recording evidence and cannot be the subject-matter of adjudication in a petition under Articles 226 and 227 of the Constitution or Section 482, the Cr. P.C.

DRAFTING OF NOTICE AND COMPLAINT

I

NOTICE – ITS ESSENTIALS

Clause (b) of proviso to section 138, the Negotiable Instruments Act speaks of "the payee or the holder in due course of the cheque, as the case may be, makes a demand for the payment of the said amount of money by giving a notice in writing, to the drawer of the cheque, within 30 days of the receipt of information by him from the bank regarding the return of the cheque as unpaid."

Though no Form of Notice is prescribed in clause (b) of proviso to section 138, yet it is a *"sine qua non"* — a first step in the direction of initiation of proceedings in the Court of Metropolitan Magistrate or a Judicial Magistrate of the first class. Its essential contents are:—

(1) The notice must be sent by the payee or the holder in due course of the cheque.

(2) It is to be sent to the drawer of the cheque.

(3) It must be in writing, stating the reasons for return of cheque unpaid.

(4) It must contain a demand for payment of the amount of the cheque returned unpaid. If any demand of payment is made towards other charges by way of claim, over and above the demand of payment of the amount of the cheque returned unpaid, it must be severable from the amount of the cheque or claimed separately in the demand notice.

(5) It must be sent within 30 days of the receipt of information by the payee or the holder in due course from the bank regarding the return of cheque unpaid.

(6) Service of notice or deemed service of notice is a *"sine qua non"* for initiating a prosecution against the accused. Section 138 does not require that the notice should be given only by "post". Nevertheless, the principle incorporated in section 27 of the General Clauses Act, 1897, can profitably be imported in a case where the sender has dispatched notice by post with the correct address written on it. Then, it can be deemed to have been served on the sendee unless he proves that it was not really served and that he was not responsible for such non-service. Any other interpretation can lead to a very tenuous position as the drawer of the cheque who is liable to pay the amount would resort to the strategy of subterfuge by successfully avoiding the notice.

(7) If the case involves an element of criminality likely to invoke the provisions of Indian Penal Code, then the ingredients of such section should also be stated. In other words such allegation must be there in the notice.

(8) There is no obligation that the payee or the holder in due course of the cheque should particularly refer to section 138, or that he is going to take action for an offence under section 138 or that the payment must be made within 15 days of the receipt of notice. Non-mention of such particulars shall not make the notice invalid.

(9) It is advisable that the demand notice is sent by Registered Post Acknowledgment Due and "under postal certificate (U.P.C.)".

(10) It is to be seen that the deemed notice should not fall short of the statutory requirements under section 138 of the Act.

II

CONTENTS OF COMPLAINT

It is suggested that the complainant should give particulars in the complaint for initiation of criminal proceedings in the beginning itself to make easy for the honourable court to take cognizance of the matter.

Particulars of the Case

(1) Cheque No. ....for Rs. ....dated ....

*(2) Cheque presented through...on ....

(3) Cheque returned unpaid *vide* cheque returning Memo dated ....

(4) Intimation received from Bank on ....

*(5) Notice of demand of payment of the cheque returned unpaid sent on. ....

Note.—Notice must be sent within 30 days

(6) Notice sent by RPAD and UPC and served or deemed to be served on the drawer of the cheque on ....

*(7) Period of 15 days starts from 21-11-2005 and expires on ....

(8) Cause-of-action starts on ....

*(9) Complaint is to be filed on or before (within one month) ....

(10) Complaint filed on ....

[It satisfies section 142(b) and the complaint is filed within time.]

III

WHO IS TO BE IMPLEADED

Section 138 speaks of criminal liability. So we have to see that while initiating the criminal proceedings, this fact should not be forgotten, such as:—

(1) Proprietorship concern is not a legal person. It must be represented by its proprietor who is a natural person.

(2) Partnership firm is not a legal entity. It can be impleaded but a partner representing the firm must be impleaded.

(3) Company is a legal person and is to be impleaded but it must be represented by any person who at the time the offence was committed; was in-charge of and was responsible to the company for the conduct of the business of the Company. Both shall be guilty of the offence – the company as well as the person responsible for the conduct of the business of the company.

List of Witnesses

1. The Complainant
2. The manager or any authorized representative of.............bank with ledger and other relevant record pertaining to the account of the complainant from .... to ....
3. The Manager or any authorized representative of...............bank with ledger and other relevant record pertaining to the account of the accused from .... to ....
4. Any other witness with the permission of the honourable Court.

Complainant

Through Advocate

List of Documents Enclosed

1. Original cheque No. ....dt. ....for Rs. ....issued by the accused.
2. Dishonouring of cheque Memo dt. ....issued by the..............Bank.
3. Copy of Notice issued to the accused along with Postal receipt and U.P.C. receipt.
4. Original Acknowledgement Due card received back through Postal Department.

COMPLAINANT

Through Advocate

Note.—*It is to be noted that persons are of two kinds, natural and legal. Natural persons mean human beings. Legal persons mean beings and things which are treated as persons by law. Thus, "legal person" includes those things which are treated in the same way as human beings for the legal purposes.*

IV

COMPLAINT

Where the Accused is Individual/Proprietor of a Concern

IN THE COURT OF CHIEF METROPOLITAN MAGISTRATE/CHIEF JUDICIAL MAGISTRATE AT—

Complaint No. ....of................

IN THE MATTER OF

.... Complainant

vs.

.... Accused

COMPLAINT UNDER SECTION 138 READ WITH SECTION 142 OF THE NEGOTIABLE INSTRUMENTS ACT, 1881

Most respectfully showeth:—

1. That the complainant is Proprietor of ...., dealing in grocery provisions and the accused is a regular customer taking grocery items on credit basis and clear the accounts by the first week of the month for the purchases made by him in the previous month.
2. That the accused made purchases for the month of .... to the tune of Rs. 6290 and issued cheque No. ....dated .... drawn on .... Branch, New Delhi
3. That the said cheque was presented through .... Branch on .... and was returned unpaid by cheque returning Memo dated .... with the remarks "Insufficiency of Funds/ Refer to drawer/Payment stopped/Account closed. The said bounced cheque along with cheque Returning Memo was received by me from my bankers on ....
4. That the said cheque was issued by the accused in discharge of his liability and the same was returned unpaid as the accused having failed to arrange for its payment.
5. The complainant informed the accused about the dishonour of cheque and the accused assured that he would make the payment in cash within a week. Having failed to make the payment, the complainant sent a demand notice on .... both by RPAD and U.P.C. The said notice was received by the accused on ...., as per Acknowledge Due but failed to make the payment within 15 days. The said period of 15 days expired on ....
6. The complainant, waited for a further period of 15 days and finding no response was constrained to file this complaint.

Prayer

It is prayed that the honourable Court may be pleased to take cognizance of the complaint and punish the accused according to law and also pass orders against the accused under section 357, the Cr. P.C. and award compensation to the complainant

Delhi. Complainant

Dated.................... Advocate for the Complainant.

V

COMPLAINT

Where the Accused is a Partnership Firm

IN THE COURT OF CHIEF METROPOLITAN MAGISTRATE/
CHIEF JUDICIAL MAGISTRATE AT—

IN THE MATTER OF

.... Complainant

vs.

.... Accused

COMPLAINT UNDER SECTION 138 READ WITH SECTION 142 OF THE NEGOTIABLE INSTRUMENTS ACT, 1881

Most respectfully showeth:—

(1) Give introductory remarks about the complainant.

(2) Give introductory remarks about the accused.

(3) Brief details of the transaction against which the cheque was issued to discharge the liability in part or in whole.

(4) Details of presentation of the cheque(s) and its dishonour for the reason stated in the cheque returning Memo.

(5) Intimation of dishonour of cheque, demand of payment in lieu of dishonoured cheque and that the notice is issued in time (within 30 days of the receipt of information from the bank about the dishonour of cheque. [Refer clause (b) of proviso to section 138]

(6) Brief particulars of non-payment of amount within 15 days of the receipt of notice or deemed receipt of notice and hence this complaint. [Refer clause (c) of proviso to section 138 and section 142(b)]

Note.—*In case there is non-compliance of section 142(b), then take shelter under proviso to section 142(b) and file an application for condonation of delay showing sufficient cause for the delay to the satisfaction of the court.*

(7) Involvement of the partners. It needs to be noted that section 138 speaks of strict liability and not vicarious liability. So in order to hold any person vicariously liable, there must be a specific, clear and unambiguous assertion in the complaint against such person(s) impleaded as accused that they were in charge of and were responsible to the firm for the conduct of the business at the material time when the offence has been committed by the firm [Refer section 141(1)]. If the complainant also wants to bring the case under section 141(2), he has to plead the ingredients of the section 141(2) in the complaint.

Note.—*Section 141 envisages three categories of persons who can be brought within the purview of the penal liability by virtue of a legal fiction created in section 141. They are (i) the company which committed the offence, (ii) everyone who was incharge of and was responsible for the business of the company, and (iii) any other person who is a partner or a manager or officer of the firm with whose connivance or due to whose negligence the firm has committed the offence [Refer* Explanations (a) and (b) *to section 141].*

Delhi

Dated........................

Prayer

Enclosures Complainant

(i) List of witnesses.

(ii) List of documents.

Through

Advocate

VI

COMPLAINT

Where the Accused is a Company

IN THE COURT OF CHIEF METROPOLITAN MAGISTRATE/
CHIEF JUDICIAL MAGISTRATE AT—

IN THE MATTER OF

.... Complainant

vs.

.... Accused

COMPLAINT UNDER SECTION 138 READ WITH SECTION 142 OF THE NEGOTIABLE INSTRUMENTS ACT, 1881

Most respectfully showeth:—

(1) Give introductory remarks about the complainant.

(2) Give introductory remarks about the accused.

(3) Brief details of the transaction against which the cheque was issued to discharge the liability in part or in whole.

(4) Details of presentation of the cheque(s) and its dishonour for the reason stated in the cheque returning Memo.

(5) Intimation of dishonour of cheque, demand of payment in lieu of dishonoured cheque and that the notice is issued in time (within 30 days of the receipt of information from the bank about the dishonour of cheque. [Refer clause (b) of proviso to section 138]

(6) Brief particulars of non-payment of amount within 15 days of the receipt of notice or deemed receipt of notice and hence this complaint. [Refer clause (c) of proviso to section 138 and section 142(b)]

Note.—*In case there is non-compliance of section 142(b), then take shelter under proviso to section 142(b) and file an application for condonation of delay showing sufficient cause for the delay to the satisfaction of the court.*

(7) Involvement of the directors. It needs to be noted that section 138 speaks of strict liability and not vicarious liability. So in order to hold any person vicariously liable, there must be a specific, clear and unambiguous assertion in the complaint against such person(s) impleaded as accused that they were in charge of and were responsible to the company for the conduct of the business at the material time when the offence has been committed by the company [Refer section 141(1)]. If the complainant also wants to bring the case under section 141(2), he has to plead the ingredients of the section 141(2) in the complaint.

Note.—*Section 141 envisages three categories of persons who can be brought within the purview of the penal liability by virtue of a legal fiction created in section 141. They are (i) the company which committed the offence, (ii) everyone who was incharge of and was responsible for the business of the company, and (iii) any other person who is a director or a manager or officer of the company with whose connivance or due to whose negligence the company has committed the offence [Refer* Explanations (a) and (b) *to section 141].*

Delhi

Dated.........................

Prayer

Enclosures

Complainant

(i) List of witnesses.

(ii) List of documents.

Through

Advocate

VII

COMPLAINT

If Element of Criminality is Involved

If the case also involves element of criminality add Para (8) to the complaint.

(8) The cheque given towards discharge of liability, knowing fully well that there is no amount in the account and that the cheque when presented shall be dishonoured, is a clear indication that the accused had dishonest intention not to pay even at the time of issuance of the cheque and that the act of issuing the cheque, which was dishonoured, caused damage to his mind, body or reputation and thus the accused has also committed an offence punishable under section 420, the I.P.C.

Note.—Write – *Complaint-filed under section 138 read with section 142 of the Negotiable Instruments Act, 1881 and section 420, the I.P.C.*